Cricket Crisis

CRICKET CRISIS

BODYLINE AND OTHER LINES

JACK FINGLETON
Introduction by Michael Parkinson

THE PAVILION LIBRARY

Contents

Introduction

Like all great dramatic events the bodyline crisis has attracted both the historians and the poets, the seekers after truth and the weavers of dreams. Fifty years on it has inspired a novel, a mini series for television and a feature film for the cinema.

Curiously enough the man who first spotted its dramatic potential was Ben Travers, one of the great writers of farce. Ben refused to take anything seriously and soon after the bodyline crisis, when people still referred to it in hushed tones as if speaking about a war averted he wrote his cricketing farce called *Put to the Test*.

Mr Travers' sense of humour was nothing if not Puckish. Not content with the basic heresy of making fun of cricket, he dared to cast that master farceur Mr Robertson Hare as the Captain of England. Some might say that by using a comedian thus he was merely predicting the future. Be that as it may, the play had a mixed reception. Mr Travers noted: 'The farce was thought very funny except in Australia.' Which is a bit like saying everyone enjoyed the fight except the poor sap who got knocked out.

The real danger in the bodyline crisis was not that people lost their sense of humour, but that they lost their sense of proportion. Which is why we were lucky that Jack Fingleton was around to absorb every moment of it as a player in order that later he could write *the* definitive book about it: *Cricket Crisis*.

Jack Fingleton was uniquely equipped to interpret and understand the whys and wherefores of bodyline. As a player he was unflappable and courageous. When some of his colleagues showed a public dislike of short pitched bowling, Fingleton followed the dictum of the great Maurice Leyland who once observed: 'None of us like it but some of us don't let on!'

Harold Larwood once told me that of all Australian batsmen who faced him in the bodyline tour, none was braver than Jack Fingleton. 'I could hit him, but I couldn't knock him down,' he said.

Jack Fingleton was also a journalist and a very good one. He was clear eyed and meticulous in pursuit of a story. Being Australian, he had a native loathing of hypocrisy and humbug; he could spot a phoney a mile off. His years spent reporting Parliament gave him a rare insight into the ways of men and the abuse of power. Above all, his splendid sense of fun, his ability to see humour in everything gave colour and radiance to his personality.

All that I have remarked about Jack Fingleton will become obvious to the reader as he unravels what follows – the most extraordinary story in all of sport. The decision to reprint the book was easy if you believe as I do that the anniversary of a special event deserves its proper testament. *Cricket Crisis* is Jack Fingleton's masterpiece and stands as fresh and intriguing today as when it was first published.

The first thought of re-publishing it came to me some time ago in Australia when my old friend Keith Miller arranged a luncheon party in my honour comprising Harold Larwood, Bill O'Reilly, Fingo and himself. I dined that day in the Pantheon. During the lunch the talk turned to the bodyline series and I became intrigued by the passion still simmering in old men. The lunch turned into a regular event and every meal became another chapter in the bodyline story.

Larwood in particular fascinated me. I was reared on the legend. My father told me he was the greatest fast bowler that ever lived. Jack Fingleton swore he was the fastest. So did Tiger O'Reilly, who as a genuine tail ender, was never in danger of being bounced, but who, as a normal human being, could see no sense in facing up to a missile being projected towards him at ninety miles an hour with only a piece of wood as a means of defence.

Being Irish, and therefore of an imaginative nature, he devised his own particular way of playing Larwood. As he explained it to me this involved standing in the approximate vicinity of the square leg umpire and dangling the bat from arm's length in front of the wicket. He told me that from this very position he once observed a strange phenomenon which would give him some indication of Harold Larwood's speed. Batting in the Adelaide test he witnessed Mr

Larwood run up to bowl. He didn't actually see the ball leave his hand but he was perfectly placed to see one of the bails collapse into a little pile of sawdust.

Whether this was caused by a direct hit or by the ferocity of the draught as the ball passed nearby, Mr O'Reilly left to my imagination. Now the point of this story is that when it was told at one of our lunches everyone laughed at the yarn except Mr Larwood who nodded in agreement at Mr O'Reilly's hyperbole.

At another lunch Harold Larwood produced from his pocket a silver ashtray wrapped carefully in a yellow duster. Engraved on the ashtray were the words: 'To a great fast bowler from a grateful skipper. D. R. Jardine.' To this day Harold Larwood refers to Jardine as 'Mr Jardine' or 'The Captain'. This link, enduring today, even with Larwood in his 80's and Jardine long dead intrigued me. What was the bond between the Nottinghamshire miner and the aristocratic Captain? They were the architects of bodyline, Jardine the strategist, Larwood his assassin.

But why? Why invent a means of attack which was based on physical intimidation of the most brutal kind? Why approach a game of cricket as if it were a military operation?

Such questions would be irrelevant today when most sports condone intimidation – both physical and mental – to the point where the basic philosophy of sport is not simply challenged, rather ignored. Nowadays you can only place sport in the context of the age we live in. Attitudes in sport are mere echoes of what is happening in society. The ugliness of behaviour in sport today is merely a reflection of society's countenance.

In the early 1930's, when the Bodyline crisis occurred, things were different. Or, at least, people imagined they were. In those days, the map of the world was largely coloured pink which meant that most chaps understood the meaning of 'It isn't cricket'. Today the phrase is merely an epitaph on a gravestone. Fifty years on it has no meaning except as a relic of a different society. But in the early 1930's it was still a creed by which men ran their lives. It is significant that when Mr Woodfull, the Australian Captain chose to condemn the tactics being used against his team, he simply said 'There are two teams out there. One is playing cricket, the other is not'. It was a mild, even insipid rebuke by today's standards. Yet what Woodfull said precipitated the real political crisis because what he had done was to challenge the fundamental basis not of a cricket match but of a way of life.

The story is even more piquant when you consider that the architect of all this chaos, D. R. Jardine, epitomised the kind of English establishment figure who firmly believed that cricket embodied every virtue of life and manhood. Jardine had much to recommend him as a leader of Englishmen in the society of the 1930's. His background – Winchester and Oxford – was impeccable. But he was a man possessed and driven by an ambition which in the end destroyed his own career and that of Harold Larwood.

Jardine's obsession was not just to defeat Australia but to grind them into the dust. More than that, he intended to show that Donald Bradman could be reduced to the level of an ordinary player. It is difficult to know which was uppermost in Jardine's thinking – his hatred of Australians or his desire to knock Bradman off his pedestal.

Jack Fingleton is in no doubt. As he says in the book: 'Bodyline was nothing more nor less than a revolution against Bradman'. As such it worked. Bradman found it difficult to cope with Bodyline. (Who didn't?) Australia lost a series and Jardine, by his standards, had achieved a goal. But still fifty years on people argue and debate not just on the legality of his tactics but the reasons and the repercussions. The story still intrigues and fascinates.

Of the key protagonists, only two remain. Donald Bradman keeps quiet in Adelaide. His self-imposed silence on this and other cricketing matters is sad to those who regard him – quite rightly – as one of the game's great historical figures. Bradman as a player and as a legend has a unique place in the story of cricket. His greatness made him the first super-star of sport; he adorned the game and it was lavish in its rewards. It is a pity, therefore, that he chooses not to articulate on his career both as a player and an administrator.

His tormentor in the bodyline tests, Harold Larwood, lives quietly with his family in a suburb of Sydney. When he comes to town on a rare visit wearing his trilby at a jaunty angle, it is difficult to imagine this slight figure as the most feared fast bowler of all time. His voice is quiet, his manner diffident. To this day he sees himself not as some ogre who nearly destroyed an empire, but a simple cricketer who only did as his Captain ordered.

Larwood and Bradman remain but rarely meet. The man who knew them best of all and observed them most closely is Jack Fingleton and he is dead. His book remains. It is not simply a brilliantly observed record of momentous events, it is a perfect epitaph to a very remarkable man. In the book – written in 1946 – Jack shows his warmth and humanity, by suggesting that Australia should make a grand gesture and invite Larwood to pay a visit. At the time Jack knew that Harold was suffering dreadful neglect in England and was terribly unhappy.

Typically, Australia heeded the suggestion and Harold Larwood didn't just go on a visit, he ended up living there. Jack Fingleton regarded this as one of his greatest triumphs and it provided one of his best anecdotes. Larwood arrived in Australia in the late 1940's.

Jack arranged for him to meet the then Prime Minister, Ben Chifley. Jack introduced the two men then left them so that they might chat together.

After about ten minutes, the Prime Minister came out of the room shaking his head. Jack asked what was wrong. 'Be blowed if I can understand a word he's saying,' said the P.M. According to Jack he then spent the next hour sitting between the two men interpreting the Nottinghamshire dialect into Australian and vice versa.

As you read the book two things emerge. One is Fingleton's talent as a reporter, the other the feeling that the writer was clearly an exceptional human being. My friend was indisputably the best Australian cricket writer there has been, and certainly in the best four or five of all time no matter where they were born.

London, 1984   Michael Parkinson

Foreword

THIS BOOK POSSESSES AN UN-
usual interest; first of all, it really is the work of the great cricketer
whose name appears as that of the author. Of most books on the
game signed by players it is dangerous to say anything belittling –
one never knows who may really have written them. I made the
acquaintance of Jack Fingleton – an acquaintance that has ripened
into friendship – long before I knew he was a cricketer of unusual
talent. Years ago he sent an article on cricket to the *Manchester
Guardian* (I had not visited Australia then, and when I first glanced
over the MS. I made a mental observation about the confidence of
the uninitiated; for it is the hardest thing in the world for anybody
excepting a good writer to count himself amongst the contributors
to the *Manchester Guardian* – at least, this was the situation in the
days of Montague and Scott). After I had read a couple of pages, I
decided that Fingleton's article would pass the test; the prose style
was not decorative – which was a welcome change in the *M.G.*'s
main style (we regarded the adjective the ally, not the enemy, of the
noun!). Jack Fingleton's article appealed to me because of natural
ease and conciseness of expression, and, important, here was a man
who knew what he was talking about.

It is a curious fact that few cricketers seem able to describe the
game from that point of view which gives them an advantage over
the most brilliant adornment of the Press-Box proper. On the
whole, they cannot make use of the important fact that they *do* see

and experience everything 'in the middle'. From the boundary's edge, or from the Olympian height of the Press-Box, the keenest scrutiny must inevitably miss many a technical secret. But if you ask the average cricketer for an account of a piece of subtle play, in which he has taken part at close quarters, the chances are that he will talk the platitudes of the most routined of laymen reporters. Ask him what sort of a ball it was that bowled Bradman, and most likely he will grossly answer: 'One out of the bag; he was too late at it.' Years ago, in the days of the pomp of Hobbs, the question of how he was ever clean bowled became a matter almost involving some slight assumption of an interference in the scientific course of nature. I saw Hobbs's leg-stump sent flying by E. A. McDonald one morning at Kennington Oval; and as I was watching from the far horizon of the Vauxhall-end (it was possible to run five in those days, before they shortened the boundary, for a drive travelling in the direction of Vauxhall – and the Houses of Parliament) I could not be quite sure of what the ball had 'done'. At lunch I asked one of the players who had been favourably placed to deliver a convincing and enlightening explanation. 'It was a pretty quick one – beat him all the way.'

In this book Fingleton writes from the 'middle'; not only that, he *feels* the game and every action as a player who from long experience has acquired that professional 'extra sense' which sends him to the essence or root of the matter, with no need to go round and round by way of the layman's necessarily inferential ways of approach. The species of bowling known in the days of 'old unhappy battles long ago' has not, to my recollection, been defined, analysed, objectively presented and judged with as much observation, acumen and fairness as in these pages. Such an account of a controversy of historical importance was urgently needed to clear away a confusion and an ignorance that might easily have done harm to the technique of fast bowling, even in a future willing to forget an unfortunate page in the past. Nobody, after studying Fingleton's *post mortem*, will ever again – surely – protest against a high rising fast ball *as such*; or work himself into high blood-pressure at the sight of a slow bowler angling for catches to a well-packed field to leg. And Fingleton does not, for the purposes of truthful description and analysis, detach events from their dramatic context; we are taken into the technical laboratory, by way of a vivid remembrance of how it all thrillingly happened – a remembrance written by a man who was not only on the spot, but was somewhat put on the spot. I am told by Australians that nobody took the general gruelling with more than Fingleton's silent, determined stoicism.

The point, indeed, is that the book *is* written; it is a contribution to the cricketers' library. 'Bodyline', of course, is only one theme, and not the main theme. Great players pass across the stage, and the scenes change from Brisbane to Bramall Lane, from the Hill at Sydney to the Long Room at Lord's. It is an Australian that looks at the game with the steady, unsentimental eyes of one born in Sydney. The honesty of every page is as straight as Fingleton's bat, and with the pen he is not afraid to attack; but his inborn realism always keeps his eye on the ball, so that he knows exactly where his strokes are going; there is next to no vague footwork, and in not more than one chapter does he give a possible chance. I have read the book with interest and pleasure, and it is with pleasure that I write this introduction.

Sydney, August, 1946.   NEVILLE CARDUS

Author's Note

IT HAS NOT BEEN EASY TO WRITE this book. It is easy to imagine many cricket devotees will express the opinion that it would have been better for the game had it not been written. I cannot judge of that, because of my somewhat central position. I am aware, of course, that a book on such a contentious subject as Bodyline must reopen old wounds, leading to many recriminations and bitternesses, but that is certainly not my purpose.

Three principles have actuated me: – (a) No Australian player of that series has yet given his middle-of-the-wicket impressions of Bodyline; (b) lapse of time permits of a calm, dispassionate analysis of the subject, and (c) I very much doubt whether many players really understood what Bodyline was and whether the legislators and players learned the lessons it so plainly taught.

I think Test cricket lost something during the Bodyline series that it never regained in pre-war years. Considering the terrific upheaval it caused, it was perhaps understandable that Bodyline should have been followed by an era of extreme righteousness in Test cricket. Everybody was so very, very careful to do the right thing that the red-blooded fast bowler who so far showed his distaste of modern marl wickets and modern batting methods as to bowl an old-fashioned 'bumper' found, while hysterical onlookers were feverishly shouting 'Bodyline', that he was regarded in the best quarters as a bit of a bounder – if not, perhaps, an utter cad.

In such a manner did Bodyline recoil on that poor, humble soul who, of all people who willingly take up a life of drudgery and sweat, stands most in need of sympathy – the Test fast bowler!

The Rise and Fall of Bodyline is a long story with much behind the scenes, and this is my attempt to tell it. For any ill-feeling that arises from this book (and I know how easy it is, as a Journalist, for the Press to whip up sensational stuff) I apologise to the Game of Cricket – but I hastily add that I think I know the game well enough to believe that no work which attempts an honest analysis of those days can do the game any harm in the ultimate end. Cricket is too all-embracing and resilient for that, and if there are any lessons to be drawn from the past, surely now is the time to attempt them, when Test cricket is gingerly about to find itself again after six years of world nightmare.

And so, like the Jester, 'I have a song to sing-o.' I hope I hear the answer, 'Sing me your song-o.' Some of the notes will be discordant, I fear, but I hope not too much so. It is to be remembered that I deal with the most contentious era known to sport – not only cricket – and it is also to be remembered that the happenings of which I write came perilously close in 1932, 1933 and 1934 to wrecking, if only temporarily, the game of international cricket. It should, therefore, be realised that the chords on which I strum are highly sensitive.

The word 'Bodyline' itself quickly became common usage. It was a coining popularly attributed to a newspaper colleague of mine, Hugh Buggy. Writing in 'telegraphese' he ran two words into one, after the old international, Worrall, wrote of the English bowling in Australia in 1932 as being on the line of the body. Previously, the distinguished critic of the Sydney *Referee*, J. C. Davis, expressed misgivings at the selection by England of a battery of four fast bowlers. He wrote this: 'If the battery achieves success it may be done by contravening the spirit of cricket.'

While the late Jack Worrall claimed that he had invented the word, it was after it had been blazoned in an Australian newspaper heading based on Buggy's 'telegraphese' coining that the term Bodyline achieved wide acceptance.

Neither Buggy nor Worrall could have forseen the storm which this type of bowling was to produce. Nor could they have known that the term Bodyline in a few weeks would come to cover not only cricket tactics, but all forms of conduct which could be interpreted as hitting below the belt. The word and its implications nauseated everybody. It prompted recrimination whenever it was used, and an international newspaper understanding throttled it out of Empire usage at a time when everybody was hoping for a little cricket peace for a change.

Feelings were too heated at the time to permit calm discussion. A misguided nationalism obtruded itself with emphasis, and most people automatically ranged themselves behind their country. It was said on the one side: An Englishman would not behave like this; the MCC side is obviously too good for the Australians, and, therefore, the Australians must be squealers. It was said on the other: Australians have proved to the world their sportsmanship, in addition to their fighting qualities. If the Australians are objecting, the Englishmen must be doing wrong.

As soon as that brick wall was built up, a wall of unyielding resistance, the sun of reason was overclouded and a solution of the problem became more and more remote.

Followed a period of quick appeasement and reconciliation. A concerted hush-hush policy on the part of the Marylebone Cricket Club and the Australian Board of Control (its many critics called this the Board of No-Control at the time) bundled Bodyline from the public gaze.

Was this the best way of dealing with the biggest sporting upset the world has known? Possibly it was at the time, but Bodyline will always remain on the records, and cricketers of the future will certainly want to know all about it. They will wonder whether it was simply fast leg-theory to which the Australians took such violent exception, or whether there was more below the surface than that. They are entitled to as much data on the subject as possible, so that they can form their own opinions; but just as vitally concerned as the cricketers of the future are a host of players and spectators of those 1932–33 days who even yet have no clear perception of what constituted Bodyline and what all the fuss was about.

This was one of the disadvantages of the Munich-like policy of appeasement which swept Bodyline and its story off the stage. There have been several English interpretations of the theory. Larwood wrote a book, to which Jardine supplied an introduction; Jardine also wrote a book, and Warner, the manager of that 1932–33 MCC team, allowed his skates to skirt thin ice in another publication. Much of that thin ice was of Warner's own refrigeration, but the point I wish to stress is that this is the first Australian interpretation of Bodyline and the atmosphere of those days by one who played in the series.

I hold no brief for those people (some of them prime muddlers in the affair) who shudder visibly, look askance and finger their tie when the word Bodyline is mentioned. 'Oh, I say, old boy!' they usually mutter, 'none of that, surely. Bygones be bygones, you know.' They are mostly appeasers who refuse to look facts in the face, and if we continue to acknowledge and consider them, fast bowlers and the game of cricket will be done an irreparable wrong. You do not really settle a controversy by locking it up in a cupboard like a family skeleton. It can be settled only by stating the facts without passion and allowing informed judgement to decide what lessons are to be learned from them.

In his book, *Cricket Between the Two Wars*, Sir Pelham Warner writes of the much-publicised and notorious dressing-room scene he had with Woodfull during the Adelaide Test of the 1932–33 series. That was when Woodfull, just before hit by a Larwood ball over the heart, told Warner that one team on the ground outside was not playing cricket and it was time such tactics were stopped. Warner writes this in his book: 'Unfortunately, a member of the Australian Eleven who was also a Pressman was in the room at the time, and next day the story was blazoned all over the newspapers.'

No name is mentioned, but the inference is obvious. Others in that room had associations in one way or another with the Press, though I was the only professional journalist present. I wrote to Sir Pelham, and his answer left no doubt that he considered it was I who had 'leaked' the story to the Press. I regard that as a very serious charge; it was also clumsy. Sir Pelham is a barrister, but I doubt whether he would have had much confidence in putting forward an argument in court that a newspaper story emanating from a room in which there were about a dozen people, including a professional Pressman, must necessarily have come from that Pressman. I do know as a Pressman that if I wrote Sir Pelham's story about the 'leak' on such flimsy circumstantial evidence I would be treading a measure on any self-respecting editorial carpet in double quick time.

I was in an operational area in 1942 when Warner's book was sent to me, and I keenly resented his allegation. I know who gave the Woodfull–Warner story to the Press (unlike Sir Pelham, I have the evidence, see p. 98), but, apart from writing to Warner and telling him he was wrong, there was little else I could do. Warner answered that he would be pleased to make a correction if I gave him the facts, but the damage had been done, and, on reflection, I thought the best thing I could do was to write my own impressions of the Bodyline imbroglio.

Sir Pelham Warner is frequently mentioned in my narrative, but he comes naturally into the Bodyline story. He was chairman of the MCC selection committee which chose the English team for Australia, and, moreover, he was the manager of the side on the tour. He was just as much a principal in the drama as either Jardine or Larwood.

The leading figure of the whole cast, however, was Bradman. He was the problem child of cricket, for never in the history of the game had an individual so completely captured records, attention and publicity. There had been W. G. Grace and Trumper, but not even these, all things considered, matched Bradman's personality. He towered above his fellows; he dominated the stage so much that at one period it almost seemed that the game of cricket was subservient to the individual Bradman. Hence, so to put it, Bodyline!

Had there been no Bradman there would have been no Test Bodyline. I am positive of that, as I am also positive that had Bradman been an Englishman and whipped the Australians as he did the English, the Australians (provided they could devise such a method of attack and had Woodfull not been captain) would have been tempted to use some such drastic theory against Bradman. And what a howl there would have been had that happened at Lord's!

It has been a problem to know how best to deal with Bradman in this book. He knew little privacy during his active career. The spotlight shone full upon him, of course, on the cricket field and within its precincts, but even miles away from the ovals he was quickly recognised and lionised. His record-breaking deeds had the effect of making his life barely his own. I would much rather have left out the semi-private part of his cricketing days, but when I reflected that my task was to give a pen-picture of the place he held in the game and the terrific influence he possessed (which, as will be seen, I consider the prime reason for Bodyline), I found it imperative to discuss Bradman in a personal manner. Indeed, this must be done if all aspects of the Bodyline case are to be set down and understood.

The basis on which to consider Bodyline is to get away completely from the question of which country employed it. The practice must be considered on its merits and facts. Some said that Bodyline typified the personality of Jardine. That may not be true, but an important suggestion is that Jardine, by his bitterness, his stubbornness, his hatred of the Australian barracker, allowed the theory to sway and dominate the MCC team and grow away from all reason. From the aesthetic cricket viewpoint it must never be forgotten that Bodyline caused a bowler of Tate's superlative ability on Australian wickets to be cast on the Test scrapheap, and the highly accomplished Verity was surprisingly omitted from the one Test which England lost that series.

There was no necessity to go as far as the MCC team did under Jardine. If the Englishmen resented the manner in which Bradman dominated the game, they had their answer to him in legitimate bumpers. The Englishmen made a very important discovery during the Fifth Test at Kennington Oval in 1930, and they could have exploited that in 1932 without going to extremes. There was no need to bowl bumpers with vicious intent and rub the salt in with a closely packed leg-field. Then, again, the English had no field quarrel with the other Australians. Why, then, turn the panzer tactics against them, bedraggle the fields and dressing-rooms with casualties and create bad feeling on all sides?

I got on well with Jardine in the little I had to do with him. I did not admire the tactics of his team, but I had a liking for the man, and few Australians will be found to say that. I once offered my Editor to write a story on Jardine, as I found him. 'And how do you find Jardine?' I was asked. 'He has his good points,' I replied. 'No, thanks,' said the Editor, 'the Australian public has made up its mind on Jardine.' Probably it was his unflinching courage in the face of most intense barracking that gave me my admiration for him, but I had that long before he sought me out in Adelaide and commiserated with me on making a 'pair of spectacles'. He had also performed the feat and knew what it was like!

Bodyline apart, I consider Jardine the most efficient, scientific and shrewdest Test captain I played with or against. His mind was delightfully analytical, and those with and against him knew they were engaged to the hilt in a Test match. Next to him – and little behind – was Victor Richardson.

I found Larwood quiet, modest and likeable. To a certain extent, I think both Jardine and Larwood were the victims of circumstances – and I will leave it at that for the present.

I hope I can do the game some service with suggestions in this book. I owe the game much. It has given me many intense days of pleasure in the sun and in the good company of cobbers all over the world. To be a Test cricketer and a touring Test cricketer is, in itself, a very fruitful education and experience in life. The game gave me, also, my wife, whom I met on shipboard on the voyage to England in 1938.

My thanks are due to many. Neville Cardus was most encouraging, and so were Hugh Buggy and William O'Reilly. They talked many things over with me and gave me the benefit of their advice and experience. E. H. M. Baillie helped me with statistics I could have got from no other source. I have also to thank warmly those international players of many countries who most eagerly replied to me with information which I sought. They prefer to be unnamed.

Canberra, August, 1946.   J.H.F.

PART ONE

Bodyline

CHAPTER ONE

'It isn't Cricket, Sir!'

THE BODYLINE STORM WAS SLOW in breaking. It hovered ominously in the English and Australian dressing-rooms before the dark and angry clouds became visible to outsiders, but once it burst there was no mistaking its fury. It thundered and flashed lightning, engendered a spiteful nastiness before a startled sporting world, and, even after it had appeared to pass on, there were mutterings and reverberations over English, West Indian and Indian cricket fields and in the highest places of English and Australian diplomacy – places where goodwill between two countries of the Empire was of much more importance than a mere game with bat and ball.

I vividly recall the day the storm broke officially. Bats, pads and flannels in disarray gave the Australian dressing-room the usual scene of a match in progress, and the smell of bat-oil and embrocation recurs to me as I recall how William Maldon Woodfull, his ribs badly bruised a few moments before on the field by a Larwood thunderbolt, lay on a massage table and spoke slow and deliberate words to Warner and Palairet, the managers of the Marylebone team.

Nobody could accuse the Australian captain of being a garrulous individual. Nature made him taciturn, and study at the Melbourne University, where he earned the degree of Master of Arts, taught him the value of words. The cricket world knew him as a man of quiet dignity, of resolute character, and all this added emphasis to the words he addressed to the English managers who had crossed the Australian threshold to extend the hand of sympathy.

'We have come,' said spokesman Warner, 'to offer you our sympathy.'

'I don't wish to discuss it,' replied Woodfull.

In naive fashion, considering all that had gone before, Warner asked, 'Why?'

And these were the Woodfull words which went beneath the English skin, which brought the bodyline case out into the open and made the English managers, the Marylebone Club and the Australian Board of Control face up to a situation which, for weeks before and despite what their eyes saw and their ears heard, they had been vainly trying to convince themselves did not exist.

'There are two teams out there on the oval,' said Woodfull, motioning to the doorway. 'One is playing cricket, the other is not. This game is too good to be spoilt. It is time some people got out of it.'

They were simple words, simply expressed, with no flavour of heat or anger. The sting was in their meaning, and Warner, for once, could not produce the soft, sweet words which fell so readily from his lips. He was of the diplomatic type, a type which chooses its words carefully and walks ambassadorial carpets with suavity and confidence; but on this brilliant summer day in Adelaide of January, 1933, words failed the usually ready Warner. He turned in embarrassment. With Palairet at his heels, he strode quickly from the room.

The heat of doubt was soon to be turned full-fire on this MCC team. In a few days the Australian Board of Control was to send to the MCC committee in London its famous or infamous cable alleging unsportsmanship against the English team. In themselves, however, it would be difficult to conceive words better suited than Woodfull's to disturb the feelings of an average Englishman, particularly an Englishman of the Public School type, a type whose representation and influence were more pronounced in this MCC team than in any other to visit Australia.

Warner had worn the colours of Rugby before he went to Oxford; Palairet was Repton and Oxford; the dour, unsmiling Jardine, leading the team on the Adelaide oval, was Winchester and Oxford; Brown was Leys and Cambridge; Allen was Eton and Cambridge; and the Nawab of Pataudi was of Oxford.

These formed a most representative band of English Public School and Varsity men. Their shoulders, doubtlessly, had often been smitten by the hand of their school captain as he told them to 'Play up, play up and play the game.' Moreover, they were of the traditional English type whose first lesson in life taught them that to do anything mean, ignoble or even doubtful was 'not cricket, sir!'. Such a term fashioned their way of life, it moulded their code of ethics.

Woodfull had thus snubbed Warner in no uncertain manner. His accusation against the Englishmen of not playing cricket was followed by his tribute to a great game which, in its charm and tradition, transcends mere victory and glorification of the individual. It would be irksome for a player of international standing to be read this first lesson in the ethics of the game, but particularly was it irksome for cricketers who were Englishmen, descendants of those who devised the game and of those who preserved its traditions down through the years.

It was not a matter for wonder that Warner walked embarrassed from the Australian dressing-room with no word in reply or defence. It was no wonder, either, that from that day until the bodyline hatchet was buried, some few years later, Englishmen and Australians should become resentful when they recalled the events which preceded and followed the Adelaide dressing room scene of 1933.

The next shot in the barrage and counter-barrage was fired with intense publicity when the Australian Board of Control, a few days after the Woodfull-Warner incident, belatedly sent off that renowned cable, the first of a series, protesting to the MCC against the 'unsportsmanship' of its team in Australia. I use the term belated advisedly, because, whether the tactics of the MCC team were sporting or unsporting, the fact was that these tactics were begun in Australia early in November. It was true, also, that these tactics had never been modified, but, indeed, had been intensified, and the high noon of January in Adelaide of the Third Test was somewhat late in the day for official action.

Inwardly, no doubt, such an accusation from Australia against its team made the MCC committee squirm. Outwardly, it did not cause much trouble. The MCC committee ordered up the heavy artillery piece of finance and cracked off this cable broadside to the Australian Board on the eve of the Fourth Test:

'If you feel disposed to cancel the remainder of the tour,' said the MCC cable, 'we would reluctantly be compelled to agree.'

That sent the Australian Board scurrying to its foxholes. If it was doing nothing else, this particular series of Tests was making huge profits. Sportsmanship or no sportsmanship, the Tests must go on. Before the next Test had commenced in Brisbane the Board sent the MCC a cable that the sportsmanship of its side was not in question – which was, whichever way you care to look at it, rather a remarkable reversal of opinion.

But I am a little ahead of my story. The legal profession had invariably been well represented on the Australian Board of Control, and season 1932–33 was no exception. There was thus reason to expect that the Board, finally deciding to take its cable step, would have framed a judicious and tactful cable. But diplomacy went for a walk the Adelaide morning the Board strung together its first cable. The Board first tried to induce Woodfull and Bradman to put their names to a cable to the MCC and leave the Board out of it, but the two players told the Board, in effect, that as it had been elected to govern the game in Australia it, perforce, should govern and do its own cabling job.

And the Board did do its own cabling job. It shot off the accusation of 'unsportsmanship' so loudly at the MCC that it resounded around the sporting world, and it did not help matters of state, either, that the text of the cable should have been in the hands of the British and Australian Press sooner than in the MCC committee rooms in London.

This was the cable:

'Bodyline bowling assumed such proportions as to menace best interests of the game, making protection of body by batsmen the main consideration and causing intensely bitter feeling between players as well as injury. In our opinion, it is unsportsmanlike. Unless stopped at once it is likely to upset friendly relations existing between Australia and England.'

In its report at the end of the 1934 English season, the MCC clearly stated that this type of bowling was unfair and must be eliminated, but that was after it had been seen by MCC eyes. Imagine the impression the above blatant Australian cable would have on MCC temperaments! Fowler once wrote that the English temperament has a stubborn, national dislike of putting things too strongly. There are many examples in English history of objectives achieved by adroit understatement, but even Australians (and we are renowned for our national bluntness) recoiled at the clumsy, blustering manner in which the Australian Board of Control publicly conveyed across the world its self-satisfied charge and verdict that English cricketers were perpetrating something rotten in the Commonwealth of Australia.

The walls of the Long Pavilion at Lord's must have shaken their historic photographs and the busts of the immortals trembled on their pedestals the day that ugly accusation of unsportsmanship obtruded into the cricket holy of holies. Those who saw Larwood bowl bodyline as only Larwood could might not have hesitated in so classifying the theory; but, if the case was clear to Australian eyes, it should have been just as obvious that Marylebone Cricket Club members, 12,000 miles away, who had never seen intensified body-line as Australia was seeing it, could not be expected to see the position immediately in the Australian light. The case had first to be put, and there was a right and a wrong way of putting it, especially when the other party was the MCC. Would one announce himself at the Pearly Gates on the Last Day by making aspersions on St Peter?

The Woodfull–Warner incident and the Board's first cable were two facets of a tour that came to be known as the bodyline tour, played – but mostly wrangled – in Australia in the season of cricket disgrace, 1932–33. It was startling copy for a modern Press with a flair for the sensational, and the whole battle of the offensive and the defensive rolled backwards and forwards with splenetic fury for all the sporting world to witness.

There were rows, fights and arguments in clubs and pubs. 'It is preventable cruelty,' claimed the old Australian captain, M. A. Noble. 'The Australians are squealers,' came back cables from England, and at the height of it, with one authority saying this and another that, with one applauding and the other decrying, the poor, humble follower of the game, he who made such Test tours possible by his few shillings at the turnstile, did not know what to think. He was completely baffled and befuddled and even now, years after-wards, is not too certain what all the fuss was about, who was right and who was wrong.

In calm perspective, it is interesting to look back over those years. I do not know whether Dr W. G. Grace placed the game before himself. From what I read, there were times when he didn't.* If he did not and had atoned for his sins it would have been a happy moment had the ghost of the Old Man happened along that season, taken a few principals and officials of both countries by the scruff of the neck, soundly dusted the seat of their flannels, placed them down and admonished them to get on with the play in the spirit of the game and not the spirit of themselves.

Had something like that happened, bodyline would have been killed soon after birth and years of squabbling would have been avoided. The theory is now no more. It was killed by a ruling of the MCC, as it was conceived by a team of the MCC, but, before its extermination, there were unseemly incidents in England, India and the West Indies, and MCC batsmen, who did not make one gesture of protest when it was their bedfellow in Australia, later struck outraged and indignant attitudes on English fields when their old love was turned against them.

* The stories of the manner in which the Old Man lorded it in the game are legion. This is an example. He was alleged to have been bowled, the off bail alone falling off. He stooped, picked it up, put it back on the stumps, and said to the umpire: 'Very windy to-day.' 'Yes,' agreed the umpire, 'but I'm not. You're out.'

Counties squabbled with counties and cancelled fixtures. Duckworth had several ribs broken; Hammond had his face gashed; Wyatt's jaw was splintered in the West Indies, and Hendren walked out in protective armour one day at Lord's like a knight who faced a strenuous joust.

It was not, however, until the pastures of leading English counties were banned to the bad Notts wolves, Larwood and Voce, that the MCC fixed bodyline with a cold stare and beckoned it to the lethal chamber.

Cricket was done an irreparable wrong in those few years. Rich in history, in art, in association and tradition, the game was dealt a staggering blow by the theory itself, but it did not end there. In their hasty desire to bury the body, the MCC and the Australian Board combined to deal the game another sickening blow. The unctuous anxiety of the two international committees to be good friends and self-effacing, to forget the bad old days, led to a passive period in which every fast bowler was forced to put on his party suit and display his nicest manners. The ambitious fast bowler who dropped a ball short at the half-way mark on the pitch, irrespective of whether the leg-side was packed with fieldsmen, was simply not invited. He stayed at home or watched from over the fence. That was the other extreme from bodyline and a bad one, too – a swing from wild bowling derring-do to correctness, almost to delicacy.

What was the origin of bodyline – what was its meaning? Was it something that existed only in the minds of the Australian batsmen or the sensational section of the Australian Press? Was it something that had its origin over-night, or was it the culmination of years of planning?

The more I think of those years, and particularly the years preceding them, the more I am convinced that something akin to bodyline was unavoidable. It was inevitable and because of one man, or, to be more precise, because of a youth just out of his teens. That youth was Bradman, who had turned the cricket world topsy-turvy by the time he was twenty-two years of age.

Bodyline was conceived for Bradman, born and carefully nurtured for him, and, when one reflects on the seasons preceding 1932–33, it might be agreed that not even a Bradman had the divine right to pre-suppose that he could indulge himself in gargantuan feast of runs and not pay the penalty of something like bodyline indigestion.

In those days of 1932–33, when the ball reared about Australian ears and noses, it was apparent that bodyline was Bradman's indigestion.

It plagued him day and night; it tortured him mentally (it did not do so physically until the final Test, when Larwood caught him a resounding blow on the upper arm), and in all this, while living, playing and travelling with Bradman, I often wondered whether he realised that his record-breaking sins, so to term them, had found him out.

I think he did. I recall his reply in London, in 1938, when Hutton had broken his Test record of 334 and I asked Bradman whether he might, some day, set out on the task of beating Hutton.

'One does not go seeking records,' was Bradman's reply. 'They simply just happen.'

That was the Bradman of 1938 speaking. He was a Bradman far removed from the hustling, ambitious Bowral stripling of the early 1930s, when all the cricket world to him was a stage and he played the Hamlet of the piece. But, conceding Bradman his 1938 thoughts of records, I doubt whether one could find a single established bowler of his early career who would agree with him that he did not seek records.

It was the record feat of making 320 not out in a country cricket final that first drew attention to him. The spotlight of that record shone on him an invitation to present himself at court in Sydney, and in as much time as the average player takes to accommodate himself to the change from concrete matting wickets to turf, Bradman swept through Sydney grade cricket to first-class ranks to the Test heights. An ordinary mortal might have paused at any of these stages to catch his breath in the bewildering delights of such a meteoric transition, but Bradman was in too much of a hurry to spare time for convention.

Bradman's mind was resolute from the first moment he stepped off the train on the long, sombre Sydney station that there would be no going or looking back to his former country pastures. His batting genius was magnificent. He had a natural aptitude for learning. His ambition was unlimited and truly remarkable in one so young and inexperienced. Many a player down the long years of Australian cricket, from Bannerman to Macartney, had made his string of centuries and received his due meed of praise; but the long-sighted Bradman, his batting genius closely interwoven with a remarkable business shrewdness, told himself that it was not sufficient to make centuries. Had it been only a century he made in that bush game the feat would not even have merited mention in the City Press. It was the number of days he batted and the score he made that developed it into a believe-it-or-not marvel and brought him to Sydney.

Bradman never forgot the first lesson of publicity and its causes which he learnt in the Australian bush. When he made a century, he made himself comfortable and settled down for two; when he had made two hundred he cocked an eye for three, and if, by pushing himself a little further, it meant pushing somebody off a record pedestal, then, hey, presto! Bradman called upon his superabundance of energy and magnificent concentration. The record became his and at such a pinnacle as to frighten all but a Hutton.

Not even Bradman could have thought it a coincidence that nearly all the records known to the statistician came his way. No Test bowler did. They will give it as their opinion that Bradman sought records against them in cold, deliberate fashion, and many, knowing the circumstances of those years, will agree that Bradman knew only too well in that 1932–33 season that his record-breaking chickens had come home to roost.

Together with the other Australian batsmen of the period, Bradman made a close study of that MCC side when it was announced. He saw there a top-heavy bowling list with Larwood, Allen, Voce, Bowes, Tate, Hammond, Verity, Brown and Mitchell. He saw something most unprecedented in that four of those bowlers, Larwood, Allen, Voce and Bowes, were fast bowlers.

What could this history-making battery of fast bowlers mean? It meant only one thing to Bradman. They were after his batting skin, and before a single ball had been bowled on that Australian tour, and because of what had gone before in the English season of 1930, Bradman knew only too well that their general plan of skinning would not be along the staid lines of orthodoxy.

CHAPTER TWO   *An Over at the Oval*

IN JUNE, 1930, THE TIMES HAD this to report of the Notts–Somerset games: 'Hunt received a bad body blow from Voce and afterwards battled left-handed when facing Voce, but ordinary right-hand against the other bowlers. Then Case, when endeavouring to avoid a ball that rose head high, hit his wicket. Case was so disturbed that he returned to the pavilion carrying one of the stumps instead of his bat.'

This savoured of bodyline. It had the ingredients that were to become so well known in Australia two years later, the ducking to avoid a hit and the actual hit on the body. So far as Australia knew it, this was the first publicised start of bodyline. Leg theory, of course, had been sleepily plodding its negative way for years. Slow to medium spinners, our own immense Armstrong among them, had long exploited a strongly packed leg-field, with the ball pitching on the leg stump or just outside of it.

In 1938 almost every English county had such a bowler, of the Sinfield, Root, Goddard type, who could dispense this leg-theory with remarkable accuracy and economy of runs. It was, as I have written, a negative theory. It so obviously said to the batsman: 'Here I go past your leg stump. I won't worry you very much, but if you want runs, you will take all the risks.'

It was this theory which the MCC, in the later years of bodyline, making its loyal and valiant last-ditch stand by Warner, Jardine and Co, said had been wrongly termed bodyline.

'The practice of leg-theory bowling has been in vogue in this country for years,' cabled the MCC in defending the tactics of its team in Australia; but that deceived nobody who saw the theories in action. Leg-theory and bodyline were barely nodding acquaintances; the only relationship they knew was that in each theory the ball was pitched at the leg stump or outside of it.

The ideal leg-theory bowler was one who could spin the ball from the off. It was customary to bowl from round the wicket, with the ball in its flight coming in to the batsman's legs to break away again with the off spin. It was essential that such a ball should be of perfect length. No matter how much spin it carried, a ball short in length or over-pitched would present no difficulties to a batsman, and in this basic fundamental of length was the first distinguishing difference between leg-theory and bodyline.

The ideal height off the pitch for a bodyline ball was at the ribs or the head (the 'bean' ball, as it is known in baseball) and, to a less extent, the thigh. No good length ball could rise so high, and thus, to get the necessary height, it follows that the perfect length for a bodyline ball was short of the usual good length for an ordinary ball. It should thus be apparent that no slow or medium bowler could traffic in bodyline, for such a bowler, pitching short in length, would be a gift to the batsman. An obvious essential for bodyline, therefore, was speed; for pace alone could give the ball lift off the pitch, and pace alone could give bodyline its very flavour of intimidation.

The fast bowler never tied up white laces who did not let one or two deliveries 'fly' every now and then at the batsman. Some batsmen became fidgety if bumpers were bowled at them; others, again (for instance Badcock, who was the world's best I saw in dealing with a short ball), would have gloried in bumpers until the end of cricket time, and it is of particular interest that Australian Interstate captains, though operating in a time of scarcity of really fast bowlers, invariably give their fast bowlers orders to bump a few at Bradman. 'Let one or two go now and then at the little bloke,' was a standing order in Australian cricket in my time.

It was believed in Australian cricketing circles that Bradman did not like it when the ball was bumped at him. Similar Australian thoughts were held of Nourse, of South Africa, and Barnett and Hutton, of England, to quote a few. It is of interest to know that had McCormick been chosen for Australia in that final Test match at the Oval in 1938, he would have had no pangs of conscience in bumping a few at Hutton and undoubtedly incommoding him, as he did later in the festival game at Scarborough.

In defending Jardine's tactics of 1932–33, critics pointed out that Gregory and McDonald hit many an English batsman in 1921. That was true, but what of it? Nobody can point the finger at a fast bowler who happens to hit a batsman with a legitimate bumper, but the bodyline case differed because the thick English placing of the leg-side field on the batsman's 'blind spot' tied down and cramped the batsman and did not give him a cricketing chance to deal with a bumper. Moreover, this brought the physical element into the case. Because playing the ball would have given a catch to the leg trap, a batsman often took the ball on his ribs instead, because the very speed of the ball did not allow him to get his body out of the way. The leg-side field was just as much a part of bodyline as the fast bowler and bumpers.

A leg-theory field had its men distributed evenly on the leg side. A bodyline field had a cordon of short-legs and fine-legs, with an outer cordon to cover them. Thus, the bodyline field was concentrated; in other words, it had to tie the batsman down while the ball played about his ribs and ears. He was 'cribbed, cabined, confined' – and battered.

This theory, not termed bodyline until early summer in Australia in 1932, was the one Voce exploited in England in 1930, and which the Australians met in that season's game against Nottinghamshire. The Australians decided among themselves that they would prefer Voce not to play in the Tests, and so to Richardson and McCabe, two gifted in the pull stroke, was deputed the task of hitting Voce out of the Test firing line.

Voce pounded down his short deliveries, Carr packed the leg-side (though not to the extent which Jardine did later), but the harder Voce bowled, the harder the Australians hit him and the further he faded from Test speculation. Voce was a good bodyliner, but he was not a Larwood. There was only one Larwood, and Voce lacked the Larwood degree of pace and control which paid the richest bodyline dividends. Voce did not make the Test side on that occasion, and the Australians went to bed in good content.

Then came the final Test, and when rain arrived one day Bradman and Jackson were in complete batting control. It seemed there would be no more play for this particular day, but a strange decision was made by the umpires that play should recommence at 6.25 pm. That means there would be time for only one over.

There was no mistaking the reception which the Australians gave to that decision. In bad temper, the not-out batsmen, Bradman and Jackson, dawdled to the wickets and were roundly hooted. Larwood prepared to bowl the only over, and in that over – so it is claimed by those who were there and are best qualified to judge – was born the plan for the 1932–33 Australian season of bodyline.

Larwood emulated his fellow-countryman, Voce. He bumped the ball short and it reared viciously off the wet wicket. Jackson, unconcerned, and Bradman weathered the over, but in those few

11

balls Bradman revealed something the Englishmen had never before seen from him while he was making 123 and 112 (Tests) against Chapman's team in Australia in 1928–29; 132 for NSW against the same side; 157 next season for NSW against an MCC team passing through to New Zealand; 334 at Leeds, 254 at Lord's, 232 at the Oval; 131 at Trent Bridge (all Tests); 236 at Worcester; 205 at Canterbury; 191 at Southampton; 185 at Leicester and 117 at Taunton. In that over Bradman showed unmistakable concern when the ball bumped.

It could be said of Bradman that he was rarely at ease on a wet wicket. The opposite was the case on a true wicket; for the world has not seen his equal, nor anybody approaching his equal, in the consistency and degree of his big scores. I particularly stress the word consistency. Some of aesthetic tastes might have preferred the cultured charm of a Kippax or a Jackson to Bradman's flaying piece; I saw Macartney and knew his genius to be of a different mould from that of Bradman. Repute also has Trumper to be of a different mould; but, in the sheer consistency and robust profligacy of their respective arts, Bradman far outshone all others, the English eras of Grace, MacLaren, Hayward and Hobbs not excluded.

Other individuals might have been noted for fast footwork, unerring judgment or brilliant eyesight. Bradman possessed all these; but, if there was one faculty which made him superior to others, it was in being able to judge, almost as soon as the ball left the bowler's hand, the length, spin and merit of that particular delivery. Therein lay much of his greatness – a quicker brain, a quicker judgment than any other batsman I have seen.

But a batsman does not place himself on a pinnacle such as Bradman occupied by virtue of any one, two or three outstanding gifts. Bradman was richly endowed in all that went towards making the champion, and in none more so than in his twinkling, magical feet. I have tried to dissect their movements from the distance of the pavilion and from the closeness of the opposite batting end; but Bradman's feet were almost too quick for me, especially against slow bowlers.

A friend of mine once had an interesting conversation with Ponsford about Bradman's batting. When asked why it was that Bradman made bowling look so easy, Ponsford, with his usual modesty, replied: 'The reason is very simple. Don sees the ball about two yards sooner than any of the rest of us.'

Ponsford meant by that exactly what I have written – that Bradman was able to judge the merits of the ball two yards or so sooner than any other batsman. This, in turn, gave him what I consider the greatest advantage he possessed over all contemporary batsmen. He played forward more, he played up the wicket more than any other first-class batsman I knew, and no bowler likes to see a batsman coming forward with confidence and attacking good length balls. Unusual height with its long reach enabled Woolley to cover by forward play ordinarily good length balls; Bradman, a smallish man, got to where he wanted by quick footwork. J. M. Taylor hit Tate hard off his back foot; Bradman hit him hard off his front, delighting to the fact that Tate's excessive pace off the pitch gave his additional speed off the bat. Where most batsmen instinctively swayed on the back foot to cope with this Tate pace off the pitch, Bradman went forward gleefully to make the most of it.

His batting stance was unique. His bat touched the ground between his feet, not behind them, like every other batsman and photograph I have seen. He stood perfectly still as the bowler approached; the end of his bat did not act as an escape conductor for energy with that nervous tap, tap, tap on the pitch so common to most batsmen as the bowler ran to deliver the ball.

Bradman at the wickets was completely at ease and at rest until the ball began its apologetic advance towards him. His lithe, compact body was a power-house of latent electricity until the switch of a ball released was turned, and then his brightness flashed in all directions. His feet took him into immediate position to offset swerve, swing or break bowling; his running feet took him three and even four yards up the pitch to slow bowling to kill the break and take advantage of the gap in the field which his eye had detected. He was at his best in making the placement of a field look foolish. He was at his greatest against slow bowling (he took 30 off a six-ball Freeman over at Folkestone in 1934), for he moved far out to the ball on the full or drew back to destroy its length and pull in that unorthodox manner which grew with him on the concrete wickets of his country youth.

I remember Bradman in his first appearance at the Sydney nets. There was a breeze of the bush and bygone years in the braces he wore, but there his rusticity ended. He was the cynosure of all eyes, and well-intentioned critics, as they always do, converged on him at the finish of his net and talked to him of his stance, his unorthodoxy on the leg-side. They would have had him change this or do that, but Bradman gave them a polite ear and then promptly dismissed them from his thoughts, internationals and ex-internationals though they were. Even at that age Bradman possessed pronounced qualities. Confidence in his own ability and interpretation of the game was one of them.

The story is told of him in those years when he was first chosen, a mere slip of a country youth, in the New South Wales touring team. An admirer had presented him with a touring cricket bag and he had gone to choose it.

'I want something big to carry plenty of equipment and I also want something that will last a long time. It is going to have a lot of work to do,' airily said Bradman to the storekeeper, and that story quickly went the rounds.

His selection, like that of others at the time, was purely in the nature of an experiment, a commendable New South Wales experiment of the period which paid and repaid handsome dividends. Mere lads were chosen in first-class games. Some fell by the wayside, others bore rich fruit (Jackson and McCabe were two), but Bradman did not consider that there was anything problematical in the scattering of his seed and its ultimate harvest. Youths walked blushingly and full of awe into the precincts of Macartney, Taylor, Andrews, Kippax, and others, but Bradman came supreme in his own confidence, determined to go his own way. And he did!

In a few short years he had the Australian sporting firmament at his feet. No Prime Minister, no inventor, no medical genius of the calibre of McCormick and Hunter, no South Pole explorer like Wilkins or world-acclaimed airmen like Kingsford-Smith, Ross and Keith Smith, Hinkler or Ulm knew the publicity from the Australian Press that Bradman received.

He rose to the heights in a period of world uneasiness, the depression years and the early rumblings which were later to develop into the avalanche of European troubles. Hitler had just commenced his rise to power; economic conferences were being held in London; gold standards were crashing; Wall and Throgmorton streets were dizzy with speculation, and one of the representatives of world finance, Sir Otto Niemeyer, had just delivered to Australians a depressing lecture on how to run their country – a lecture dictating financial belt tightening in a land of primary abundance.

As the Irish poet and author, Eimar O'Duffy, had it:

> The banker in his counting-house counting out his money;
> The land was overflowing with bread and milk and honey;
> The shops were full of good things, the factories likewise;
> The banker shut his books and said we must economise.

Bradman's colossal feats with a piece of willow gave editors a chance to depart from their usual mournful run of depression news. His deeds were so remarkable that they spilled over from the sporting pages and gave the window-dressers of the Press an infrequent opportunity in those days to instil a little brightness, some light relief, into their usually gloomy leader columns.

He became the most discussed person in Australia, conceding the limelight for a short period only to the then New South Wales

Premier, John T. Lang, when that turbulent politician became embroiled in a Government Bank crash, a constitutional tilt with Governor Sir Philip Game and a ribbon-cutting episode at the opening of the Sydney Harbour Bridge.

Bradman became the continent's number one idol, not merely because of his prodigious batting feats, but, in a sense, because they happened at a time when Australian national life was sick and apprehensive. Business men on the verge of bankruptcy said, 'To hell with business' (it invariably finished there, anyhow, in those days!), closed up their doors and went out to forget their woes and themselves with Bradman. It was usual to see thousands leave the ground when Bradman was dismissed. The atmosphere and most of the interest in the game walked back with Bradman to the pavilion, a bitter pill for previous headliners to swallow and none too happy a prospect for those who had the interests of the game at heart; but circumstances and his own genius surrounded Bradman with an atmosphere and a publicity value no other player could approach.

People who had never been to a cricket match before, who did not know a bat from a ball, flocked to see Bradman. A carnival spirit hung over every ground on which he played, and the first sight of him as he emerged from the pavilion was sufficient to send the whole ground into ecstasies of delight. No other batsman in my time, which corresponded with Bradman, could approach his terrific skill with the bat or his unlimited popularity with the crowd. He was the planet, solely inhabited; the others revolved around him, shining intermittently in the early 1930s in his reflected glory.

His colleagues frequently felt that they were mere lay figures or items of scenery to be arranged to provide a background for the principal actor, but, from a public point of view, Bradman was responsible for a very great percentage of the enormous public interest in cricket between the two wars.

He seemed to bring out through the gate with him a breath of power and a confidence which made everybody feel that the whole fortunes of the game would be changed by him – as they invariably were. He walked slowly to the wickets with a slight rolling gait, the slowness so that he could accustom his eyes from the dark of the pavilion to the light of the ground (a gentleman named Lyon took him to task for this slow walk, in England, in 1930, but as Lyon had also played the game he should have known better).

Where 99 batsmen out of a hundred make their last few yards to the wicket with a grim, haunted look on their faces, determination alternating with nervous hopefulness, Bradman's mien when at last he reached the creases was one of supreme and disarming happiness. A few seconds' business with the umpire and then he looked about him with a huge grin. That grin was the cheekiest, the most challenging, and the most confident thing I have seen in sport. It was such as to rip the innards out of any bowler, sending him hurtling down to spreadeagle the stumps of this cocky young man, but always the tale was the same. Bradman opened his score with the cheekiest and most confident of shots, and there he was at the other end or walking back down the pitch from a boundary shot, grinning, grinning, grinning!

The crowd loved and adored him for his tradesmanlike activities at the wickets. His worth was apparent and intrinsically honest. He gave them even more than they asked for their admission money.

He was at once the despair of the bowler, the captain and his fieldsman, the batting worthy struggling at the other end and his comrades in the pavilion. He made it all look so easy, so simple, so prearranged. He always made the onlooker feel that a loose ball would be lifted for four to the very place on the boundary to which batting science required that that ball should be sent.

He was the genius absolute. To bat with him was an education and revelation, not given by any other batsman of the period. Great artists like Trumper and Macartney varied the direction of the shot for sheer artistic satisfaction, but Bradman was implacable. He was more interested in runs than art, and in the days when he was playing for Australia you would have searched a long time before you found an onlooker who seriously disagreed with him. He was the undisputed hero of the new-found public, the broadcasting public. He was the darling of the spectator's heart – and justifiably so, because no batsman in history had been so prolific and none of the moderns could approach the standard he set for consistency and sheer honesty of batting purpose.

Sydney citizens asked the visitor whether he had seen our Harbour, our Bridge and our Don. It was embarrassing to walk down the street with Bradman, to ride in a street car or dine with him. He was instantly recognised and acclaimed, even staid professors permitting themselves a childlike chuckle as they obtruded a pen and a piece of paper on Bradman for an autograph. The life of the champion seemed to be one long succession of autographs. The post disgorged hundreds of them at him daily, and almost the only peace he knew from them was while he was at the wickets – which was probably a reason why he stayed there so long.

In all this adulation, in all this hero worshipping, which came at its flood when he had just passed his 21st birthday, Bradman never lost his balance. He never allowed his head to expand in the vapourings of flattery. The ground was always in contact with his feet, though once established he did not temporise with any challenges against his domain.

Once in a game in Sydney against Victoria there had been the bold claim in a newspaper that Ironmonger, who had taken his wicket in the first innings, had the measure of the champion. It was dangerous for Ironmonger that such stuff should have been written. Bradman made a close study of what the critics wrote. His most spectacular innings in Australia was played in Sydney (Fleetwood-Smith being the chief operating medium) the day after a leading critic had written that he did not possess the spectacular flair of a Trumper or a Macartney.

As he opened his huge mail this other Sydney morning he casually asked several of us if we had seen the particular article about Ironmonger and himself.

'Yes,' somebody answered, 'we did.'

'It will be quite interesting,' said Bradman, with a smile, 'to see what happens to-day.'

The tone in Bradman's voice suggested that he himself was in no doubt. Ironmonger was to be put through the Bradman hoops, but Bradman was not boasting. In his 'it will be interesting to see what happens to-day,' he was letting us know that he had accepted the Ironmonger challenge, and he wished us to note how he accepted it.

Until he reached the sobriety or comparative sobriety of his late twenties, Bradman was always impish in his batting. It amounted almost to a point of honour with him, as I have written, to take at least a single from the first ball bowled to him, but in this innings against Ironmonger, the innings which was to prove whether a mere bowling mortal could hold a cricket god in chancery, Bradman's audacity took on the flavour of contempt.

It was not sufficient for Ironmonger first to be subdued and then flayed. A Jackson or a Kippax might do that. Ironmonger, or rather the critic, had to be put in his Bradman place.

From the very first ball Bradman took the most daring risks. He cut Ironmonger fine off his middle stump, he flicked him off his stumps to the fine leg fence, he on and off drove him, hit him high to the outfield (always difficult with Ironmonger), and then, in a final flourish of contempt for the critics, Bradman hit Ironmonger over the fence. No batsman could have done more against a bowler, and in all this it was difficult not to believe that Bradman was laughing hugely, not at Ironmonger so much, but at those critics who suggested Ironmonger held an option over him.

Bradman returned radiant to the pavilion. 'What was in that article again?' he asked.

That was Bradman's nature. He liked nothing better than slaughtering bowlers and critics alike.

There was another occasion, on the eve of a charity game in which Mailey and Bradman were opposed, when a statistician found that Mailey, then a cricket veteran, had taken Bradman's wicket several times. The newspaper displayed the fact. It was an interesting news item, but for Mailey it could mean only one thing, even though the game was a charity one. It meant for Mailey his offering on the sacrificial altar of Bradman's greatness, for the little chap never missed a cricket item in the newspapers.

I lunched with Mailey that day and he was obviously ill at ease.

'They shouldn't write stuff like that,' he said, referring to the newspaper item.

Mailey knew his Bradman. He knew, as a consequence of that item, that there would be a hot Bradman reception awaiting him.

Thousands thronged the small ground, and there was a buzz of excited expectancy as Bradman made his customary slow walk to the wickets. The test was to be immediate. Mailey was bowling. As Mailey apprehensively twiddled the ball from hand to hand at the other end, Bradman meticulously took his guard and looked about the field as if to say: 'So Mailey, one of the Old School, has my measure. Well, well! Let us see if there is anything in this rumour. I'm ready when you are, Arthur.'

Mailey began his ambling run, his arm came up and over – and Bradman was running yards down the wicket with his bat poised aloft. There was a succulent swish of Bradman's bat and away in the distance, as if fearing what was to come, the ball lost itself in the crowd.

Then followed cold and deliberate cricket murder. Mailey's deliveries speeded to the fence and over the fence, and from one of the latter soaring hits came the tinkle of falling window-glass, the orchestral accompaniment to a stage plot of murder that had thousands calling for blood, blood, still more Mailey blood. Bradman put Mailey in the stocks that day for all to see. Then he hanged, drew and quartered him. Mailey was butchered to make another Bradman holiday.

That was another glimpse of Bradman. He was the dominant cricket figure of his age, and if fate delivered to him one of an older generation, then his treatment would be such as to suggest that Bradman was the dominant cricket figure of all the ages. Mailey had then retired from the first-class stage and was far past his best, but had he been in his prime I venture to say the story would have been much the same. Bradman paid respect to no bowling save bodyline.

All bowlers, with the possible exception of O'Reilly, whom he first met in a country game, came alike to Bradman. At one time or another he took up Tate, Larwood (before bodyline), Geary, Voce, Freeman, Verity, Constantine, Francis, Griffith, Grimmett, Fleetwood-Smith, Ebeling, Blackie, Ironmonger, Oxenham, Quinn, Bell, Morkel, McMillan and the rest of the world's best. He was wary and respectful always with O'Reilly, but the others he closely analysed and then slashed them apart before he left them bewildered, abashed and out of breath.

I hasten to add now that all this concerned Bradman the Great, of the Good Wicket. In that category he stood alone. He was towering, majestic, omniscient – until the patter, patter on his palace roof told him that the rains had arrived. Then he put off his majestic plumes and stole out to mix with the rabble, his features indistinguishable in the ranks of the wet-wicket mediocrities.

Bradman's repeated failures on wet wickets must forever remain the mystery of his career. I saw him bat on innumerable occasions on damaged wickets, but only twice did I see him succeed – once for NSW against England in 1933, again for Australia against Yorkshire at Bramall Lane in 1938.

The strangest thing about Bradman on a wet wicket was his attitude. Nobody likes beginning an innings on a damaged wicket. The difficulties are many, but any batsman who has made runs on a 'sticky' has no two thoughts of the intense pleasure and thrill it has given him. He must have a certain amount of good fortune to aid him in the early stages, the stages when he senses the tricks of the pitch, but he must also be proficient and gifted in not playing at the ball which will miss his wicket. He must be highly skilled in the art of 'dead' bat play, the sensitive touch of the fingers on the bat which drops the ball at the batsman's feet and keeps it out of the short-fieldsmen's hands.

Kippax was an excellent wet wicket batsman. Leyland and Hammond gave a masterly display of 'dead' bat play on one of the worst Melbourne wickets imaginable in 1936–37. History records that many of the older brigade, Trumper especially, could rise superior to the vagaries of a disturbed wicket. Trumper often top scored for Australia in Tests on gluepots. Bradman, also, should have risen far above his contemporaries on wet wickets, for he possessed in marked degree the qualities so essential for success on such pitches. He had the necessary eagle eye, footwork and judgment, but Bradman, instead of rising above his fellows under such conditions, fell far below many.

It always seemed that Bradman refused to take wet wickets seriously. There was not in his gait to the wickets that slow, measured tread so common to him. He came in a hurry and invariably left in a hurry, as if he were in the middle of a telephone conversation in the pavilion when his turn came to bat and had asked the caller to hold the line – he would not be long. It seemed he could not bring himself to be interested in such wickets; that he knew the good wicket which would soon come along would provide him with his customary big score, thus effacing any memory of this transient failure on a bad wicket.

I saw Bradman fail often, as I have written, on bad wickets, and that usually by careless or indifferent batting. I saw him succeed twice, and that was sufficient to prove that Bradman, had he driven himself to the task, could have been a good batsman on bad wickets.

And now you will be wondering what all this bad wicket talk has to do with bodyline. It has this. Bodyline was conceived for Bradman in that one over at the Oval in 1930, when Larwood dropped the ball short on a wet wicket and Bradman showed concern when it lifted round his ears.

It is not difficult to believe that bowlers' thoughts of Bradman were hard ones. Imagine yourself as Tate, Mailey or Ironmonger. What would your thoughts be of Bradman? If you had spun the flesh off your fingers; if you had planned and sweated for aching day after day until your shoulders were heavy and your heart despondent; if you had done all this and seen your honest offerings treated with the smile of contempt, what would you think if you suddenly saw Bradman show concern?

The shock would be too great to be missed. You would keenly analyse such a phenomenon. It would certainly set you thinking, and thus it started off a train of English thought after that Oval over. The next Test series would be played in Australia. A theory was very problematical if it had to rely on wet wickets to make the ball rise – but wait! Fast bowlers bowling short on the truest of wickets could always make the ball rise, make it rise as high as the head, if necessary.

Doubtlessly, there were such thoughts in some English minds as the 1930 Australian team was waved farewell from Tilbury. Those cricket heads went into English hibernation with a glint in their eyes, which, incidentally, were both wide open.

CHAPTER THREE   *Reflections on the Stoep*

Between the 1930 australian tour of England and the visit of Jardine's team there were two international tours of Australia. The West Indians came in 1930–31 and the South Africans the next year, and each tour, particularly that by the South Africans, had its place in bodyline history.

The West Indies team was the first from there to come to Australia. South Africa had been before, in 1910–11, with Sherwell, Faulkner, Schwarz, Dave Nourse (Dudley's father) some of the leading players, but Australia, unlike England, had not made a practice of inviting teams from other countries. England enjoyed a continual whirl of teams from Australia, South Africa, West Indies, India and New Zealand. The incidence of summer in those other lands made it a little difficult for Australia to send and receive teams, though New Zealand, for all the help and encouragement it received from the Commonwealth, might well have wondered over the years whether Australia really was just across the Tasman Sea or perched at the back of Chinese Turkestan.

These tours, therefore, were in the nature of innovations. Each began with great promise, for there was something delightfully fresh in the manner both countries played cricket. It lacked the dourness of the Australians, that of the South Africans especially, although actually it is dour determination which enables the Australians to take advantage of a situation. If an Australian made 20 or 30, for instance, he invariably took the control which such a good start gave him and went on to a big score; if a South African made 20 or 30, he usually became light-hearted and proceeded to take risks. And Tests are not won that way.

Neither the West Indians nor the South Africans could pace it with the Australians on the Test field. The Australian public's international appetite had been fed on English–Australian games. They received these other international teams with great preliminary interest, but that interest faded when the Tests became one-sided affairs. Some Tests were even finished in two days, and each tour, in consequence, was a financial loss and a great worry to the Australian legislators – who were bound to take a poor financial view of it when the MCC suggested the very next season that two of the profitable bodyline Tests should be cancelled!

Individually, the West Indians possessed some of the most gifted cricketers in the world. There was no more polished batsman than Headley. He ranked with Bradman, McCabe, Hammond, Nourse and Compton, for he was delightful in his footwork, a powerful on-side player (the best I have seen), and he drove the ball like a flash to the off. O'Reilly had not then made his international bow, but Grimmett and Ironmonger were at their spinning zenith, and anybody who could take a Test century from them needed to be flawless in his batting. Headley did so, but received poor batting support from his team mates, particularly Constantine.

I cannot think of anybody to rival Constantine as the then world's greatest all-round player. Hammond, to be true, was the world's greatest slip field, but stayed only in that position. Constantine could field there also, and could whisk to any position in the field – and sometimes, in fact, did range over two or three positions to one delivery. He compared with Captain Stephenson in that; it was no surprise for a batsman to bend to his task with Constantine in his mind's eye at short fine-leg, and then find him flinging himself for an almost impossible catch to a stroke played to mid-on. Five yards either side of Constantine in the field was dangerous ground, for he swooped and darted like a swallow and had the ball on its return journey to the wickets before one could say Emmet Robinson.

I may be allowed to digress here, for I adored fielding. Given a band, sun and breeze, good fielding surface and batsmen playing strokes and I could field for ever. Give me seven Constantines in the field, Cameron, Tate, Grimmett and O'Reilly, and I would send them confidently against the greatest batting team of Grace, Hobbs, McLaren, Trumper, Bradman and the rest that the world has seen.

That is what I think of Constantine as a fieldsman; that is also what I think of the importance of fielding even against the greatest batsmen. Ask any batsman what he thinks when ordinary boundary shots are repeatedly cut off and yield no runs, or when aggressive fielding keeps him penned in his creases! And ask any bowler what heart that gives him to go on with his job!

To return to the West Indies tour. Constantine was potentially the greatest all-rounder Australia had seen since J. M. Gregory. It required one big in heart and stature to be an all-rounder on modern wickets, especially in Australia, but brilliant as Constantine undoubtedly was with the bat, he revealed few instances of it in Australia.

One was unforgettable. It was against NSW, when Constantine had the field strung out like the competitors in a married women's race. One ball he put halfway up the Hill; another he bounced on to the Paddington stand roof and over into the Show Ground, and yet another he put high on the roof of the Sheridan grandstand. Langton's hit on to the Railway grandstand at the Wanderers in Johannesburg was the biggest I ever saw, but these of Constantine's were little inferior, and, in addition, he drove along the ground with the speed of a bullet. Constantine has since expressed the opinion that this Sydney innings was the best he ever played.

Constantine was a glorious batsman, but he could not fathom Grimmett, and was a sorry Test performer with the bat.

His Test scores in that series were 1, 14, 12, 8, 9, 7, 7, 10, 0, 4 – a total of 72, and an average of 7.2 per innings. Woeful stuff for such a class cricketer!

Roach was another capable West Indian batsman, and no happier or more exuberant team had been seen in Australia than this West Indies one in its opening games. Never had such vigour been seen in the field. It was not sufficient for one fieldsman to chase the ball. Often three joined in a joyous, laughing dash; but it was not long before Bradman and Grimmett happened across the happy West Indians and left a withering blight in their wake.

Grimmett oppressed all, with the exception of Headley, but more than anything else it was Bradman's blade which dulled the West Indians' happy outlook on life and cricket. Their hours in the sun changed from happy to long and laborious ones as their bowlers went the way of all bowlers against Bradman. They developed aches here and pains there when Grant called them to the bowling crease when Bradman was in command, but, had they been as wise in Australia as in Manchester in 1933 when they followed in England's bodyline footsteps, the West Indians could have called a much different tune.

They were capitally equipped for bodyline. Constantine could have played the Larwood role, with Francis and Griffith in the lesser parts. At his bowling best, Constantine was only slightly inferior to Larwood. He had a smooth, flowing action to the creases. Like Larwood, he had perfect control of the ball, and if his bowling in Australia was often desultory (he had come from a Lancashire engagement) there was one Sydney occasion when he took six NSW wickets and rose to real Larwoodian heights of pace. Constantine later regarded this as his best bowling feat of all time. In that spell Constantine was very little below Larwood's speed, and of all fast bowlers in the world at that period he was best fitted next to Larwood to bowl bodyline successfully with the necessary control.

Constantine would have caused a sensation that Australian season had he attacked Bradman in such a manner. Bodyline, however, was then only in its first pangs of English birth, and, moreover, it required as leader a rugged individualist who would see things through. In that capacity, one could not think of the mild G. C. Grant, who went after the tour to do missionary work in Africa, in the role Douglas R. Jardine was to play later.

It was several years after that the West Indians heard of the white man's 'magic', aped it, sent Wyatt home from the West Indies with his jaw broken in several places and, through Constantine, gave England an unpopular sample on the somnolent Manchester wicket in 1933 of what Larwood and Voce had given the Australians a few months earlier in Australia.

Bradman did not let the West Indians off lightly in their first tour of Australia, but he dealt even more severely with the South Africans the following season. He met them quietly with a modest 30 for NSW, and that introduction gave the South Africans great heart for the future.

'Hobbs is always at his best,' wrote Cardus in 1919, 'even if he fails to put up a big score. This is no paradox. There are cricketers who can give a glimpse of their mettle even in the very process of being clean bowled, just as a tyro may hit a ball to the boundary time after time, yet only to convince us of his total lack of art.'

That could not have been written of Bradman in his first innings against South Africa. He was most unlike his real self. Not a gesture in that innings hinted at the trouble in store for the South Africans, and they, eager in the first blush of the tour to assess their opponents, were delighted with what they saw of Bradman, fiddling to the slow bowling of McMillan, spooned back a simple catch.

That happened soon after lunch on the Saturday of the game. It rained later that afternoon and play ceased temporarily. No country breeds sportsmen of such friendly natures as South Africa, whether it be cricket or rugby, and the visitors were no sooner off the field than they came visiting to the NSW dressing-room to meet our players. With Dalton on the mandolin, they introduced us to their wide repertoire of songs.

The South Africans loved to sing. In 1937 I was to travel with their Springbok Rugby team around Australia and delight in their compulsory hour's sing-song each day on shipboard. Of that cricket introduction to the South Africans in Sydney I remember Sarie Marais, Da la la Ding, Dalton's renowned Fly Song and a cricket song, credit for which they gave to Newman, of Essex, and which is well worthy of reproduction.

It runs:

> 'If your bat wants to score, well let it.
> If a four you can get, well get it.
> Don't be too slow, just have a go,
> All the folks will hear about it and the crowd will grow.

> 'If a duck is your luck, never mind.
> Someone else will get two, you'll find.
> So just have a go and forget it,
> And if your bat wants to score, well let it.'

There is no better cricket philosophy than that, but what impressed more than the South African songs that day was their general feelings of elation. The reason was not hard to find. Their broad smiles made it obvious that they had looked at close quarters at this ogre Bradman, this Bradman who had terrorised English cricket, and they were not frightened by him.

The poor South Africans! Pity their bland innocence! They had the temerity to think that in one innings they had gauged the measure of this cricketing immortal. 'O bring my terug na die ou Transvaal, daar waar my Sarie Woon,' they happily sang, and as they sang you could imagine their thoughts back at the Wanderers (Johannesburg) that Saturday evening, back amid the conversation of their friends as they told each other in that pleasant, high-pitched voice of the Veld, 'Man, but our lads in Aussie have the measure of that fellow Bradman.'

The vision was short-lived. It faded almost overnight, for on the Monday there came a period when Bell, the fast bowler, found that the customary band in attendance was interfering with his run to the wicket. He had Cameron stop the music, but it was Bradman, even then, who was giving the South Africans more trouble than had all the bands of the Aldershot Tattoo been present.*

Bradman was taking his first calm look at the South African

---

* Bell complained that the band put him off his run, and, unfortunately, for they added atmosphere to a big game, bands ceased playing at Sydney until January, 1944, when an Air Force band played Lord Gowrie on to the field during a Service game. Cameron's veto of the band recalls the story of the racehorse owner called before the stewards for an explanation when his horse, the favourite, ran poorly. The owner claimed that the band had played so out of tune as the horses were going to the post that it had upset his horse. The explanation was accepted!

bowling wares. Quinn, then perhaps the deadliest left-hander in the world, and who was fated to have the cruellest of fortune in dropped chances off Bradman, was not playing; but Cameron had Bell, Morkel, McMillan and Vincent at his command, and Bradman coolly looked over the offerings of each. The red light of danger was flashing when Bradman batted like that, an innings of calmness rather than of highlights. It meant that he was probing each bowler, indexing him for the accounts ahead and indexing him, moreover, in so thorough a manner that, had he chanced to meet the same string of bowlers in ten years' time, he would remember immediately the talents and wiles of each.

Bradman made 135 in that dissecting innings. The South Africans speedily changed their minds about him, and any lingering doubts of his ability were dissipated in the first Test at Brisbane, when he made 226. Thrice before he was 20 in that innings he was missed, Mitchell dropping him twice in the slips off Quinn. This medium paced left-hander, who swung the new ball both ways, was to have execrable luck against Bradman, but the lives he was given at Brisbane sufficed to inject Bradman with any confidence he needed against the South Africans.

The Bradman appetite had found itself. Following his dish of 226 in Brisbane, he played himself to 219 for NSW against South Africa in Sydney; 112 in Sydney again, in the Test match; an unpalatable hors d'œuvre of two in Melbourne (caught Cameron, bowled Quinn – both, alas! now dead), followed by 167 in Melbourne and, to cap it all, 299 not out in Adelaide.

If Bradman was gorging himself at the South Africans' expense they, for their part, were heartily fed up with him. Quinn told the story against himself of how, after a day's slaughter by Bradman, a weary, dispirited band of South African cricketers emerged from the ground and wended their slow way hotelwards through the gates. They were met by a pack of autograph hunters and one pushed pencil and paper under Quinn's nose.

'Give me your autograph, please, Mister,' he was asked.

'Don't worry me, sonnie,' said Quinn, trying to put the lad off, 'I'm not a cricketer.'

'No, I know that, Mr Quinn,' brightly came back the lad, 'but give me your autograph just the same.'

Bradman was repeating for the South Africans the treatment he had meted out to English bowling in 1930. He was stamping the South African feelings in the green grass of all the Australian grounds and there began, as there invariably began against Bradman, mutterings on the field of 'Haven't you had enough yet?' and 'It takes a lot to satisfy you.'

But mutterings on the field against Bradman were no new experience for him. In the first partnership I shared with Bradman, while he was making part of his 352 not out against Victoria, I heard wicket-keeper Ellis make many caustic remarks to Bradman's back. The red-faced Victorian, who was also a Councillor, might just as well have been addressing one of the council meetings in his Melbourne suburb for all the notice Bradman paid him.

Bradman ignored the mutterings, ignored the meaning glances, and proceeded merrily on his unhesitating, unconcerned way against the South Africans – until near the end of his unfinished feast of 299 at Adelaide.

Then came the moment when the patience of Bell could stand it no longer. He was the only bowler of pace in this South African side, and that in itself for a touring team on Australian wickets was enough to break the heart of any man. Week in, week out, month after month in a blazing sun and with the concrete-like popping creases driving boot sprigs deep into the soles of his feet, Bell toiled and sweated with as much heart and vigour as the Voortrekkers in opening up the hinterland of his own country.

Bell was a big, powerful man, an ideal type for lock in a Rugby scrum (or Number Eight, as the Springboks call him), and an unusual type of delivery, in which his hand swept down and out from his head, took additional toll of his grand physique. Any man who had been through Bell's experiences would have done, perhaps, precisely the same as Bell did to Bradman.

Late in that mammoth innings in Adelaide Bell lost all patience with the Australian champion. He flung himself into a last burst of speed on this docile wicket (a wicket as peaceful as the hills in the background), and in that last dying attempt he dropped the ball short in line with Bradman's body. It bounced at Bradman's ribs and, as at Kennington Oval in 1930, Bradman showed that he did not altogether appreciate it.

Bell wiped the sweat from his brow. Could this be true? Did his eyes deceive him or was Bradman ruffled out of his complacent mastery? What irony, if there was a chink in the Bradman armour, that it had taken the South Africans four long Tests and two Interstate games to discover it! But no matter, the South Africans gossiped among themselves. There was one final Test waiting to be played in Melbourne. It was easier to bounce the ball there than on Adelaide, Bell remembered, and there was still time enough to see whether there was anything in this suggestion of Bradman sensitivity to bumpers.

The South Africans looked to that Melbourne Test with interest unequalled in any other.

But they were destined never again to see Bradman at the batting creases. Heavy rain preceded the final Test, and ten minutes before the South Africans went out to make 36 on the world's worst sticky wicket, Bradman slipped in the dressing-room and wrenched his ankle. He did not field in that innings and he did not bat; he fielded next day in the final South African innings of 45, when the game was finished in two days.

The South Africans could forgive fate for many things on that Australian tour. I never met a finer or brighter band of sportsmen. They did not take themselves over-seriously, as some touring Test cricketers could be accused of doing, but laughed and sang most when their cricket clouds were darkest. I played my first Test innings against them on that bad Melbourne wicket, and, after opening with Woodfull, experienced the despair of seeing Woodfull bowled by Quinn for nothing with an absolutely unplayable ball. When I got to that end, Quinn – and for this I will always remember him – presented me with a full toss to get over the prospect of making none in my first Test innings. Few Test bowlers would be as generous.

The South Africans, however, were like that. Cricket, to them, was always and only a game, not a war of attrition or grim upholding of reputations. One in a position to know has told me that the South African team is always by far the most popular visiting team in England, and I can well understand it.

Their disappointment in Australia was intense. Though a team of brilliant parts, their collective ability made a poor showing against Australia, which that year had one of the best attacks in history. Wall still retained his pace and swung the new ball away in the very last moment of its flight, that late swing which is a nightmare to the opening batsmen. Grimmett, Ironmonger and O'Reilly played as brilliant and varying a symphony of spin as any Test side would wish to hear, but, despite this, the South Africans had the batting ability to do something big.

The South Africans did, in fact, do relatively big things, but they were too seldom and unrelated. Cameron might succeed one day and the others fail. It might be Mitchell's solo turn next and then Viljoen, followed by Dalton, Christy, Curnow or Taylor, but when the other team possessed an entire batting side itself in Bradman, to say naught of Woodfull, Ponsford, Kippax and McCabe, it was wholly insufficient for a lone South African voice to sound in reply. What was wanted was a choir, a choir of concerted and sustained effort.

There was not in the world a better wicket-keeper, even though saddled with the captaincy worries of a losing team, than Cameron, and there were also few, if any, superiors to him as a punishing batsman. Morkel was a good all-rounder, Bell a splendid opening bowler of vicious in-swingers, Quinn's splendid left-hand capabilities I have mentioned, Vincent was a Verity-type of left-hander, and McMillan, on his day, a slow bowler of class.

It will be seen that this was a team of possibilities, of rare possibilities indeed, but its tour record was ignominious. It did not win nor look like winning a Test. Had Mitchell taken either of those two catches in Brisbane off Bradman, the story might well have been different, because such errors, especially with a Bradman concerned, play a big part in the loss or gain of confidence at the beginning of a tour.

All these disappointments the South Africans accepted like true sportsmen. They could forgive fate for many twists in this most distressing tour of Australia; but there was one blow they could neither forget nor forgive, and that was when a wrenched ankle kept Bradman from them in the final Test on a wet wicket.

It was Bradman more than the rest of the Australian Eleven who had disgraced the South Africans and debased their standard of play. The whole, long blazing summer he had rubbed their noses with disdain in the green Australian earth, and then, when this heaven-sent chance happened along for them to rub his nose in the Melbourne mud for a change and revenge, he was denied them. They could not forgive that.

A wet wicket in Sydney gave the West Indians a belated chance to mollify their feelings against Bradman (bowled Francis for none) in their final and only victorious Test. All the South Africans asked, Bell in particular, was two overs or even one over against Bradman on that Melbourne gluepot. Bell had his bumper theory to exploit, but bumpers or not, a wet wicket would have given them a chance to avenge their feelings for all the Bradman scouting they had done that year.

At the end of the tour there was one South African who did not return home to sit in sad soliloquy on his stoep. Shrewd, hard-headed Herby Taylor went on a visit to England instead, and he took with him interesting reflections on Bradman.

If the men of the old order change in cricket, yielding place to new, they do so with keen, analytical thoughts. It is all, apart from memories, that is left them. The modern champion begins always from behind scratch; for is it human to expect the older brigade, the feats of bygone years enhanced and mellowed by age, to be anything but intensely or bigotedly loyal to his generation? But Bradman presented a poser, for who, in any generation that had gone before, could compare with him and his fabulous records?

Taylor was one of the Old Brigade. He was a stylist and a theorist who had worn well. He was past his best when he came to Australia, and it was seldom there flashed from his bat a suggestion of the glory of other days. It is not in the eyes, arms or judgment that a cricketer first begins to wander sadly downhill. It is in the legs, the poor, faithful old props whose every creak as they go to and fro tell the sad tale to their bearer of departed elasticity, that elasticity which enabled them to move in unison with judgment.

So it was with Taylor. For unceasing hour after hour he had summoned his fatigued feet to take him backwards and forwards to his fielding posts while this Imp of the Younger School, who treated derisively the deeds of Taylor's contemporaries, cut and drove merrily, pulled and glanced, and cared not a whit for any cricketing soul, present or departed.

When the time came for Taylor to strike a blow for his generation, to show, in contrast, the merits of the Old School, he found that his spirit was willing, nay, most revengeful, but his legs, indeed, were weak. Time marches on and nowhere more tellingly than in a sportsman's feet and legs.

Human nature being nothing but human nature, it might have been at the end of the season that Taylor's reflections on Bradman were somewhat soured. To no South African more than Taylor did Bradman outstay his batting welcome. Taylor was a theorist, an ardent theorist. On Adelaide Oval one day he went to pains to show me how Bradman, in playing back defensively, did so wrongly. He took up a bat and showed how Bradman's feet pointed up the wicket, bringing him full face to the ball instead of, as Taylor contended, his back foot pointing to point with the body half face to the ball. Hobbs and many other champions, incidentally, played back defensively in a similar manner to Bradman.

Bradman, Taylor considered, would find it a very difficult matter to get runs on a turning wicket. I thought, sardonically, considering his scores of 135, 226, 219, 112, 167 and 299 not out, that if this was the silver South African lining to the Bradman cloud it was rather dim, but what impressed Taylor most at the end of that tour was not any theoretical notion of how Bradman played back defensively, but how he reacted to bumpers.

Taylor went on to England and naturally discussed the Australian tour. A very reliable old bird told me that he discussed it in high places, and what more natural than that Taylor should talk at length on the few bumpers Bell bowled at Bradman in Adelaide?

Possibly English heads nodded together in agreement with Taylor; possibly they remembered the Oval Test in 1930; possibly the bodyline plan was hatching.

CHAPTER FOUR   *Bradman Unlimited*

Iℕ THE TWILIGHT OF AN OCTOBER
day in 1932, Bradman, McCabe and I left Sydney on a five days'
railway journey across Australia to Perth. Richardson and Lonergan were to join in Adelaide, and the five of us were to form with six
West Australians a team known as an Australian Eleven. It was to
play Jardine's MCC team in the second match of this momentous
Australian tour.

We three New South Welshmen (Bradman had not then been
attracted to Adelaide) had to travel 2,761 miles to Perth. That
meant we would cover 5,522 miles, or almost half of the trip to
England from Australia, before we reached home again. All that for
one single cricket match! It was no comfort to think that one might
travel that distance only to be bowled first ball.

A touring cricketer spends much of his Australian and South
African summer in a train, although the Pacific war has shown many
Australians that distances in the south are not comparable with
those in the north. No English team has yet seen that far north of
Australia. When Darwin and Townsville become big cricketing
centres – and the Pacific war has made that feasible – visiting teams
will find that the mileage covered then will more than double that
travelled by previous tourists.

South Africa has also had to contend with this major travelling
problem, although the air, naturally, will solve such difficulties in
the future. Of the days just past it is interesting to compare

31

travelling in the Dominions and England. One did not emerge from an Australian or South African train after two or three nights and welcome a first-class game. In England, on the other hand, one could finish a game at Lord's at 6.30, have dinner at one's hotel, and, catching a glorious, gliding train, emerge at the other side of the Kingdom in broad daylight, have a night's sleep and be fresh to play next day.

It did not do to ponder on what cricket fate had in store at the end of this long Australian journey. That, I remember thinking, could work itself out. It was sufficient for me that I was to play my first game against an English team, for what English or Australian cricketing youth, from the time he first fingers a cricket bat or ball, does not imagine himself walking in the steps of the mighty?

Does he not mouth their names with fervent awe, fighting, if necessary, for the reputation of his heroes? He saves their portraits on cigarette cards, records all their deeds, scavenges, if need be, for their autographs, and is faithful to his ideal long after the critics or time have humbled his heroes in the dust.

Love of cricket is something that just happens. The doting parent cannot push or coach his offspring into it. If he tries to do so he will more likely achieve the reverse result. His purpose will be better served if he pushes a bat, a ball or a ticket to a big game into his offspring's hand and then promptly allows atmosphere to complete the conversion.

We never lacked atmosphere in our Sydney suburb of Waverley. There had been a long string of internationals down the years in Syd Gregory, Carter, Hendry, Kippax, Collins, Jack Gregory and Mailey. The club numbered other most accomplished players in Dr L. O. S. Poidevin, Charlie Gregory, Frank O'Keeffe (who died soon after accepting a Lancashire engagement), Norman Callaway (killed in the 1914–18 war and who critics aver was a world's champion in the making), Forssberg, one of the best hitters I've seen, and many others.

Our local ground was unenclosed. Friday was always a big afternoon, for we would hasten from school and field like terriers in the outfield while our heroes batted in the nets. We hung on every piece of gossip from them and learnt our cricket in a hard school, for the caretaker, 'Boss' Reid, a tall, dignified man with a van Dyck beard, did not take kindly to urchins desecrating his carefully-preserved and beloved turf. A state of war always existed between generations of Waverley urchins and Reid. To beat him we had to rise very early in the morning and post scouts, who gave warning when they saw him in the distance. We would then make a hurried retreat over the oval fence with bat, pads and stumps.

This element of danger gave zest to our cricket education, although it was difficult to observe the principle of both eyes firmly on the ball when one generally had an eye cocked for an outflanking movement by Reid over the top of the hill at the rear of the ground. The Waverley oval was a shrine of veneration to us small boys, and often my school-mates, Frank Conway and Jim Holm, who both later worked a thrilling path up through the various Waverley grades, would sneak with me over the fence in the dark of night and play imaginary cricket in the centre. We would dash helter-skelter up the wicket for short runs and, fired by association with such revered turf, play brilliant innings in the moonlight until time told us we should be off home to neglected lessons.

All this would probably take place near one of Reid's magnificent wickets which he had zealously prepared for the morrow. No wonder he was always ready to scalp us. The high standard of Waverley wickets died with him, for cricket on that oval in my time was never an easy or a pleasant task. The wickets used to powder and crumble, and no wickets are harder to play strokes on, because of the uncertain rise and pace of the ball.

Carter, the famous wicket-keeper, was our hero. He played the most amazing shovel strokes round to the leg side – strokes I have never seen the like of since. It mattered not that the ball pitched several feet to the off. Carter would whisk his right foot across, drop his right shoulder and make a scooping action with his bat like a man throwing soil. Away the ball would sail to the leg side. Carter was the district's undertaker, and there was a strong boyish furphy* that this stroke had been perfected by his profession.

Carter, born in Yorkshire, was full of cricket personality with his little quick steps and mannerisms at the wicket. He loved the game. He smiled hugely and accepted all challenges when captains sent two and three extra men to the leg side to catch him on his shovel stroke. He played almost entirely off his back foot, alternating leg-side shots with chops down the gully. No player could have had more worship for another than he had for Trumper. He never tired of talking about him and would not listen to comparisons. 'Put Vic away up high, then talk of the rest,' he used to say.

I have never known such awe as when, at the age of 16, I played my first grade game under his captaincy. He always played in an old discoloured Australian cap. He was a veteran at the time, but

---

* The word furphy, which sprang to my mind, stands in need of explanation, as it is an Australianism. Furphy was, and is, a manufacturer of implements at Shepparton, in Victoria. In the 1914–18 war he had a contract to supply water carts and also other metal containers associated with the sanitary contracts for the camps. For one reason and another, a story of a gossipy kind which obtained currency among the troops came to be known as 'a furphy'.

proudly disdained to stand back to fast bowlers. He was at his best on a spinning wicket, the test of a true stumper, and some of his stumpings on the leg-side bordered on the miraculous. I venerated him, along with the other youngsters of my time, and would willingly have tried to walk on my head had he asked. Umpires always trod carefully with him, for he knew the rules by heart. It was Carter who put Armstrong wise to Tennyson's blunder in the 1920–21 series, when that English captain made a closure unpermitted by the rules, but temporarily permitted by the umpires.

Kippax, then making his name with flowing, graceful centuries, was a god to us. He was regarded as the second Trumper and the whole district went into savage mourning in 1926 when he was passed over in the team for England. Collins, a selector of that team, was also a member of the Waverley club; but the club, generally, took Kippax's non-selection so much to heart that it snubbed Collins by refusing to accord him the customary farewell, even though he was captain of the National eleven.

Some of the critics alleged temperament against Kippax. He had to fight his way to the top when Collins, Bardsley, Macartney, Taylor and Andrews (all New South Welshmen) were considered Test certainties. Fledglings such as Woodfull, Ponsford, Victor and Arthur Richardson and Kippax had to scramble for the few crumbs left over. Ratcliffe and Punch were two other magnificent New South Wales cricketers who also found it hard to push their noses into recognition. Of Kippax I would say that I have seen no better wet-wicket batsman, and wet-wicket batting is surely a test of temperament.

Once I travelled a whole section past my usual tram-stop when I discovered that I was sitting opposite Hendry. I regret to admit that I joined a stupid, childish voice in barracking against that very gifted student of the game, Dr L. O. S. Poidevin, who later (unbeknown to him, of course) returned good for evil in many ways with his learned advice to me and kindly encouragement. The Doctor played Davis Cup tennis for Australia and was, in fact, chosen for Australia in a Test match, but an injury kept him out of the side. He would have been the only double tennis–cricket international but for that. He played later with Lancashire and, together with Dr E. P. Barbour and J. C. Davis, made a trio of Australia's most talented cricket writers, expertly knowledgable and understanding in the difficulties of players.

Our greatest thrill of those early days was once when we called a truce with 'Boss' Reid and entered the sacred precincts of the pavilion to assist on the scoring board the day Carter and Hendry played their first game after returning from England in 1921. We deserted the board to stand alongside the two as they walked on to the field. Had they just returned from Saturn we could not have been more impressed.

Carter, incidentally, made a glorious, if lucky, century. He gave fast bowler Scott, afterwards a Test umpire, severe treatment.

It will readily be seen, therefore, what a game against England meant to one with such a cricket upbringing. It was a feature of our test games in those years on our Old Trafford (a piece of parkland) that if we won the toss with the choice of names or innings, we immediately chose names. Then we could be England, and being England gave us the very maximum of glamour.

It also gave us, as he went with the country, the little cockney from down the street who claimed that he had once seen Hobbs bat at Kennington. If he had, he did not learn much from the experience, because the first straight ball invariably spelt doom to him, but he was considered to have 'colour'. Being England also meant that you (being Hobbs, of course) could talk condescendingly to your urchin partner as you walked to the creases, telling him that must have been a good innings he played last week against the Varsity at Cambridge. Do I hear the oaks rustling at Fenners!

I smiled at these recollections as I lay full-stretch on my sleeping berth the first night out to Perth and watched the moonlight on the swiftly-receding countryside. It was all very thrilling to play against the South Africans and West Indies (against the latter I almost impaled myself on the Sydney pickets in my enthusiasm in the field and received a stitched eyebrow in consequence), but, due respect to the others, the Englishmen were blood of the real cricketing blood. They were cricket itself, for they represented Lord's and Canterbury and Bramall Lane; Grace, Hobbs, Fry, MacLaren, Spooner and Tyldesley. They represented years of tradition and it seemed unreal that I was travelling westwards to play against such giants as Hammond, Larwood, Sutcliffe, Leyland, Jardine, Allen and the rest.

I wondered whether I would be nervous fielding to Hammond. I wondered whether I would have the good fortune to be in the covers to that thrilling stroke of his. And Larwood! Four years before as a schoolboy I had seen him bowl in Sydney, and thought then that it was miraculous anybody at the other end should even see the ball, let alone play it, so fast did he appear.

Alas for those idealistic dreams of youth! They are worth mentioning, worth describing, for in the reality of my first Test match against England, in the first bout of the bodyline Donnybrook, I was to look back cynically on those vain glorious moments of youth when all Test players were gods and the green grass they trod was paradise itself.

If, in those Test matches, one did permit his mind to wander back on what he had imagined Test cricket against England to be, a rib-tickler from Larwood or Voce soon aroused him from his reverie and taught him that Test cricket, like life, was real and very much in earnest, though the goal, in this series at least, was somewhat doubtful.

Members of the Board of Control took the three of us to lunch in Melbourne, and I recall my amazement when I heard the chairman, Dr Alan Robertson, gloomily predict that this coming tour would be a financial failure. 'Cricket is doomed in Australia,' Dr Robertson told us, which was, I thought, a strange opinion for the Number One man in cricket officialdom to express, even if he thought it.

Four years later, at the conclusion of the final Test in Melbourne which gave Australia the Ashes, Dr Robertson made a speech from the grandstand balcony to the crowd below, in which he said he was sorry England had not won that game and the Ashes. That also was a strange statement to fall on the ears of Australian players who had fought uphill after losing the first two Tests; but the period was one in which the Board and the MCC, after the bodyline dust had been laid, were each anxious to outdo the other in friendly sentiments.

The financial failures of the West Indian and the South African tours had depressed our cricket legislators, but it is interesting to recall that Dr Robertson expressed his pessimistic thoughts in the presence of Bradman, the greatest crowd-magnet the game had known, and whose presence in the game in Perth was soon to cause amazing enthusiasm and provide that ground with record attendances.

In that October of 1932 Bradman was at the very height of his fame. When the train was on its long run across the Nullarbor Plain, lonely men and women of the outback travelled many miles to catch a glimpse of this cricket magician. Piping little voices travelled the length of the train calling 'Bradman, Bradman, Bradman,' when infrequent stops were made at night along that desolate, dreary line. At Quorn, a sleepy little hamlet drowsing in the hot sun, the Mayor came down to the train to accord us a civic reception in the shade of peppercorn trees.

Kalgoorlie, with its famous, bearded 6 ft 6 ins Mayor Leslie, wearing a sombrero hat (he was always remembered by the Prince of Wales), gave us another reception. Further down the line at Coolgardie hundreds of enthusiastic miners flocked to the station calling for Bradman. His patience had worn thin by this time. He locked himself in his cabin, but the miners were determined to catch a glimpse of him. They began to ransack the train, several windows were broken and the conductor thought it time he moved out of Coolgardie. The train drew out from a tumultuous scene, with a sequel storing up for the return journey.

We must trace his history to know the real Bradman of that period and the influence he had on the game. He came to his first Interstate trip a raw country youth, and he came, moreover, when there was great jollity in the NSW team with the remnants of what was known as the 'Portuguese Army'. Why so called I do not know, but this frolicsome band left a legend of fun in its wake.

A bright prospect faced the veterans of the 'Army' as they assembled at Sydney station for the annual southern tour. They were relieved of business and office worries for two weeks while they moved in the sun of Adelaide and Melbourne. They nudged each other as they looked over at the several youngsters in the side. It would be good fun telling them tall stories in the train and pulling their legs. And this fresh-faced lad from the bush, Bradman, looked as if he would be good game.

The train had hardly found its second puff of steam before the leg-pullers were at work. It was all done in good fun and passed the time. They set to work on Bradman.

'What else,' asked one, 'do you do besides play cricket?'

Bradman said he played the piano.

'Ah,' was the rejoinder, 'it is no wonder then that you are good at cricket.'

Nobody could see the connection.

'Piano playing tunes up his wrist and back muscles,' explained the leg-puller.

At this there was great argument while Bradman and the other youngsters looked puzzled. There was talk of wagers, money changed hands (to be returned surreptitiously later), and Bradman agreed to prop himself on the edge of the carriage seat and go through the motions of playing the piano. The arbiters were to feel the muscles of his back and make their decision.

They found it difficult to decide. Would Bradman mind taking off his shirt so that they could the better see his muscles in operation? No, of course not, and while one hummed 'tiddley, tiddley, umpty, ump,' Bradman again went through the motions of playing, and the judges, struggling to restrain their mirth, ran their hands over his back muscles. They could not agree on a decision. Bets would stand over until Adelaide, where, if Bradman would oblige on a real piano – and so another innocent was put through his introductory hoops. Bradman was not alone in being duped. All incoming youngsters went through a similar baptism.

The Bowral boy smiled later when he recalled his introduction to the cricket mighty. In a few short months he had given the old-established players an entirely different view of himself. In a few short years he had pushed every other Australian individual off the stage, and it was certainly a new experience for some of the older players (and in some quarters not altogether a relished experience) to see the galmour which they formerly shared now taken, enlarged and monopolised by this slip of a country lad.

Convention taught that an Australian youngster on his first tour of England should conduct himself modestly and gauge the differences between English and Australian conditions for future occasions. Bradman snapped his fingers at convention and reeled off record after record, and it was tribute to his skill that on all the vary-paced wickets of England – and they vary considerably – he scored his hundreds and thousands of runs in brilliant fashion.

It was only natural that such phenomenal efforts should single Bradman out from his fellows. He became tremendously popular with the English public, and anybody with an appreciation of news value could understand Bradman being highly featured in that 1930 season, and featured, moreover, to the exclusion of his team fellows, many of whom had had a good press in their previous English days. It was not a pleasant sensation for some of them to find themselves out in the publicity wilderness, and this, in itself, created a vacuum between Bradman and some of his fellows.

There were other contributory factors. Nothing succeeds like success and Bradman found favours and gifts raining in on him. One admirer gave him £1000 when he made the record Leeds score of 334 in a Test. The same benefactor gave Hutton a similar amount when he toppled Bradman's figures. Some members of the Eleven, their outlook not submerged in the juice of sour grapes, did not mind Bradman being given such recognition, but what they did resent was Bradman's apparent lack of effort to bridge the widening gulf between himself and the rest of the side.

They rarely saw him. He was always busy with an engagement here or an appointment there, and practically the only time some of his team mates met him was when he walked with them through the pavilion gate. 'Who's the stranger?' was the sarcastic quip.

Bradman did not make friends easily nor did he court popularity. Possibly he carried this to an excess, considering the high position he held in cricket and the veneration extended to him by younger players. In later years, when he was captain of the South Australian team, his opponents rarely saw him off the field, and he did not observe that time-honoured custom of visiting his opponents' room and meeting the new-comers to the side. In one game against NSW, in Adelaide, he made history by closing his innings through another party over the loud-speaker system,* and then, later, sending a message to the visiting room to ask NSW to follow-on.

---

* This was a peculiar business. 'Announcement, announcement,' came a voice over the amplifiers. 'The South Australian captain hereby declares his innings closed.'

One in Bradman's position was unwise to leave himself open to criticism in such a manner. The successful one is always a ready target for criticism in Australia, and Bradman had hit a new Australian high in success.

Some of the older players, possibly resenting the manner in which he had turned their cricket world upside down, never went out of their way to be particularly friendly towards him. Bradman did not mind that, because he had enough to engage his attention. Four years before, his world revolved around a village best known as a warning for a refreshment stop on the journey between Sydney and Melbourne. In 1930, when he was a mere 21 years of age, the whole cricket world revolved around him, and this, to put it without stress, was a most unusual transformation.

At his inexperienced age in 1930, Bradman evidently did not think he was doing wrong in cutting himself off from the rest of the team at the end of a game, although he did much the same thing in 1938 when the team of which he was captain in England never saw him again on tour after he had injured himself in the fifth Test.

Nor, when he returned to Australia in 1930, did Bradman think he was leaving himself open to criticism when he left the ship at its first port of call and proceeded across Australia ahead of the team in what was a triumphal and somewhat commercial procession.

He made appearances at city theatres. The original conquering hero had no greater welcome from civic authorities; but for the others, trailing behind like Mrs Murphy's cows, the barriers between Bradman and themselves were built even higher. One said they felt like apologising for themselves when, in the wake of the regal Bradman entry and exit, they came after the champagne into an atmosphere of stale beer.

Bradman did not come home to rest after his English labours. On his return from England he hit the business front as spectacularly as he had hit the cricket front. Bradman bats, Bradman hats, Bradman boots, Bradman shirts, Bradman suits, Bradman gloves and pads rolled off the assembly line like parts of Spitfires during the English blitz.

This part of his career must be mentioned. It had a connection with his cricket and serves to give an impression of his associations with other players. The manner in which he bestrode the cricket world like a colossus, on and off the field, should be truly assessed, for what more likely than that all this played its part, and a big part, in the trap of bodyline set for his downfall?

The next time Perth saw Bradman after he had hastened away from his team-mates of 1930 was when he came to play against Jardine's team. This followed upon much preliminary shenanigan. One moment Bradman was going to play in Perth; the next he wasn't and the next he was. Perth was in a fine flutter. It was like that cryptic record of the tram inspector Finegan who itemised a derailed tram thus: 'Off agin, on agin, gone agin, Finegan.' Only Bradman could have dangled and angled legislators in such a manner and got away with it.

No prince could have had a more regal entry into Perth. As the long and dusty eastern train jolted to a stop thousands crammed the station, the adjoining roofs and buildings, the exits and the streets outside. Police had to force a passage for Bradman, and the Palace Hotel, where we stayed, was in a constant simmer by day and night.

We might have seen portents in that trip to the West. Together with the Englishmen, we journeyed 50 miles to York to a country race meeting. From memory it was the only time on that tour that Australians and Englishmen fraternised socially; portents of the squabbles ahead were possibly seen at the racecourse when two small boys simultaneously arrived to sell Jardine a race-book.

Jardine was in a quandary which one to patronise, when suddenly gloves were produced and the boys set to with a will. It was a spirited bout, but Jardine stopped it by buying a book from each. It was the only known diplomatic move he made in Australia.

All Perth seemed to have deserted its business posts when Bradman came to bat on Saturday morning. The Englishmen had batted for two days on a good wicket. It rained on the Friday night and on Saturday we walked out to bat on a damaged pitch. Bradman came twice to the creases and made 3 and 10. Perth was intensely disappointed.

Bradman knew then what was up the English sleeve. I played golf with him prior to the cricket game, and he told me of his anxiety to get runs, because he was under the impression the Englishmen thought he would be daunted by pace. There were no bumpers that day. Allen was the lone fast bowler and Allen was not a bodyliner.

Of that match Hobbs wrote in his *Fight For The Ashes*: 'The mighty Bradman came and went twice for scores totalling 13. The ground hushed as if a national calamity had occurred, and any true interest the crowd had in things was instantly killed. Once Don went to a splendid one-hand catch by Hammond, standing wide at second slip. Next time it was Pataudi who got him. In the first instance I thought that only Hammond in the side could have taken the catch. The second time some of us thought that Bradman did not care a lot for the fast bowling of Allen.'

Allen was certainly fast that day, and the English camp was watching anxiously for any Bradman reactions to speed. Hobbs's notes show that the English were pleased with what they saw. The lynx-eyed Jardine missed so little on the field that he noticed if a sprig of grass shed its seed. Sutcliffe, with a high advisory position as leading professional, also missed little, and keenly watching from the pavilion was Warner, whose right index finger was always on the pulse of cricket, as if it had grown on his hand specially for that purpose.

The bumpers and the leg-side field were to come later, but what the Englishmen saw in Perth on that trip convinced them that their plan looked like working out. It was a happy MCC band which caught the train with us back to the East – a far, far happier band than any which had trudged off English fields in 1930.

At Coolgardie, on the trip back, happened the sequel of which I wrote earlier. The miners came again to the train, but this time to see McCabe and present him with a ball. Mailey pointed me out as McCabe, and as the train stayed only a few minutes I thought it would save explanation if I accepted the presentation and made the speech. I hope everybody was satisfied.

CHAPTER FIVE

Bradman and the Board

A REMARK MADE BY BRADMAN on that homeward journey from Perth aroused our interest at the time and took on added significance a few weeks later when a trial of strength between Bradman and the Board seriously threatened to deprive Australia of his services.

It was a night after Richardson and Lonergan had left us when Bradman, McCabe and myself were discussing the season's prospects.

'Don't be at all surprised,' said Bradman, 'if I am not with you chaps this season.'

It was a strange and mystifying remark. The functioning of an Australian Eleven at that time without Bradman would have been like a cigarette without a light or like playing Hamlet without the Prince of Denmark. We pressed him for an explanation, but he laughed and would say no more.

What reason could Bradman have had for making such a statement? Was it that the few portents of the preceding seasons had given him an inner revelation and he saw the signs of things to come; was it that he had weighed on the financial scales and found wanting the prospects of playing Test cricket and being fettered by the voluminous regulations of the Board as against not playing cricket and being flattered by the offers of press and broadcasting organisations?

Or, and this might have been a consideration, did he see in not playing in the series a chance of vindicating his feelings against the Board when it fined him £50 for infringing his contract on the 1930 English tour by writing for the press?

It might have been one of these reasons which prompted Bradman's remark; it might have been a combination of them or it might have been none of them; but let it be recorded that Bradman had no love in his heart for those Board members who had fined him £50.

So that, perhaps, the player might be given moral strength to evade temptation if it urged him to forget his Board contract in England, the Board holds £150 of his bonus. This he receives in Australia at the end of the tour, provided the manager gives him a clean sheet in his observance of the contract.

The contract tries to make nothing clearer in its long twelve pages than that no player shall write for the Press, directly or indirectly. The Board keeps itself aloof from the Press. Its meetings are always behind closed doors, and poor encouragement is offered the Press to give the big publicity to cricket which it does give. The Board takes every precaution in its English contract to see that the players and the Press do not meet in any business sense. Only the captain is empowered to give an interview, and with all its involved verbiage the Board can be said not to leave any ambiguity in its contract regarding writing.

While the 1930 team was in England there appeared a series of articles entitled 'My Life Story', by Bradman. The manager of that tour, W. L. Kelly, considered that Bradman had infringed his contract by writing in England, or causing to be written, his life story. Bradman was reported and in his final account with the Board was given his bonus less £50, which he was fined. Had some of the Board members had their way, I learned subsequently, he would have been fined the full £150. Bradman, however, did not think he had been let off lightly. He intensely resented the principle of the fine and held it against the Board.

In the year 1932, two years after the return of the side from England, the principle of this fine still rankled with Bradman. He might have decided that this coming series was his chance to get even with the Board; that he would sit aside and write and allow the inevitable lack of glamour which his absence would cast on the Tests to recoil on the Board's collective heads.

Like most well-known Australian Test players of the past thirty years, he had little in common with the majority of the Australian Board of Control; but Bradman, when he recalled the £50 fine, what he considered to be its principle and spirit, and also what his success on that 1930 tour had meant to the coffers of cricket, thought he had more reason than others to dislike the Board and its ways.

In 1932 he held a three-cornered business contract, shared by a newspaper firm, a broadcasting company, and a retail store. He entered into this contract some time after his return from England when there was a possibility that he would accept an invitation from the Lancashire League and be lost to Australian cricket.

He was not in any sense of the term a journalist by profession, though, unlike most other prominent sportsmen whose names appeared from time to time at the head of a column, he was not 'ghosted'.*

Before the 1932–33 series started Bradman wrote to the Board and, in view of his contract with the Sydney *Sun*, asked for permission to write on the Tests as a journalist.

I must explain here the difference in the Board's attitude to journalists playing cricket for Australia in England and in Australia. On tour in England no player is allowed to write, irrespective of whether he is a journalist or not. In Australia the Board is not so strict, for it allows a full-time journalist, one whose sole occupation is journalism, to write on Test matches and still be eligible for Test selection. Several provisos are imposed by the Board, and a player, if he wishes to continue playing and likes peace, imposes others. The Board will not allow him to comment on the selection, before and after, of the Test side, and the permission, if given, can be withdrawn at any time.

I do not know whether Bradman thought he would be given permission to write when he made his application. I was the only full-time professional journalist playing first-class cricket in Australia and Bradman and I applied to the Board about the same time. They refused Bradman permission, but granted it to me.

Bradman was quick to issue an ultimatum. 'If I am not allowed to write,' he stated in an interview, 'I will not play.'

Here was a pretty 'how d'you do'. An Australian Eleven without Bradman! It was unthinkable and the public and the newspapers lost no time in saying so. Though the MCC was then playing its preliminary matches, the sporting topic on everybody's lips was whether Bradman would play in the Tests, whether the Board would recede from its stand?

* 'Ghosting' is a term well known to newspapermen. In essence it means this: If Smith becomes a well-known figure in some sport, a certain type of newspaper (unfortunately, for journalists, a type too common) will decide that it is of news value to have Smith's name splashed across its columns. An offer is made to Smith for the use of his name. He consents, and a newspaperman is given the job of 'ghosting' him. That means the newspaperman will have a talk to Smith and then write the copy which appears under Smith's name. More often than not Smith, whose number three iron travels faster, more interestingly and more concisely on the subject of golf than his mind, will leave it to his 'ghoster' to write what he likes. The job is intensely disliked by newspapermen. They do the job, while Smith gets a fee few journalists can command.

It was an awkward position in which the Board found itself. Had this been any ordinary Tom, Dick or Harry who was flouting it, the Board would have washed its hands of him and seen to it that he certainly did not play Test cricket again.

Mailey, a faithful old war-horse of Australian cricket, had gone out of the game in the evening of his cricket days in such a way. His sole occupation in 1928—29 was newspaper work, but he had offended the Board by applying for permission to write after he had written. True, he had written only a few lines on an Interstate game in Brisbane. It was an oversight on Mailey's part not to have applied earlier for permission, but the Board condemned him and made him unavailable for Test selection. A very worthy cricket servant thus passed from the game, unhonoured and unsung.

I do not remember any newspaper outburst on Mailey's behalf, but Bradman was a different matter. Mailey was in the evening of his career; Bradman, who was Bradman, was at the high noon. The sporting public literally howled at the Board, and its members, thinking of the Big Six of 1912,* wiped their collective brow and hoped, like Mr Micawber, that something would turn up.

The Board–Bradman battle raged for several weeks with intense public interest and spirited controversy. Bradman had the public and the Press stoutly behind him, but what could the Board do? The precedent of 1912 had been established and there was also the Mailey case. It was unthinkable that the Board should bow the knee to any individual player and this the Board righteously told itself;

---

* The Big Six were Trumper, Carter, Armstrong, Cotter, Hill and Ransford. In those days it was a rule of the Board's constitution that the players should choose their manager to England, with the Board having the right of veto. In 1912 the Board took the selection of the manager out of the players' hands. Frank Laver, who had been the player-manager of two preceding teams, and, incidentally, who had headed the Test bowling averages of each tour, was the choice of the players, but the Board did not favour Laver. The players asked for a reason. They were not given one, but simply told they could choose anybody but Laver. In the midst of the storm Laver sent a telegram to each of the Six: 'Don't bother about me. Go to England.' But the Big Six stood by Laver and refused to tour England. Feeling was very high and the Sydney Town Hall was packed in a protest meeting against the Board. Prominent speakers were W. A. Holman, later Premier of New South Wales, and R. Long-Innes, subsequently Chief Equity Judge of New South Wales. There was talk of legal action to restrain the Board from sending the team, but it went without the Big Six and experienced a lean tour. Armstrong came back into the game to captain the magnificent teams of the 1920–21 periods, of which Carter was a member. Trumper died in 1915, Cotter was killed at Bersheeba, in Palestine, and Ransford and Hill did not play Test cricket again. The 1912 incident was the thin end of the wedge for the Board. The officials of every team since have been Board members. It is of particular interest, as I write, that Bradman is reported from London as saying that he hopes to return to England with the first Australian Eleven after the war as manager. Bradman has since issued a public denial of this report. He has also since become a member of the Board.

but as soon as the Board permitted itself to sink back into the complacency of righteousness it was jolted by the thought that dealing with a mortal like Mailey was vastly different from dealing with a god like Bradman.

For the first few weeks of that MCC tour Bradman provided the Press with good copy. He had a contract to write, he said, and he intended to fulfil that contract. Did that mean, he was asked, he would not play for Australia if he could not write? If the Board persisted in its attitude, said Bradman, then unfortunately it meant that he would not play Test cricket that season.

It was an anomalous attitude for the Board to adopt, for it gave its tacit blessing to the many players who trod a well-worn path from the dressing-room to the broadcasting microphone to tell, in between puffs of cigarette and other advertising, their story of the day's play. Their comments over the air were duly reported in the Press next day, so that it was difficult for the Board to justify its boycott of Press activities.

But victory was to go to the Board of Control, even though it was only a victory of sorts. The late Sir Hugh Denison, managing director of the newspaper with which Bradman had a part of his multiple contract, stepped into the breach and announced that he would release Bradman from his writing contract. I did not have Bradman's confidence on the matter and I never asked him any questions. Thus I do not know whether he was pleased with the terms of settlement.

Press interest passed from Bradman and focused again on the MCC team. The Englishmen had journeyed through the peacefully rich country of South Australia and come to rest on that lovely Adelaide ground where the river winds slowly by, where green and russet-brown trees peep into the ground and the purple hills of the Lofty Ranges in the distance, Australia's most beautiful hills, join with the adjacent cathedral spires in giving benediction to the play.

Nobody who knew that season will question that that particular Adelaide game was the only one of peace and cricket-like calm of the whole tour. Bitter feelings were evident or simmering in almost all the others, and press pencils were always sharpened for the incident that was just around the corner, or imagined to be there.

The Adelaide game was the calm before the bodyline storm. The Englishmen came twice more to Adelaide on that tour, and once a Bastille-like tumult enveloped the ground while the Larwood guillotine fell inside. Mounted troopers surrounded the Oval outside in grim readiness for the imminent riot. That was the third and inglorious Test. The next and last time Jardine led his forces on the Adelaide field, the South Australians made the only effort by an Australian team – and a pathetic one it was, too – to emulate bodyline. In all this the cathedral spires looked naked and ashamed, and every now and then a fortuitous heat-haze clouded the Lofty Hills. Of such happenings in such a setting, Reginald Weber might well have written his immortal lines: 'Though every prospect pleases and only man is vile.'

CHAPTER SIX   *And Then Came Larwood*

Aᴜsᴛʀᴀʟɪᴀ's ɪɴᴛʀᴏᴅᴜᴄᴛɪᴏɴ ᴛᴏ bodyline was in the first Melbourne game of that tour. Voce bowled it in a modified form with a forward short leg, two short legs behind the wicket and a man covering them in the deep. Compared with the later din, it passed off relatively quietly.

Larwood did not play in that game. He was a natural athlete and did not require hard and consistent work to bring him to his top. He bowled only six overs in his first game in Perth and followed that with a leisurely five overs in Adelaide, where he skinned his toes. The leading actor of the bodyline tragedy (I write not of the management or producers!) was quietly resting in the wings, and he emerged in the next game for bodyline's full Australian dress rehearsal. Be it noted that Jardine was not a participant. R. E. S. Wyatt captained the side, which suggests that the theory was an accepted part of the team's tactics.

Bradman came from Sydney to play in this match, an Australian Eleven versus England. I did not see the game and I quote Hobbs in his description of it, pointing out that Hobbs was one person in Australia at that period who could appreciate what was happening in the middle. Only a few short months before, at Kennington Oval, the famous Surrey batsman had caused a profound sensation by volubly protesting at the wickets when Bowes bumped short balls at his head. And the Oval crowd also vociferously hooted Bowes for his tactics.

Hobbs wrote of this Melbourne game: 'Woodfull and Bradman did not get going against our excellent bowling. A ball from Larwood struck Woodfull over the heart. Bradman jibbed at the fast stuff. He mixed bad strokes with his good ones, put a ball from Bowes between the short-legs and, when six, sat down in coping with what he thought would be a bumper from Bowes. This was a queer incident. Bradman sat on the wicket with his bat somewhere over his left shoulder and the ball hit it, going for a single between the umpire and mid-on.

'On the Tuesday the wicket rolled out pretty well, with a certain amount of damp from rain on the previous day. Larwood and Allen bowled at a terrific pace. When Bradman came the bowling became even faster – really demon stuff – in an attempt to shake Don's wonderful confidence. It seemed that this was done. For the fourth time on this tour Bradman failed to make a big score. The expresses of Allen and Larwood were too much.'

Further describing the game, Hobbs wrote: '. . . this brought Bradman in front of Larwood. The first ball was enough. Bradman, in drawing away to cut a shortish delivery, completely missed the ball, which hit the top of the off stump. And, oh! once again, the crowd's silence. The bowling looked very dangerous stuff. These were real shock tactics. Bradman, wonderful player though he is, ducked away like anyone else. Most of all, I was impressed with the form of Larwood. I don't think he has ever bowled faster.'

Larwood was rested the next game against New South Wales in Sydney, but Voce played and gave almost as vigorous an exhibition of bodyline as any seen in Australia that season. With the exception of Bradman, who had seen the theory at close quarters a few days previously in Melbourne, it took the New South Welshmen completely by surprise, for, although McCabe and Kippax had seen Voce in action at Trent Bridge in 1930, the Voce of the faster Sydney wicket and under Jardine was different from the Voce of the Carr–Nottinghamshire association.

There was nothing half-hearted about Voce's bowling. He bowled with studied intent at the body, the ball pitching at the half-way mark and sometimes shorter; he had four to five short-legs with two men covering them in the deep. Voce bowled Bradman, but for the main purpose the stumps were intended to serve, they could well have been left in the pavilion. Most of Voce's deliveries, if they did not meet a New South Wales rib in transit, cleared the leg stump, or a space outside the leg stump, by feet.

This was bodyline in deadly earnest. It was apparent and intentional, its malice unaffected by the frequent contacts of body and ball, for a blow on the ribs would, of a certainty, be followed the very next ball by a delivery of similar length, elevation and direction. For a time several members of the English leg-side trap either offered apologies when a batsman was hit or gave a rubbing palm in solace; but a continuation of such courtesies would, in the circumstances, have been hypocritical and embarrassing to the giver and receiver alike. The batsman was later left to do his own rubbing in the privacy of his imprecations.

Those early games gave birth to the bad feeling between the two teams which was blatantly obvious throughout the series. Players snapped at each other and never gave a thought to mixing off the field in social enjoyment or in cementing those oft-quoted 'bonds of Empire' which this game of cricket, allegedly more so than any other sport, had fostered over the years.

One Australian player, possessed of a bullet-like throw, used to hurl the ball back in retaliation at the wickets as if he were at a coconut stall at the fair, thus drawing many a scowl to himself from the side-stepping batsman. At the tour's end not one Australian player bade farewell to the MCC team!

I realised the full significance of bodyline the afternoon of the Sydney game against the MCC team which Jardine led. I opened the innings for New South Wales, made a century and carried my bat through the innings. I should have been deliriously happy as I returned to the pavilion, for was this not a complete realisation of a youthful dream? Could one have wished for a better answer to one's prayers, with Test selection against England also in the offing?

There was, on the contrary, no wild thrill about it. I was conscious of a hurt, and it was not because of the physical pummelling I had taken from Voce. It was the consciousness of a crashed ideal. Playing against England in actuality had proved vastly different from what boyish dreams and adventure had imagined it to be. The game was not the thing, but almost seemed to be the last thing.

Bradman had yet another bad match, scoring 18 and 23. His scores in six innings against the Englishmen were in marked contrast with those he had made in England in 1930. They were 3, 10, 36, 13, 18 and 23 – just 103 runs. Four of his 1930 Test scores in England were 334, 254, 232 and 131.

More remarkable, however, than his small scores was the manner of his dismissal in the second innings for New South Wales against England. He was on the march near the wide mark on the off while his middle stump was being knocked by Voce from the ground behind his back.

This was the most un-Bradmanlike happening of his whole career. Had it befallen a young player, one trying to push his way to the top, he would have found it difficult to avoid eternal damnation as a consequence; but with Bradman it served to prove further, as

Hobbs had written in Melbourne, that his wonderful confidence had been shaken.

I find it interesting to recall a conversation I had in after years with a member of the Board of Control regarding that particular game, and I recount it because of the part the Board was later destined to play in the bodyline affair. This member told me that Bradman had related to him his experiences in Melbourne, where, so Bradman alleged, the Englishmen had deliberately bowled at him.

'I refused to accept that,' said my Board acquaintance, in most judicial manner. 'I preferred to wait and see the MCC–NSW game in Sydney and then form my own impressions.'

'And what were those impressions?' I asked.

'That the MCC bowlers certainly did not bowl at the man,' he answered.

I was flabbergasted. 'You are not serious, are you?' I asked.

'Certainly,' said he.

'But,' I replied, 'I spent some hours in the middle of the ground that day and I formed, together with the evidence of a somewhat battered body, an entirely opposite opinion.'

'Well, then,' said the Board man, in a manner suggesting that this settled the matter for all time, 'you were wrong.'

Contrast this attitude with that of the Right Hon Herbert V. Evatt, famous Australian statesman and some years after that 1932–33 season to become a leading official of the New South Wales Cricket Association. 'I was revolted by that particular day's play,' this Australian High Court Judge told me. 'It made me feel that I never afterwards wanted to see a single day's play of that series.'

This feeling was shared by my Mother. A keen lover of the game, she saw that NSW game against England and refused to witness another game, shunning even my First Test against England.

I have written earlier that bodyline was brought to Australia for Bradman's own especial benefit, and it can be said at once that it paid rich dividends. Bradman in that Test series was only a shadow of his former self. He averaged 56 runs with an aggregate of 396, a Test average that would have pleased anybody until Bradman himself arrived on the Test scene and made the scoring of 50 runs a matter of almost small moment. Then, again, had not Bradman made almost that aggregate in one innings in England two years before?

It was in his batting, in his demeanour at the wickets, that Bradman showed how this type of bowling really upset him. There was always a defined streak of the unorthodox in his batting. He made his own rules and his imagination did not recognise the limitations which the average Test batsman found himself obliged to

51

observe. But even unorthodoxy blushed at some of Bradman's capers against bodyline.

This was exemplified in his first Test appearance against England in that series. He withdrew, because of illness, from the first Australian Test team. Australia was overwhelmed in that game (despite McCabe's 187 not out, the best innings of the series), but all Australia thought it would be a different story in the second Test when Bradman returned to the side.

He came to the wickets in Melbourne after Woodfull had been dismissed cheaply and the thronged ground gave him a reception of which I have not known the equal. The atmosphere at that moment was one of gleeful and confident expectancy. Men turned to each other with the smile of delight which Bradman's appearance always engendered, and told themselves that now they would see about Larwood, that now the fun would begin and it would be fast and furious.

Never could there have been such a dramatic anti-climax. I was at the other end and saw Bradman take his guard. Bowes, whose pace in Australia was not comparable with that of Voce, let alone Larwood, began his lumbering run, and to my surprise I saw Bradman leave his guard and move across the wicket before Bowes had bowled the ball.

The first natural and obvious principle of batmanship is not to make up one's mind before the ball is bowled. Not even Bradman could flout the canons of the game in such a manner, for if much could be done and accepted under the guise of unorthodoxy, that unorthodoxy itself had its earthly limitations and did not embrace a miraculous foresight which told by the bowler's run to the wickets where the ball would pitch and its direction.

Bradman was outside his off stump when the ball reached him. He swung at it and hit it into the base of the leg stump. A hush fell on the ground, an unbelievable hush of calamity, for men refused to believe what their eyes had seen. Bradman left the wickets in silence.

The Bradman of the next innings was completely different. It was as if he had slept upon his seven consecutive failures against the Englishmen and had decided they were more than enough. The stumps on this occasion were always behind his body or his bat, and he made a century, not like the old Bradman, for there was an absence of the spectacular, but a century rich in the honesty of purpose.

Some of the Melbourne crowd showed its appreciation of Bradman's return to runs by having a 'bob-in' fund for him – to buy a grand piano!

It should be stated, for the sake of records, that the Melbourne wicket of that game was strangely unlike an Australian pitch. The Englishmen had strong suspicions about its preparation. The truth is that a deluge the previous week necessitated covering the pitch with a tarpaulin for several days, thus deadening the soil.

We won the toss and I recall my mixed feelings as I walked with Woodfull to open the Australian innings, for the Melbourne wicket before lunch on the first day is renowned for its liveliness. This is often caused by the moisture still in the wicket from its preparation; but although Jardine had banked on this reputation and the English team congested itself with Larwood, Voce, Allen and Bowes, all fast bowlers, this Melbourne wicket was as docile as an intruding male in a meeting of feminists. I saw three hours of it in the first innings.

That century was the only innings of its nature Bradman played in the series. In Adelaide, when Larwood returned to bowl after a rest, Bradman hit a swishing six off Verity at the other end in such a manner that the veriest schoolgirl sensed suicide was in the offing. That innings, like others he was to play in Brisbane and Sydney when he moved feet to the off and then feet to the leg before Larwood delivered the ball, brimmed over with the gambler's spirit and sent the thousands delirious with delight. It was all very thrilling if one did not stop to think that this was a Test match, not village green cricket, and that Australia was staging a burdensome uphill fight.

Inside and outside the cricket circle there began murmurings against Bradman. The old Australian Eleven captain, Noble, took him severely to task on the air one night during the Adelaide Test. He charged him with letting Australia down and he criticised Woodfull for not checking him in his style of play.

'Bradman suddenly developed a sensational desire to score off everything,' broadcast Noble, 'and that regardless of the safety of his wicket. His opposition revelled in his indiscretions and laughed up their sleeves, because he was doing just what they wanted. Bradman evidently forgot he was playing in a Test match and that the winning of the game was paramount.'

Hobbs wrote of Bradman's display: 'Off Verity's next delivery Don made a wild hit to wide long-on and was lucky to hit it in the middle of the bat, for he failed to get anywhere near the pitch of the ball, which, as it chanced, did not turn. A little later he hit a similar ball for six and off the next delivery he was well caught and bowled by Verity. There was a good deal of grumbling round the ground as Bradman went – people said he had thrown his wicket away as soon as he saw leg-theory.'

Hobbs again criticised him in Brisbane and Sydney. Of Brisbane, when Bradman lost his wicket at a time when Australia was making its best stand of the series, Hobbs wrote: 'He tried to cut a ball from Larwood on the leg stump and was bowled. I was convinced that Bradman would not have leg theory as bowled by Larwood. [Hobbs, incidentally, was not too keen on it as bowled by a much dimmer light in Bowes. – Author.] If a schoolboy tried to cut a ball on his leg stump you would smack his head. Yet here was Bradman doing it.' And of Sydney, Hobbs wrote: 'At any rate, Woodfull played for his side, which was more than Bradman did.'

Cricket has not known a more Alice-in-Wonderland innings than that played in Sydney by Bradman in the final Test. When Larwood was still two or three yards from delivering the ball, Bradman was on the move. First he went to the off, then to the leg. Bradman made 71 and barely a stroke he made was known to the text book. It was the riskiest and most thrilling batting imaginable, and that in a limitless Test in which the sum total of risks, ordinarily, would be counted on the fingers of one hand.

Bradman's stumps were left wide open not once but a dozen times. An ordinary straight ball from Larwood would have been sufficient then to end Bradman's innings, but it really seemed that the stumps were of minor concern to both Bradman and Larwood. It seemed that Larwood was anxious to claim a hit on Bradman in this final Test – a thing the Englishman had not done previously. And Bradman seemed just as determined Larwood shouldn't. Larwood got a hit, late in Bradman's innings, with a stinging blow high on Bradman's left arm.

In some quarters Bradman drew criticism upon himself for this type of batting. In others he was given lavish praise for the plan he had evolved, so it was said, to defeat bodyline. Was it not better, it was claimed, to die thus than to a simple, popping catch to the leg-trap?

Larwood made the blatant statement on his return to England that Bradman was frightened. The taunt stung Bradman.

'I resent Larwood's accusation and deny it emphatically,' he said. 'According to Larwood's ideas, it would seem that to adopt ortho-dox methods and get hit is displaying courage. Any other methods whereby his theory might be defeated evinced fear.'

'Actually,' continued Bradman, 'my method of playing Larwood exposed me to considerably more danger than the orthodox way. Anybody who understands cricket knows that.'

These divergent opinions of the two leading actors in the bodyline drama are worth recording, though Bradman will not find an Australian batsman of that series to agree with him that he took more risks of physical hurt than they did.

When an acquaintance wished Bradman luck as he was leaving for the fourth Test in Brisbane, he replied: 'I would sooner return from Brisbane with a pair of "ducks" than a pair of broken ribs.' The person to whom that was said was amazed at what seemed to be Bradman's lack of thought for Australia's Test prospects; but Bradman, at this stage and much earlier, saw bodyline clearly for what it was.

It was the Australian poet, Adam Lindsay Gordon, who wrote:

> 'No game was ever worth a rap,
>   For a rational man to play,
> Into which no accident, no mishap,
>   Could possibly find its way.'

No person is entitled to have things made to order for him in sport. The Englishmen, thinking of the many times Bradman had made exceedingly merry at their expense, might have said so to Bradman. He could have replied that there was reason in all things. I saw one of my schoolfellows killed by a hit on the temple from a cricket ball, and there was no doubt this danger, despite Jardine's opinion in Tasmania that the theory was not dangerous, was always present. 'My constant dread,' said Hele, who umpired in all the Tests, 'was that a batsman would be killed.' 'If this goes on,' said Hobbs of Bowes at the Oval in 1930, 'someone will get killed.'

Australia's best known Test umpire, A. C. Jones, who had retired the season previous to the bodyline one, told me that he would have had no hesitation whatever in banning bodyline at once under the rule of fair and unfair play.

What would have happened had Jones lasted another series as Test umpire and no-balled Larwood under the rule of fair and unfair play? It is difficult to hazard an opinion. Had Larwood been 'called' during some of the tensest moments of the series, when the temper of the crowds was surging to fever heat, I am positive there would have been an ugly scene, perhaps a riot which would have besmirched the grand game in living memory.

The question, however, automatically arises: Did Jardine assume that because the umpires took no action he was justified in continuing and intensifying the policy of body battery? Was the silence of the umpires to be taken as tacit admission that the bowling was fair – within the letter of the law, let the idealists say what they like of the spirit of the law?

I wonder what would be the interpretation by the dominant Jardine of the famous lines of Lord Tennyson, grandfather of one of England's most gallant Test captains – lines from the lips of the goddess of cold reason:

Self reverence, self knowledge, self control.
These three alone lead life to sovereign power.
Yet not for power: power of herself would come
Uncalled for; but to live by law,
Acting the law we live by without fear,
And, because right is right to follow right,
Were wisdom in the scorn of consequence.

There were many theories about Bradman in that series. I am certain of only one point. Bradman refused decisively to be made an Aunt Sally, and I do not know that anybody would desire to blame him on that account. This, rather than any vague theory of beating bodyline, was probably the essence of his amazing and unorthodox capers at the crease before the ball was bowled. Like Peter Doody, his life, judged by Bradman standards, might have been a short and a gay one, but it also had the merit of being, as far as possible, somewhat safe physically. He received only the one blow, whereas Woodfull, Richardson, Ponsford, McCabe and myself carried a multiplicity of bodyline brands for the entire season.

Bradman's playing of bodyline did not make it any easier for the other Australian batsmen, particularly Woodfull, who, though slow on his feet, tried valiantly to make the best of a bad job. Woodfull gave his bowlers instructions that rather than take the risk of a bad blow they were to sacrifice their wickets. But this instruction applied only to the bowlers. Nobody knew better than Woodfull the difficulties of bodyline, but he expected his batsmen to share these difficulties, and there were times when he was displeased with Bradman's methods.

The Australian batsmen came that season like buds to a tree in a prolific spring. They fell like autumn leaves. The side was close to demoralisation on one or two occasions. Woodfull was not certain he was playing in the second Test, let alone that he would be captain, an hour before the game began; such world-renowned batsmen as Kippax and Ponsford went overboard after the first Test, although a line was thrown to Ponsford for the third and fourth Tests, only for him to be cast adrift for the fifth.

At the end of that season the nerves of all the Australian batsmen had worn thin. I do not think there was one single batsman who played in most of those bodyline games who ever afterwards recaptured his love for cricket. Bradman never regained his 1930 poise, and his batting in the early games in England in the 1934 season made people wonder whether he was identical with the Bradman of four years before.

Above, A Four at Lord's. J.H. Fingleton hooks a ball from J. Smith over the heads of the leg-fieldsmen in the game Australians v. M.C.C. at Lord's in 1938. Others in the picture, left to right, are Farnes, Compton, Wyatt, Maxwell and Human.
Left, Bradman out to a brilliant catch by Bell – South Africa v. N.S.W. at Sydney. Cameron is the wicket keeper.

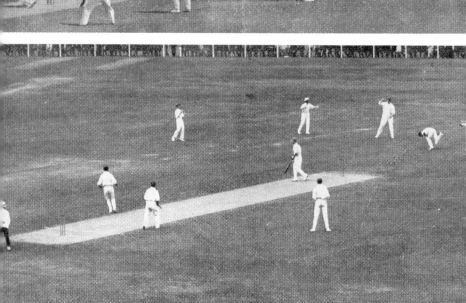

Above left, Full of Action. Demonstrating the vigour of the West Indians, this photograph shows Constantine making a vain effort to catch Rigg.

Centre left, Woodfull struck on the back by a ball from Larwood as he 'ducked' to dodge it. Note the packed leg field – Larwood's crowd of short-legs and leg slips. These would be covered by two in the deep, leaving only two on the off-side.

Below left, H. Carter makes one of the most sensational catches ever seen behind the wicket. E.A. McDonald is the bowler, and Jack Hobbs the batsman.

Top, McCabe Suffers a Hit. This was in the first Test. Note how Pataudi, Allen and Sutcliffe move to him in sympathy. Such gestures ceased as the tour progressed.

Below, Larwood's 1928 field. The great English bowler had two short legs, Hendren and Hammond. Note Woodfull's rather complacent attitude – with no thought of ducking!

Above, A memorable run. Jack Hobbs, in
Adelaide, starts off on the 100th run of one of
his many centuries.
Below, Bradman Gets a Duck. The Australian
hero out first ball in the Melbourne Test to
Bowes. Note his position, wide on the off.
Larwood is in the foreground.
Right, D.R. Jardine. As he strode to the
wickets, a tall, austere acidulated Englishman
with his Harlequin cap rampant and a white
'kerchief knotted around his throat, he strode
into the vision of many as the very
personification of the Old School Tie.

Above, This extraordinary field shows the venom of an Australian 'sticky' wicket. Duckworth has just caught Lonergan in Perth. Verity is the bowler. Other Englishmen are Sutcliffe, Mitchell, Hammond, Leyland, Paynter and Jardine. *Left*, Hammond falls to a Fairfax catch at gully slip. Fairfax was the Australian who walked off the Sydney ground when barracked, never to return.

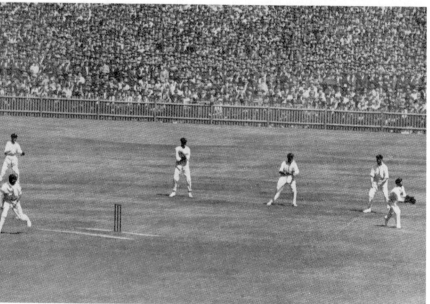

Above, The stroke of a record breaker. This shows the great physical effort which Bradman put into his strokes.
Below, Oldfield makes his greatest catch in Sydney from Jack Hobbs off Gregory (famous Hill in the background). Hobbs was out for one of his very rare 'ducks'.

Top, Woodfull Hit Over the Heart. This was a terrific blow and the beginning of intense barracking at Adelaide, especially when Jardine, with Woodfull still groggy, accentuated the leg field for the very next Larwood ball. This led to the Woodfull-Warner incident, when the English manager came to express regret, and had much to do with the Board sending a cable of protest to the M.C.C. on its team's tactics.

Below, Oldfield Hit at Adelaide. This was not entirely due to a Larwood bumper, Oldfield being the first to state that the ball came off his bat. Concern is seen on Larwood's face.

Above, Lucky Hardstaff! An O'Reilly victim that escaped. The Englishman pulls a ball off O'Reilly in the Sydney 1936 Test. All eyes follow the catch, which was dropped. Obviously Hardstaff stepped on his wicket in making the stroke, but he was given not out!

Left, South Africa's Best. Dudley Nourse plays the perfect square cut on the Wanderers, South Africa's famous Test ground which is now no more. Ames is the wicket-keeper.

CHAPTER SEVEN   *Not Even Trumper*

An ENGLISH NEWSPAPER COULD
have had a rare scoop in the 1932–33 season had it quickly appreciated the bodyline mishap at its true news value and sent off a
Cardus, a Fry or a Robertson-Glasgow by flying-boat to report
proceedings. Cricket knowledge was necessary to understand the
position, and newspaper ability would have enabled the critic to
present all the ramifications of the case. Indeed, a direct Press
approach to the crisis at that stage might have brought all the
principals quickly to boot. It should be remembered, also, that
when certain Australian writers described bodyline accurately some
Editors were none too pleased.

But no such expert came from England. An army of them came
with Allen's team of 1936–37 to lay the bodyline dust, but they were
four years too late for the real stories.

Pertinent questions could have been asked of certain people in
1932–33, and the answers, together with the evidence the eyes of a
Cardus, a Fry or a Robertson-Glasgow could not have missed,
would have pin-pointed the crisis and avoided much trouble and
accusations that year and in after years. In addition, it needed one
gifted in the technicalities of the game to write the bodyline case as it
stood.

Bodyline had to be seen to be understood. Years afterwards I met
a Hong Kong evacuee who told me all about bodyline. He had some
fatuous idea that Jardine began it because Perth schoolboys had

barracked him. He had never seen bodyline, he admitted, but he understood it. He was talking through his hat. Similarly were those good Johannesburg folk talking through their hats in 1935 when they angrily shouted 'bodyline' at McCormick when he bumped a few balls at Nourse, and also the Leicester people in 1938 who screamed 'bodyline' when McCormick struck a batsman.

That was not bodyline. It was not a semblance of it. The theory began only when the fieldsmen herded to the leg-side and the captain and the bowler both realised that, to justify and maintain those men in their positions, the ball had to be delivered so that it came to the batsman high on his body.

This point must be stressed and understood, because high-bouncing balls without the field packing would have been as ineffectual and uncontrollable as a rudderless ship. One was the counterpart of the other; they were as inseparable as the Siamese twins.

The fielding captain had to be certain – 80 per cent of the territory under his command being devoid of fieldsmen – that when a batsman made a stroke it was confined to square and fine leg. The short and leg-slip fieldsmen were grouped in a semi-circle about the wicket, and they were covered in the deep by two and sometimes three men. For these men to serve their purpose it was imperative that the ball should be bowled, not quite at the stumps, but to the left of them – that is, in line with the body.

A technical explanation might explain this. A short ball bowled at the stumps can be hooked or pulled from mid-on to fine leg. The direction in which it is played is determined by the distance the batsman moves his right foot across the wicket, thus putting his right shoulder outside the line of flight of the ball for the stroke.

To the ball on his stumps the batsman has the widest possible range for his onside stroke, but when the ball is on the line of his body that range quickly contracts. The shoulders must be unlocked to play the stroke, and that can be done only by moving the feet. When the batsman moves his right foot across to the off, as he must to free and unlock his shoulders, the only direction left in which to pull the ball is to square-leg and behind it.

So far as I see it, there is only one possible alternative – an unorthodox forward pull shot, in which the batsman puts his left foot up and wide on the wicket to pull with his face outside the line of flight of the ball. Nobody tried that dangerous experiment against Larwood and nobody will wonder at that.

It will thus be seen that the first essential of bodyline was control. And Larwood had control. It is my conviction that had Larwood not been in the 1932–33 side and bodyline had to rely for its existence on Voce and Bowes, the theory would not have survived the first Test.

Allen, though, incidentally, the best fieldsman on the side to bodyline, would not bowl it, although he would have been possibly a more dangerous bodyliner than Voce, as he was faster. It was rumoured that Jardine approached Allen to bowl bodyline, but he was given a deaf ear. It is to be remembered that Allen was in the side in a privileged position, as he was an amateur. He never once departed from the orthodox methods of a fast bowler, methods which made him a very useful and successful member of the side. He reserved to himself the right to bowl an outrageous 'bumper' whenever he felt like it or felt that the batsman would not like it. Further than that he would not go.

Bowes had the bodyline spirit, but lacked the pace, and even though Voce, swinging into the batsmen with the new ball, could be exceedingly difficult at times, he had neither the sustained pace nor control of Larwood. Larwood was the master. Voce merely the coadjutor, whose haul was rich because he followed in the steps of his master, usually from the opposite bowling end.

I will never see a greater fast bowler than Larwood. I am sure of that, and at this moment pay a tribute to him as a truly magnificent bowler. His genius that season with the ball was of the same mould as Bradman's with the bat in 1930. He had the advantage of a canny, astute captain in Jardine, who carefully nurtured him in quick, small bursts of bowling and who, moreover (apart from the bodyline placing), was as artful a skipper as you would meet in a day's walk in smelling out the weaknesses of batsmen.

I, for one, will never cease to sing Larwood's praises as a bowler. I saw so much of other fast bowlers from all other lands that I do not hesitate in placing him on the highest pinnacle by himself (I never saw E. A. McDonald). One could tell his art by his run to the wickets. It was a poem of athletic grace, as each muscle gave over to the other with perfect balance and the utmost power. He began his long run slowly, this splendidly proportioned athlete, like a sprinter unleashed for a hundred yards dash. His legs and arms pistoned up his speed, and as he neared the wickets he was in very truth like the Flying Scotsman thundering through an east coast station. He was full of fire, power and fury – or so he looked at the batting end just before he delivered the ball at you at an estimated speed of 90 miles an hour.

The first time I was in runs with Larwood bowling I was watching, naturally, the batsman at the other end as Larwood ran up. Just as Larwood approached the crease I heard a loud scraping sound and the thought flashed across my mind that Larwood had fallen. He had not. A few yards from the crease he gathered himself up and hurled all his force down on to a stiff right leg which skidded along the ground for some feet. How his muscles and bones stood this terrific test over the years is a mystery to me. Curiously enough, this leg gave out on him in the final Test of the bodyline series.

Larwood's first trip to Australia was under Chapman in 1928–29. He had appeared with pronounced success in the fifth Test at the Oval in 1926, when England recovered the Ashes from Collins's team, the Test in which Old Man Wilfred Rhodes was the colossus.

It was in Melbourne in the fourth match of the 1928–29 tour that Larwood first released his speed of abounding energy to an Australian crowd. Bowling in short spells in accordance with the tactics to which Chapman strictly adhered throughout the series, Larwood took 7–51. It is more than probable that he would have taken the other three wickets in quick time had his captain wished to facilitate such an honour by possibly overbowling him.

There was an incident from that match worth repeating because of the uncomfortable position in which Ponsford placed himself. Ponsford was then a player-writer, whose articles were syndicated throughout the land. In the article on this game he was permitted by his Press sub-editor to publish the view that 'Larwood was not really a fast bowler.' Ponsford had been one of Larwood's seven victims in that innings and he himself suffered most of the repercussions. He failed to reach double figures against the Notts express in the first innings of the second Test in Sydney, and in playing a defensive shot in the first over he was struck on the hand. A fractured metacarpal bone put Ponsford out of the rest of the series.

I met only one other man who expressed doubts about Larwood's pace. He was that delightful old character and former Australian fast bowler, Ernie Jones. 'Jonah', as he was known throughout the cricket world, snorted if anybody went into rhapsodies about Larwood's pace in his hearing.

'Fast?' would expostulate Jones, who was once reputed to have bowled a ball through Doctor Grace's beard, the sheer pace beating the Old Man. 'Him fast? Why, s'welp me, he wouldn't knock a dint in a pound of butter on a hot day. Don't tell me he's fast.'

But 'Jonah'* was merely being faithful to his own generation. Sir Stanley Jackson, whose experience covers many generations, said in 1944 that Larwood was the best fast bowler he had ever seen. Sir

---

* 'Jonah' was one of the personalities of the game. He was a big, hearty, raw-boned chap who got much amusement out of life. I always enjoyed a chat with him in Adelaide. For a time he had a job in Western Australia and, off Fremantle, was reputed to be the first Australian to welcome successive English teams. He would hire a row-boat and be out there in the dusky dawn as the liner dropped its anchor in the stream. 'Jonah' would then row round and round the liner, dropping his oars every now and then to pick up a huge megaphone through which he roared to the boat: 'Hundred to one England in the Tests.' One of the MCC teams, which was quarantined in the liner for a week off Fremantle, got very tird of 'Jonah's' propaganda. He visited the precincts of the liner every morning with his megaphone, relating amazing tales of the Australians whom the Englishmen would later meet.

Stanley, by the way, appealed to Australians as an eminently fair critic.

I had this interesting experience from batting against Larwood. The first dorsal interasseous muscle, between the thumb and the index finger, ached for a week after batting against Larwood, so severe was the concussion of the ball hitting the bat. I experienced this against no other fast bowler.

I still retain my mental picture of Larwood and I remember that he could move the ball in the air when it was new. A ball that came to me one day in Adelaide on my leg stump in the air knocked my off stump flying. He could move the old ball in from the wicket with what is known as a body-break, and the pity of it all was that a bowler with such rare gifts of art and nature should, whether at his own or another's desires, have prostituted his genius when it was at its full lustre.

Hobbs wrote that Larwood of that year was at the peak of his career, and his figures, compared with those of four years before when the Australians batting was not so compact nor established as in 1932–33, lend support to his contention. A proportion of his success, and a considerable proportion, was obviously due to the intimidatory nature of bodyline; but the truth is that Larwood was so fast and so skilful in the 1932–33 season that his figures would still have set a standard in history had he contented himself with orthodox means of attack.

I write this with conviction and a true appreciation of the ability of Woodfull and Ponsford, of the might of Bradman, of the individual artistry of Kippax and McCabe and of the rugged honesty of Richardson.

That orthodoxy would have had to include the occasional bumper, a necessary shaft in the armoury of all fast bowlers worthy of the name. It could also have included a concentration on the line of flight of the ball to the hip, a delivery which gave Hendren many a catch at short leg.

One or two of the Australians might have grumbled at the bumper, as one or two batsmen of any country would, but they would not have received a word of sympathy from their team-mates or the public. Nobody, either, could have made out a winning case against a battery of balls rising on the hip, even if the leg-side were packed; but the case passed from this category into that of bodyline as soon as the ball went higher than the hip, when it reared about the chest and, particularly, the head. This, together with the cramping leg-side field, was intimidation and bodyline, for a batsman's first thought, of necessity, was his personal safety.

Larwood had the control to concentrate on the hip theory which I have just described. Had the English oligarchy been satisfied with that and left its exploitation exclusively to Larwood, the team would have sailed home with blameless and victorious colours.

Neither Larwood nor Voce, however, made any attempt to keep the ball within uncomplaining limits; nor were they given anything else but a free hand in this regard. The English adopted bodyline in all its nakedness and without shame. The Australian batsman at the other end reported that Jardine said: 'Well bowled, Harold,' when Woodfull was hit over the heart in Adelaide; it is also on record that Richardson, batting first on his leg stump guard, moved his guard a foot outside the leg stump in Adelaide and still the ball followed him. This proved conclusively, if further proof were necessary, that the body and not the stumps was the main target. Richardson's was the classic experiment which justified all Australian Press criticism.

Bodyline demanded an occasional hit or near miss. It was part of the plan and inherent in its nature.

I come now to this most important and controversial point – could bodyline have been mastered?

There were two ways in which it could have been beaten, with the bat or by retaliation. Some of the Australian team favoured retaliation and pressed Woodfull accordingly, but he, the peace-loving son of a minister of religion, would have none of it.

'We will play cricket in the manner in which we think it should be played,' was his answer. Then he turned his other cheek.

This was a noble and pious sentiment, which reflected credit upon Woodfull. If any dignity was left to Test cricket at the end of that 1932–33 season it was due entirely to Mr W. M. Woodfull, but bodyline was a grim and ruthless battle into which a leader of mild gentility came somewhat poorly equipped.

The red-blooded Richardson, unless I misjudge him, would have staged a counter attack. Bradman also. Collins would have raised his whimsical eyes at the MCC tactics and asked Jardine whether this was really how he wanted to play cricket.

And I tremble to think what the War Lord of cricket, Armstrong, would have done had bodyline been used against his men. He would have snorted, not so much with rage, but at the cool audacity of anybody who would try his patience or tempt his imagination to such limits. Then, indeed, would mailed Mars have bestrode the Test battlefield 'up to his ears in blood'.

Mercutio covered bodyline as well as love when he spoke these lines to Romeo in the street of Verona –

'If love be rough with you, be rough with love;
Prick love for pricking, and you beat love down.'

No captain needed excuses to justify retaliation if he were the finest offended, and possibly no Australian captain in recent years, other than the peace-loving, studious Woodfull, would have stood more than half a Test match of Jardine and the MCC tactics.

All that happened in after years proved conclusively that had the MCC team been pricked with bodyline, it would have been beaten down. It was said that Australia had no Larwood and therefore could not have retaliated. True, Australia had no Larwood – but it was not Larwood in England in 1933 who made the Englishmen weary, bodily and mentally, of bodyline. It can be claimed that with the possible exception of one stormy match against Lancashire in 1934, England saw only a faint glimmer of Larwood and bodyline as Australia knew them. Larwood broke down in his last Test match in Australia, and it remained for lesser lights to give England its fervid distaste of bodyline, suggestive proof that it was not necessary for Australia to possess a Larwood to have inconvenienced the MCC tourists.

Wall would have been a substantial bodyline lead for Australia. On a green-top wicket in Adelaide on the first day of the third Test, on a wicket responding with the moisture still in it from preparation, he caused the Englishmen pronounced concern when the ball lifted. His field was orthodox.

In view of what passed between Warner and Woodfull later in the dressing-room, it is interesting to recall the prophetic words of Hammond as he spoke to an Australian at point after being caught off Wall from a ball that kicked.

'If this is what the game is coming to,' grumbled Hammond, as he walked by, 'it is time a man got out of it.'

With a packed leg-field, Wall would have been a nasty bodyline proposition, but the best of all would have been that mysterious fast bowler, Laurie Nash, who served a purpose in two Tests. In the first, against South Africa the previous season, he was most successful, but the only other time he was hailed to the Test colours (and that against the strong wishes of certain Board members, the Board having to approve of the selection of players after they have been chosen) was in the final game of the 1936–37 series, when his presence was to suggest diplomatically that if Voce were tempted to bowl bumpers, Nash might also be tempted.

On this 1936–37 occasion, the Australian Test Selection Committee threatened to resign if they could not keep Nash in the team. The Board members yielded to pressure.

For some unknown reason Nash was not a popular figure with Australian officialdom. The migrating Tasmanian played cricket as he played Australian Rules football (in which he was a leading star), and that was with no beg pardons. He was intensely keen. He would have liked Test orders of any description, and would have had no scruples had those orders been to open fire on the leg-side with elevation high.

With Richardson as captain and Williams, only medium fast, as the agent, South Australia tried bodyline against the MCC in the final Adelaide game, but it was a hopeless failure. The excitable Alexander, on his own initiative and without a leg field, bowled bumpers at Jardine in the fifth Test (catching him, incidentally, a terrific whack in the ribs, which the imperious Englishman would not deign to rub) after Jardine had complained against Alexander running on the wicket after delivering the ball.

So far as Woodfull was concerned, however, he washed his hands of bodyline and saw that his team also was above reproach. The only suggestion of Australian retaliation, if one may so term it, was when Bradman let the wicket-keeper have the full force of his bullet-like throw when Sutcliffe, Number One professional of the side and also a selector, was at that end. Sutcliffe was forced to do a hurried jig aside, glowering meanwhile at Bradman.

Some Australians thought that Sutcliffe's hands were not too free from bodyline taint. There was a mystifying action in the fifth Test which suggested that Sutcliffe, befitting his high professional post, held a strong arbitrary place in the team. Bradman had just arrived to bat. Jardine threw the ball to Allen to bowl. Sutcliffe hurried across, took the ball from Allen and threw it to Larwood.

Australia certainly could have retaliated. It is a moot point whether retaliation would not have been the best and quickest way out of the mess, and whether it would not have quelled the jibes of squealing which assailed the Australians from many points at that time and in after years.

As Woodfull would not permit retaliation, the only means of combating bodyline was with the bat, and this opens up one of the most contentious aspects of the whole bodyline affair.

Many of the older generation shook their heads and derided the efforts of the Australians to beat bodyline with the bat. They 'shouldered their crutch and showed how fields were won' in their day, condemning, meanwhile, those Australians, with the job on hand in the middle, as too slow on their feet or too timid in their hearts.

Only the batsman hemmed in by fieldsmen while Larwood thundered the ball at his ribs and head knew the difficulties of the job. It was easy – also perfectly safe – to talk and demonstrate with a walking-stick in the far-off pavilion; what was not easy was for the critic to put himself in the position of the batsman with all the disabilities of the situation.

There was the distinct possibility before the series commenced that Bradman would not play in them. Had he not played posterity would have remembered his colossal feats and accepted for granted that he would have successfully handled Larwood and his bodyline. The facts, however, are that Bradman did play, that he did not rise superior to bodyline – and who, since cricket's inception, was more endowed than Bradman to deal with any bowling theory?

Others in that Australian side were also well equipped to deal with bowling eventualities. Despite their stringent limitations of stroke-making on that tour, Hobbs frequently wrote that the Australians attempted more strokes than the English. Seeing that the hook or pull shot was the only stroke by which Larwood could have been hit out of the body firing line, it should be stated that with Kippax, McCabe, Richardson, Ponsford and Darling, the latter coming into the last two Tests, Australia, with Bradman added, had a wealth of brilliant batsmen most proficient in playing that particular shot.

This point should be stressed and further emphasised by stating that thousands of Australian spectators would have great difficulty in recalling a single hook shot by Hammond in any of his three tours of Australia.

Woodfull and I relied upon the perpendicular bat common to most opening batsmen and rarely indulged in the hook shot. Glances and forcing strokes to the on would have brought us runs against the average fast bowler, but Larwood's leg-trap did not permit such strokes. So Woodfull and I, to make the runs we did against bodyline, were forced almost entirely into defence and ducking against Larwood, in the process of which we took a considerable hiding.

As Larwood had the last laugh, I must mention a cheeky device I used against him in the second Test in Melbourne. He was able to send down a glorious ball which was a nightmare to an opener. It came down on the middle stump, or thereabouts, moved slightly in the air towards the end of its flight, and then went away off the pitch. I had the confidence of youth in those years and preferred to take the chance of a hit rather than have this other nightmare ball bowled at me.

Woodfull and I opened and very early in the piece Larwood bowled a short ball to me. I walked further down than where the ball pitched and ostentatiously patted the wicket. I intended Larwood to infer that if he pitched the ball much shorter he would be in danger of hitting his toes. I repeat – I was then very young.

An infuriated Larwood bounced the ball at me more than ever. This was just what I wanted, because Larwood in his fury never gave a thought to that other ball. Several of the Australian side did not think my tactics were clever. They argued, and perhaps with some logic, that Larwood was dangerous enough without being baited.

It might have been a coincidence that Larwood, in that innings, had his poorest bowling period of the Tests. He had to wait for the tail-enders before he got a wicket, taking those of O'Reilly and Ironmonger for 52 runs.

Larwood had his laugh in the next Test when, possibly under Jardine's instructions, he switched his tactics, helped me to a 'pair' and had me temporarily out of the Test business in no time.

Of the Australians of that period there were many as gifted in the hook shot as most batsmen in cricket history, though Kippax, a glorious hooking batsman, was discarded after only one Test. The English tactics caused the bottom to fall temporarily out of Kippax's game, which was not to be wondered at, because the season before he was close to death's door when a fast ball from Queenslander Thurlow went from his bat to his head, splitting his skull just above the temple.

The inability of Bradman, Ponsford, McCabe, Richardson and others to beat bodyline gives rise to the question of how Trumper, Macartney, Ranjitsinhji, Hobbs, Fry, Gunn, J. T. Tyldesley and others of earlier generations would have dealt with Larwood and his tactics.

Those of the old brigade who saw Larwood deal out devastation in Australia in 1932–33 had no doubts that the giants of their time would have given comrade Larwood and his totalitarian tactics short shrift. I once asked the natural question concerning Trumper and Larwood of my very good friend, Carter, and I knew the inevitable answer before he gave it. Carter cockily declared that he, himself, would have had a preference for Larwood from both ends. Carter meant it, because there was no limit to his confidence or disregard of the ability of any bowler when he had a bat in his hands; also, the unorthodox and risky shovel stroke over his shoulder, in which Carter delighted, had more chance of paying dividends against bodyline than the orthodox pull stroke. Carter, though, was the only batsman I saw who played the shovel shot.

In my conversation with Carter, years after bodyline, I knew that he thought poorly of the efforts of my generation to play it. He admitted his idolatrous reverence of Trumper, a reverence attributed by him to the fact that Trumper attained his greatest triumphs in the face of extreme adversities. He told the tale of when the first South African team was in Australia and a Test match in Melbourne was postponed a week because of bad weather.

Bemoaning the postponement, Sherwell said he had hoped to get Trumper on a sticky Melbourne wicket. Llewellyn, who had played against Trumper in England, told Sherwell not to think that he had missed anything.

'I'd sooner bowl against Trumper on a good wicket,' said Llewellyn, and added, 'he tries too hard on a sticky.'

Carter held the opinion, and I do not refute it, that an Australian Eleven player not prepared to take all that was coming to him in the centre had no right to be there. Others of his generation held the same view and were generally critical of the Australian batting of 1932–33. How, then, would the old brigade have stood up to Larwood's modern tactics? Nobody can say conclusively one way or the other, because the case rests on supposition, but it is interesting to toss a few considerations into the ring.

In 1944 Sir Stanley Jackson was reported in Australia as saying that Larwood was the greatest fast bowler he saw. If Sir Stanley was correctly reported, his opinion is full of interest, because he saw most fast bowlers and had playing associations with those of the early part of this century. Consequently, his opinion merits the highest respect.

Another interesting consideration is that the magnificent English bowling combination of Foster and Barnes beat Australia even more decisively in 1911–12 than did Jardine's team 21 years later. Warner was captain of that team. Illness allowed him to play in only one game, and there are those who believe that the memory of Foster's fast bowling at the leg stump in that tour remained ingrained in the minds of some English authorities, particularly Warner.

In personal absolvement, Foster related in 1933 how Jardine came to him before the team left for Australia and asked for his field placements in Australia 21 years before. Foster vigorously denied then that his bowling and Larwood's had anything in common. He declared that he bowled at the leg stump and never, at any time, aimed at the man.

Hobbs, also a tourist in 1911–12 and by far the most distinguished batsman of the series, wrote in 1932–33 that the bowling of Larwood and Voce often reminded him of the deadly Barnes–Foster combination.

From this might be deduced two propositions which suggest that Larwood was more physically hostile to batsmen than Foster. There is Sir Stanley Jackson's opinion that Larwood was the greatest fast bowler he saw; there is Foster's denial that he bowled at the man, which Larwood undeniably did.

Keeping this in mind, one turns to the feats of the Australians in 1911–12 against Foster. It was a season studded with names of brilliant Australians. There were Trumper, Syd Gregory, Bardsley, Kelleway, Hill, Ransford, Macartney and Armstrong. Those names, even though time might have blunted the edge of original brilliancy of one or two, are juicy enough to satisfy any cricket historian. Yet most of these renowned men revealed a marked inability, Bardsley especially, to cope with Foster's fast bowling at the leg stump.

Foster took 32 Test wickets at 21.62; Barnes 34 at 22.88. Here are the Australian batting averages for the Test series: Gregory, 36; Armstrong, 32.40; Ransford, 31.50; Trumper, 29.88; Hill, 27.40; Macartney, 26; and Bardsley, 16.12. These averages are mediocre and it is particularly interesting to compare them with Bradman's average of 56 in 1932–33 – a season in which it was considered that he did poorly and in which he was freely criticised.

I am not sure that something is not pegged against the older generation by Hobbs' violent dislike of bodyline when it was bowled against him by a second-class bodyliner in Bowes, although, in justice, it should be added that Hobbs was then in the gloaming of his bright days.

These little tit-bits are not, perhaps, without some importance in the general discussion of how other generations would have faced up to Larwood and his works. One really telling story remains to be told.

Two Sussex cricketers, Ranjitsinhji and Fry, were making huge scores on the perfect Hove wickets towards the end of last century and the beginning of this. One day a fellow English player said to Ranjitsinhji: 'Ranji, I could stop you and Fry making those big scores at Hove.'

The Indian prince was amused.

'How?' he asked.

'By packing the leg field and making the fast bowler aim at your leg stump,' was the reply.

Ranjitsinhji thought for a while, and this was his response, significant in its conception of what then constituted a proper outlook on the game:

'Yes,' said Ranjitsinhji, 'that *would* stop Fry and me to a great extent, but surely you would never do *that*.'

I saw Hobbs, Macartney and Bardsley bat. I pay tribute to them and also to the others, Trumper especially (even to those who never saw him bat, Beldam's perfect photographs of Trumper playing a drive show how glorious he was), but I cannot conceive that any of the Old Masters could have been arrayed more brilliantly than McCabe in the first bodyline Test when he scruffed the theory to make 187 not out.

McCabe that day wore the mantle of Trumper. I believe that because of what I have read and been told of Trumper and of what I saw from McCabe in that innings. It made description seem hollow; it will forever be quoted as a standard work in cricket's Elysium.

'Come and look at this; do not miss a stroke of it,' called Bradman from the Trent Bridge balcony in 1938, when McCabe was playing another of his three immortal innings, this time for 232. Bradman was calling to fellow Australians doing odd jobs inside the dressing-room. 'You will never see the like of this again,' added Bradman, and from such a genius this was the highest praise. Yet McCabe's 187 at Sydney was perhaps a more brilliant effort because of the odds he faced.

Those who saw it will never forget. I have seen the dignified gentry of the members' pavilion grin like truant schoolboys as Bradman passed through them after one of his devastating batting whirlwinds; but never, before or since, have I seen respectable gentlemen give vent to such exuberant feelings as that day when McCabe returned to the pavilion. They roared, cheered and clapped all at once until they were red in the face; they threw their hats, sticks and luncheons away in their ecstasies, and, if space had permitted, they would have turned catherine wheels to give expression to the feelings which McCabe's innings sent surging through them.

McCabe took bodyline in his teeth and scruffed it as a terrier would a rat. He played it with ease and mastery and, moreover, did as he liked with the strike, thus giving tail-ender Wall an unusually long if tenuous stay at the wickets.

If McCabe did all this, it might seem fallacious to argue that bodyline could not have been mastered, that Trumper and giants of bygone days would not have risen superior to it.

My answer is that Trumper, Hobbs, Macartney and the other luminaries would probably have shared a similar fate to McCabe's against bodyline – brilliant when fortune favoured them; dishevelled and negative when it didn't.

In that innings of 187 not out McCabe completely mastered bodyline. The Englishmen would have been justified after the first Test in never again bowling a short ball to McCabe on the leg-side.

But did they give McCabe best in their bodyline quest? They did not. Larwood, Voce and bodyline were at him again when next McCabe came to the wickets. They did not always get his wicket, but they unbalanced his play, so that the scores in his following nine Test innings were: 32, 32, 0, 8, 7, 20, 22, 73 and 4. In nine subsequent innings McCabe made a few meagre runs more than he made in that first Test innings.

McCabe tried again and often the strokes of that memorable innings which crashed up against the boundary fence and kept the fieldsmen as busy as secretaries at a Big Three conference. Almost ever afterwards, however, in that only pull shot which the bodyline theory allowed, the ball flew high and came to rest in a fieldsman's hands in a manner which made McCabe look rather futile.

This in no sense belittles McCabe's Sydney innings. I say again it was the greatest I have seen, but the dice of the leg-side field was always heavily loaded against the batsman, and McCabe will be the first to agree that the pull shot behind square-leg to a rising ball is the biggest of all gambles in placement. If that little piece of good fortune is with the batsman, well and good; if not, he finds, as McCabe afterwards did, that he just cannot steer the ball clear of the crowded field.

They tell the story of the two Hardstaffs, father and son, and two of the finest characters to walk on a cricket field. Father Hardstaff was umpiring in a game in which Joe was caught out on the pull shot. That evening, over the family meal, the father ignored young Joe. He never spoke to him. The only recognition he gave him was late in the meal, when he addressed himself to his wife in a forlorn, doleful voice which suggested that the family had fallen on evil days. 'Mother,' said Hardstaff, Snr, 'son's a gambler.'

All Trumper's vast array of strokes would have been useless against a theory which allowed him only a pull shot behind square-leg. A diagram of McCabe's strokes in his big Sydney innings shows where this batsman, whose cover drive and square cut cried art to the highest cricket heavens, made only 16 runs – 16 paltry runs, I emphasise – in front of the wicket on the off side out of 187.

You will see now what I mean when I write that bodyline prostituted the art of batting. It knew not the delicacy of the back-cut; it denied the grace of a cover drive, cricket's most graceful stroke. The glorious straight drive, majestic off drive or lofty shots over the off field might never have been born for all the birthright bodyline conceded them. The thoughts of such strokes, thoughts which once tumbled over themselves in the minds of gifted men, rarely entered into the scheme of things, because Australian batsmen were so circumscribed by bodyline that they had, of necessity, to think first of their physical safety and then of the negative aspect of the only stroke left to them.

The text-book did not know most of the strokes played that season against bodyline. There were cow and dog strokes, so called, and a form of aeronautical loop-the-loop shot more in keeping with the rough surfaces and the uncultured minds of village green cricket. They had little to do with the smooth, circumscribed actions and thoughts of a Test sphere that had been moulded and hallowed by generations.

There was a concession, nay, a right, to the champions of all other days, and that was to die at the wickets a death of dignity. A ball of rare deceit and cunning might have cut short in its infancy the innings of a Grace, a Trumper, or a Johnny Tyldesley, but in his downfall the champion always looked his class; a quick and clean death did not rob him of his rightful due of immortality and he did not leave the creases humiliated.

Bodyline caused everybody, from Bradman down to the merest nondescript, to cut the most ungracious capers. It made them shuffle, sway and bob; duck, weave and dodge. They were soul and art destroying moves, and a batsman ran hot with shame when, as so often happened, his feet took him into such unaccustomed positions that they momentarily forgot their rightful places when a ball of ordinary accuracy and height came along to spreadeagle his wicket.

Larwood took 33 wickets in those Tests. That he clean bowled 16 of them (nine batsmen, seven rabbits) had nothing to do with the bodyline case, as was so often argued. The knock-out blow in a boxing bout is not always the hardest. What goes before wears the opponent down and prepares the way.

Batting is an art and the complete artist must possess, in addition to his own individual technique, a quick eye, judgment and foot-work. He must be free from fault in these essentials and then, with a facility for timing and placing, he must possess a temperament that will answer the ordinary Test demands – and those demands are not inconsiderable.

Bodyline refused to grant any of these a rightful recognition. It made a batsman think first of his physical safety, and no mortal, be he a Trumper, a Ranji or a Bradman, could do justice to his art under such conditions. The split second in which he decides his stroke and then proceeds to execute it is gone if first he has to decide the ball is not going to hit him.

It was said of many Australian batsmen that season that they were hit because they were too slow on their feet. What are the facts? Larwood bowled at an estimated speed of 90 miles an hour. That means it took less than half a second for the ball to reach the batsman after it had left Larwood's hand (the batsman has a yard off the 22 yards pitch at his end and Larwood would gain almost a yard at the other). Larwood's intense speed over the 20 yards allowed the batsman only that small fraction of time to do his thinking and follow it with actions – actions circumscribed by the small area on the leg-side.

To avoid being hit, one would have needed feet of quicksilver to get out of trouble after taking up an initial and correct position to defend one's wicket. There were times, often, when one simply had to move one's bat aside (while in the correct defensive position) and take the ball on the ribs, because playing it would have meant a catch to the leg-trap.

Small wonder, then, in this Australian bodyline season that there were incidents galore, oaths aplenty and unorthodox movements of strange design. The batsman was deterred on many sides, but bodyline knew no limits. It went undeterred by Jardine, by the team managers and the MCC. It went undeterred by retaliation and, lastly, and let it be written hastily, undeterred by the spirit and traditions of a grand and noble old game.

Bodyline reminded me of that Rugby story in which the players of both sides were mixing more brawling than football. Of a sudden the ball was kicked over a neighbouring fence and 'play' was suspended while a search was made for another ball. A burly forward, seeking retribution for one eye already closed and a nose streaming blood, pushed his way up to a meek little referee.

''Ere,' he said, 'let's forget about the ball and get on with this bloody game.'

CHAPTER EIGHT

Introducing Mr Jardine

I̠N THE ENGLISH SEASON OF 1921 an Oxford undergraduate made a slow but decisive way towards the first century of the season against Armstrong's invincible team of Australians. English cricket had not then recovered from the paralysis of the first European war and Collins's AIF team. Douglas's MCC visit to Australia in 1920 had not re-established the English standard, and against this Australia, with its grand stiffening from the AIF team, had moved from strength to strength.

That 1921 tour was the most dismal for England in all its long history. In addition to the paucity of talent, accidents befell leading English players and the selectors called an inordinate number of men to the colours. It was in vain. To the time of which I write, Armstrong's team had walked rough-shod over English cricket and feelings, and not a single home man had topped the century against them.

Enter the Oxford undergraduate! By precise batsmanship and with a straight blade which never wavered a point from the perpendicular, he passed his half-century and moved cautiously through the difficult seventies and eighties to the apprehensive nineties. That most distinguished century, of all the 1921 season, was only a stroke or two from him when he was beaten by time and a concession for which the Australians had fought vigorously – a day of rest before a Test match.

The three-day game against Oxford became a two-day game. The undergraduate who did not get his century and was left not out at 94 was (Yes, you've guessed it!) Douglas R. Jardine.

That was Jardine's introductory bow to Australians, and one might well wonder whether the memory lingered. None could blame the Australians for seeking a playless day before a Test. In their homeland they knew only six, or even less, first-class games in an average season and, in addition, played cricket only in their club games of a Saturday afternoon. Many an Australian found that the grind of playing cricket for ceaseless day after day in England turned a pleasurable game into a dull duty. As Oxford, however, had met the Australians half-way in depriving themselves of a day from their fixture, the Australians might well have exerted themselves to play an extra over or two to see whether Jardine could make his century.

When the Australian team captained by Victor Richardson was dealing harshly with South African cricket in 1935–36, the South African teams often agreed to play extra time on a second day so that a game could be finished. Bradman made a gesture to Edrich on the last day of May, 1938, when that player wanted a few runs at Lord's to complete his thousand for the month. Bradman did not present Edrich with his thousand. In declaring the Australian innings closed he merely gave Edrich a chance which he accepted.

I do not know the full circumstances of this Oxford game in 1921, and of those I have asked who were there, none could tell me. I do think, however, that extra time should have been made in some manner. Instead, there was talk of a train to catch, there was a hurried finish and, human nature being so, an undergraduate was left behind to ponder and doubtless regret that the single honour had so narrowly eluded him.

At that impressionable age, when the first-class sphere was just unfolding to him, Jardine possibly felt resentful in some degree towards Australians. It was only human – though many Australians often wondered whether Jardine was blessed with such a quality – and it is not beyond belief that Jardine always remembered this first meeting with Australians, and was never afterwards prepared to show them any mercy or consideration.

Jardine, born of Scottish parents in India, made his first trip to Australia in 1928–29 with Chapman, and his flannels had barely emerged from their first laundering before he had made up his mind that he liked neither Australia nor the average Australian. Even at this early stage feelings were reciprocated.

Jardine was not a good mixer. He was not the hail-fellow-well-met type, like Chapman and Gilligan, whom Australians love to meet from the old country. An Australian likes to make a quick decision about the person he meets. He does not stand upon ceremony himself and, especially in sport, wants to be on a friendly basis with a visitor as soon as he shakes his hand.

Jardine was not responsive. He did not proffer his hand more than was necessary. He was aloof and discerning with a cold, judicial mind in gauging people and events before committing himself. He did not want to be rushed with friendship and gusto – he preferred to do his own picking and choosing. He was of that proverbial English type which shares a railway compartment on a journey and never enters into conversation. Their Australian proto-types, in comparison, would be playing poker together and possibly addressing each other by Christian names by the time the first station flashed past.

Nothing could better serve to illustrate the difference in disposi-tion between Jardine and Chapman, his predecessor as captain in Australia, than an incident on a New South Wales railway station. At a train halt on their way north to the first Test in 1928 the three amateurs of the English side – Chapman, Jardine and the bowler who commanded respect and popularity wherever he went, J. C. White – strolled along the platform to stretch their legs.

A stranger accosted them with a cheery greeting. His garb was of the country, but he was a prominent identity of the district and a fairly accomplished sportsman. Jardine's reply was a supercilious stare and complete ignorance of the proffered hand.

I am neither blaming nor criticising Jardine for his attitude. To him the strange gentleman's approach, perhaps, was not *comme il faut*. The correct introduction was lacking. It was, however, in accord with Australian manners, for such men of the bush, who live a lonely life of solitude for month after month on their outback stations, readily and happily grasp their few chances of conversation and friendliness with passing strangers. Chapman and White warm-ly shook hands with the countryman, for they, like most amateurs who have visited the Commonwealth with English sides, invariably thought it proper to show some appreciation of the manners of the country of which they were highly honoured guests.

There is no better prey for many Australians than the overseas man on his first visit. Possibly because of its youth or remoteness from older centres of civilisation, the Australian feels he must publicise his country, and in no time the visitor is told that Australia has the best this and the best that in the world. The thing to do is to profess belief in such tales, and the Australian, cautiously wonder-ing whether you are pulling his leg in turn, is delighted to know you and to do anything for you.

But Jardine was not amused by such understandable insularity. He was bored immeasurably, and that, in turn, nettled Australians, who abhor bored and critical visitors. The Australian wants to like his visitor; just as important, he wants his visitor to like him.

Had Jardine come to Australia in the late 18th century and been vested with the authority of that time, his coldness and indifference would have been in keeping with that grim period. Australia was founded in 1788; Marylebone Cricket Club a year later. That was the period when London was known as the City of the Gallows with rope-twisted bodies swaying in the breeze on Finchley Hill, on Tyburn, at Execution Dock on the Thames, at Wapping, below Purfleet, and at Woolwich.

Dr Johnson deplored the suggestion that public hangings should be abolished and 160 crimes were punishable by death. Women and children were burned, flogged and hanged. In 1810 Sir Samuel Romilly was heavily defeated in the House of Commons when he moved that transportation to Australia be introduced in lieu of death in cases of stealing from dwellings. The stealing of articles of 2/– and over in value was punishable by death and humane juries often defeated this law by finding victims guilty of 'stealing a diamond tiara, valued at 1/11'.

Had Jardine come to Australia in that 18th century and been cloaked in authority, he would have strutted the stage with the early Governors. Coming when he did, an Englishman needed a new approach, and many Australians considered that Jardine did not have that approach. He was incapable of unbending and his attitude to Australian newspaper men travelling with the MCC team was always one of icy aloofness and frequently of downright rudeness. For a time in 1932 he was inaccessible to Australian journalists, while still ready to discuss team news with the Fleet Street men who accompanied the side.

When Australian reporters once asked him for the names of the English players selected for one of the Tests his reply was: 'We are here to win the Ashes, not to make stories for your newspapers.' His rare Press conferences took on something of the atmosphere of a Press interview with Winston Churchill. Rather than have to parry awkward questions on bodyline from Australian reporters, he used 'Gubby' Allen as a sort of liaison officer to meet Australian cricket writers.

Canon Hughes, a kindly old man of wide culture, who was president of the Victorian Cricket Association in that turbulent period, was very upset by Jardine. It was not the Canon's nature to speak strong words, but of Jardine he said this in an interview: 'I saw more of Jardine than most people did, and I do not like the gentleman. He does not like me and publicly insulted me in Sydney.'

What was there about Jardine that irked so many Australians?

Was it that he was the leader of a successful side and the Australians did not like being beaten? That accusation was made, but it appears untenable. Only four years previously Chapman had led a more successful English side through Australia, and Chapman was an Australian idol. Did Jardine lack tact? Was he a snob? Did he make obvious his hate of Australians?

For a beginning, and in Australia it was a particularly bad start, he first presented himself for analysis in 1928–29 in a Harlequin cap. Let that facet of his history not be underwritten, for in the loud and resplendent colours of that cap was woven much trouble for Jardine.

The Harlequins comprise Oxford University players, Blues and a few who have narrowly missed being Blues. Their counterpart at Cambridge is the Quidnuncs, and amateur traditions allow a Harlequin or a Quidnunc to bat in that cap when playing for any other team. When fielding, however, it is not amateur etiquette to wear any cap other than that of the team with which the man is playing.

An Australian who has toured England and the many Australians who have, themselves, been either Harlequin or Quidnunc know of these traditions; but the average Australian does not comprehend such privileged niceties nor does he countenance flaring caps or startling ties that announce, so he considers, that this player or that went to some particular Varsity. In effect, the Australian says this: If it is a school or a Varsity match, wear your caps by all means; if you are representing your country, represent it from the head down, for no cap should take precedence over that of a man's country.

Australians will not tolerate class distinction in sport. They could never understand why, in England, amateurs came out of one gate and professionals another. Members of the last Australian Eleven in England deeply resented a Lord's article written by Charles Fry, an Oxonian, a Harlequin, a Test player, a Royal Navy officer and therefore a gentleman who might have been more charitable, in which he described the second Test and used the occupations of the Australians in ordinary life to preface their names.

'In all this Australian team,' wrote Fry, 'there are barely one or two who would be accepted as public school men . . . and while I am writing this, curator—— has just bowled another maiden over.'

Australians do not accept people at cap or public school value. They come to the face and work underneath, and though I have no wish to prick the susceptibilities of people whose modes and standards differ from ours, my point is that we must try and understand the Australian outlook on such matters in analysing Jardine's first trip in 1928–29.

His first public action was to gather exclusively the Varsity men of the South Australian team and wine and dine them. His second was to wear his Harlequin cap, and though other Englishmen had worn such caps in Australia before him, there was something about Jardine in a Harlequin cap which nettled Australians.

As he strode out to bat, a tall, angular acidulated and seemingly aloof Englishman, with a gaudy cap rampant and a silk handkerchief knotted around his throat, he walked into the vision of many Australians as the very personification of the old school tie. Perhaps, like most batsmen, Jardine was superstitious and wore such a cap for luck, but as he strode along with that stiff-legged walk so characteristic of him many Australians resented him, because they thought he was putting on 'side' in his Harlequin cap.

The Hill of Sydney and the Outer of Melbourne, always quick and eager to judge a new man on the flimsiest of impressions, welcomed him with open mouths, and ragged him.

'Eh, eh, Mr Jardine,' roared a barracker, 'where's the butler to carry your bat for you?'

They considered him a barracking gift from the gods, but Jardine could have won them to his side at that very moment had he doffed his cap and gaily waved it to them. A Churchill would have done that and added a victory sign for good measure. Any crowd likes to be recognised and acknowledged. One such act from Jardine and the barrackers would have accepted him – gait, cap, 'kerchief and all.

But who, even with the imagination of a Shakespeare, could imagine Jardine making the concession with such a cap to an Australian crowd? His face set more sternly, his walk became stiffer, he froze more antarctically beneath his cap of many colours – and the barrackers became more voluble, and less respectful.

In such a manner did Jardine walk into Australian cricket. It was not that he hadn't been warned of the temperament of the crowds and of the many ways and means a man of tact had of winning them to his side. Every amateur who left England knew that the Australian barracker democratically leaned to the professionals and that an amateur was always a ready mark for criticism. Johnny Douglas (reverence to his memory!), Chapman and Arthur Gilligan knew well that all that was needed was a grin to the Hill or a cheery wave to the Outer when they were being barracked . . . just this to show the common touch . . . and they were the barrackers' friend for evermore. No crowd is quicker to condemn, no crowd quicker to applaud, than the Australian, and none is more easily won over.

It is necessary that something should be known of the Australian barracker, for the red-herring of barracking was drawn across the bodyline trail by the MCC as the crisis developed.

Barrackers are much the same the whole world over, and no country can afford to point the bone at another. It is all a matter of partisanship, and that partisanship, naturally, is noticed most by the visiting team. I heard a demonstration at Cape Town on New Year's Day, 1936, when Richardson and Wade said the wicket was unfit for play, that would have taken the honours in any land. I was the central figure at Trent Bridge in 1938 in what was as bright a barracking show as any I have heard or seen in any land. Even Sydney's renowned Yabba, with all his foghorn hoarseness and sarcasm, was no better barracker than that renowned woman who used to sit near the scoring board at Surrey's Oval.

Barrackers also differ in their home countries. Those of Adelaide are much more subdued than their brethren in Sydney and Melbourne; the people in the north of England are chirpier and more critical than in the south, although in 1938 I noticed that members of the Oval had much to say – and abusively at that – when Bradman refused to work his few bowlers into the ground before a Test and batted instead of making Surrey follow on.

Any Australian of the last trips home has no two opinions of the Trent Bridge gentry when they are in full voice, which means when an Australian pokes his nose on to the Notts ground.

It can be said, and no Australian will gainsay it, that the Trent Bridge crowd had patriotic reason to feel bitter against Australians. The bravest action seen on any cricket ground was that of a diminutive parson in 1934, when he walked through a hissing and booing crowd and clapped the Australians on to the field. The concerted clap-clap-clap of thousands all round Trent Bridge in 1938* was as crude a piece of barracking as that seen on any sporting

* This was the occasion when I light-heartedly and momentarily sat down on the field, all else having failed to humour the Trent Bridge gentry. Australia was fighting a losing battle and our only chance was a draw. Brown and myself set about playing for time. The batting, naturally, was dull, but everybody knew it was our only game. Then came that concerted clap-clap-clap as the bowler was running up, which increased in intensity. I might mention that many of the grounds in England have no sight board at one end, and it is regarded as very bad form if anybody should move in his seat behind the wicket while the bowler is running to the wicket. The batsman will immediately withdraw from the wicket and the bowler starts his run again. That is accepted, and so also should be the principle that there is comparative quiet while the bowler is running up. What the barrackers do after that is of no consequence. Bradman sent out a message that if this clapping continued while the bowler was running up we were to withdraw from the wicket. I told the messenger that they were not worrying me. They weren't. He said: 'Those are the skipper's orders.' I told Hammond and he agreed with the orders. I therefore drew away. Next time I drew away and stopped Verity in his run-up, Verity squatted on his haunches and I went one further and sat on the turf. As I said, the barracking did not worry me, but I carried out orders. The Editor of Wisden's said: 'The barracking was never more than mild, certainly not hostile, and from only a small proportion of onlookers.' He and I must have been at different grounds that day, and, if what he claims was the case, Bradman would hardly have sent out orders. It came from around the ground, was continuous and loud, and, if I may say so, in execrable taste. Bradman, himself, later drew away from the wickets when these tactics were directed at him.

ground. Yet the Australians could understand the underlying feelings of the Nottingham crowd. Their loyalty to Larwood and Voce, their townsmen and the principal actors in the bodyline drama, came uppermost, though a country which had such essentially unsporting barracking in its midst could ill afford to accuse other countries.

From Thomas Wood's 'Cobbers' can be quoted a very interesting deduction on the toughs of Sydney.

'Sydney,' Wood writes, 'has more than its fair share of toughs. They are larrikins, deadbeats, grass-chewers, louts; gangs of youths and young men who live how they can where they can and take their fun as they find it. Their steadiest interest is spotting a winner.

'They watch games, though they neither play them nor understand them, and they speak their minds. They, principally, are the barrackers, whose jeers and horseplay spoil many a good match. They get more publicity than they deserve.'

The opinion is good, but the point is that it could have been written of many lands, and, furthermore, that type did not comprise principally the barrackers in 1932–33. We have far too many horse races in Australia. I am always amused when I see a press photograph of some corpulent gentleman at the races, cigar in mouth and glasses over his shoulder, with the caption beneath running – 'that well-known sportsman.' Why, he'd have a stroke if he tried to run ten yards! One of the curses of Australia is over-gambling. It obtrudes itself at the slightest chance, and there are, at a Test match, quite a number of bad losers who 'can't take it' if their side is losing, and turn their tongues to abuse.

Dr Wood has given a good description of such a type, but they would form a minute minority of an Australian Test crowd. By far the greatest number of people at an ordinary Test match in Australia never utter a word, and those who do can be divided into several classes.

First there is the 'blah' type, whose loud voice speaks his vacant mind. He utters the same old parrot-cries that have come over the fence for years, and they are as boring to everybody as they are unoriginal.

'Get a bag' or 'Get the fire brigade to put him out,' he roars and he expects people to laugh at him. That barracker should have been drowned at birth.

The next is as much part and parcel of the game as the bat and ball. He is the real man of humour.* He does not spoil himself with

---

* Here are instances which come to mind. Jardine was fielding on the fence one day in broiling heat. The flies were worrying him and he made vicious passes at them. From a voice at his back came this cry in offended terms: 'Hey, Jardine, you leave our flies alone.' Clarrie Grimmett, who had just written a book entitled 'How to Get continual chatter, but breaks out occasionally with the flash of humour and genius that sums up a situation and causes people to rock with merriment. He is an ornament to the game and, I might add, an essential, who helps many to sit through a grim Test.

Another type peculiar to Australia is the 'baiter'. He will join in to make a chorus with anybody to rag a person susceptible to barracking. I can best describe him by a little story of my experience at Randwick (Sydney) races. Just before an event I met a friend who intended backing a certain horse. That horse won, and as many punters thought his previous form had been inconsistent and that he was, in fact, a 'roughie', they formed a ring adjacent to the weighing enclosure and loudly boo-ed the horse's connections. To my surprise, I saw my friend there.

'You've only got yourself to blame for this,' I said to him – and he was boo-ing louder than anybody. 'You did intend to back him, you know.'

'Oh,' he replied, 'I backed him all right.'

I was surprised.

'Then why are you boo-ing?' I asked.

'Oh, well,' he answered, 'I wouldn't miss a bit of fun like this.'

In dealing with Australian barrackers the only thing to do is humour or ignore them. The fatal mistake is to show resentment, for then the barracking is intensified. I know players who have come through turbulent games and do not know that there has been barracking, so intent have they been on their job. I know others who have kept a sensitive ear cocked for anything coming over the ropes and their play has suffered accordingly.

Barracking in Australia, as in other countries, has put many a player off his game. A case in point is that very capable all-rounder from Oxford R. H. Bettington. He returned to his home in Australia at a time when it seemed he would win a place in a Test team against Chapman's MCC side, but in one of his very first games in Sydney Bettington had the misfortune to drop several catches in slips. The best fieldsman in the world could have done so, but Bettington had the added handicap of having just returned from England with publicity surrounding his name.

Each succeeding time Bettington played on the Sydney ground the barrackers reminded him volubly of the catches he had dropped.

Wickets', was toiling away in Sydney, and though the score was mounting he hadn't taken a wicket. At the end of one of his overs a voice from the Hill called out to him: 'Hey, Clarrie, go home and read your book again.' Phil Mead had made no runs in twenty minutes. 'What's wrong with you, Mead?' boomed a big voice. 'Have you got white ants in the legs?' Herbert Sutcliffe's meticulous scraping and patting of the wicket was met with the stentorian advice: 'Hey, bring him a b—— pick and shovel.'

They never allowed him to forget it, and I think Bettington tired somewhat of his home crowds. He did not make the Test side, but he won the amateur golf championship of Australia a few years later. He finished with cricket prematurely.

Fairfax was another Australian of recent years whom barrackers upset. The Australian barracker by no means confines his voice to visitors; and Fairfax was one of many Australians who incurred the crowd's ire. He dropped a catch one day, or was slow to move to the ball, and the barrackers trained their voices at him.

Fairfax had his own way of dealing with them.

'I've had enough of this, Kip,' he called across to his captain, Kippax, and he walked off the ground in the middle of an innings, accepted an offer to go to England from Sir Julien Cahn, and never again appeared on an Australian first-class cricketing ground.

The whole subject of barracking can be summed up this wise. It is harmful or harmless, depending upon the temperament of the man barracked, and when a player has won his way to Test ranks his temperament should be such that he does not care a fig about it.

Hendren knew how to handle Australian barracking. He had a jovial chat with them on the fence and no cricketer stands higher in Australian esteem. He had a sense of humour, too, which the barrackers loved.

'Eh, Patsy,' he was asked once on the Sydney fence, 'why isn't so-and-so in this English team?'

'Ah,' replied Patsy as he turned that incorrigible Irish face of his to the questioner, 'they'd only pick good-looking blokes in this side.'

Patsy belonged to the Hill evermore, and so did the Nawab of Pataudi when a Hill-ite asked him once whether he wanted the barrackers to address him as Your Highness.

'Just plain Pat to you boys,' replied Pataudi with a grin, and he, also, was considered a good fellow.

Like Hendren, Pataudi also had a quick sense of humour which won him immediate Australian friends. There was the occasion of his first Melbourne appearance, when a beery barracker offered him the deadliest of all insults by yelling out – 'Hey, Gandhi, where's your goat?' Pataudi, instead of behaving like one or two other people who could be mentioned, turned around with a smiling flash of teeth, pretended to identify the man in the dense crowd and said, 'Ah, so there you are; would anybody lend me a piece of rope?'

King George VI (when Duke of York) and the Prince of Wales revealed in Australia the democratic touch that made them, like their father, such firm favourites with Australians; but Jardine, unhappy fellow, was of that English type which just did not know how to unbend, how to relax. When they called to him from the Hill, he remained with his back to them, a Gibraltar-like figure of bleak immutability.

Had he turned about and swapped an occasional remark with them, it would have tickled their fancy, their importance, and broken down the barracking he received. They would have gone home that evening and proudly told their families they were on speaking terms with Jardine, and, moreover, he was not 'stuck up', as people said, but a decent sort of bloke.

Jardine, however, did not make friends easily, even among his own team. It was rumoured, when he left the 1928–29 team in Melbourne to make an early return to England, that he bade farewell to only a few in the side. It was not necessary, because of the barracking he always received, for him to analyse his thoughts on the 1928–29 homeward boat and decide that he did not like Australians.

Four years later, when a certain plan of campaign had been decided upon by somebody in England, the powers-that-be looked about for a captain who would carry the plan through. He had to be a captain above the ordinary. He had to be dogged, tenacious, remorseless, and who better in the whole of England, they told themselves, than the Cromwellian Jardine? He was the man to carry through the job. No task would be too big for Jardine. Indeed, with his temperament, with his inexorable sense of duty, he would have been the ideal type to have sent to the Ruhr Valley at that time to see that the Germans never rose an inch above themselves. It was a pity, both in a cricket and a worldly sense, that Jardine did not go to the Ruhr instead of returning to Australia!

Not for one minute do I think Jardine was directly responsible for bodyline. He was not a selector, and I mention again that those selectors chose four fast bowlers.

'Jardine came to me,' wrote F. R. Foster, the fast left-hander who bowled leg-theory in Australia when Warner was captain in 1911–12, 'and he asked me for my leg-side placings. I gave them to him, but had I known to what purpose they would be put in Australia, I would never have given them.'

That is interesting, but does not the evidence suggest that Jardine was a bodyline accessory after the selection act? The first bodyline exhibition in Australia was given under Wyatt's captaincy. At that, Jardine was the only English present-day cricketer I met whom I could have conceived as a bodyline captain. I never met A. W. Carr.

'You bowl another over like that,' Chapman threatened Voce at Folkestone just before the 1932 MCC team left for Australia, 'and I will take you off.'

Voce was bowling his bumpers. He bowled another such over and Chapman, who was deputising for Jardine, whisked him off.

Gilligan was another English captain who would not have stood bodyline for half an over.

Jardine struck immediate press trouble at Perth in 1932. It is a wise Prime Minister, actress or sporting captain, on a quid pro quo basis, who makes the path easier for the average working pressman; but Jardine, so the flock of eastern pressmen said who met the team, was most autocratic. He would not play 'ball' with them in announcing his team to suit publication purposes, and, with other things added, he made quick enemies. Pressmen soon debunked the advance propaganda from England that Jardine was a changed character.

When he reached the Eastern States he was the same aloof Jardine. He was still unbending and he had the ground closed to the public in Adelaide before the third Test because a number of onlookers had chirruped at him at practice the preceding day.

Poor, unfortunate Jardine! Troubles never ceased to dive-bomb him all the time he was in Australia. Some of it emanated from his own team, incidentally, for a side which came so overloaded with bowlers was asking for internecine strife. Never once, however, did Jardine deviate from what he considered to be his path of duty. He was convinced he had been given a certain task to carry out. That task came within the laws of the game, and, by the beard of Grace, he would carry out that job and all the barracking in and out of Australia would not deter him.

Enter, now, the new crop of Australian barrackers. When you visualise those huge crowds of 90,000 and 80,000 which sometimes daily saw those Tests, imagine there thousands upon thousands of Australian grade, pennant and junior players, whose knowledge of the game was not elementary, but, indeed, very practical.

'I was sitting one day in Adelaide,' the Right Hon R. G. Menzies, later Prime Minister of Australia, once told me, 'and it was before play had commenced. I was chatting to the man next to me, whom I didn't know. He was quietly-spoken, cultured and most interesting. We spoke of many things before the game started. That was the day Woodfull was struck by Larwood. I looked at that man again and he was a changed person. He was on his feet and his face was choleric. He shouted, he raved, and he flung imprecations at Larwood and Jardine because of what his eyes had seen.'

The noisy barracker is always with us in Australia, but this was a new type. This was the one who sat in his thousands for Test day after day and never uttered a syllable because of his cricket self-respect and his love of the game; this was the one in 1932–33 who, knowing the game and appreciating what was going on in the middle, deeply resented his countrymen being hit and turned into Aunt Sallies.

Larwood was bowling to an orthodox field that day in Adelaide when Woodfull was hit. Woodfull moved across rather awkwardly to the bumper, which appeared to be about the off stump. There was a great uproar, but this was intensified when, Woodfull having recovered sufficiently to take strike again, Jardine swung the field across immediately to the leg side and Larwood proceeded to bowl a succession of bumpers. Jardine's action at the best was a terrible error of judgment. I thought that the crowd would split the skies. If it had not been that the match was in Adelaide, the 'City of Churches', many of us felt that the crowd would have come over the fence and the match would have broken up in disorder.

The hitting of Woodfull could be discounted to a certain extent. It was the immediate swinging across to the leg field while he was still groggy and sick on his feet that created the real ill-will, even among onlookers who up to that time had taken a fairly detached view of the matter.

I have good reason to believe that Jardine himself very speedily regretted the decision he made on that occasion, but on the field he was cold and impersonal, oblivious of the near-rioting crowd.

Not even a rioting crowd on the field about him, however, would have deterred Jardine, that apostle of faith in the Englishman's power to do no wrong. From his dominating height he would have surveyed the milling crowd and probably called up the wicket, 'We appear to have some extra men, Larwood. Would you like a few more across on the leg side?'

The MCC case against Australian barracking fell flat to the ground on this count. The unusual and intense barracking of that bodyline season was directly caused by bodyline. He was blind who could not see where bodyline was heading after the first Melbourne and Sydney games, before a Test was played, and the Englishmen could not expect to have it both ways – such tactics by them and not an outcry of protest by the Australian crowds.

A wise man, a tactful man, would have looked for a path out of the maze after the first few games of bodyline, but Jardine's nature never admitted that a maze even existed. In the middle of the season he laconically observed from Launceston that leg-theory appeared to have had its birth in Australian newspapers.

'We knew nothing about it when we came here, but we have learnt a lot since,' he said. 'The practice is not new and there is nothing dangerous in it. I hope it goes on being successful.'

Cardus wrote that Jardine had no moonshine in his make-up; that he was a Scot who was in the habit of counting his change in any match, whether against Australia, Lancashire, Yorkshire or the blue blood of Middlesex at Lord's.

'He is armed with common sense and irony,' wrote Cardus. 'His batting lets you know what his conception of cricket is like. He takes nothing for granted, not even a long hop. None but a man of remarkable character could have stuck to his guns with Jardine's cool purpose in the face of a whole country's rage and indignation. It is easy to court popularity nowadays, so much so that we have come to the stage where the worst we can say of anybody is that he is popular. The sure sign of greatness is an ability to stand alone and to accept as inevitable the feeling that people are saying behind your back what they would not dream of saying to your face.'

Jardine certainly stood alone at the end of the tour so far as the Australian public was concerned, but they said nothing behind his back that they did not say to his face. He was the most hated sportsman ever to visit this country, yet there was something indefinably magnificent and courageous in the resolute manner in which he stuck to his bodyline guns. They shouted, they raved, they stormed at Jardine in Australia and they cabled, but he remained calm. He remained coldly indifferent to the point of seeming boredom as he marshalled his fielding forces and kept them pegged all the season within picking distance of a batsman's pocket.

We never saw his captaincy under its greatest strain, more the pity. I would like to have seen his reactions had the Australians, too, employed bodyline, and whether he could have kept at a distance those elements in his team who would certainly have implored and beseeched him to stop Larwood and his tactics (as happened in England later). Jardine, the disciplinarian, would probably have been too strong for them. He would have fought them, pointing out that he was not going to forsake the taming of Bradman to save them a bruise or two, but, whatever happened, Jardine himself could have been battered black and blue and never cried 'enough'. He was chockful of courage.

Jardine was a magnificent captain in his knowledge of the game and his analysis of those he played against. To those who condemned him because he played cricket as if it were a war, he might have replied, had he so deigned, in the clipped, cryptic voice common to him, 'Have not the Australians always played Test cricket in such a manner?'

I saw much in Jardine to admire. I am not prepared to put the whole bodyline blame on his wide, courageous shoulders and leave it there, nor on those of Larwood, either. Each did a job, and the great pity of it, in the final analysis, is that two such eminent and gifted cricketers should have departed from the game under such an unmistakable cloud.

Larwood was a professional cricketer, and it is a fair deduction that he bowled as he was ordered. He was greatly upset when Oldfield was injured in Adelaide. He had no great personal liking for Bradman, whom he considered conceited; but Larwood, in his nature, in his outlook on life, was rather a meek soul. There was his quiet reply at Ballarat when an irate busybody crossed Larwood's name off a list which had just been posted at the Englishman's hotel showing the team for the morrow.

'I hope,' said this foolhardy soul to Larwood, 'that you never play cricket again.'

Larwood did not break out into a fury. 'You say that,' he said quietly to this fellow, 'when cricket is my life, my means of livelihood.'

CHAPTER NINE   *I Appeal to All –*
Sir Pelham

I<small>T WAS NOT ONLY IN BOWLING</small>
that the English team of 1932–33 came armed to Australia at all
points. It was that way also with managers, for two came for the first
time in history. They were Sir Pelham Warner and R. C. N.
Palairet, who were, in passing, both old Oxonians and Harlequins.

Warner had been to Australia twice before as captain. Because of
his eminent standing in the English cricketing world, his long
experience abroad and at home, and his profound knowledge of the
game, he was regarded in Australia as the figure-head of the party.
He was the chairman of the selection committee which chose the
team – the others were Perrin and Higson – and he has since written
that the job of selecting the 1932 team for Australia commenced in
1931.

'All our ideas, workings and selections,' he once wrote, 'invariably had the team for Australia in view.'

Sir Pelham had written extensively on cricket in England, and as
he was so highly placed in English authority and reputation, it is of
more than passing interest to note his opinions, particularly those
concerning Bradman and a certain incident at Kennington Oval.

Bradman had more than a big influence on Warner in his first
English trip of 1930. He positively frightened him, and I find
nothing more interesting in my cutting-book than this view which
Warner expressed in the London *Morning Post* after Bradman had
made his record score of 334 at Leeds: 'England must evolve a new

type of bowler and develop fresh ideas, strategy and tactics to curb his almost uncanny skill.'

At the end of the fifth Test Warner wrote: 'Bradman must have a tremendous influence on the future of the game. One trembles to think what lies in store for the bowlers during the next fifteen or twenty years.'

Sir Pelham Warner, as chairman of the selection committee appointed to choose the English team to go to Australia and attempt to quell Bradman, had that amasser of runs very much on his mind as he meandered around the English countryside in early 1932. He was engrossed in his task, when suddenly there cut across his path an incident that evidently greatly disturbed him, as it did many others in England.

Surrey played Yorkshire at the Oval, and Bowes bowled bodyline at England's greatest batsman, John Berry Hobbs, then in the evening of his career.

Hobbs did not take bodyline exactly bobbing down, for he made obvious and indignant protests. He walked down the pitch and remonstrated with Bowes, a precedent, be it noted, that no Australian batsman followed in the five Tests and other games of rib-crunching by Larwood and Voce in Australia. The Oval crowd also hooted with vigour.

Hobbs was not alone in his indignation. Sir Pelham fairly bristled, and next day in the *Morning Post* he delivered himself of this bitter denunciation, which, if it did not make Yorkshire sit up and take notice, should go on record as very conclusive proof of Warner's immediate opinion of such bowling tactics.

'I am a great admirer of Yorkshire cricket,' he wrote. 'I love their keenness and the zest with which they play, but they will find themselves a very unpopular side if there is a repetition of Saturday's play. Moreover, these things lead to reprisals, and when they begin goodness knows where they will end.

'All this may sound like a sermon, but I have no desire to preach or lay down the law in any way. I do love cricket, and on Saturday Yorkshire fell from her pedestal and her great reputation was tarnished.

'Once again I appeal to all who control Yorkshire cricket, the president of the club, the committee, the captain, to men like Sutcliffe, to see that things are altered. I have written, I hope, honestly and fairly, and I am certain I echo the opinion of all who care for cricket and who wish to see its high traditions and prestige maintained.

'We saw protests on the field from Hobbs, then the crowd shouted for Bowes to be taken off, and later Macaulay sent down two fast full pitchers to the Surrey captain. Very coolly Mr Jardine ducked and the first header went for four byes; the second was taken by the wicket-keeper.'

Warner did not write that stinging criticism in the heat of the moment and then wish to forget it in the cool reflection of another day. He returned to the attack again in the *Cricketer* with this censure:

'Bowes should alter his tactics. He bowled with five men on the on-side' (Larwood and Voce usually had seven in Australia) 'and sent down several very short-pitched balls which frequently bounced head high and more. That is not bowling. Indeed it is not cricket, and if all fast bowlers were to adopt his methods there would be trouble and plenty of it. Bowes is a fine natural bowler. He must stand 6 ft 5 in and therefore brings the ball down from a great height. He would be a far better bowler if he concentrated on length and cut out all this short stuff. He is not doing justice to himself, his ability or to the game by such methods.'

In the light of all that happened soon afterwards in Australia, it is well to remember these Warner sentiments. It is well to remember, also, that they were written by an Englishman of another Englishman of happenings in England before the tour of Australia.

I stress this point, for it is to be noted that Warner (vide his recent book) considered the Board's first cable to the MCC to be 'hardly diplomatic.' The wording of the cable was: 'Body bowling has assumed such proportions as to menace the best interests of the game and to make protection of the body by batsmen the main consideration. It is causing intensely bitter feeling between players as well as injury. In our opinion, it is unsportsmanlike, and unless stopped at once it is likely to upset the friendly relations existing between Australia and England.'

This Board opinion was reached after three Tests and other games of such bowling. Contrast that cable with Warner's opinions of Bowes after one single innings, and it will be found by comparison that the Board's effort was a milk-and-water affair.

'They will find themselves an unpopular side if there is a repetition,' wrote Warner of Yorkshire. 'These things lead to reprisals and when they begin goodness knows where they will end . . . Yorkshire fell from her pedestal . . . Bowes should alter his tactics . . . that is not bowling . . . it is not cricket . . . if all fast bowlers were to adopt his methods there would be trouble and plenty of it . . . not doing justice to the game . . . I appeal to all who control Yorkshire cricket to see that things are altered.'

Moreover, there were these marked differences between the two cases. The Oval incident in England was in a match between two counties; that in Australia between two countries, in which the maintenance of good feelings and the ethics of the game were of infinitely greater importance. Furthermore, the sands of time were running out when the Board sent its cable. The season was more than half over, the theory was intensifying instead of abating, and it was a matter requiring urgency and directness rather than any deft diplomatic deployment.

And yet I am not certain I disagree with Sir Pelham when he writes that the Board's diplomacy could have been bettered. Had I been the Board of Control and failed to negotiate a satisfactory parley with the MCC managers in Australia or the MCC committee in London by the long-distance telephone, I might have been tempted to send a cable such as this: 'Appended is verbatim criticism of your manager Warner regarding game Surrey versus Yorkshire at the Oval several months ago. It describes perfectly similar set of circumstances, only worse, which has arisen here. Would you please acknowledge?'

This question asks itself: How could Warner, who, as he stated himself, loved cricket and wished to see its high traditions and prestige maintained, reconcile his expressed thoughts of the mild Oval affair with what he saw and officially countenanced for a period of months from Jardine, Larwood and Voce in Australia?

Aldous Huxley once wrote of some of his fellow-countrymen: 'The ethical standards of Englishmen undergo a rapid change as they pass from the essentially peaceful atmosphere of their own country into that of their conquered and militarily occupied Indian Empire. Things which would be absolutely unthinkable at Home are not only thinkable but do-able in India.'

Did Warner consider that things unthinkable at Home but do-able in Australia were justifiable temporarily because they quelled Bradman? Was he prepared or forced to suffer bodyline in Australia and then condemn it (as he afterwards did) when the storm had passed by?

These are pertinent questions. Some might regard them as even impertinent, but somewhere among them must lie the truth for the attitude or vacillating lack of attitude which Warner adopted when manager of the 1932–33 MCC team in Australia.

On that tour he was to Australians, and still remains, a cricketing enigma. Nor, possibly, was he so only to Australians. He has written that confusion existed in England over what really constituted bodyline. He claims that such confusion still exists in some quarters, but surely the one person who could have dissipated this confusion at the outset was Warner himself.

'It is a most remarkable thing,' wrote Noble at that time, 'that in all this fuss over bodyline we have not heard one single word from the MCC managers. Where does Warner, in particular, stand on these extremely doubtful bowling tactics?'

Cardus wrote in the London *Observer* on January 29, 1933: 'The Australians object to a deliberately planned attack made up largely of half-pitched, high-kicking balls which look to be dangerous to limb, if not to life, and which compel a batsman to think first of all of his personal safety. If the bowling of Larwood and Voce in Australia has not in any way justified this impression of it, why have we not received an emphatic denial of these accusations by somebody in responsibility on the spot?'

Cardus could have meant nobody other than the managers and, in particular, Warner. If the public did not know where Warner stood then, they know now, for this is what he has written in his book, *Cricket Between Two Wars*, of the war in cricket between the two other Wars:

'Much confusion,' he writes, 'has been caused by a very large number of people thinking that bodyline was but a term for leg-theory – a form of bowling which has been in use in this country for fifty years. Bodyline is absolutely and entirely different, and this fact was not at first generally recognised in England nor is it still in some quarters.

'One of the strongest arguments against this bowling is that it breeds anger, hatred and malice, with consequent reprisals. The courtesy of combat goes out of the game.'

These sentiments, of course, are no different from those Warner expressed about Bowes. Knowing, therefore, what he thought of bodyline before and after the Australian tour, we are left wondering only what Sir Pelham thought of bodyline in Australia. And that, I think, is a most important phase of the bodyline affair. Where did Warner stand, and what were his feelings when, as the figurehead of the MCC, he travelled from bodyline battlefield to battlefield in Australia and saw his tattered and beloved MCC flag fluttering over the now-conceded suspect deeds of his henchmen and his charges on the field below? That flag, as he was so fond of claiming, had never flown over an MCC defeat. There was Warner consternation in Sydney one morning when it was lost for an hour before being discovered with a cleaner, who was using it as a duster.

'What!' said the amazed workman. 'This here a flag? You're not kiddin' me, are you?'

The faded piece of precious bunting was run to the flagstaff in time to witness another MCC win on this tour.

Is it any wonder Sir Pelham regarded this historic piece of bunting with sacred affection? It was his banner when he led the 1903–4 team to triumph in an Australian series, the period which has often been described as the Golden Age of Australian cricket.

Again it was his banner when, as captain for the second time, he recovered the Ashes for England in 1911–12. Owing to ill-health

Warner did not play in the Tests of that series. Sydney Barnes and Frank Foster were the knights of the ball who wreaked havoc among our gifted batsmen.

When Collins' team was in England in 1926 Warner was one of the MCC selectors. This very flag flew from the mast on the ivied keep at Lord's during the second Test. England recovered the Ashes.

To Sir Pelham the flag had become more than a standard of triumph. It had become an identity, a symbol of supremacy in every clash with Australia with which he was personally associated.

Bradman was the giant who had to be slain when Warner made his third crusade of recovery in 1932–33. Again a selector and this time manager, he was committed to maintain the victory tradition. With what reverence and ambitious thoughts must he have folded the flag which was destined to float over the scenes of hostility on the Test ovals of Australia!

But where, I reiterate, did Warner stand during these stressful moments of hostility; where did he stand during cricket's most momentous era in history?

Sir Pelham Warner was an inordinately proud man when he left England as manager of the MCC team. Cricket to him was a religion and the MCC was its high priest. He had led England often before on international jaunts, but his cup of pride was filled to the brim when he saw the English cliffs fade astern and he looked with a proud and fatherly eye upon his 16 charges (the 17th, Maurice Tate, came by a later boat after an illness). Warner was serving his beloved game and the MCC in a most exalted and responsible position; he was keen to justify himself and, as well – for there was no more intensely patriotic Englishman – bring home the Test bacon! This, on the face of it and remembering Warner's oft-quoted opinion that Bradman must be curbed, seemed possible only if Bradman was shorn of his loins or some of his glory.

Warner was looking forward to renewing associations with people and places of happy memory, as he termed Australia. He was apparently happy, also, in the strength of his side, for it is a fair assumption that as chairman of selectors, he received much of his own way – even to the choice of Bowes, who, despite his malfeasance at the Oval just previously, had apparently not entirely blotted his Warner copybook.

'Bowes had only five days to make preparations for the tour,' Warner writes in his book, suggesting that Bowes owed his selection to a last-minute hunch. If the hunch was not Warner's, at least he found himself in agreement with it, for he continues in his book, 'and when it was suggested it was a bit late to invite Bowes I replied, "Lord Roberts got ready for South Africa in three days".'

The soul of good-fellowship, Sir Pelham beamed his way ashore at Fremantle and spread himself in his first interview to the Australian Press.

'The very word "cricket",' he told the scribbling newspapermen, 'has become a synonym for all that is true and honest. To say "that is not cricket" implies something underhand, something not in keeping with the best ideals. There is no game which calls forth so many fine attributes, which makes so many demands on its votaries, and, that being so, all who love it as players, as officials or spectators must be careful lest anything they do should do it harm.

'An incautious attitude or gesture in the field, a lack of consideration in the committee-room and a failure to see the other side's point of view, a hasty judgment by an onlooker and a misconstruction of an incident may cause trouble and misunderstanding which could and should be avoided. This is the aim of the Marylebone Cricket Club, of which I am a humble if devoted servant, in sending teams to all parts of the world to spread the gospel of British fair play as developed in its national sport.'

There is something slightly mysterious about that statement. Such *cliches* roll readily from the tongue of any manager at the beginning of a tour, but through this introductory statement of Warner's appears a vein of apprehension, a foreboding of something evil in the scheme of things. It was almost as if Warner feared an evil cricket sprite would jump from behind the stumps at any moment and scream 'boo' – or 'bodyline'!

For which country's benefit did Warner deliver his oration? Did he foresee trouble and was he setting himself or his team up on the pinnacle of good sportsmanship, to rise above the dust of discord which he sniffed in the offing?

This is what F. R. Foster, the highly successful left-hand bowler who came to Australia under Warner's captaincy, had to say of his former leader: 'In the whole history of cricket there have never previously been two managers sent to Australia with an English Eleven. Warner was sent to keep the peace. The cable sent by the Australian Board of Control is evidence that he failed in his object.

Not even Edward the Peacemaker could have kept things on an even keel in that season, but, compared with other years, what peace was there to keep? There had always been Australian barracking, but this was accepted as part of the game. Sir Frederick Toone, who certainly had not possessed anything like Warner's practical experience of the game, had been manager of the two previous sides to Australia, and he never had to worry about keeping the peace. He travelled through his tours and the incidents common to such tours, exuding good sportsmanship and happy feelings without any noticeable effort. So, too, in the tour of 1936–37 did Rupert Howard.

Did Warner recognise, at the time he made his Fremantle statement, certain elements within his side? Did he know that the premeditated tactics of his team to quell Bradman would sail pretty close to the wind? More pertinently still, did Warner have any hand in those tactics?

It is regrettable that Sir Pelham, going so far in his book in discussing bodyline, goes no further to tell us whose idea it was that bodyline should have been bowled by the MCC. And, also, what efforts, if any, were made inside and outside the team to disown the theory on tour. Sir Pelham whets our appetite. He gives us little morsels, but he leaves us hungry for facts in the end.

The indisputable facts are:

1. Warner was chairman of a selection committee which chose four fast bowlers for Australia and two of them, Voce and Bowes, had already bowled bodyline in England.
2. Bodyline was bowled by the MCC team continuously in its Australian tour of five months.
3. Warner, representing the MCC, remained manager of the side to the end of the tour.

The evidence would seem to suggest that at some time or other Warner cocked an agreeable ear to the suggestion – he might even have suggested it himself – that the way to quell Bradman was with fast bowlers bowling short to a leg-side field. He had seen for himself and been told of Bradman's reactions to short, bouncing balls; he probably also remembered that Foster (considered by the eminent Australian authority, J. C. Davis, to be the originator of fast bowling to a leg-side field) had taken 32 wickets in five Tests in Australia in 1911–12 when bowling to the leg field. Foster, however, did not consistently bowl short nor did he bowl at the batsman. He claimed this vigorously and none has gainsaid it. He had a beautiful, rhythmic delivery and kept an excellent length.

As a highly important official of the team, Warner would naturally play a part in the team's tactics. It might have been that he never committed himself further than to countenance an occasional bumper or two for Bradman, and if so, possibly that commitment troubled him when he saw Larwood and Voce in full Australian blast.

One well entitled to express an opinion told me: 'Warner was terribly distressed about the whole business and I really think did all he could to stop it. He and his co-manager, of course, were approached on the subject by members of the Board in Adelaide before the cable was sent. Warner was right up against the tactics and sent a report to the MCC after the first Test in Sydney roundly condemning bodylining and urging prompt action to stop it.

'How much backing, if any, he received from Palairet I do not know, but I do know that he could make no impression on Jardine and was a most unhappy man. Marylebone, itself, did not believe things were as bad as they were, and though they subsequently scotched the business, they had only a pale, pink perception of the real, ruddy rumpus we had in Australia and have not yet seen bodyline as we saw it in Adelaide.'

No Australian who knew him will credit that Palairet, Warner's co-manager, became fussed over the subject. The only known opinion Palairet uttered in Australia had to do with the alleged shortcomings of Australian railway porters, and, so far as Jardine was concerned, it would appear that he and Sir Pelham were often at loggerheads. This is suggested by these lines in Warner's book, but more particularly by what is unwritten between them:

'The 1933 season was not a happy one,' Warner writes. 'Larwood's interviews in the Press and Jardine's book did not help matters and a certain section of the Press seemed determined to make trouble. Larwood might well have said, "Save me from my friends", and he had some pretty bad ones. I begged Jardine not to write a book, and later Larwood also came out as an author, Jardine supplying the introduction. The cricket world was indeed upside down. Nerves were frayed and people known for their courtesy had some strange lapses. I felt particularly sorry for Larwood, and here I think the Nottinghamshire committee might had done more to guide him and to keep him from being stunted by certain newspapers.

'I had suggested Jardine as captain in an appreciation of the position at the end of June, 1932, and any difference was a constant source of worry to me. Here was a great captain who had, in my view, encroached on the ethics of the game. Loyalty is a great quality, but loyalty to an individual should and must take second place to a cause or even a game. Moreover, I should have been going back on my previously expressed views. It is not unfair to say that Jardine was occasionally "difficult" and did not always recognise who were his best friends.'

The truth was that Warner did not know which way to turn in Australia. His cricket ideals and his standing crumbled and crashed around his unhappy ears. As well as any man in Australia he knew what effect the English tactics were having on the game and the individuals playing it, and he knew also that the repercussions would be prolonged and intensely bitter.

'Don't put so many men on the leg-side, Douglas,' he was once reputed to have pleaded with his captain when the storm was at its height, but Jardine by then was in his blackest Scottish mood with the Australian barrackers and paid not the slightest heed. He intensified his leg-field.

'I see,' Jardine once coldly observed in Melbourne when Pataudi ignored his call to go from the off to the on-side after Woodfull had been struck, 'I see that His Highness is a conscientious objector. You go across, then, Hedley,' he said to Verity, and that, incidentally, was the Indian Prince's last Test of the tour.

Warner left England better equipped for his post than any other manager in history. Why, then, was Jardine too strong for him?

'The tactics of the captain on the field have nothing to do with me as manager,' parried Warner half-way through the tour when he was approached by Board members at Adelaide on the subject; but that was either a confession of weakness or a sparring for time.

Nobody knew better than Warner that the tactics of the captain on the field were very much his concern as manager. Fowler says the word manage means to control, to take charge of. The manager is blessed with full authority, and in no place more than on the field do a team's tactics reflect upon the club or country it represents.

If the MCC managers could not control or discipline Jardine's behaviour on the field, surely they had the requisite power to do something off the field. Jardine could have been dropped from the team, from the captaincy, or even recalled to England.

When Warner parried the Board in Adelaide possibly he knew then that Jardine was too strong for him. He knew he did not have the support of Palairet or the MCC, although, in view of the allegation that Warner sent a condemnation to the MCC of the team's tactics after the first Test, it is interesting that the MCC should later have replied to the Board's first cable. 'We have no evidence to show that our confidence in our team has been misplaced.'

Warner knew at that period in Adelaide that he had been forced into a corner, and, in his desperation, he put on as bold and as brave a face as possible under the mask of 'loyalty' – loyalty to the MCC team, if not to the game of cricket, of which he spoke and wrote so often in grandiose terms.

Holding to his office of manager, Warner probably prayed every night for the end of the season and the avoidance of incidents, but incidents and bodyline went hand in hand. A scene such as that between Woodfull and himself in the dressing-room was always imminent. He writes that the publicity given that incident was responsible for much bad feeling between the sides, but what had gone before left little additional room for more ill-feeling between the teams.

I was one of the Australians in the dressing-room when the Woodfull–Warner incident took place, and in his book Sir Pelham gives me the dubious honour of making the story public.

'Unfortunately,' he writes, 'a member of the Australian Eleven who was also a Pressman was in the dressing-room at the time, and the story was blazoned all over the Australian papers on Sunday.'

I had the chance that tour to write stories fit to water any editor's mouth, but my newspaper employers never once embarrassed me by asking that I should trespass upon knowledge which the dressing-room gave me. A journalist very early in his career learns to hold his tongue, and he learns, moreover, that information comes from most unexpected quarters. I did not give the story out, and it is regrettable, from my viewpoint, that Sir Pelham did not check his facts before he made such an ill-founded statement. I know, as do others, who gave the story out, and unlike Sir Pelham, I can give facts, but the publicity given that scene was merely incidental. The bodyline fire had been burning furiously for months before that.*

Warner tried to soften the sting of the dressing-room scene by giving the Press this statement: 'Mr Warner states that Woodfull has expressed regret for Saturday's incident to Messrs Warner and Palairet. The incident is now closed and we are now the best of friends.'

To that Woodfull replied, 'I did not apologise to Mr Warner for any statement I made. I merely told him that there was not anything personal between himself and myself. I strongly repudiate any suggestion that I tendered any apology to Mr Warner for any statement I made.'

All this made Warner's position even more uncomfortable. At that stage only one course of action was open to him, and the taking

---

* The story as told me by Claude Corbett, then writing for the *Sun* and a colleague of mine, was this: 'I got a ring on the phone that night at our hotel. It was from Don Bradman, who told me he wanted to tell me something. Don was also working in a third-sense for the *Sun*, being associated with a broadcasting firm and a sports store. We arranged a rendezvous on North Terrace and, while we sat in his car, he told me all about the Warner–Woodfull incident. It was too hot a story to run on my own, and I gave it to all the Press.'

I have always held it against the Don that he did not own up and clear me. Warner himself had a cheek to think such a sensational story would not leak out, as there were several in the team who maintained a 'leaking' connection with the Press.

Bradman obviously didn't like what I wrote about him in *Cricket Crisis* and for years ignored me. Then one night we were both with the English team at dinner at Government House, Perth, and throughout the evening we studiously ignored each other. I thought it all too silly and wrote the Don accordingly, and we agreed to bury the hatchet. No doubt this explanation will unearth the old feud again, but I think I owe it to myself to tell the story as Claude Corbett told it me. At least Don Bradman was a very good and observant reporter. He had every detail correct. (Taken from *The Immortal Victor Trumper*, 1978.)

of it would have been justified by all he said previously and subsequently about bodyline and cricket, and also by what happened when the theory was eventually condemned. If the MCC would not support him, if Jardine and Palairet paid no heed to him, Warner should have issued this ultimatum to the MCC. He should have insisted that either Jardine abandon his tactics or resign his captaincy, or, as the alternative, he himself would resign his managership.

Warner idolised cricket. He was keenly and naturally partisan, like many Australians, in that he wanted his own side to win, but all his writings suggested clearly that the game was his chief concern. What could it mean to him had his team won the whole cricketing world if he lost his cricketing soul? Cricket to him was life and religion, but when the MCC committee recanted on him and suggested that he should accept or do nothing about the dogma of bodyline creed, Warner became an apostate from his convictions and sought solace for his cricket soul in what he was pleased to term loyalty.

Over five months, five Test matches and other games of bodyline, Warner did not resign his managership. His eyes and an innate conception of how cricket should be played told him that what was going on under the auspices of the MCC was grievously wrong. His blind allegiance to the MCC, however, would not allow him to do anything publicly about the matter. He heaved a soulful sigh, had his tattered MCC flag run to the mast-head and took as his slogan: 'My MCC team, right or wrong. Bodyline as usual.'

This was the man, be it remembered, who made such a spirited and public appeal to Yorkshire when Bowes ran his mild bodyline riot at the Oval. 'I *appeal* to the president, to the committee, to the captain, to men like Sutcliffe . . .' and so on *ad infinitum*. Surely one who made such a hullaballoo over one game of such tactics would have turned the cricket world topsy-turvy rather than allow them to prevail and succeed under his proprietorship, under his managership, with his name forever afterwards linked with an official concurrence. Silence in such a case could be construed only as consent to the embracing of bodyline.

This English manager, whom Australians regarded as the figurehead of the party and one of the outstanding personalities of the cricket world, baffled Australians. Clem Hill, the famous left-handed batsman of earlier days, was one of a party in Adelaide who listened to Warner's distressed voice one day. Somebody had asked Warner why he did not do something about bodyline.

Warner said: 'But what can I do? What can I do?'

And Hill made him this reply: 'You can come down off the fence for a start, Plum.'

Warner was the unhappiest manager who ever came to Australia, but the manager of a team makes his own managerial bed. Before he arrived he said he was looking forward to meeting again 'faces and places of happy memory,' but no one was more pleased when the miserable tour finished.

When he arrived back in England he might, or might not, have quoted Whitman to Jardine:

> 'O captain, my captain! The fearful trip is done,
> The ship has weathered every rack,
> The prize we sought is won.'

CHAPTER TEN   *An English Pot-pourri*

No GOOD PURPOSE IS SERVED BY resurrecting many of the happenings of the cricket world in the seasons immediately following that year of bodyline in Australia, but there were important aspects, especially English reactions, which merit a proper acknowledgment. Indeed, they should not be side-stepped in the general story of bodyline, especially if a moral is to be drawn from the whole sorry tale.

It took years for the dust to settle, years which saw occasional flarings of temper and mutual cricket mistrust between England and Australia. Out of it finally emerged ponderous legislation which was advanced by Australia, embraced by the MCC, and was the cause of scenes behind the scenes in which the humble fast bowler, as if his burden on somnolent wickets were not already heavy enough, was forced to do penance for Larwood's sins of offence by pitching the ball only on that spot marked X and blessed by officialdom.

In Melbourne, in 1937, when Bradman and Allen each had a potential bouncer up his respective sleeve in Nash and Voce, there was a general pow-pow half an hour before play began. Umpires and everybody concerned had a say as to where a ball could legitimately be pitched. That was the decisive Test of the series, and such a prior dressing-room scene had nothing to commend it. Incidentally, for that Test, the Australian selectors had to adopt a very firm stand with the Board to keep Nash in the side.

I never saw a more incongruous scene than that in Adelaide in

1937 when an umpire, obviously acting upon instructions, surveyed the bowling talent of Australia there assembled to do honour to Grimmett and Richardson in a testimonial match and to do credit to their own ability with the 1938 tour of England in view. I would not be too certain that Grimmett, who speeded through the air what he called a flicker and which made pace off the wicket, was not suspect, but he was one of the few bowlers not summoned to an ante-room to be told where he was expected to pitch the ball. A sad moment that cricket had come to such a pass, but not altogether without its piquant flavour, for the one chosen to deliver the ultimatum was umpire Scott, than whom no fast bowler ever delivered more pronounced bumpers.

The many books written after the Australian tour did not help matters. They were mostly splenetic, especially those written by principals of the tour. The embers of the fire were still too warm for feeling not to enter into the controversy. The sportsmanship of Australians, who were widely called 'squealers', was questioned in many quarters, and in the early welter of accusations it was comforting to read these words from the renowned Sir F. S. Jackson: 'One of the things I wish to say, and that without the slightest hesitation, is that I have racked my mind for recollections and I know of no instance of Australian cricketers with whom I could possibly find fault.'

Warner and Allen did not return with the MCC tourists to England. They came on by a later boat from New York. As the main party was nearing England, Sutcliffe, presenting Jardine with a token from the team, had this to say: 'We can never say how much we all appreciated playing under you. We all admired your skill, courage and fighting spirit and the manner in which you upheld the best traditions of English cricket.'

There were many in England, however, not so sure of the position. That hard-hitter of other days, Gilbert (Croucher) Jessop said: 'This bowling is dangerous to life and limb. Intimidation is opposed to the spirit and traditions of the game. Better to lose a match than lose the respect of your opponents. It is unthinkable that our camaraderie with Australia should be threatened by a method with so little to defend it.'

As the MCC team landed, it was emphasised that there was perfect harmony in the side. That might or might not have been the case, but it was obvious that if there were any feelings of resentment among embittered cricketers who found their own particular art unwanted in Australia, those feelings were submerged in the common cause. As Heine wrote of other parties, the MCC cricketers might have been Roundheads, they might have been Cavaliers, and as such looked askance at each other, but they never ceased to be

Englishmen, and, therefore, were at once homogeneous and united against the common enemy.

So the party, including that portion of it unwanted in Australia because of bodyline (and which had a tie struck for itself, dubbing its club second division), put on a mute, inscrutable face and pledged loyalty one to the other, though that loyalty, of which Sir Pelham has written at length, became rather frayed at the cuffs later when the party took liberties with each others' ribs.

Larwood, who had broken down in his last Test in Sydney, where he was cheered as enthusiastically for a brilliant 98 as if he had been on his own Trent Bridge ground, came home ahead of the team, and was escorted like royalty through his home town to a place where a sign 'Larwood's Batteries' told him that he had found home and an abode of peace at last. Recharged, as it were, he emerged and plunged into an abyss of books, controversies, royalties, serial rights and talkies, and was reported to have quintupled his Australian wages and allowances by a week's exhibition of bodyline at Gamage's.

It was rather fitting, because of his position as Secretary for War, that Lord Hailsham should have become the new MCC president, and, at the dinner to Jardine's conquering heroes in London, he spoke words which, it was noted, caused Jardine to blush.

'Jardine is probably the best captain in the world to-day,' said Lord Hailsham, 'and his gallant band of sportsmen has worthily upheld England's reputation.'

Those at the dinner, who had had more than a fill of the bodyline squabble and were hoping for more peaceful days, regretted the tone of Jardine's speech. It was stiff, said one report, lacking in grace and humour, and with not one single conciliatory gesture towards the Australians. Some of his paraphrases bordered on bitterness.

The Australian High Commissioner and former Prime Minister, the Right Hon S. M. Bruce, stated a neat Australian case and gave excellent advice in his speech. In an analogy which he drew between Jardine's cap and his spats, he said that Australians had objected when he once returned from England wearing spats.

'I was not going to be beaten by the newspapers,' said Mr Bruce. 'I ordered six more pairs from England and had to wear the wretched things for four years.'

Mr Bruce had this interesting criticism of Australian people: 'There are true sporting instincts in Australian crowds, and only when they are roused and believe they are right will there be any ill-feeling. Whenever it is necessary to straighten out troubles, do it, for God's sake, by personal contact and not by exchanging notes.'

103

As the Walrus said, the time had come to talk of many things, and Lord Hailsham and his entourage withdrew behind the glass in the Long Pavilion at Lord's and got down to bodyline business. Lords Hawke, Ullswater, Bridgman and Belper were there, and also Sir Stanley Jackson and Sir Kynaston Studd, together with Warner and Palairet.

There was intense public interest in that first meeting, but no statement was issued. News-hawks who peered through the window were stirred to see Warner bobbing and ducking as if demonstrating the actions of an Australian batsman against bodyline. The members sat and watched him with grave faces, and it was regarded as ominous that the father of the committee, Mr A. J. Webbe, should have allowed his pipe to go out three times. The committee appointed a sub-committee to nurse the baby.

The first ball of the new English season had barely been bowled on May 1 when there came a cautious and somewhat hasty observation from the Warwickshire secretary that the game Larwood played in Australia would be unsuitable to English conditions.

Doubts were also stirring in Sir Pelham's troubled breast. Of the occasion when he was called to give evidence before the MCC sub-committee he writes in his book: 'The question was not understood in this country. Very few people here had seen bodyline in full blast, and I was of the opinion that, if let loose in England, the pavilion critics would condemn it and that in a short while spectators would begin to leave the ground. That I was correct in holding these views was later proved by the happenings in certain matches. However, some people who had never seen bodyline held that I had got the wrong perspective.'

Thousands in Australia would have howled with disappointment had Warner's counsel been accepted and England not seen an example of what had caused the fuss in Australia. Actually it so happened that, with the possible exception of the following year, when Larwood (who had not recovered in 1933 from his Australian accident) opened out against Lancashire at Trent Bridge, England never did see bodyline on a scale approaching that in Australia. At that time, however, all Australia was waiting for the English fun to begin. Bradman publicly gave the West Indies advice to bowl bodyline in their English tour, which was just starting.

'No bodyline bowling palaver can dim the glory and success of the MCC team in Australia,' augustly ventured *The Times* at this juncture. 'If the Australian Board had not been cajoled into recording the displeasure of the Australian people, Larwood's achievements would now be regarded in their proper perspective, namely, reminding the world that cricket does not rely entirely upon huge scores.'

It was followed by this dig at the Australians: 'Youth must be chosen against the West Indies so that England will be prepared for Australia in 1934 – should the Australian authorities decide that cricket is still a good game.'

In the issue of the *Cricketer* on May 20, 1933, Warner paid this tribute to Jardine, and, despite Warner's many protestations on the general subject, it is of interest to note that he admired Jardine's placing of the field.

'Jardine,' wrote Warner, 'is one of the best English captains, brave and tenacious, an acute observer and thinker, who admirably managed his bowling and placing of the field.'

From the *Sunday Graphic* came this sentiment, which found hearty reciprocation in Australia: 'We must make the fullest use of bodyline in order that England may determine for itself whether there was any justification for the Australian protest.'

And at that time A. W. Carr, stormy man of English cricket and captain of Notts, declared that he would use bodyline and Larwood to the fullest extent against other counties. No Australian either hoped or asked for more.

On May 21 the West Indians, Constantine and Martindale, recorded their first English hits on Joe Hulme, the Arsenal footballer and Middlesex cricketer. Dryly observed the *News Chronicle*: 'Hulme's football colours are red: his cricket colours are likely to be black and blue.'

Two days later a strangely muffled figure emerged from the Lord's pavilion and shuffled to the wickets. It was Patsy Hendren in his anti-bodyline three-peaked cap.

'My wife doesn't object to my looks being spoilt,' drolly explained Patsy, 'but she draws the line at my head.'

Die-hards dozing in the Lord's sun and discussing the good old days were electrified by this sign of the times.

On May 25 Warner wrote of the dignity of the game and chided Australia. 'I admit that England must say one or two things to Australia, but Australia can hardly take that amiss. She has said a few things herself and must expect to be answered. I plead for peace, and hope that everyone will refrain from comment detrimental to the dignity of the game.'

Hey, presto! His words about dignity and peace had barely been uttered when, next day in fact, New South Wales had the backing of old South Wales at Cardiff, when the crowd angrily demonstrated against Bowes as Turnbull and Clay were hit. Recalling the MCC's protest in one of the cables series against offensive Australian barracking, it is well to note the anger of the Cardiff crowd. On June 5 Bowes knocked Watson senseless at Old Trafford amid uproar. Things were indeed beginning to happen.

One by one Jardine's men emerged from under their blanket of silence and Duckworth got this off his voluble chest:

'The whole thing in Australia boiled down to the simple fact that some of the Australian wizards were frightened to death by Larwood,' quoted George, who is an admirable fellow.

He was not to know then that fate and his old team mate, Larwood, had several hard things in store for his own ribs in that stormy match I have mentioned against Lancashire. Duckworth had several staved in.

All this and the rising current of disapproval and ill-feeling running rapidly through the English county clubs should have been sufficient to tell the MCC that bodyline begot offensive barracking. But the MCC, sticking tenaciously to the barracking stand it had taken against Australia and stoutly contending there was no such thing as bodyline – it was merely fast leg-theory, which was known to Caesar – resolutely refused to correlate the two evils. The cabling war continued apace and continued to bore and abhor people beyond measure.

In Australia Mailey had these words to write of the barracking angle: 'If the Board did nothing to stop offensive barracking, Jardine did less. I did not expect him to rush to the fence and plead on his knees to the patrons of the Hill, but I expected him to be a little more tolerant and understanding and not indulge in subtle tactics that were meant to irritate and not pacify. Those half-hourly rests for refreshments in Adelaide in the third Test were unforgiveable. Here was a chance to be nice, but the cool and imperturbable Douglas probably said to himself: 'You gave me a hell of a barracking last time I was here, and now I am going to annoy you.'

'If the MCC wants offensive barracking to cease it has the remedy in its own hands – don't send Douglas Jardine out here again. That is rather severe on one of the brainiest captains who ever came to Australia, but I am sure Jardine would willingly make the sacrifice for the sake of cricket.'

A correspondent writing to the *Star*, London, said that since the MCC had blessed bodyline (which it had ingeniously tried to confuse with leg-theory, he added) the committee should carve the following distich on the pavilion at Lord's:

'Since all is fair in love and cricket,
Bowl at the batsman, not at the wicket.'

At the annual University match at Lord's, Wilcox, the Cambridge captain, had Farnes bowl bodyline against Oxford ribs and feelings. Seven MCC members, including Sir Home Gordon and Lord Suffield, in a joint letter to *The Times* decrying the Varsity bowling, expressed regret 'that the tactics seemed to savour of those employed in the Australian Tests, which would destroy the whole charm, spirit and enjoyment of the game.'

English opinion was taking a decided switch towards Australian sentiments on bodyline, and particularly was this so when the West Indians did their bodyline best in an unsustained burst in the first Test against England at Manchester.

I am credibly informed that the West Indians bowled bodyline in that match on an agreed understanding with some influential members of the MCC who wanted to see what the theory was like. Grant, the West Indies skipper, was agreeable, but some of his fast bowlers protested, and with reason, that if there was to be a bodyline exhibition it should be on some more responsive wicket than Old Trafford, which is notoriously lifeless.

Even at that, the West Indies, with Constantine, Martindale and Griffith, greatly inconvenienced the Englishmen. Hammond had three stitches put in a gaping cut that stretched from eye to ear and he looked a very sick warrior when he was out after making a few runs against the theory. Jardine, full of pluck as usual, batted 65 minutes at one stage to score 14 runs.

The only other occasion on which the West Indies bowled bodyline on that tour was at Harrogate against Yorkshire.

Wisden had this to say of the Manchester experiment: 'We can at any rate be thankful to the West Indies for showing us what an objectionable form of attack this kind of bowling can be. Most people in England, whichever way they inclined, were to a large extent ignorant of the effect it had upon cricket, and there can be no doubt whatever that the exhibition given at Old Trafford confirmed opponents of it in their views and caused hundreds, who had open minds on the subject, to turn definitely against it.'

In that 1933 season the county captains met and decided that as the MCC could not deal with the matter they would not pack the leg-field. Fourteen of the seventeen came to what was known as the Gentlemen's Agreement, the three standing out being Jardine, Carr and Jupp.

Carr, whose statements about bodyline and his leading of Larwood and Voce generally created trouble, agreed that he was opposed to direct attack, but contended that neither Larwood nor Voce exploited it. He might as well have added that the moon was made of cheese.

It is of interest, however, that in the game later against Leicester in 1933, E. W. Dawson and Carr mutually agreed that they would not tolerate bodyline. Carr made this press statement: 'Somebody is going to be killed if this sort of bowling continues, and Mr Dawson and myself considered that the game would be much more pleasant if it is stopped. Sooner or later something will have to be done, so why not do it now.'

'It is strange,' wrote Cardus about that period, 'how circumstances have consistently conspired to prevent Lord's from looking upon an authentic demonstration of bodyline methods by one or other of the heroes of Australia. What is sanctioned by Lord's and thought good enough to beat Australia is legal and presumably desirable in this country, yet I have met no cricketer this summer who wants bodyline. Everybody is getting to hate the sight of the leg-trap and the short bumper. Bodyline would vanish to-morrow if cricketers here governed the game.'

The Right Hon R. G. Menzies, who went on an official visit to England in 1935 as Australian Attorney-General, told me that talk of bodyline met him at every turn. It was fortunate for Australia that there was at Home a man of such standing and cricket knowledge to put its side of the case.

He had told me the tale of a Yorkshire Mayor who conferred the honour of his city upon him.

'I am delighted to meet you and to bestow the honour of my city upon you,' said Mr Mayor, and then added, in an aside to Mr Menzies: 'But I think I should tell you that I do not like your cricketers. I think they are squealers.'

When he got the chance, Mr Menzies put this question to the Mayor: 'Did you think the Australians squealers in 1928 when Chapman, who also had Larwood with him, gave them a bigger drubbing than Jardine's team?'

Mr Menzies then told of bodyline as he saw it, and the Yorkshire Mayor admitted that he had not thought of it like that.

Mr Menzies put the case often on that English visit, once outside The Temple, after a Privy Council appearance, to Lord Hawke. In his book Warner suggests that Mr Menzies came into the Australian firing line after the first cable was sent from Adelaide, and he thinks, possibly, Mr Menzies was responsible for the change of Australian front in the cables. That was not so. Mr Menzies had no hand in the cables at all. He rather thinks he was asked about the first cable after it was sent! He advised Woodfull not to become embroiled in a Press controversy, but to approach Jardine privately and tell him his tactics must be stopped. If they were not, Jardine would then have to take all responsibility for them.

'The dressing-room story of one side playing cricket and the other not set English backs up. The Australian case could have been handled much more tactfully,' said Mr Menzies to me once when we were talking in King's Hall in Parliament House, Canberra.

Mr Menzies had just related the delightful tale of how the news of the declaration of war had come to Lord's in 1939. He illustrated how workmen came into the Long Pavilion and carried off the bust of Grace.

'This,' said one of the Oldest Members in definite terms, 'can mean only one thing. This is war.'

Inside the House the Brisbane Line controversy on Australia's defence was being waged in all its intensity.

'We Australians,' said the former Prime Minister, nodding towards the Chamber, 'indulge in a deal of what I might call slang-banging, but it probably does not mean as much as people think.'

To return to 1933. The thoughts then of the committee of the MCC must have been very mixed. The polyglot bodyline chickens were coming home to roost day by day, and because of the stand it had taken against Australia at the beginning, the MCC had to give them sanctuary, if only temporary sanctuary, no matter how dowdy and ruffled they looked on the Lord's rafters.

Jardine, also, was rapidly becoming a problem child. Probably many of the MCC committee wished he would go and shoot off his bodyline ardour at lions in Africa until things quietened at home, but Jardine was very much on hand. As the MCC had condoned and blessed him in Australia, they had to continue taking him under their Lord's wing, and he emerged to be blessed and sent to India as captain of the MCC team again, a blessing possibly given with the MCC fingers very tightly crossed for luck.

India was almost Australia over again. Larwood, Voce and Bowes were not there, but Jardine, Clark, of Northants, and the bodyline field were sufficient for a hot curry of trouble.

This is a portion of what happened in India: Merchant had his chin split; Naomal had his eye cut open; a ball at Madras narrowly missed the Maharajah of Patiala's turban and bitterly incensed the crowd; Dilawar Hussain was hit on the head in the Calcutta Test, and, like Oldfield in Adelaide, was carried off the field; Clark, at Colombo, amazed everybody by walking down the wicket and deliberately scraping with his sprigs that part of the pitch where a good length ball would land. Clark's action was so blatant that the MCC batsman at the other end apologised to the Cingalese captain, Dr Gunesakari.

The renowned Australian and Middlesex all-rounder, Frank Tarrant, who umpired in the Calcutta Test, told me that when Clark hit Hussain he told Jardine he would stop Clark from bowling.

'I will stop you from umpiring,' was Jardine's retort, according to Tarrant; and he did!

'Clark would say as he passed me,' said Tarrant, ' "he will take this one" OR "there will be some bobbing to-day". Every cricketer knows what that means. I sent a report on the whole matter to the MCC. All I know is that Jardine did not play for the MCC again.'

109

Everybody at this stage was heartily sick and tired of the word bodyline. They hoped for cricket peace, but at a time when the Australian tour to England in 1934 hung in the balance, Jardine, Larwood and Voce caused more trouble. Jardine cabled to England from India that he had no wish to play against the Australians again; Larwood said the same, and, remarkable from two professionals, Larwood and Voce publicly criticised the MCC.

At the end of 1933 *Wisden* commented: 'We hope that we shall never see fast leg-theory bowling, as used during the tour in Australia, exploited in this country. It is definitely dangerous, creates ill-feeling, invites reprisals and eliminates all the best strokes in batting.'

At that time the MCC sent this cable to the Australian Board: 'We agree, and have always agreed, that a form of bowling which is obviously a direct attack by the bowler upon the batsman would be an offence against the spirit of the game.'

What, then, one might ask, was all the fuss about? Was this not what Australia had claimed from the beginning? If Australia had been given credit for having the spirit of the game just as much at heart as the MCC; if Warner and Palairet had interpreted their managerial duties correctly in Australia and stood up to their responsibilities, would not all this fuss and trouble have been averted?

Many thought it would be better if the Australians did not come to England in 1934. It was thought it would be best if Test cricket were forgotten for a time and the position allowed to settle, but there were other reasons why the tour should take place, not least important being the financial cricket dependence of both countries on Test tours.

It was in a still cloudy atmosphere that Woodfull took his team across in 1934. The absence of Jardine, Larwood and Voce from the English side lessened interest in the game, and many considered the real Test atmosphere was lacking. It was on the assurance from England that bodyline would not be bowled that the Australians made the trip, and only once was that agreement broken – not surprisingly, perhaps, by Nottinghamshire.

The county sent eleven professionals into the field against the Australians and Voce was the bodyline culprit. Woodfull sent for the county secretary at the end of the day's play, and he told him that the agreement under which his side came to England had been broken. The county committee could please itself, said Woodfull, but if Voce took the field next day, the Australians would consider the game finished and would return to London.

The Nottinghamshire committee imposed a 'diplomatic' illness upon Voce next day and he did not take the field. Spectators sensed that something was amiss, and the Australians were roundly hooted as they walked on the ground. One who was there told me that he has seen nothing braver than the action of a diminutive parson who tucked his hat under his arm, walked along with the Australians through the hooting crowd and clapped them right to the middle of the ground.

As this Voce incident led to much trouble in the Nottinghamshire county club, and had something to do with the eventual disposal of Carr as captain, it will be fitting here to quote part of the county committee's report:

'The committee yield to none in their admiration of Larwood's great bowling feats in Australia and elsewhere,' ran the report, 'and we would point out that the regrets expressed by this club do not relate to Larwood's bowling nor do they reflect on him in any way. The committee have never had occasion to question the fairness of Larwood's bowling.

'At a joint meeting held at Lord's on 23rd November, 1933, of the Advisory County Cricket Committee and the Board of Control of Test matches at home, at which the county captains were present, the question was discussed and the following conclusions were arrived at: It was agreed that any form of bowling which is obviously a direct attack by the bowler upon the batsman would be an offence against the spirit of the game. It was decided to leave the matter to the captains in complete confidence that they would not permit or countenance bowling of such type.

'Three charges of direct attack were brought against our team during the past year, and we regret to say that we have been bound to admit that two of the charges have been proved. Although only three formal complaints have been made, it is within the knowledge of the committee that grave dissatisfaction against some of our bowling exists among several of the first-class counties. It has been freely suggested that Carr has not observed the agreement of 23rd November, 1933, to which he was a party and at which time he stated that he was strongly opposed to bowling of the type mentioned.

'The Nottinghamshire public can have no idea of the widespread nature of the complaints and appears to be under the impression that the controversy is with Australia alone. This is far from being the case. It was freely stated at the Test match at Trent Bridge, when leading cricketers from all parts were assembled, that action from more than one direction was contemplated in the near future.

'Lancashire wrote on 21st June, 1934, stating they were unable to renew fixtures with us for 1935. The umpires did not uphold the Lancashire complaints and the Notts committee took no action. In the game against Australia, the umpires gave their opinion that the charge of direct attack bowling was fully proved. The committee decided that there was nothing left to be done but to express regret. It sent the following resolution to the secretary of the MCC: "This meeting deprecates the bowling of Voce on the Monday evening of the Notts–Australia match at Trent Bridge in the two overs referred to, and will take the necessary measures to prevent its recurrence."

'In August, at Lord's, against Middlesex, the Middlesex committee registered an emphatic protest against the manner in which Voce bowled during the match. Notts again apologised and said they would take such measures to effectively prevent any possible grounds of objection in the near future. We shall take such steps as may be necessary to prevent this club again being placed in such a humiliating position.

'At the end of 1934 season Lancashire had refused to renew fixtures, Middlesex had a genuine legitimate grievance against us, and we can definitely state that our friendly relations with some other counties hung but by a slender thread. It was clear that unless an entirely new spirit was created there might be a general refusal on the part of other countries to renew fixtures.

'The most important question to consider was the captaincy, which was the key to the situation. The full committee appointed S. D. Rhodes and G. F. H. Heane joint captains for 1935. That the decision of the committee in appointing a new captain was justified is clear from opinions recently expressed by Carr and which have appeared in the press. He is reported to have said: "I saw Voce bowl, there was nothing unfair. If I had been captain, Voce would have bowled even if the Australians had walked off the field. When I am captain, I shall not restrain anyone from bowling as they think fit."

'It is obvious from these statements that Carr's view of fair bowling is so far different from that of first-class umpires and many leading cricketers that a recurrence of trouble under his captaincy would be practically certain to arise. The statement that he would allow bowlers "to bowl as they think fit" proves that he fails to appreciate one of the chief responsibilities of a captain. We wish to make it clear that in future the committee will require whoever may be captain of our team to be fully responsible for the conduct of the team on the field.'

And so Carr was sacked.

Voce later apologised to the MCC and came again, somewhat apprehensively to Australia in 1936. He was warmly received with not the breath of a boo against him and was a better bowler, with a ball running away magnificently, than he had been four years previously when he pelted his gifts into his own side of the pitch.

At the end of that 1934 season the MCC made this report: 'There was evidence that bowlers had made direct attacks upon batsmen in the season of 1934. This attack could be defined as persistent and systematic bowling of fast, short-pitched balls at the batsmen standing clear of the wicket. The MCC has always considered this type of bowling to be unfair and it must be eliminated.'

The MCC said that the umpires, being the judges of fair and unfair play, had the power to deal with direct attack.

The MCC ruled that once the umpire had decided that a bowler was adopting direct attack methods, he should caution the bowler, and if the caution was not effective he should inform the captain of the fielding side and the other umpire of what had happened. If that were not effective, the umpire was then empowered on a repetition of direct attack to call 'dead ball' and call the over completed. The umpire was then to request the bowler's captain to take the offending bowler off immediately. He was to report the incident to the captain of the batting side and then, later, report the whole proceedings to the MCC.

If a bowler had been ordered off, as above, he was not to bowl again during that innings. The umpires were assured of every support from the MCC, and, furthermore, they were also asked to make a report if any player or captain disputed their decision or even showed resentment, on or off the field, of the umpire's decision.

It is somewhat lamantable that the only victim of the new ruling in Australia was the Queensland aborigine Eddie Gilbert. Early in his first-class career Gilbert had been accused of throwing the ball, but that had not militated against his selection, and he became a virtual regular member of his State eleven, more hostile on his home wickets than in the other States.

In a Sheffield Shield match in 1937 against a New South Wales team, not at full strength, Gilbert retired from the bowling crease after completing an over of medium pace. The Press and public took it for granted that Gilbert had ricked a muscle.

The news broke the following day. It transpired that umpire Borwick had ruled that Gilbert's deliveries were dangerous – of the bodyline pattern. He did not bowl again that innings.

There was but a passing storm. The Queensland players were resentful, but they had accepted the verdict passively. The New South Wales players, realising that anything Gilbert could do with the ball was but a mild shadow of the Larwood assault, were inclined to be sympathetic. No violent objection had been made by the batsmen. No voice of protest had been heard from a barracker. After the match Borwick went south to umpire in a Test against Allen's team. The ripple his action had caused passed almost unnoticed in Australia and probably received no mention overseas.

113

The MCC's ruling and direction to umpires marked the practical end of bodyline, a theory and a controversy that did the game incalculable harm. The moral of it I will try to draw in the next chapter, but surely it must be undoubted that the whole affair was badly bungled at its beginning, and the consequence of that bungling was the embarrassment of the game and of many players for years afterwards. Even as late as 1938 in England I heard heated discussion on the case and, in many quarters, Australian players of 1932–33 were always suspect.

Why was the whole business bungled so badly? Was it because of incapable or die-hard legislators in both countries; of English lack of confidence in the Australian Board of Control, most of whom to those abroad were not even a name in the game; was it because of the managerial ineptitude of Warner, particularly, and Palairet?

Your opinion and guess are as good as mine. I would like to have known more of the English scene behind the scenes – who was the initial instigator of bodyline, for instance, and whether Jardine did as Warner told him or Warner as Jardine told him. The bodyline history is incomplete without these answers, but, in the final analysis, there are certain conclusions which I am prepared to accept.

I itemise them thus:–

(a) Bodyline was invented purposely to quell Bradman and it succeeded.

(b) The theory kept Tate, one of the greatest bowlers the world has known, out of the side for five Tests, despite the fact that he got Bradman, Kippax, McCabe and Bill in his first game of that tour for 22 runs.

(c) England was good enough to win that year without bodyline and with Larwood bowling to a normal field with an occasional bumper.

(d) Bodyline cost England the series in 1934, due to the absence of Larwood and Voce and their effect upon certain Australian batsmen, and again in Australia in 1936–37, when circumstances would not allow Allen or Voce to bowl legitimate bumpers.

(e) Bodyline recoiled upon bowlers, in that it deprived them of the bumper, a stock ball in trade.

(f) Had not War intervened, Australian fast bowlers would have ignored the ponderous bumper rule in their dealings with the new Test record holder, Hutton, in Australia in 1940–41.

Most surprisingly – and for no apparent reason – Hammond lifted the lid somewhat on bodyline in mid-August, 1946, in an article in the London 'People'. Fourteen years after the Australian season Hammond strongly and unconditionally condemned bodyline, saying that he and other prominent Englishmen would have left the game had it been continued. He said he believed that only good luck was responsible for no one being killed by it. The Australians thought the same (as did Umpire Hele), but this seems to join issue with Hammond's further declaration that Jardine, Larwood and Voce never tried to injure or intimidate their opponents. If Hammond, Hele and the Australians got the impression that a fatal injury was just around the corner surely something of this impression must have occurred to the three team fellows Hammond mentions. Hammond names Carr, Fender and Jardine as the tacticians who evolved the bodyline scheme in conference with Larwood and Voce. This is interesting, but does not account for the fact that none of the three was a selector of the team to Australia, which, as stressed often, included four fast bowlers, two of whom had already bowled bodyline. Hammond's article 'out of the blue' was written almost on the eve of the English team, of which he is captain, sailing for Australia. The fact that Hammond should utter such sentiments 14 years later is proof of the bond of loyalty which the 1932–33 MCC team kept. An expression of such an opinion in 1932–33, even unofficially, would not have justified the MCC committee saying in one of its cables that it had no evidence that the tactics of its team were unsporting.

CHAPTER ELEVEN

The Money in Cricket

W HEN A PRINCIPLE OF CRICKET was at stake in 1933, the Australian Board of Control, which had raised the principle, quickly dropped it when the MCC committee suggested cancelling the rest of the tour, including two Test matches.

Part of the Board's cable from Adelaide read: 'In our opinion, the tactics of your team are unsporting.' From Brisbane, before another Test ball had been bowled, the Board turned this remarkable cable somersault: 'We do not regard the sportsmanship of your team as being in question.'

What was the reason for such a sudden change? As Napoleon once said, there are two questions that cannot be asked too often. They are how and why.

In 1928–29, in Australia, the gate takings for five Test games against England were £75,324. In 1932–33 they were £70,352. In 1936–37 they were £90,909. What frightened the Board of Control more than bodyline in 1932–33 was the MCC suggestion that the rest of the tour, with its two remunerative Test matches, should be cancelled. No deadlier yorker had been bowled in any Test series.

The MCC committee was possibly sincere in its suggestion that the rest of the tour should be cancelled, although this might have left the bodyline subject up in the air for all time. But if it was a battle of tactics the MCC certainly cabled a shrewd, strategical move. Finance from the game meant as much to the English counties as it did to Australia. It was essential for both countries that the game should continue and the turnstiles kept clicking. As the MCC called this tune, the Board had to dance to it, and, of course, the Tests went on, bodyline, moral-line or any other line notwithstanding.

Each country treats its players generously. It costs no small sum to assemble 16 or 17 players, send them first-class on a luxurious steamer to the other end of the earth, house them in the best of hotels, attend to their every want and give them, as Australia did her players, £600 out of pocket expenses for an English tour.

The gates had to click right merrily to maintain this state of affairs, and, in the case of Australia, there were deficits to be made good on the South African and West Indian tours.

The members of the Australian Board were all esteemed business and professional men, and, as a band, strove with commendable vigour to advance the interests of the game – as they saw them. Test players, squatting on one another's lap to peep through their dungeon-like dressing-room windows at the play in Melbourne, might have grumbled over the years at the opulent and luxurious quarters and lavish fare of the legislators in the stand above, but none could deny the eagerness of the legislators to see the game flourish.

The only query arises in the definition of the word flourish. It might have been argued against the Board that too many of its members thought their legislative ability was judged by the financial success or otherwise of a tour.

I do not wish to be unkind to the Board. I am merely being analytical. Unlike four of my Test friends, McCabe, O'Reilly, O'Brien and Fleetwood-Smith, who toed a Board line in 1937 and do not know why to this day, as they had no charge preferred against them; unlike Bradman, who was fined £50 for an alleged misdemeanour; unlike Mailey, who was barred from Test selection; unlike Ponsford and Kippax, who were not allowed to go to India in 1935 on a privately arranged tour; unlike the Big Six of 1912; unlike these and others I was never a victim of any Board autocracy and thus have no vengeful axe to grind. But as a player, when he submits himself for Test consideration, is the plaything of the critics, so also, in some measure, should be legislators who aspire to the highest cricket positions.

The predominant feature of the Board of Control at any time of its history was the absence on it of people who had played a decent standard of cricket. When it is considered that the Board is in supreme control of the game in Australia, it surely must be a most amazing state of affairs that, since its formation in 1905, only four legislators of international cricket standard have found seats on the Board. It is just as amazing that New South Wales, the home of

Australian cricket personalities (to wit Trumper, Noble, Carter, Macartney, the Gregorys, Collins, Bardsley, Cotter, Duff, Bradman, McCabe, Kippax, Taylor, Oldfield, O'Reilly and innumerable others), and Victoria, next important producer of types and personalities, have not yet been represented on the Board by one who has played international cricket.

Season 1932–33 was no exception to the rule of international paucity, or to the rule of Interstate, first grade or even district representation paucity. Only two names, Hutcheon and Hartigan, both from the Cinderella State of Queensland, will be found in *Wisden's* lists of spurred-and-booted cricket players in this Board personnel of 1932–33: Dr Robertson, Dr Mailer, W. L. Kelly (Victoria); R. A. Oxlade, W. C. Bull, F. M. Cush (New South Wales); B. V. Scrymgour, R. F. Middleton, H. Hodgetts (South Australia); R. Hartigan, J. Hutcheon (Queensland); S. H. D. Rowe (Western Australia), and H. Bushby (Tasmania).

Rowe, always a good friend of the player and a magnificent manager in South Africa in 1935–36, was up to Test standard, I was told once by the late Prime Minister, John Curtin, who, as a fellow West Australian, often played against Rowe.

This Board, by virtue of the very realism of things, could not have possessed in any marked degree a practical appreciation of what was happening in the middle of the ground. This was the Board which sent the first cable; this was the Board which did its double-shuffle dance the minute the MCC piped its first note on the financial flute. It was not the MCC offensive against Australian barracking which started the Board hopping. It was the threat to liquidate the Test goose laying the golden egg. That was a master-stroke by the MCC committee, because it knew precisely what finance from a successful tour meant to Australia – as, indeed, it meant to the English counties, most of which drew their main sustenance from a share of Test gates.

Big cricket was big money. In 1938, at Lord's, in a four days' Test between England and Australia, the gate receipts were £28,164. In a three days' game at Leeds the same year they were £14,189. (Incidentally, revenue from Tests in England would be immeasurably greater with more adequate accommodation.) Big cricket, therefore, was decidedly big business, and it is not surprising that some players caught the infection of the money virus from some of the legislators.

This was particularly noticeable towards the end of the 1920s – the depression period, be it noted – when the increasing inroads of the game made it necessary for a player in both England and Australia to be either his own employer or have sympathetic employers.

A tour of England monopolised eight months of the working

year, a big slice out of the career and initiative of the ordinary young man making his way in the world. To quote two cases only, Bradman and McCabe were both on the graceful side of thirty after they had each made three trips to England, one to America and Canada, McCabe to South Africa, and each, apart from the ordinary first-class games in Australia, had participated in five Test seasons in Australia.

The average Australian business man is intensely fond of sport, but no ordinary mercantile concern could afford to carry a cricketer who was incessantly absent from his employment. If prominent cricketers were to continue playing the first-class game in Australia and abroad, if they were to keep an eye on their business future after their cricket days had ended, it was necessary that they should be associated with sporting businesses. Many of them were.

Some were engaged in business with partners. Others were associated with firms and, as the practice of having royalty-paying names on autographed bats and other goods crept in and developed, so, too, inevitably, developed the habit of individualism. It was not sufficient to hold a place in a team and hold it with credit. To shine above his fellowman and create a special market and demand for, say, the Bill Blobbs bat, it was necessary for Bill Blobbs to carry to the middle with him a Bill Blobbs special, and there lay about him with such gusto as to suggest that his willow was superior to other autographed bats.

Competition was keen and firms spurred on their representatives. It was said facetiously of two Test players, inseparable on tours, that the only rift in the lute of their friendship was that one received as royalty sixpence a bat more than his mate.

Could one blame individuals of outstanding ability who, improving the shining hour, developed such an outlook on the game? The game, I think, lost a certain element as a consequence, but players had only to look about the pavilions as they walked out to bat to see sad instances of heroes of other days who had given much time and energy to the game to the detriment of their pockets and their future. Moreover, the period when this spirit became most noticeable in Australian cricket, and I think this was also England's experience, was the period of depression when youths left school and found little besides an unemployment queue awaiting them.

Legislators plainly showed their concern for the financial side of the game. If the game made such demands upon their time, surely players were justified in giving a thought to themselves and their future when, the age of adulation ended, they were again like any ordinary citizen who had to shoulder his responsibilities.

It was inevitable, then, that somewhere about the middle twenties Australian cricket should have become more individualistic. Quite often it became a matter not so much of the team as the individual, for this was the period when the sensational section of the Press was establishing itself. That type of newspaper did not want a combination of individuals to share the praise and limelight it was eager to lavish.

It was of little use for this particular Press's purpose to feature as a story that eleven men preferred to sleep on their right side and wore night-shirts in preference to pyjamas; that they were all simple, humble souls who never forgot their old nurse and twice yearly sent her red roses. An interview with a hero's mother was considered of more news appeal than a description of the hero's innings.

The world was crammed at the time with pole-sitters, marathon dancers, marathon pie-eaters or individuals eager to push a companion far and wide over the countryside in a wheel-barrow. The stunt or flapper Press, as it was known, wanted a single entity, whether a pole-sitter, a barrow-pusher, a cricketer or a horse, to set up on the publicity pedestal for the masses to wonder at and read about.

There were two Australian cricketers of that period who were born to fill admirably that intensely individualistic bill. The first was Ponsford and the second Bradman.

Ponsford was a true product of the monopolist age. He guided records and runs into his own exclusive cartel by hooking, driving and cutting for hour after hour with the precision and certainty of a machine. His bat looked twice as broad as any other batsman's; his appetite for runs appeared as if it would barely be appeased when Judgment Day sounded.

On only four first-class occasions has a score of over 400 been made. Ponsford made two of them. Four of his first-class tallies were 437, 429, 352 and 336. In four successive innings in first-class cricket in Australia, in 1926–27, Ponsford made 437, 202, 38 and 336 – a total of 1,013 runs.

Only those who have made a hundred in a first-class game, and more particularly in a Test, know what concentration goes into the effort. The occasion, in itself, before crowds ranging from 30,000 to 90,000 is a test of the individual. His brain never knows peace. For the whole innings his concentration must be at its tensest to see that no slip is made, that the eyes, arms and legs co-ordinate to carry out the dictates of the brain. Every move of the opposition must be seen and circumvented, and the individual's play must be accommodated to the changing phases of the game.

All this saps the average individual to such an extent that he is quite prepared, indeed eager, to call it a day when he reaches a century. He is tired, physically and mentally, but happily aglow with the thrill of achievement. With infinite peace of mind he allows his concentration a little respite. His thoughts wander and he thinks of the cooling shower in the pavilion and possibly a glass of deliciously cold beer that waits to be sipped in the glowing reflection of a century.

To the average cricketer, this is the superb and sublime moment of happiness. He looks at the scoring-board and sees there the three magic figures opposite his name. He thinks back on his failures, his tremulous fears at the beginning of his innings, and he laughs at them. He thinks of his apprehension a few minutes back as he fought his way with furrowed brow through those difficult eighties and nineties and he smiles again. This is his hour of triumph. None can deny it and his innings, small wonder, becomes a death-or-glory affair. He accepts all challenges, flirts with disaster and is not sorry when his end comes. He has done his job; somebody else can carry on. In five minutes he will be out of dripping flannels; his hand will be wrung in warm congratulation; there will be the cold shower and the glass of beer, soon to be followed by a string of congratulatory telegrams. Happy thoughts, indeed!

Ponsford, more so than any batsman in history up to his time, ignored the simple merits of a century or a double century. His ambition sought Olympian heights of satisfaction. Like Bradman, who was to follow closely in his steps, Ponsford did not know the meaning of the word pity in its application to bowlers. The lore of mercy with Trumper was rich in legend. It was said of him that when he had made a century he looked about for a deserving bowler, one who had tried bravely or, perhaps, a youngster in need of encouragement, and he gave him his wicket so unostentatiously that not even the bowler was cognisant of it. Ponsford and Bradman, contrariwise, lived in a materialistic age. They were realists who tempered their batting with no mercy.

Ponsford humiliated the humble Tasmanians in 1922–23 to make the then world's record score of 429. He sharpened his bat on the Queensland grindstone in 1927–28 to make another world's record of 437. Once in Australian cricket he performed the magnificent feat of hitting eight centuries in twelve innings.

Ponsford was a popular player with his fellows. Away from the batting creases he had a good sense of humour, but he religiously put that off when he put on his pads.

The story is told that when he made 352 of Victoria's record score of 1,107 against New South Wales, Ponsford looked as if he would bat on into eternity; but at 352, enough runs for any team's total, Ponsford played a ball from outside his stumps on to the wicket. As he turned to see that his ears had not played him false he made this remark in a most doleful voice: 'By cripes, I *am* unlucky.'

Though in itself a tribute to Bradman, it was in essence unjust that Ponsford's really magnificent performances should have been practically forgotten in the rise and reign of Bradman. Sporting glory is as hollow as all earthly glories, but it is well to note that Ponsford retired from cricket at 34, an age at which Dr Grace was cutting his second teeth in the game.

O'Reilly, whose opinions were moulded in the blistering fire of experience, considered Ponsford the greatest batsman he bowled against, superior even to Bradman.

'I always gave myself a chance against Bradman,' O'Reilly once told me, 'but Ponsford seemed to be a different proposition. Like the elephant, he never forgot. He was ready for every little trick up your sleeve.'

It is of more than passing interest that Grimmett also thought Ponsford more difficult to bowl against than Bradman.

As with Bradman, wet wickets upset Ponsford. He did not like them and took no pains to hide his dislike. On coming to breakfast on tour, players never asked whether it had rained during the night. The question was, 'Did "Ponny" wake during the night?' If he did, it was assumed to have rained, for it was reputed that the merest trickle was sufficient to rouse Ponsford and cause him to toss uneasily on the thoughts of a sticky wicket for the next day.

Like most Australian youths who rise and decline much more quickly than their English contemporaries, Ponsford began to play competitive cricket at an early age. He was 14 when he first pitted his skill against Melbourne district players, but his youth would have earned him no compassion.

Australian sport is not like that. I remember playing competition cricket against an uncle when I was 15. He was a magnificent all-rounder who never wanted for runs or wickets, and I had vain thoughts that family pride would have pleased him to see me against his bowling. I actually thought I might even get an easy one first ball! But not a bit of it. The sight of me to him was inflammatory.

'The confounded cheek of this,' he seemed to snort as he ran up to bowl against me, and his roar for lbw, which could have been heard chains away, sent the umpire's finger skyward. (I am pleased to say that I had my revenge on Uncle some years later.)

The average Australian youngster learns in a hard school, and so it was with Ponsford. The impression of keen competition left its imprint on his youthful mind, and the first lesson he learnt was that if he wanted any encouragement he had to make it himself.

He once told me that he always followed advice received when a youngster. That was to get as many runs as one could on every occasion, because one would never know when a spin of misfortune would come along. Ponsford was no dreamer. It is an axiom that every first-class cricketer has had his run of outs, his spell in the doldrums.

'I don't think I had the intention of big scores at the start of an innings, but when runs did come along I guess I thought to myself that this same opportunity might not happen along again and that I would do well to make the most of it,' he declared in describing his big-scoring motives.

'I played on those principles. I did not think at the time that big scores took much out of me. Now I am not so sure, for I certainly suffered after-effects.'

The task of keeping himself on the pinnacle to which he had climbed undoubtedly took its toll of Ponsford. It exacted heavy nervous energy and prematurely killed his love of the game. At the age of 34 he felt that he never wanted to see a bat or a cricket game again.

Ponsford was a magnificent cricketer and I pay him homage. Justice will see that his worth is not forgotten, but, stupendous as Ponsford's deeds were, they paled when Bradman made his entrance.

Bradman did not allow Ponsford even a few short years to bask in a rightful glory. The true perspective of Ponsford's deeds had barely dawned on the game when Bradman ruthlessly thrust him from public thought with the most stirring string of big scores ever known.

The Ponsford wounds of 437 against Queensland had barely healed when Bradman reopened them and rubbed in salt with 452 not out – not out, if you please – at the end of 406 minutes at the crease, with 49 fours!

The mere simple centuries in Bradman's first-class career seem poor meat for him. He made over fifty of them, but it is his scores of 200 and over that tell the tale of his supreme mastery in first-class games. They are: 452 not out, 369, 357, 340 not out, 334, 304, 225, 254, 232, 252 not out, 236, 205 not out, 223, 258, 220, 299 not out, 226, 219, 238, 200, 253, 244, 206, 233, 270, 212, 212, 278, 258 and 202.

If Bradman plays no more first-class cricket, his career will have finished in his 31st year. He had then made 92 centuries in 274 first-class innings. Dr W. G. Grace had 1,493 first-class innings for 126 centuries, and Hobbs 1,315 innings for 197 centuries.

The condition of wickets in the time of Grace was vastly different from those which Bradman and Hobbs enjoyed, but, to strike an illuminating comparison on the figures of all three, it can be estimated that Bradman would have made approximately 501 centuries had he played as many innings as Grace, and 444 if as many as Hobbs.

Further, it is to be observed how many of Bradman's 92 centuries ran on into double, triple and one quadruple three-figure tallies.

His figures are the criterion of his domination of first-class cricket, except in the bodyline year, when he made only one century against England. It is to be noted, also, that in the bodyline year he had begun on his usual string of big scores with 238 and 52 not out and 157, all against Victoria and all played before he appeared in his first bodyline Test.

Bradman dedicated his early manhood to the business of making runs. It will be said of him, and argued in the years when cricket connoisseurs recall the past in warm debate, that he lacked the flowing or artistic brilliance of some of the past masters; but the truth is that Bradman could have been a batsman of soothing glides and graces had he so desired. He was too long in the head for that. Others might have gloried in the ripple of delight and applause which greeted a flick to the leg-side or a flash through the slips, but such strokes invariably yielded only a single and in their making revealed only a fraction of the face of the bat to the ball. Bradman could play all these pretty strokes and in fact did so when moved, but for the most part his bat did not indulge itself in sly, covetous glances of ones and twos. It looked at the ball with a broad face of impish impunity and demanded four. He took risks aplenty, but when those risks were analysed it was generally found that Bradman's bat was full face to the ball.

Such tactics assuredly paid the richest dividends. One of Bradman's contemporaries, in a tone of voice suggesting that the cricket gods were unjust in their distribution of favours, once charged me to note how many full tosses and long-hops Bradman received. It is true that Bradman received more such bad balls than other batsmen, but the reason was easy to discover. A bowler who saw a batsman plank his legs in front of the wicket and then flick the ball off them to fine leg was always willing to be in such a party; a bowler who saw nothing else but the full-face of Bradman's offensive blade coming up the wicket to meet him began to think of the weeds in his garden or some other place where he could more pleasantly and profitably spend his time. The truth was that Bradman's bat found many a bowler's heart wanting and made loose deliveries for himself.

We succeeded one year in sobering Bradman down. It was in Adelaide in December, 1938. After Bradman had made his usual confident beginning, I decided, as captain of New South Wales, and with the help of O'Reilly, to play an extra cover, a little deeper, with another man extra on the on-side, between square and mid-on and back a little. We decided to forget about the slips, and the result was that we cut the usual Bradman fours down to ones. He made 143 in 230 minutes, probably his slowest big score of all time, with only 11 fours. He took 185 minutes to reach a hundred and had hit only six fours. But we could not have done that against the Bradman of the early 1930s.

We met the Queenslanders in Melbourne on their way across to Adelaide, and I told my good friend and fellow-opener, W. A. Brown, of my plan. He liked it and thought he might also try it. Bradman made a double century. I asked Brown later about the match and he answered sorrowfully that he had tried the scheme.

'I had no sooner done so,' he said, 'than Bradman called out to me: "I see your little game, Brownie. I was going to get out after I had made a century, but I'll make two now."' And he promptly did!

There was no limit to Bradman's confidence. He showed that to its greatest extent in the period just before he went to the wickets. That is the worst time of all for a batsman. Once the job is in hand the average Test batsman does not worry one bit. The 50,000 or 90,000 spectators might as well be in Timbuctoo for all they mean to him, but the batsman is a touchy and jumpy individual in the pavilion just before he goes out to bat. He replies in monosyllables; he avoids everybody, for he is then as highly strung as a boxer about to enter a ring.

Bradman never knew such human frailties. Hooker, the New South Wales bowler, who holds the world's record last wicket partnership of 307 with Kippax, spoke to me once of this difference between Bradman and all other batsmen.

'If I said to them before they went out to bat, "Good luck to-day," most would just grunt or nod their heads. They did not want anything to break in on their concentration. Once, as Bradman was going out to bat in a first-class game in Sydney, I said the usual thing to him and he replied, "Thanks, Hook. Now let me see. It is five minutes past twelve now. Seventy minutes to lunch. A quiet 60 will do me."'

When lunch came Bradman was in the sixties. Hooker commented that everything was proceeding according to plan.

'There's no doubt about your confidence,' said Hooker.

Bradman grinned.

'One must plan,' he said. 'I'll be 200 by tea.' And he was!

That is an insight into Bradman's make-up. While the average batsman walked to the wickets with mixed thoughts, wondering whether luck would be with him, whether the bowler might send along an unplayable ball in the first over, Bradman never gave a thought to such things. In his bright lexicon of youth there was no such word as failure. It was a case of how many would he be by lunch, by tea, or whether he would bat for one, one and a half or two days.

Tennyson's words aptly described Bradman and the spirit which he brought with him to the creases:

> '. . . strong in will
> 'To strive, to seek, to find, and not to yield.'

In an article once in *Wisden* on Bradman, Dr Evatt wrote that his batting was functional, and it was, inasmuch as it was always adapted to the main purpose in hand – that of winning the game. Bradman considered that it was the first duty of a batsman to get the greatest number of runs possible for his side. And this he always strived to do.

To no other batsman in the world had newspapers given over the whole of their poster to a play on a cipher when Bradman, as several times happened, failed to score. 'O BRADMAN' said the posters, for Bradman failing to score was big news. Bradman in an illness in England in 1934 was again big news and the subject of hourly bulletins and special editions. When Bradman made 270 in the third Test in 1936–37 one London newspaper issued a contents bill with two words: 'HE'S OUT'.

In all the games I played with Bradman I never once saw him show disapproval, even by the faintest gesture, of an umpire's decision or a streak of misfortune. It might well be thought that things have come to a pretty pass when one is complimented on observing the ordinary courtesies of a game, but international sport has become such a commodity on the world publicity stage and the Press has plastered individuals with such disproportionate importance that some time the glamour creeps into, and – finding plenty of room there – expands the cranium. Those so affected take not kindly to reverses. It is a simple matter to be a gallant, smiling sportsman – your happy outlook obvious to all within the orbit of the oval – when things are going well, but it is when the rubs of the game happen along, together with the inevitable bad decision, that the sportsman shows out in his true colours.

With the exception of the early part of the 1934 English tour, his game still grievously troubled by the bodyline after-effects, Bradman knew little of the ups and downs of the average Test cricketer. He was dropped after his first Test against England in Brisbane in 1928 (team mate Kelleway, off the field a contributor to an Australian newspaper, volunteered an opinion that Bradman was not up to Test standard), but these were the only notable checks Bradman received in his magnificent career. He was thus not tested in misfortunes as an ordinary player would be, but I saw enough of him to know that he accepted with grace the few rubs that came his way.

The test of a champion is often not on the international field, before the public gaze. Maybe it is on some remote country green where the Great One is apt to act as lord of the domain with the others the necessary serfs with no feelings. I remember Bradman playing in a country game at the height of his career. His name had been advertised in the district for weeks before. From far afield came the adulating ones, who sat ready in their thousands to pay homage to the champion, but alas for the exhibition they were to see! Fate had one of the umpires at the end from which his nephew was bowling to Bradman, and family pride overcame the old chap's better parts. Most enthusiastically he gave Bradman out first ball to his nephew's wild appeal – a frightful decision. The only two happy people on the ground were the umpire and his nephew. In this year of grace, 1946, they still continue to be the town's outcasts.

Bradman left the wickets with a broad, wide grin. He saw the humour of it. That umpire contrasted with the English one who sternly castigated the young village bowler who loudly appealed for leg before wicket against Dr W. G. Grace. 'Not out, m'lad,' said the umpire, 'and let's have no more of your nonsense. The people have come to see the Doctor bat, not you bowl.'

No one can question that Bradman was the most arresting personality in all cricket's history. If there are any doubters on that score I will settle them by quoting what I consider to be this most conclusive evidence. The greatness of Bradman was shown by the fact that a theory such as bodyline had to be invented to beat him. No such tribute, for such it really was, had ever been paid to the old masters – Grace, Hobbs, Trumper, MacLaren and others.

Bodyline was nothing more nor less than a revolution against Bradman. It was an uprising of bowlers against their lot, a lot over the years which had yoked their honest shoulders to doped wickets and limitless Tests; and Bradman, with all his genius, with all his concentration and remarkable stamina, with all his ruthlessness, was the last straw.

Bradman was the counterpart of the French King Louis, enforcing his batting taxation on the bowling masses. Warner was the Rousseau; Jardine the Danton; Larwood the Robespierre, and, as in all revolutions, heads rolled. Bradman, after the revolution, was never again the same cheeky batting monarch, and the cricket heads of Larwood and Jardine fell to the crash of the legislative guillotine.

History shows that bowlers have always been the miserable and unfortunate outcasts of the cricketing family. In the early 19th century there was grumbling because the pitches had improved considerably; runs were flowing and the bowlers were still restricted to the under-hand delivery. Crumbs were thrown to the bowlers every now and then. The hole in the ground evolved into a stump, another came and later another on top of the two. The stumps broadened and heightened, but with pitches improving in texture batsmen continued to hold the upper hand.

Then came a crisis in 1826. Two brooding bowlers of Sussex, Willie Lillywhite and Jem Broadbridge, took their courage and the ball in their right hand and let both go at shoulder level. (Legend has it that a woman first invented round-arm bowling!) The storm was terrific, for those were days of peace. No roaring exhausts clouded the sky or main roads, and the rashness of Willie and Jem was debated in village pubs and haunts for days and even years.

Lillywhite and Broadbridge lived cricket lives of outcasts until 1844, when officialdom opened the rule book to round-arm bowling and made it legal. Peace reigned, as they once used to write of Europe, until 1862, when a certain Edgar Willsher, surfeited, bored and tired by the batting monopolists of his day and the legislation always prone to make it easier for the batsmen, took his arm high above his shoulder at Kennington Oval and let the ball go at that height. He was no-balled, peculiarly enough by a Lillywhite, and Willsher left the field in utter disgust. A near-riot followed. The bowler's cap was in the ring again, and in 1864 came legislation to allow the ball to be delivered at any height. That is the present position.

The bowler has always had to fight for concessions. There was irony in the legislative crumb thrown to him in recent years of a leg before wicket decision to an off-break pitched off the wicket. The truth was that no bowler could turn a ball from the off in the first few days' play on most Test wickets. Over the years the batsmen have been the petted and spoiled darlings of legislators and groundsmen. They have been nursed solicitously; as someone once put it, they have been rocked to sleep in the cradle of perfectly doped wickets.

Two of the evils of modern cricket have been doped wickets and limitless Tests – one the counterpart of the other in the Test sphere. It might be considered trite justice that the country which sowed the seed of limitless Tests should have reaped the retribution of body-line, for if, on the face of it, there was justification for the Australian lament that teams should come and go 12,000 miles without reaching decisions in most of the Tests, there was also a suspicion that the huge gates Tests attracted had more than a little to do with the advocacy of limitless Tests.

It was of little use staging a limitless Test if the wicket was not there to pace the days with it. Sometimes accidents did happen, as, for instance, in the four days' fixture at Leeds in 1938, when one of the best Tests in all history was over in three days. That wicket was under-prepared, according to modern standards. The usual wicket for a limitless Test has to be prepared to withstand a siege of seven days or more.

The last limitless Test before the war was so limitless it never finished. At the end of ten days in Durban, England and South Africa had to pull stumps so that the visitors could catch their steamer home.

Limitless Tests and doped wickets were good alike for the batsmen and the gates. But a pertinent question is: Were they good for the game? The point at least opens up a wide field for debate.

Let us look at it first from the viewpoint of the bowler. Here was a person who began his career on a village green in England, a coir mat or a piece of parkland in Australia. He found that by cutting his fingers underneath the ball, it turned from the off; by twirling them over the ball, it turned from the leg. Such a sensation of achievement thrilled him. It gave him incentive to explore the bowling path. He still had to become a master of flight, deception and length if he wished to combat batsmen of class, but the initial experience of seeing the ball cut in from its line of flight and weave its way past the bat to the stumps gave him his first encouragement to persevere in his calling.

If he was not a spin bowler and relied upon pace, he was equally delighted when the life he gave to the ball was responded to by the pitch and the ball went through smartly and brightly.

Was a bowler entitled to such flatterings of his vanity? I think he was, if only for encouragement; but whatever ideas he might have had about his ability to turn a ball at will on ordinary wickets he soon had all this stuff and nonsense knocked out of him when he ascended to the first-class heights, particularly if he was an Australian.

These youthful miracles of spin, as he wistfully regarded them in after life, passed into the limbo of unknown wiles when he got down to the real business of his cricket career on doped wickets, on pitches prepared for limitless Tests against monopolistic batsmen. The somewhat uneven pitches of his youth, which registered every degree of spin and sometimes gave break where none was intended, gave way to smooth, somnolent strips of rolled, rerolled and doctored turf. Their very nurtured nature kept them aloof from the temptations of spin, and the bowler became a slave to his art. He moved in a world of sweat, curses, drudgery, tattered shirts and broken boots, and the wonder of it was that Grimmett, O'Reilly, Verity, Tate, Geary or any of the labouring and toiling trundlers did not drop in the tracks from a broken heart.

I remember the first time I played against Grimmett. I did not lack advice and it was splendid advice. I was told to forget about break and play every ball from Grimmett for a straight ball. Of course I did not do that. I did what practically every other batsman did when he first met Grimmett. Fascinated or mesmerised by the little chap's violent twisting of his hand as he delivered the ball, I played for a leg-break and was promptly out leg before wicket to a ball which fizzed straight through.

I knew better after that. I knew neither Grimmett, O'Reilly nor anybody else could turn a ball for at least two days on the average first-class Australian wicket. The surface of the wicket was too smooth for the ball to grip and give effect to its spin. The ball thus naturally skidded through on its original course.

I give full credit to Hutton for his world's record at the Oval in 1938. Anyone who bats as interminably a time as Hutton did deserves all the praise he gets, but Hutton will be the first to admit, I think, that nobody could have turned a ball on that Oval wicket for two days at least. It was the same that year at Trent Bridge; it would have been the same had play been possible at Old Trafford, and it has been the same on many grounds the world over for some years. Who will deny that most wickets have been over-prepared with water, liquid manure and fertilisers? All life has been rolled out of them and all life has almost been knocked out of bowlers asked to do duty on such pitches, particularly in limitless Tests.

The bowler, the ugly duckling of cricket, generally accepted the snubs and rough edges of life uncomplainingly. There came a time when even the little niceties, the little knick-knacks of his profession, so to speak, were denied him. He must not use resin; he must not raise the seam.

There was a delectable scene in Adelaide once when Leyland, under orders, accused Ironmonger of using resin. On that peaceful Adelaide wicket it would have made no difference had a spin bowler borrowed Aladdin's lamp and given the ball a rub against it before each delivery, but, custom being custom, Leyland took his point. He wagged an admonishing Yorkshire finger at Ironmonger.

"Ee, laad. Thou'st using resin,' said Leyland.

Ironmonger snorted. A look of injured virtue flitted over his face. 'As if I would use such a thing,' he barked.

He dived his hand into his pocket, took out a handkerchief, waved it furiously and defiantly – and clouds of something that looked like resin floated in the atmosphere!

The dice was loaded against the bowler, but there was nothing he could do about it. I remember a Test occasion when a bowling worthy took his cap from the umpire at the end of his over and walked down the pitch on a line between the stumps. Perhaps he piously hoped that a sprig or two of grass would come up with his boot sprigs. He whistled as he went and he had a faraway look in his eye as if communing with nature.

I eyed him suspiciously.

'Excuse me,' I said politely, 'but you are walking on the wicket.'

He jolted back to earth.

'What's that?' he asked.

'The wicket,' I replied. 'Would you please walk off it?'

'Oh!' said he, looking as innocent of intent as a habitual criminal making a statement from the dock, 'Oh, the wicket! I am so sorry.'

'Excuse me,' I said again at the end of his next over, 'but would you mind walking off the wicket?'

'Tch, tch! How careless of me. My thoughts were far away.'

'Excuse me,' I barked at the end of his next over, knowing I had right on my side, 'but would you mind walking off this —— wicket!'

As I wrote, there was precious little the poor bowler could do about his fate.

An Epilogue
to Bodyline

Bodyline was not a cricket revolution which grew overnight. Unrest among bowlers, because of the difficulties and injustices of their job, had been simmering for years. It was purely a coincidence that Bradman, bringing to the game a particular outlook, should have synchronised with a period when the art of doped wickets was at its height. All it required to touch off the fire of bowling revolution was somebody like Bradman, somebody who could throw into bold relief just how one-sided this game of cricket had become in its lauding of, and consideration for, the batsman, always at the expense of the bowler.

It naturally followed that a batsman became more of a publicised individualist in cricket than a bowler. Circumstances kept a bowler's feet on solid earth, kept his nose to the pitch, so to speak, but there was nothing to stop a batsman from soaring to any heights. With this individual flavour so pronounced, it was not surprising that some first-class batsmen should have become rather selfish mortals.

Some became masters in the dubious art of keeping the strike or leaving it to somebody else if the going was difficult. If you watched one or two batsmen carefully you would notice almost an indecent anxiety on their part to take a single off the last or second last ball of the over so that they would be on hand to take strike to the next over at the other end. This was done for self, not side.

It was not a general habit. Most players were prepared to take the rub of the game and the strike as it came; but that the habit existed at all was evidence of the individualism that had crept into the game. I recall an evening in Melbourne in 1932 when a leading Australian batsman very forcefully denounced bodyline to members of the English party; yet I doubt whether that critic was actuated by regard for the game or regard for the fact that bodyline had caused the bottom to fall out of his own particular cricket world.

Bodyline was not in the interests of the game, and the 1932 MCC team did cricket and England a grave disservice. There can be no doubt of that. How often have we heard it airily said that if Hitler played cricket there would have been no war. Had Hitler played in that 1932–33 series he would have thought war inevitable. The whole cricket world would have been a battle-field had bodyline been condoned, for it negated the very principles and good feeling for which cricket was renowned.

True, it took the genius of a Larwood to demonstrate its effectiveness in the Test sphere, but as one moved down the cricketing scale it was not necessary to have a Larwood to inconvenience batsmen of lower degree. Some Australian junior teams copied Larwood's tactics in their parkland games that season, and there was a long record of brawls, disturbances, hospital cases, police intervention, and bad feeling.

Bodyline denied the game its essential batting art, but the point is that it did not suffice to ban bodyline, put the fast bowler at a disadvantage he did not know before bodyline, and then imagine, by waving a wand of good-fellowship to the accompaniment of glib phrases, that all was right and proper in cricket again.

All was not well in cricket prior to the War, and that was solely because legislators ignored the lessons bodyline so blatantly taught. I make bold to say this now – and probably I took as big a hiding from bodyline in 1932–33 as any Australian – that the theory might have been justified, that it might in the end have indeed been a good thing for the game had its lessons been learnt.

In the 1930 tour of England, Bradman the Individual took precedence in many minds and in many quarters over cricket the Game. That state of affairs was not approved by those who knew the art of the game, who knew of Bradman's very human frailties on a wet wicket and who had seen champions come and go with the game going on for ever.

A few short years are infinitesimal in the life of cricket; a few years in the life of a champion bring the inevitable diminution of eyesight, vigour and the confidence of youth. Here to-day, gone to-morrow, forgotten next week, is as true of cricket as life. In a few short years Bradman once more would have returned to the ranks or gone over to the immortals while cricket continued on its pedestal.

It can be of no lasting good to any game if an individual is thought to be the greater. That was proved in Australia in Bradman's own time when thousands left the ground at his dismissal; when crowds at the NSW–Victoria Sheffield Shield game dwindled from 35,000 to 7,000 and 8,000 in a few years, and when Bradman, himself, invited to South Australia for the principle of the gates, became so accepted that Adelaide gates fell below the crowds of the Victor Richardson-Nitschke-Lee-Ryan days.

What was the significance of all this? Did it mean that Bradman, by his huge scores, by his consistency in producing century after century, had dulled the cricket appetite of the Australian crowds for anybody else than Bradman, for no cricket but Test cricket and for no score under a hundred or, as Bradman made a hundred so simple an affair, under two hundred?

Bradman did not have an inspiring influence upon those who played under him. His leading bowlers did not regard him as a good captain. In the first place he was not an idolised leader of men, as Richardson was, for instance. The Australian team in South Africa in 1935–36, without Bradman and under the captaincy of Richardson, pulled better together and was a superior all-round side to the Australian Eleven Bradman led in Australia in 1936–37 and in England in 1938. No one made a score of 200 on the South African tour, but the fifties, sixties and centuries of the players gave the side all the margin McCormick, Grimmett, O'Reilly and Fleetwood-Smith desired for victory.

The presence of Bradman in a side, because he was such an intense individualist, often had a bad effect. He swamped the others and made them indifferent. Only a batsman knows how difficult it is to score a century, but Bradman made that poor meat and he made the scoring of 50 in a Test match, once considered a splendid feat, go almost unrecognised.

The Australian Board of Control made itself look foolish in 1937 when it found itself unable to comprehend that a Test side including Bradman should have been beaten in two successive Test matches by Allen's MCC team. (England twice caught us on wet wickets, though the result could well have been the same had this not happened.) They summoned McCabe, the vice-captain, O'Reilly, O'Brien and Fleetwood-Smith before them (for what reason nobody has yet discovered), but in between the summoning and the appearance, Australia won a Test and the Board committee, feeling uncomfortable, bought the players a drink and shook each warmly by the hand.

I once saw O'Reilly playing in Sydney for the Australian team that had been unbeaten in South Africa. It was the beginning of the next Australian season and the other team was captained by Bradman. That Australian team was pardonably proud of the unbeaten record it had in South Africa, but thoughts of its record had to be cast aside when Bradman came to bat. It was Saturday morning and just prior to lunch. O'Reilly was in magnificent bowling form and had taken several quick wickets. He was immediately taken off. He was itching to get at Bradman before he settled down, but the afternoon crowd could not be risked. It did not matter about O'Reilly's reputation or the unbeaten record of his team. The sole consideration was that Bradman should be at the wickets at the adjournment. On this occasion there was but one excuse. The match was a benefit for Jack Gregory and Warren Bardsley.

Bradman had no part in this. He would have preferred his duel with O'Reilly to be immediate, but the gate transcended all such considerations. Bradman had then such an influence on the gate that legislators congratulated themselves if he was not out at an adjournment or over-night.

O'Reilly did not bowl at Bradman until long after lunch. He was then settled, made a big score and Richardson's South African team suffered its only loss.

I am not blaming Bradman in any manner for this state of affairs. He was a victim of circumstances, although those circumstances were largely of his own weaving. He could not have foreseen when first he committed himself to big scores, unlimited, that they would create bodyline and that he would reap the retribution of his own mastery.

The people to blame for bodyline in the main were those who could see no further than huge scores, doped wickets and limitless Tests.

In the final analysis these factors could not be for the game's good, as bodyline proved. 'Ill fares a land,' wrote Oliver Goldsmith, in his immortal lines, 'to hastening ills a prey, where wealth accumulates and men decay.'

This sentiment could be applied to any game.

None can gainsay the importance attaching to the financial side of cricket. Intermittent tours were carried out on a grand scale; business buildings were constructed in cities in the name of cricket, and hundreds of players throughout the world, not only in English counties, depended upon cricket for their livelihood. To them cricket was, first, a means of livelihood and, secondly, a game.

Money was the essence of limitless Tests, because Test matches could always be relied upon for big gates. Why confine a Test to three or four days when it could go on for more?

Had not War intervened, this concern for the financial side of the game, as typified by limitless Tests, would have given cricket its greatest set-back in history in Australia in 1940–41. Hutton, Edrich, Compton, Gibb, Hardstaff, Barnett, Hammond, Ames and others were capable of batting against the attack Australia would have presented for three or four days in one single innings. The ten-day unfinished Test at Durban would have been the forerunner of many more. One such match in the middle of a season would have disrupted a tour; two would have disrupted the game.

I often wonder what would have been Hutton's experiences had that 1940–41 tour eventuated and had he set about emulating Bradman's big deeds. I do not think any prim compromise between the Board and the MCC would have stopped fast bowlers from exploiting the theory that Hutton did not like bumpers. And would the Australian crowds then have shouted 'bodyline' against their own bowlers?

No trite rule made for the sake of convenience should prevent any fast bowler from bumping the ball. That is where the bodyline revolution recoiled on long-suffering bowlers because a bumping ball is as much part of a fast bowler's set-up as a pair of sprigged boots. Provided that a packed leg-field does not obtrude upon the spirit of the game by tying a batsman down, nobody has any moral right to tell or direct a bowler where to pitch the ball. If a batsman does not like bumpers that is all the more reason why a bowler should bowl a bumper every ball if he feels like it. I know batsmen who delight in bumpers; I know others who abhor them.

This brings me to my final contention. No such theory as bodyline, off-theory or that incredibly dull leg-theory which is so common in England would be necessary if bowlers were given the dues that rightly belong to bowlers.

I know many will disagree when I contend that the very excellence of wickets made for stilted and colourless batting. Constantine thinks that the better the wicket the better should be the batting; but although that seems logical, my experience was that batsmen on a slow, true wicket were less disposed to take risks, their assumption being that they had only to stay at the wickets and runs would come to them. I refer, again, to Hammond on many occasions in Australia and to Hutton and Hardstaff in the fifth Test in 1938. I know that, too, from my own experience as a Test opening batsman.

Limitless Tests and doped wickets, the one the relative of the other, denied the bowler his rights. If a wicket had to be prepared for a limitless Test then the very nature of its preparation rolled all life and fire out of it. No bowler could get response from it; no bowler could make spin take effect on it. The bowler was thus driven to other means, to evasive and negative action.

Give a bowler a wicket which takes spin and lift and he will not worry about a batsman's ribs or tiring batsmen and spectators with dreary, negative bowling on the off or leg. He will attack the stumps. This will entail a greater variety of strokes, because the

136

batsman has to play every ball; he has to make the most of it while the wicket going is good.

Consider the attitude with which an opening batsman sets out on his task in a limitless Test, especially if his side has won the toss. The openers face the biggest task of the innings. The ball is new and lively, the bowlers and fieldsmen fresh and eager for a quick break through, which means everything to a side losing the toss in a limitless game. If the opening batsman survives those initial overs he has done a big job for his team, but his next task is to sit on the bowlers for as long as possible.

A limitless Test is a war of attrition and the batsman who gets out taking a risk is considered either a national rogue or a fool. Charlie Barnett, who played a glorious pre-lunch innings on the first day at Trent Bridge in 1938, watched the final limitless Test from outside the fence because his stroke-making was not wanted. I made a century in a Test against England in Melbourne once and decided that I'd hit a certain bowler, not overpopular with us, over the fence or die in the attempt. A roaring slash put a ball to the bottom of the pickets, but I faced an admonishing finger from my skipper at the other end. He pointed out, and rightly, that there was still all day to bat, and the next, if necessary.

Two of the best stroke-makers in cricket are W. A. Brown and Len Hutton. Yet I have seen each forced into a strokeless groove in a limitless Test. When a batsman is obsessed by defence for an hour or two it is no easy matter to blossom out into strokes. I think every opening batsman in the game, and every spectator, too, would welcome a state of affairs whereby a score of 40 or 50 is considered to be a job well done, as it certainly is. After scoring 40 or 50 a batsman should be entitled to take risks and play strokes.

Limitless cricket, however, does not cater for risks, because the batsman's job is to play the bowler into the ground, use up as much time as he can and bring the other side to bat when the wicket is showing signs of wear. That is the present-day Test philosophy. I have seen Hammond bore people in Australia by refusing on a perfect wicket to play strokes when past the century. Surely there can be no greater condemnation of limitless Tests.

The batsman must be encouraged to take risks, because it is good for his enjoyment of the game, good for the spectators and good for the bowlers.

How, then, can the risk element be brought back into the game? Only by one factor, I think, and that is the clock. Playing against the clock, either on the offensive or defensive, is one of cricket's greatest charms, and the way to do it, I suggest, is to play the Test series on a points basis.

The six days set down for Tests in 1946–47 is too much. Four days of cricket, from eleven o'clock to six, is enough for any Test, provided – and it is an important proviso – the wicket is prepared for four days. There was a Test match in Melbourne in 1932 which finished on a worn wicket early on the fourth day; there was a Test match in Leeds in 1938 which finished on a worn wicket in three days. I am positive these games will be mentioned years afterwards when mammoth-scoring matches have long since been forgotten.

The wicket at Leeds was under-prepared and took spin from the very first over. The Melbourne wicket, because of weather circumstances, was also under-prepared. The important point, however, is that cricket emerged from these two games with colours flying. That could not be said of the final limitless Tests in England in 1934 or 1938 nor of the unlimited Durban fiasco in 1939.

Bradman made a century at Leeds, a glorious century, which provided proof that his greatness would have been marked had wickets not been so over-prepared. All batsmen at Leeds accommodated their play to the pitch in the knowledge that it was taking spin and they had better take risks. Hassett won the game for Australia by chancing his luck in the dying minutes of the third day, but what mattered more than the winning of that game was the pleasure it gave the spectators and the pleasure it gave the players.

That is the Test cricket the world will want when the series begins again, and that is the type of cricket it is entitled to expect. With due respect and acknowledgment to Bradman, Ponsford, and Hutton (and the Indians, Merchant and Hazare, who are making records as I write), I think it serves no really good purpose if a record Test crowd sees only a few batsmen in a day's play. Cricket is at its best when a number of styles are on view and batsmen come and go with fair rapidity.

There can be no thought of battering bowling activities if wickets are falling in fair time. If batsmen are taking risks and bowlers are not driven into the ground by a deadened wicket nothing can go wrong with the game. To bring about this state of affairs, I maintain, the legislators will have to bring the clock back into the game.

Tests of limited duration need not entail wild and indiscriminate slogging. In the two sparkling matches I have quoted technique and batting culture had their rightful places.

The Australians have a time-honoured argument for limitless Tests. Why should a team travel 12,000 miles, they say, and then face drawn Test games? The argument is sound, but if the Tests are limited to four days and points given for an outright win and a win on the first innings some sort of a result would be reached in every game. The series could be decided on points, and it would make for better captaincy and brighter cricket if teams were faced with the prospect of forcing an outright win in the period.

It might be argued that teams gaining a first innings lead would be content to sit on that lead, but that is the state of affairs to-day, and ambitious captaincy might shake an opposing captain out of such complacency. At all events, the stage would be set for risks in captaincy, and I aver that risks are not taken in limitless Tests. Captaincy is given limited scope. Much too limited.

Cricket will have many difficulties when the time comes in 1946–47 to resume Tests; but the game has always risen superior to its crises, and there is no reason why it should not do so again. I think, by very virtue of experiences in the last eight years, that the new generation of players will bring better spirit and atmosphere to the game than that existing in my time. We were inclined to take many things for granted. The war taught us an appreciation of the days that had gone, and made us wish we had made more of them. The world cries out for the ethics, principles – and comradeship there is in cricket. Cricket is one of the good and clean things in life.

There has been much discussion in England on the future of the county competition and whether it should be played with two or three day games and one or two games a week. This can only be decided by the living order obtaining in Britain. There will be few, if any, of the leisured class (if such a class still exists!) able to give a whole summer over to cricket on an amateur basis. Semi-professionalism might be the answer, but I know as an Australian that visitors think far too much county cricket is played in England. Much of it is unprofitable and many clubs could not continue were it not for the Test proceeds which come their way.

The other aspect of too much cricket is that the standard and the spirit deteriorate. Five months of play, six days a week from eleven in the morning to six and six-thirty in the evening, is a tall order, particularly for Australians, who play about half a dozen first-class games in a normal season at home.

There are many times on an English tour when an Australian yearns to see more of England than 22 yards of wicket. He loses his zest for the game and becomes stale. Then there are the three 'unofficial' Tests towards the end of the tour at Folkestone, Liverpool and Scarborough, playfully called festival games, in which the touring Australian is either too worn out or played out to do himself justice.

What of the Australian road back? The completion of the War and the collection of Australia's strength from over most of the world's surface will show what our stocks are; but a point for dismay is that cricket fell badly by the wayside during the War in Australian schools. Many schools actually preferred soft-ball to cricket! This was an American influence. Players were lost to the game or their enthusiasm and education dampened by the continuation of four-hourly grade and pennant games long after they had served their purpose. It was a tall order to ask 22 players to show their mettle in four hours. Those to suffer were usually the youngsters.

More care was shown for the spectators and the gates than for the average player, who, when all is said and done, plays any game for his own enjoyment and recreation.

Australia will have to make a big effort if cricket is to regain its former prestige. Australian youths will always retain a love of the game, but there must be careful planning to see that art and culture are retained until the youngsters pick up the threads again. And that brings me again to the Australian legislator!

Airily said one of these legislators (he was a legislator when I was a boy in short trousers) when O'Reilly announced his retirement in mid-1946: 'There is no need to panic. It will make room for a young player.' That attitude is all very well if the legislators have taken steps to provide a flow of young players, but an analysis will show that Australian cricket in the mid-wars period has depended and existed amazingly well upon a thin vein of accomplished players – and these players owed their ability not to any constructive legislative work, but rather to their own initiative and enthusiasm.

When I was a lad I went one night to a lecture given by the former Australian Eleven captain, M. A. Noble. Even now I think I can remember everything he spoke about. Young, aspiring cricketers learn most by emulation. They dwell, especially, upon the words of one who has proved himself in Test cricket, but I cannot remember O'Reilly, McCabe or others of my generation ever being asked by the legislators to give a lecture or take some interest in the on-coming players. Thus to speak lightly and optimistically of the retirement of O'Reilly as making way for a young player is rather foolhardy if steps have not been taken to assure that this young player is on hand. If no such young players fortuitously discover themselves in the next Test season against the very experienced Englishmen, the series could well be a dismal failure and I repeat that there has been only a thin vein of talent in Australia in the mid-wars period.

Had it not been for the Sydney newspaper, the *Daily Telegraph*, New South Wales cricket would have fallen badly after the serious period of the Pacific war had passed. The newspaper promoted interest in Service games by offering bonuses for quick scoring or good bowling and fielding. Years before, the Sydney *Guardian* conducted searches through country districts for bowlers to replace Gregory, McDonald and Mailey. None was found, but the search created terrific interest, and it was an unforgettable day when the country elect assembled on the Sydney Cricket Ground to show their ability. These are the stunts which create public interest and following, but the point is that the legislators should not allow others to do their work. Further, no official attempt was made to keep the attractive Pepper in Australia and, at the time of writing, the equally attractive Keith Miller is talking of taking his talents to north of England professional cricket. Australia cannot afford to lose such cricketers. Young, virile legislators are needed as much as young players. Some of the present Australian legislators have seen three generations of players pass.

Why is it that since the formation of the Board in 1905 only four of its members have had international cricket experience? The four were Hill, Darling and Jennings, of South Australia, and Hartigan, of Queensland.* Not a single representative from the rich cricketing talent of New South Wales and Victoria, the leading States, has ever sat on the Board. This surely must be the oddest state of affairs that has ever existed in any sporting organisation.

Consult the committees of the MCC over the years and you will see there innumerable names that have figured largely on the field of play. In Australia, however, it would seem that one of the greatest disabilities facing a man seeking Board honours is to have played international cricket.

It might be said that an active player is too busy in the game to concentrate upon the legislative side of it, but that applies only if a post has to be built up over the years. There was the recent example of McCabe, who allowed his name to be nominated for election to the NSW Association. McCabe is the most brilliant cricketer his club has known. It would be impossible to assess what he has meant to his club in finance and standing, yet McCabe suffered the ignominy of receiving one or two paltry votes. Why was this? McCabe was an ornament not only to his club, but to the very game of cricket. He had a vast international knowledge and the sporting manner in which he played the game suggested that he would be zealous of preserving the best that was in it. McCabe as a cricketer – yes! McCabe as a legislator – no!

Some time later the NSW Association refused McCabe when he wanted to play with and coach Sydney University, a team of young players and a club whose resources had been sadly whittled by War. In such churlish manner has Australian cricket only too often treated a faithful servant when his days of active use are nearing an end.

Board of Control representatives are chosen from personnel of the State associations. The first-class player consequently has more than one election hurdle to clear.

* Bradman was appointed to fill a South Australian vacancy in late 1945.

I was discussing this subject once with A. R. B. Palmer, a very noted Australian sports writer, who was my first newspaper editor, and his remarks threw further illumination on the partially exclusive grip which our legislators have on the plums of office.

'As you probably know,' he said, 'over a decade I scarcely missed one of the monthly meetings of the New South Wales Cricket Association. In that period questions concerning the actual conduct of play, the laws, cricket equipment and of matters in which first-class experience was of essential value to discussion frequently arose.

'Invariably such qualified cricketers as E. W. Adams, R. J. A. Massie, A. Ratcliffe, E. L. Waddy, E. A. Dwyer, R. C. M. Boyce would vote together, but in a badly beaten minority. I once asked a famous Test player why he did not represent his club on the Association. It was at the time when the larger stump was introduced, when the lbw rule was beginning to be the subject of thought. His reply was: "I stood once. They did not want me. I don't feel disposed to seek another rebuff."'

Most Australian players, who hold the MCC in the highest respect, think also that the Australian Board of Control has been unfaithful to the game of cricket from an Imperial point of view. Twenty years ago, as manager of an Australian Eleven in England and as secretary then of the Board of Control, Sydney Smith promised the Imperial Conference that Australia would attempt to foster cricket in New Zealand and India. India has been ignored, New Zealand treated with insulting neglect, the culminating factor being 1945, when the Board sent an Australian team to New Zealand in March of 1946. Cricket in New Zealand in March is something of a problem. The single 'Test' was finished in under two days.

After much wrangling with the Board, Frank Tarrant managed to get a private team away to India in 1935, but churlishly the Board refused permission to Kippax and Ponsford to make the tour, despite the fact that their Australian careers had finished. It may seem odd that the Board should dictate to private individuals whether they should or should not visit another country, but officialdom in Australia exercises considerable and remarkable control over players, who are mostly young and immature. No team, for instance, can play in a country town or make a touring jaunt without first receiving permission from the State Association.

I am not one who believes that cricketers necessarily make the best legislators. Nor am I one who believes that men who have played only a very shaky standard of the game, if they have played at all, should say yes and no on matters of highly technical cricketing importance, matters which affect the very preservation of the game.

It is a sad truism of Australian sport that those who deserve best of it, those who have given years of faithful service, often are treated the worst when their active days are over. A narrow streak of parochialism runs in Australian national life. It is not confined to sportsmen, but is evident against men in public life. Politics is a national game and nowhere more so than in sport.

'If I were young I would fight this. Now I am at a stage in life when I simply can't be bothered,' once said a prominent official whose years of faithful service did not save him from being cast holus-bolus from his sport in a trice.

It is the same in Australian cricket. Players who have given years to the game detect some undercurrent against themselves. More than likely it is the jealousy of some ambitious and nondescript Caesar. The player is anxious to benefit the game. He knows he has the knowledge and the ability to do so, but who could ask one who has trod the international fields to return to his native haunts and engage in parish-pump politics before he can render further service to the game he loves.

I refuse to believe that such men as Trumble, Trumper, Darling, Carter, Noble, Armstrong, Macartney, Collins, Ponsford, Kippax, McCabe, O'Reilly, Richardson, Woodfull, Ransford, Taylor, Pellew, Gregory and Oldfield – many of them highly successful business men – have no more to offer the game when their days of active worth are done. Yet it is a fact they and their like have been ignored consistently by Australian officialdom, and the cricketers feel very strongly about it.

If Australian cricket is to come back strongly when the game settles down again, some of these older players must be enticed back into cricket channels to help and impart their knowledge of the game. They will refuse, and rightly, to go out into the byways and highways soliciting the votes of every Tom, Dick and Harry so that they can rise up through the clubs, the associations and the executive committees to the Board room. What the Board should do, and I put this forward as a matter of cricket urgency, is to set aside three additional seats to the 13 now in being, to be filled by first-class cricketers on the votes of first-class cricketers, ex-internationals and internationals.

I wonder whether the Board will agree. It asks little and is an assurance that on all contentious matters, such as bodyline, the Board will have expert opinions on hand. I earnestly hope something on those lines will be achieved. It would be for the ultimate benefit of cricket. It would also show that the Board is anxious to refute the suggestion that it regards itself as a very exclusive body, entitled to all the plums of office.

England will have her worries, but it may be that the histories of the Wars will be reversed. The AIF team of 1919 stood Australia in good stead for many years, but the nature of the recent world conflict dispersed Australian cricket forces. A few years make a big difference in the form of a player, but an England that could send such sparkling players and personalities as Hammond, Barnett, Hardstaff, Hutton (a beautiful stroke-player, his Oval innings notwithstanding), Edrich, Bartlett, Compton (to my mind the world's most classical batsman), Yardley (a glorious on-driver and now England's 1946 Test vice-captain), Wright, Griffith, Pollard, Pope, Levett and a few Yorkshiremen for level-headedness and good measure, has little to fear – apart from a few bowling qualms.

Australian cricket will succeed despite its hoary legislators. The game is inborn with our national life, and I think the new generation will bring a refreshing and a better tang again into Test cricket. Pepper is one of the most attractive cricketing personalities in years, and the 1945 English tour showed that Miller is in the same class.

On both sides there will be the wail of no bowlers. That lament has been with us for years, but I think an in-between wars period that produced Gregory, McDonald, Mailey, Grimmett, Larwood, Tate, O'Reilly, Blackie and Ironmonger has little for which to apologise.

The Global War has cost the game much genius, but I think the charming words of the late Australian Prime Minister, John Curtin, sums up the position. Mr Curtin, who loved cricket and was directly responsible for the Services tour of England in 1945, was speaking extemporarily at a Canberra meeting to establish a memorial to the late Patrick Hore-Ruthven, son of Lord Gowrie, recent Australian Governor-General.

'The most terrible thing that has marked these days,' said Mr Curtin, 'is the frightful loss of irreplaceable human quality that the god of war has demanded. I think Patrick Hore-Ruthven embodied that kind of nature, which was not only a contribution to the fellowship of man, but a revelation of the noble aspects of life. That small book of his poems, which is in a sense a memorial to him, reveals the high thinking of which he was capable, that indescribable sense of the beautiful which had impressed itself on his mind.

'We wish to establish a monument to the youth lost in these days of struggle, in which too many young men have been cut off and the longevity of life rudely disturbed – young men, musicians, artists, poets, writers, physicists, scientists – just in the bud of their potentiality. We cannot measure the cost of this terrible war in money and material things. I doubt whether there can be any spiritual assessment of the loss. I am certain that just as many a Bradman of the future has lost the chance of development, so perhaps a Rupert Brooke, a Southey or a Dickens has been lost.

'It is not all sadness that, I think. Most certainly the soil into which they have descended will give back in some way some part of the nature that has become dust. I do not doubt that some child of a serviceman, benefiting by this fund, may restore the balance and give back to man that rich mind or great skill or other human quality of which the war has temporarily deprived us. For I believe in the continuity of man. While I acknowledge the episodic reverses that mark this history, I think if we can make the best of what is left to us that best can be a crown for the losses we have sustained.'

Those are the sentiments the British world will cherish and nourish in the years that lie ahead. The responsibility of players and legislators – and, indeed, the barrackers – is to see that they give full expression to cricket's nobility, companionship, peace and graceful art, for the post-war world will stand not only in need of such qualities, but will be anxious to atone for the years that have been lost for all time. Cricket, in its all-embracing nature, has a job to do for the Empire, and possibly never in our history has the fulfilment of that job been so urgently essential.

I have one other proposition to advance. In paying a tribute to Frank Chester, the game's outstanding umpire, I recall that many of England's former players take up umpiring when their active days are finished. I remember so many lovable characters (does any other game provide such individual types as cricket?) in Tiger Smith, Hardstaff Snr, Denis Hendren, Fanny Walden, Emmot Robinson, Bill Reeves, Lee, Newman, Len Braund and others – all magnificent personalities and champion umpires. Now, what is there to stop Harold Larwood from following in their footsteps, and, if he does, what is there to prevent the Australian Board of Control from graciously inviting Larwood to come to Australia with the next MCC team and umpire in the Test series?

I doubt whether any Australian cricketer has seen Larwood since those stormy days of 1932–33. He was not present during the 1934 and 1938 days, or, if so, did not pay us a visit. I doubt whether there are any hard Australian feelings against Larwood. I recall the tumultuous reception given him in Sydney in 1933 when he was dismissed in the nineties during the fifth Test. The whole ground regretted that he did not make a century, and I cannot help but feel that he departed the game in most regrettable circumstances, circumstances altogether unworthy of his brilliancy. I should like to see my country make a noble gesture towards Larwood, because I think the game, generally, owes him something. There is no further room for tosh and nonsense about bodyline, especially after the really serious form of bodyline England and Australia have survived integrally and proudly together over the past few years.

PART TWO

Other Lines

CHAPTER ONE   *A Yorkshire Gesture*
                     July, 1938

I̲T WAS A VIVID CHANGE TO Bramall Lane after the peace and quiet of Chesterfield. The leaning steeple of the town looked benignly down on the game against Derbyshire, and stolid, silent be-capped men, who might have interrupted a trip to market and left their cows and pigs outside the ground, sat quietly around the ropes, sucking meditatively at their pipes and solemnly wagging their heads in disapproval as the county batsmen advanced to and retreated from the wickets almost before acknowledging the introduction to their guard.

The bowling strength of the county was magnificent, approaching almost to Test-like standards. Copson found bite from the wicket and flicked the ball across from the leg stump, an achievement Copson had despaired of ever doing in this life again after a season on mute, unsympathetic Australian wickets. The tall, rangy Pope brothers did much the same thing, and Mitchell, brown eyes bubbling behind his spectacles, bowled his leg breaks with an occasional bosie and bowled them as well as ever he had bowled them.

But strength in bowling alone is not sufficient. The Derbyshire batsmen went through manœuvres as crooked as their church spire, the game was put into the records in two days and off we went in our roomy charabanc, singing and laughing through the streets of Chesterfield and across the peaty moors, bound for our Georgian home in the Grindleford hills. No better prospect than this of the morrow faced us in the whole of our English tour. A day away from the game with the green, verdant English countryside beckoning with its trees and calling with its birds!

If only it didn't rain . . . and it didn't! The sky next day was so innocent of cloud that, always excepting Manchester, one could not imagine a drop of rain in the whole of England. The sun streamed through the wide windows of the sleepy hotel; poplars, elms and oaks cut gently-swaying filigrees against the bluest of blue skies, the smell of eggs and bacon floated up from below, and doubtlessly the birds were homaging the day in rich, limpid voice; but this you were not to know, for in the room just along the corridor Brown (basking in the thrill of a glorious double-century the day before against Derbyshire) and McCormick were dueting spring in raucous voice. Along the corridor, too, O'Reilly was noisily informing the countryside that his bonny lay over the ocean, his bonny lay over the sea, and wouldn't somebody please, bring his bonny back to him. If O'Reilly did not get her, you reflected, as you indulged yourself in a glorious stretch, it would not be for the want either of volume or repetition.

On no other English morning had the team been so happy. Bantering quips and laughter chased across the breakfast table; gone were the gruff monosyllables that came with each morning of an important game, and gone, also of such mornings, was the little ball of nervous apprehension that pitched and tossed in the stomach-pit of players.

Yorkshire loomed large and serious on the cricket calendar for the next day, but what of that? To-morrow could watch its own interests. For this day it was sufficient to live in the present, and, breakfast over, a rollicking band of Australian explorers gathered in the leafy lane. There was no set plan. Apollo was climbing lazily and unthreatened. We would wander wherever our legs, our inclinations and the long, low line of purple hills in the distance took us.

Our steps went downhill and made their first of that day's many stops at the village school-hall. Derbyshire children of ten and eleven, the roses of the hills rich upon their cheeks, were as intrigued with our accent as we were with theirs, but the school-bell, ringing, took them off and we continued our ramble, meeting soon a person who took our thoughts quickly back to home, gumtrees, billabongs and magpies.

He was a tramp, a lonely, tattered old fellow who ignored our cheery 'good-days' and passed by in silence, deep in thought. In that he differed vastly from our own tramps, or swagmen, as we call them, who love to loiter in their long, dusty treks and yarn to all and sundry. But, if not friendly, the English tramp at least served a purpose. He took our thoughts back to Australia and we swung along to the bridge singing that delightfully Australian song, 'Waltzing Matilda', with Banjo Paterson's words bringing the nostalgic whiff of an Australian gum to our nostrils.

> 'Down came a jumbuck to drink at the water-hole,
>   Up jumped the Swagman and grabbed him in glee,
>   And he sang as he stowed him away in his tucker-bag,
> "You'll come a-waltzing Matilda with me."'

We swung off the road and down to the river, where some swam behind trees in Huckleberry Finn style and Badcock tickled for trout, as he assured us he had tickled many a time in Tasmanian streams. He stalked the river with a finger crooked under the water, the idea being, so he told us, to feel the trout, run the finger under their stomach to the gills and then throw them by the finger to the bank. It was all very impressive (considered not the thing, I understand, in the best sporting circles), but we saw no trout.

All that morning we lazily followed the course of the river. We shied stones at rabbits, discovered idyllic falls, shut in a wooded little glade, listened to birds and wondered what they were.

> 'To whose falls,
>   Melodious birds sing madrigals.'

As lunch time approached we made the village of Sproggett, where we quenched a man-sized thirst with man-sized pewters of cold beer preparatory to lunching, under centuries-old rafters, on cold chicken, the reddest and biggest strawberries in the whole of England, and thick, yellow cream.

We loitered and wandered again that afternoon, wishing that this perfect day would never end. It was a tired and contented Australian band that arrived back that evening to our Grindleford home.

With such a day in between, you will understand me then when I write that the change from Chesterfield to Sheffield was a vivid one, vivid in its transition from peace and rural calm to Sheffield survival of the fittest, whether steel, cutlery, business or cricket.

The sun was still friendly next day as our charabanc ran along the range of hills. We topped a rise and there in a valley ahead of us hung a pall of mist. 'Sheffield,' laconically said the driver, and in another ten minutes we were in another world. That which we had taken to be mist was the oppressive sky of modern industry, a sky belched forth by chimneys as numerous as stakes in a tomato patch. The somnolent, whispering English woods of sun, shade and birds were behind us; here was another of those strongly marked English contrasts which are so bewildering – the very rich and the abject poor, indescribable beauty within cooee of indescribable squalor, palatial Pall Mall clubs that unblushingly exist cheek by jowl with the midnight soup queue at Admiralty Gates or the tortuous procession of invalided Welsh miners which goes beggingly down the Strand.

The battle of life is there to be sniffed as one goes through the narrow, brownish-grey streets of Sheffield. It is the battle of competition and industry, the battle of fresh air and sun against the smoke fumes, and if any beliefs existed that this was an excursion of cricket peace, those beliefs dissolved as the charabanc swung through the gates of Bramall Lane, historic home of Yorkshire cricket.

It is easy to mistake the atmosphere which receives rather than greets you at Bramall Lane. It seems to bristle with belligerency, a belligerency apparent in the stares that meet your arrival and which bore through as you go to the nets before play begins. Cheery nods, smiles and calls of 'good luck' assail the Australian as he goes to a net before a match at Lord's; at Sheffield he is conscious of cold looks of calculation, which seem to bore through his flannels and demand of the wearer his right to wear them.

But this is not quite so. Sheffield connoisseurs of cricket are like Sheffield cutlery – cold on the surface, sharp in dissection, brimful of good feelings if not cut up the wrong way, and always, certainly always, seriously conscious of being Sheffield through and through with a reputation to uphold. The looks of the grim spectators, the postures and gestures of the eleven robust Yorkshiremen who wear a white rose on their caps, all issue a proclamation to any Australian within fifty miles of Sheffield on the day Yorkshire plays Australia, and that proclamation runs something like this: 'We are Yorkshire. Thou's playin' wi' cricket fire, laad, when thou comes 'ere. We are noo aboot to show thee, laad, that thou'st no sa good as thou thinks.'

Life and cricket are serious businesses in Sheffield. Nothing better sums up Yorkshire ways and means on a cricket field than that northern doggerel of philosophy:

> 'Thou must see owt and say nowt,
> Thou must eat owt and pay nowt,
> And if thou dost owt for nowt,
> Do it for th'sen (thyself), laad!'

You might think from this that the Yorkshire Eleven is made up of men with granite souls. It is not true, but in thinking so you could pay Yorkshire no greater compliment. This (and did not every brave and flamboyant Yorkshire gesture show it?) was the Yorkshire Eleven. All hail, everybody bow and let the trumpets blow! This, the other side, was the Australian Eleven. Who? demands the Yorkshireman? What'st thou doin' at Bramall Lane, laad? Hast brought apology wi' thee?

Of what use to tell them that this Australian Eleven is unbeaten to the moment in England. Where'st thou bein' playin'? Why, only in sooth! Great Scarborough cliffs! Get umpires oot, laad! Let's gi' on wi' victory!

The wicket was wet. Sellers, a pair of shoulders on him suggesting a Rugby wall at full-back, wins the toss for Yorkshire and hesitates not a moment. Australia is for it. We can bat. McCabe and I walk out, the pair of us in the middle of what is commonly known as a trot, or a period of lean scores, and I prepare to take the first ball from Bowes, noting meanwhile with trepidation that the merest touch of my sprig is sufficient to mark my block on a wicket with more moisture in it than is good for our peace of mind.

I shape up for the first ball from the bespectacled Bowes. He lumbers along and, ah! in that moment, the agony of mind of the opening batsman who takes strike on a sticky wicket, a wicket whose extent of nastiness waits to be probed!

The ball from Bowes hits the sodden turf, takes a seamful of it, and, evidently disliking the taste of it, rears violently. A nasty wicket, a cranky wicket obviously full of moods!

Bowes comes again and the ball pitches on the off. It does not rear this time, but, like a rabbit streaking for its burrow, it darts viciously in and hits me on the pad.

Bedlam breaks loose. Bowes shows his teeth, he curls one leg behind the other, looks in agony to the heavens and, with both hands apart, wails 'Owzat' with a venom which sends Duckworth pale with jealousy as he hears it in the next county.

What does a batsman think in that pregnant moment between the appeal and the decision? His eyes dart to the umpire's face and try to interpret there a ray of hope; his courage sinks to his sprigs if he thinks the umpire must justly give him out, or, if he thinks he has right on his side, his courage flutters like a spiralling dove.

English umpires cannot be hastened into a decision. A Chester remains mute for the eternity of a second and none can read his face. Then he either turns his head away from the bowler if it is not out (giving him the bleakness of an entire back if the appeal is a frivolous one) or raises one solitary finger to the batsman with the finality of a judge sentencing a murderer. That prolonged inbetween period gives a batsman more agony of mind, but the English method of calm deliberation is preferable to the general Australian one of answering an appeal almost before it has fallen from the bowler's lips.

None of these thoughts crossed my mind with the Bowes appeal. A hazy thought did occur to me that a man who wore spectacles should bear himself with more dignity and respect for his lenses, but any other thoughts I had on the subject were frightened out of me by a blood-curdling yell in my rear. The 'Owzat' of the rotund, red-faced wicket-keeper Wood split the heavens and threatened the same to my back, but it was only by a short breath that he beat nine Yorkshire fieldsmen, who faced in all directions and demanded 'Owzat'; they, for their part, barely beating 15,000 Yorkshire men and women, who frenziedly wanted to know of each other if this wasn't indeed 'Owzat'. And high in the factories surrounding the ground wee Yorkshire lassies turned from their windows and hurled 'Owzat' at their foremen.

A self-respecting batsman would not have dared to await a verdict. To such an appeal he would have dismissed himself and gone his way, but Test experience dulls such chivalries. I stood my ground, and the umpire, who has played all his cricket with Lancashire, and knew the ins and outs of Yorkshire cricket, answered with a spirit possible only to a Lancastrian. He roared 'Naht oot,' matching the Yorkshireman look for look.

This, you might be pardoned for thinking had you known not Bramall Lane, might easily have led to a crisis. Such an appeal and dismissed so contemptuously! One might have had visions of eleven outraged Yorkshiremen walking stiffly off the field to the plaudits of a sympathetic crowd, but there was none of that. The Yorkshiremen accept the decision as if nothing untoward has happened. They hitch their trousers and settle down again, thrilled in the experience that the very second ball of the day has given them the chance to show their fire and oil, as it were, their larynx.

There is a frenzy a few minutes later when McCabe is dropped, and the simmer from that has barely died away when I swing hard at a ball from Bowes. It travels to a fieldsman who has not to move an inch – and he drops the catch! This is too much. Two dropped catches and a decision against Yorkshire in five minutes! The spectators howl their fury and castigation vies with the smoke for mastery of the Sheffield air. People carefully put their capacious luncheon baskets from their laps to the ground, turn to the neighbours and demand to know what manner of game 'yon laads are playing at t' day.'

Bowes looks piercingly at the offending fieldsman and eight other Yorkshiremen strike poses that tell all with eyes to see that never, no never, would they have dropped a catch like that.

But Yorkshire has no need to worry. A few minutes more and McCabe and I are both back in the dressing-room. Yorkshire sleeves are tucked higher to deal with Bradman and Hassett.

Bramall Lane is in fine voice. Comment and advice meet every move on the field and Yorkshire fieldsmen bustle about with as much vigour and importance as the surrounding chimneys erupt their smoke (though I refuse to believe the old chestnut that every loyal tender of a Sheffield fire stokes up when the Australians bat). This is cricket to the death, with no fine flourishes or gentlemanly graces. The bowler does not conceal his intention to do to death the batsman in the worst possible manner; the fieldsmen stride boldly to their places with malevolent side glances at the batsmen.

All this does not worry Bradman or Hassett in the slightest. Each is calm and imperturbable, his full attention concentrated upon keeping the ball where it belongs for batting safety. Bowes, whose fast bowling in Australia some years before was as peaceful and as lacking in intent as a Sunday afternoon in Canberra, is a demon on this wicket. He flicks his fingers over the ball and it responds with a devilish whip across from leg; he flicks them under and, hey, presto! there comes an off-break wicked in its enmity to the stumps.

There is a roar like the salvo of concentrated fire from a fleet as Bradman's bat plays only with edgeful purpose at a coquettish ball running away to the slips. The dismissal of Bradman at any time in England is a matter of supreme national importance, but this time the crowd is chagrined as the ball comes to earth inches in front of the clasping hands of first slip. The incident in itself, however, is an occasion and so, perforce, second slip and third slip and even point dive and leap to lend colour. There is no lack of action in this Yorkshire team!

Bradman is slow in scoring, very slow, but this innings under bad conditions belies his reputation of being a bad-wicket nonentity. He is solidity itself. There are none of those thrilling pull-shots with a bat as crooked as a corkscrew. It is a real captain's innings, full of fight and merit. The wicket is all the bowlers' way and footwork, alone, enables the batsmen to survive. They dart forward to get the ball on the full or smother its devilry at the pitch, or else they play back almost on top of their stumps with a bat so dead that the ball drops at their feet.

Bradman scores a run every three minutes; Hassett is slightly faster, and Bramall Lane has plenty to discuss as it opens its big luncheon baskets. It has been a morning of dynamic action with thrills and close calls innumerable.

Bradman has chewed over more than his lunch during the adjournment. The tactics of his team undergo a rapid change on the resumption. The Australians move in to the attack, for Bradman is anxious to get Yorkshire in on this wicket. Anything well pitched is met with a full swinging bat; a ball the slightest fraction short is swung to leg off the back foot. Both batsmen take risks aplenty, the fieldsmen speed around the ground and the spectators fall again into critical mood – but what is this? Bradman has moved feet down the wicket only to miss the ball. Woods, a devilish grin on his face, clutches at the ball as a soldier would his sweetheart after years of service abroad. The bails are flicked feet into the air and the banshee wail from Woods envelops the ground. Bradman is out for 54, one of his best innings in England. Bramall Lane chirps in high glee again.

It is the breaking of the one Australian partnership. Batsmen shuffle in and out like voters at the ballot box – all except Hassett, who accepts full responsibility. He runs down the wicket to a ball from Smailes, his nimble feet miraculously bring his body into position, his bat goes up and down in a perfect sweep, his weight shifts from his back to his front foot in a trice, there is the noticeable flick of wrist and away the ball soars to the accompaniment of sweet, succulent willow-music, higher, higher and still higher, over the mid-on fence for a superb six. The applause is unstinted, for Bramall Lane knows its cricket.

The next ball Hassett repeats the same stroke, only this time the ball flies higher and further to lodge, at last, in the top of the Members' Stand. Two successive sixes! Bramall Lane just rocks in a frenzy of delight. To be true, this is treating Yorkshire cricket with ignominy, but there will be time and enough later for castigation. Bramall Lane thrills in Hassett's charms and pays due deference.

A lovely little cricketer, a charming batsman of grace – but, confound it all, says Bramall Lane of a sudden, what is this that is happening out there now? Hassett is doing what he likes with the strike. He is away for a single almost before the bat touches the ball and every time Yorkshire changes over it finds Hassett at the receiving end. The deuce take him, says Bramall Lane, Yorkshire cricket cannot be treated like this!

Sellers marshals his fieldsmen and bowlers to keep Hassett away from the strike, but the little Australian calls his own tune and Bramall Lane does not like it. It does not like to see Yorkshire playing second fiddle. The crowd begins to criticise Sellers, Sutcliffe, Leyland, Verity, anybody and everybody. ''Ere, laads, wha's matter wi' thee? Play oop, Yorkshire, play oop.'

Hassett has smelt death in the rain-laden breeze. He determines to meet it with death-or-glory methods, and twice in a Robinson over he sends the ball whistling among the crowd for two more sixes. The crowd acknowledges him as if he belongs to Yorkshire. One more six for Hassett, they pray, just one more six and then let the devil himself claim this perky little Australian. But it is not to be. Hassett is out at 94 for an innings any master would be pleased to tab with his name and Australia is out for 222.

The wicket is still cranky when Yorkshire comes to bat. O'Reilly, the only Australian of this touring team who could take toll on such a wicket, is resting in the pavilion and the Yorkshire batting is as substantial as a county pudding. There are no flounces, flourishes or cuts and at stumps Yorkshire is 2–50. We leave for rustic Grindleford with our heads reeling from the noise and clamour of the day.

There is more rain that night and the wicket is wet next day and even worse. Only Robinson and Wood survive against Waite's off-spinners. Yorkshire is out for 205, 17 runs behind.

It is a bitter disappointment for the crowd, but all this is quickly forgotten as the Australians walk quickly in and out on a wicket now vile. Only Bradman is at all successful. He makes 42, Australia totals 132 and Yorkshire needs 150 for victory. Only 150 to lower Australia's colours for the first time of this tour!

The banter around the ropes as the Australians come on the field is intense. Men laugh and joke with each other and call over the heads of their fellows. 'Good old Yorkshire. Eh, laad, but it takes Yorkshire to show Aussies oop.'

Sellers sends in Wood and Verity to play out time and this they do, Verity, most expert of all batsmen in doing this, with a bat that refuses to peep at a ball one-eighth of an inch outside the stumps. We retire again to Grindleford, this time with defeat staring us in the face. The only provision we make is that Yorkshire will well and truly earn it.

The morrow sees a better wicket. The pavilion doors soon swing to behind Wood's ample body on his return journey and a piece of freak fielding removes Verity. 'Come, one, easy one,' imperiously chants Sutcliffe, that lord of cricket creation, as he pushes one to cover with his typical slice-straight bat. Sutcliffe ambles majestically and quietly up the wicket, and the modest and effacing Verity, relying on his lord that it is indeed an easy one, hurries not unduly to the other end. But Bradman goes for the ball like a flash and, by some strange intuition, Hassett tails him. Bradman stoops and scoops the ball back. Hassett, already in throwing position, catches it and away the ball speeds to the wicket with one of those delicious Australian under-the-shoulder throws. It grooves the stumps, Barnett flicks the bails off and Verity, with Sutcliffe's 'easy one' still ringing in his ears, is out. Verity leaves the field in a daze, as well he might, for the quickness of the move bewilders most onlookers.

The Pudsey products, Sutcliffe and Hutton, are now together. They are master and pupil, so it is said, but their methods and stroke-play are entirely dissimilar. Sutcliffe's nostrils are dilated with the recurring sniff of battles of other days. He is loving every minute of this, more so when he sees O'Reilly afar off in street clothes in the pavilion. He feels himself master of the situation and positively purrs. His eyes are not as keen as they were, but his supreme confidence is unchanged.

'Wait thar,' he calls. He plays the ball, peers at it, runs three yards up the wicket, crosses the bat across his chest, comes to rigid attention and then holds up a traffic-police arm to the man at the other end. 'Wait thar,' says Sutcliffe, bristling with polished dignity from sleek hair to immaculate boots.

I think whimsically of Sutcliffe, as I cross to and fro between the overs. I notice his emphatic smack, smack on his block with the bat as the bowler runs up and then his shuffle, shuffle across with his feet before the bowler delivers. No cricketer has more mannerisms; no batsman has possessed a better fighting temperament.

I like most the spit and polish of Sutcliffe when he is master of the situation and knows it. I see him in his element at Lord's, where none can match the outraged indignities he suffers when, with Lord's packed and Sutcliffe immaculate with sleek hair parted in the centre, somebody has the misfortune to move in the Long Members' Pavilion as the bowler runs to deliver the ball. Up shoots Sutcliffe's traffic arm, his planked palm daring anything to move between his end and Buckingham Palace. He draws away from the wicket, makes vigorous sweeps with his bat to the pavilion, and all eyes follow it to discover some hapless wretch (possibly a Baronet) who had dared to move in his seat at such a moment in British history.

Sutcliffe and his dignity then return stiffly to the wickets. He plays the next ball meticulously and slowly back to the bowler in a pretentious manner which calls up to the Members' Stand, 'Had you not moved in your seat, Sir, and momentarily distracted me, I should have swept that ball to the boundary.'

And everybody looks again at the Baronet, who slinks in his seat and creeps from the ground at the first opportunity, possibly never again to go to Lord's or his club.

Who could match the cool calm of Sutcliffe in Sydney in 1932 when he chopped a ball from O'Reilly hard on to his stumps? For some unknown reason the bails did not fall off and the surrounding Australians almost swooned in agony. But not so Sutcliffe. He looked at the Australians with arched brows as if to say, 'Pray, please, what is all this fuss and ado about?' Sutcliffe was 43 then; he made 194 and not a flicker of his steely black eyes suggested that anything untoward had happened, let alone the greatest piece of good fortune ever to befall a batsman.

The face of the old Yorkshire master is again inscrutable this Bramall Lane day. Runs come slowly, but he is unworried, because Yorkshire has time to spare. A run here, two there and the score board shows how surely Yorkshire creeps upon Australia.

A Yorkshire Gesture – July, 1938

Hutton, too, is full of Pudsey fight and confidence. The Australians can make no impression on either, but suddenly Hutton falls into a ball and pushes it to the on. He does not quite get over it and it skims along inches off the ground. I get my fingers under it at short-leg and one Yorkshire mainstay has gone. Barber, a talented man, is next. He and Sutcliffe are together at lunch. The board shows Yorkshire 3–83, Sutcliffe and Barber each 36 not out. Yorkshire wants only 67 for victory and all the afternoon in which to get them.

We go to lunch a quiet and chastened team. Defeat stares us in the face as surely as the roast beef in front of us. The delighted hum of the spectators below floats up to the luncheon room.

But what is that? The sound is unmistakable. It is rain and heavy rain at that. The faces of the Yorkshire men drop. This bitter fight for two and a half days and now rain!

But the shower passes and the thousands stream from their shelter as Sellers and Bradman walk out after lunch to look at the wicket. 'Good old Sellers,' the crowd calls to the Yorkshire skipper; 'Poor old Aussie,' they chaff Bradman. The crowd is again in highest spirits.

But here, now, is the sequel of this tale. You must try to imagine that setting – two and a half days of bitter cricket; the enthusiasm of the keenest cricketing crowd in England; victory just at hand for Yorkshire, and that victory waiting to be acclaimed by deep-throated Yorkshire roars and general cock-a-hoopness. Bear this in mind and consider whether you do not agree that no cricketing field has known a finer gesture than this.

Sellers walked to one end of the wicket. He took one look there and walked back to the other. Then he turned to the crowd, wrung his hands and threw them wide apart.

The game is over! Sellers' gesture was saying that the wicket was unfit for play and that the match Australia v. Yorkshire had ended in a draw.

I have seen no more spontaneous act of sportsmanship than that of Sellers. Bradman was in an invidious position. As captain of a side facing defeat he would have felt diffidence in suggesting that the wicket was unfit for play. But Sellers saved him all this. Ninety-nine captains out of a hundred would have been well within their rights in saying that they would inspect the wicket again at three, at four or even at five. Some in the position of Sellers, for he had nothing to lose and all to gain, might have pushed for play to begin immediately, because too often in cricket is the state of the wicket conditioned by the state of the captain's mind and the game. At the least, for his side and victory, Sellers could have disagreed with Bradman and called in the umpires.

Not so Sellers. He washed the game off with a magnificent Yorkshire gesture. He gave not a thought to victory, not a second thought to that intensely loyal Yorkshire crowd behind him which cried out in sheer pain at this cruel blow. Sellers did not embarrass Bradman by even asking him for a decision.

After the crowds had sadly filtered away an hour later, I was finishing my packing when I chanced to look down through the dressing-room window. I saw a dear old white-haired Yorkshire lady who vigorously shook an umbrella at me.

'Ah,' she called, 'the pity o' it, the pity o' it. And we had thee well and truly whacked. If only I could get at thee with 'brella 'twould be summat, 'twould be summat, indeed.'

CHAPTER TWO   *A Broth of a Bhoy –*
                  W. J. O'Reilly

T HE CRICKET STORY OF WILLIAM Joseph O'Reilly is one of a man big in heart, in stature and in ability. None but the brave deserves the fair, and it is just as true that none but the big in heart shall merit Test bowling fame, particularly if he is a spin bowler, as O'Reilly was, and more particularly if he flourished, as O'Reilly did, in an age when the art of prepared and doped wickets had reached its zenith of somnolent impassivity.

O'Reilly was not one to be dealt with mathematically. It could be said that in so many games he captured so many wickets at such and such a cost, but this elementary knowledge leads exactly nowhere in an analysis of the bowling powers of this Australian giant. The records book is too easy an escape for the stumped or unknowledgable critic, and, moreover, it tells only a poor portion of the story. It does not tell whether a bowler was at his best in time of crisis; it is mute on dropped catches and utters not a syllable on moral wickets, those uncredited wickets when a bowler spread-eagles a batsman's defence only to miss the stumps by a fraction. And O'Reilly, as others know as well as himself, had many of those wickets in his time.

Having snubbed the records book to that extent, I now ask its pardon and take the liberty of quoting figures which will show, in some degree, O'Reilly's worth for all time. In four Test series against England he took 102 wickets off 7,846 balls at a cost of 25.64 runs each; in two series against South Africa he took 34 wickets off

340 overs (six and eight-ball overs) at 18.97; in two tours of England he took 260 wickets at 14.52; in Sheffield Shield he took 203 wickets off 1,342 eight-ball overs at 17.43; in 15 years of Sydney grade cricket, played on Saturday afternoons, he bundled out 921 heroes at a cost of under 10 runs.

O'Reilly's 203 Sheffield Shield wickets are the most taken by a New South Welshman. When he first began in 1931–32 the habit of heading Sydney's grade averages, his 54 wickets at 7.88 had only once been bettered – in 1893–94, when A. L. Newell took 60 at 5.43.

So much for irrefutable and interesting facts, but they tell only meagrely the tale of O'Reilly the bowler and the man.

One might almost call O'Reilly a mystery bowler. He made good by stealth, for his art was not clearly apparent to those watching from outside the ropes. Larwood was different. The merest tyro knew immediately that Larwood was a great bowler, for his terrific speed was plainly there for everybody to see as the ball hurtled through to the wicket-keeper. So, too, was the greatness of Tate apparent. He made the ball hustle off the pitch with the whistle of a cyclone, and one could see from the back of the stumps or behind Tate's arm how he made the ball run away or come in to the batsman. Mailey's profligate breaks were as obvious as day after the ball left the pitch, though many a twittery batsman failed to tell the leg-break 't'other' from the bosie 'which' as the ball came spinning through the air. Grimmett was another whose wiles, if not perhaps art, were mostly apparent to the spectator.

All these bowlers and others took a spectator into the game with them, but not so O'Reilly. He covered himself up, he hid his intentions with flank movements as the 6 ft 3 in of him, elongated arms and legs flaying the atmosphere, bobbed and jostled on his long run to the wickets. He was a flurry of limbs, fire and steel-edged temper – a temper given free orders to open fire and glare fire when anything resembling a bat or a pair of pads happened within the orbit of his eyes. Much of this O'Reilly set-up was visible to spectators, but when a batsman against him was cramped uncomfortably on the defensive, when he was leg-before wicket or bowled, and particularly when he popped a dolly catch to the leg-trap, many on the outer were not quite certain what had happened and why. For that matter, many an O'Reilly victim was none too sure, either, what had gone on under his very batting nose.

That is the sense in which I term O'Reilly a mystery bowler. I could count on the fingers of one hand, leaving out the thumb, the batsmen who succeeded in understanding and recognising his wares to the extent that they could rough-handle him. At some time or other he dismissed every world-class batsman of his day, and the manner of the dismissal left no possible doubt whatever.

Bats did not go forward to meet O'Reilly with full-faced impunity and confidence. They wavered out, much like a peroxided blonde entering the surf without a bathing cap, for one could never be too certain against O'Reilly that the ball he was playing for a leg-break might not, indeed, be a bosie or, just as embarrassing, a top-spinner.

This general atmosphere of mystery made O'Reilly the most discussed bowler of his day. Few will agree in their opinion of him.

Some said immediately that he was the world's greatest bowler of his time. Others conceded – and the records book suggested they were not being over-rash – that he was fit to rank with the bowling immortals. Then lined up the doubting Thomases, among them leading critics – who saw O'Reilly from the outside, be it remembered – and they found it difficult to make up their minds whether O'Reilly was really a great bowler or a flattered bowler. Their prime argument against him was that when he was not getting wickets he did not look a world bowler.

The truth was that on his day O'Reilly was the world's leading bowler, but it must be immediately noted that his day was never one on which a wicket had not been stirred from its doped sleep. Length and variation of pace alone stood to O'Reilly on such days. Of what possible use was it to deceive a batsman with type of spin when a glazed wicket robbed the ball of all spin? And – but before going any further on this line I must break off and tell the story of O'Reilly from the beginning, because there is cricket romance in the tale of this country bowler's over-night rise to world fame.

He was a native of Wingello, a country hamlet about a hundred miles south of Sydney and typical of hundreds in the Australian outback. Wingello is some 30 miles further up the line from Bowral, the drowsy little village that nurtured the short-trousers exploits of Bradman before giving him to a doting world. Like such country villages, the life of Wingello centres around its small railway station, which notes arrivals and departures and faces from neighbouring villages. Just across the dusty way from the station houses are grouped a modest school, an equally modest church, a store that stocks most things, sparse houses which tail off into the bush down the road and which contain railway fettlers and the other workers of the district.

The houses are roofed, country fashion, with corrugated iron, which gives off a merry song of rain in winter and blistering heat in summer. In summer, also, come dry westerlies to whip up the dust and dry off the pastures, and it is then that this high southern spot is a fit preparatory school for an embryo Test bowler destined to spend long hours in the sun. O'Reilly's father was the village schoolmaster and the family lived there for years.

The Australian boy of the outback who seeks sport in the high noon of summer must have a sporting appetite well developed. O'Reilly had that appetite, and he was further blessed, though possibly he did not think so at the time, in being the youngest of four brothers: the dignity and the size of his elders taught the baby not to give himself airs and graces, essential knowledge for one destined to live with his bowling nose to the grindstone.

The family possessed one other thing in common and that was an almost entire lack of sporting equipment. That proves an attribute in the long run, because the petted child with enough equipment to turn out two sides has never yet made any team other than that which stands in need of his gear. The unspoiled and not too-encouraged is the one who grasps essentials and learns to appreciate. So it was with O'Reilly. He learned in a hard school and by the very sweat of his lofty brow.

The brothers had no ball. With great ingenuity they looked about and found a tough, gnarled Banksia tree-root that looked as if it might be persuaded into some degree of roundness. They turned to with a chisel and worked in relays on the stubborn root. It came round at last, this root that most amazingly was to see out the entire boyish days of the O'Reillys, and armed with a bat made from a piece of gum-tree the four brothers made their way down past the creek to the paddock that had been scrubbed of timber.

Again I emphasise that William Joseph was the youngest of the four, a point worth stressing because his invariable legacy – older brothers being older brothers – was the ball. His lot was a Cinderella-like one and long and intimate association taught him all there was to know about the ball. He found a knot on either side of it. His long fingers twined around each in turn, and he came to know them as the off and the leg knot. He experimented and persisted with them, telling himself as he trudged off to fox his Banksia root in the mulga across the creek that his day would come against these brothers. Time wore down the ordinary wood of the ball; time and boundaries could do little with the knots.

As the ordinary wood wore down, the knots became more pronounced. They gave a better grip to the eager, tenuous fingers. The young O'Reilly bit his lips in the determined fashion Test batsmen were to know so well in the years ahead. The day of the O'Reilly underdog would dawn – then let his brothers watch out!

He had his first official game of cricket when ten. Wingello could not make up an eleven itself, so, with reinforcements from the village above, the side set out with many more dogs than pieces of equipment. The dogs would be handy for the rabbit chases en route, and in this fashion the Wingello Eleven made its way on foot down the seven long dusty miles to Tallong. They walked there and back.

O'Reilly does not think he was successful with the ball. By far his clearest recollection of the day was being bitten by a Jumping Joey ant, though, perhaps, if one had known the pincers of a Jumping Joey at close quarters, there would be little to wonder at in that.

About this time in the home paddock the baby brother often found himself in disgrace with his elders. He was crazy concerning the reason for many a cuff he received, but the possible truth was that he was beginning to show his brothers up. There were fewer long chases into the mulga; fingers grown longer and stronger were giving more spin to the root-ball, and when off and leg-breaks were not rapping the brothers on the shins, they were mostly dinning a tune on the kerosene-tin wicket. And this, from the baby brother, bordered on cool cheek. The day of the underdog was indeed dawning.

His next big game – it is to be noted how few chances an Australian bush lad receives – was a few years after that at Tallong, when he was invited to play with the Governor's team against I Zingari at Sutton Forest. Here, again, he cannot remember his feats, but he thinks they must have been noteworthy, because the Test slow bowler, H. V. Hordern, gave him a long bowling talk after the game.

In this period O'Reilly several times played against neighbour Bradman, and, even so early when the genius of the youths was in its embryo stage, each developed for the ability of the other a regard that was to live on in their first-class careers. Bradman rose earlier than O'Reilly, and in his first book, the book of 1930 for which the Board of Control fined him £50, Bradman dwelt at length on the ability of O'Reilly, then an obscure country school-teacher.

Grown out of his father's country school, he went to college in Goulburn (NSW), where he was a sporting all-rounder rather than a cricket specialist. He went to Sydney at 17 to study and qualify in the steps of his father and, most oddly, the youth who had sought the game under the country's bleakest conditions never bothered to play the game in this city of cricket plenty.

Athletics was his love. A State record in the junior hop, step and jump showed how close cricket came to losing a champion. Nothing could wean him from athletics in those years, and he might have become an Olympian had there not happened a Saturday morning when he went as an onlooker with a student friend playing in Moore Park (Sydney) junior competition.

His friend's side was a man short. Would O'Reilly make up the team? He'd be delighted. He took the field in borrowed gear and, as a gesture towards his willingness to help the team out of difficulties, he was given a beneficiary over.

O'Reilly was a sensation, in the first sense because his long, loping run with arms clawing at the air made everybody giggle. The laugh, however, soon switched across to the other side of the faces.

The coir matting wicket on which he bowled was ideal for spin. It had as much grip in it as a parish-pump politician's handshake on the eve of an election, and O'Reilly whipped the ball across at will from either side of the wicket.

The humble juniors against him were tumbled out higgledy-piggledy, and it needed someone stonier in the heart than O'Reilly to resist the pleas of his doting fellows that he should become a regular playing member.

He did not forsake athletics. He played cricket in the morning, athletics in the afternoon, but his athletics career now became tainted with doom. To the accompaniment of crashing wickets, his fame and name spread on the parklands. It permeated senior clubs, with the result that next season brought with it an invitation to play with a grade club.

The change from matting to the spin responsive turf wickets of Sydney grade cricket suited him, and he was fast on the path to notoriety when the bush claimed him a second time. He had qualified as a teacher; his posting was to the back-blocks. In quick succession he taught at Griffith, Rylstone and Kandos, small centres, and in this second bush immersion he set himself a task.

It was to perfect a delivery he had lacked the confidence to bowl in Sydney. On that delivery his very fame was built. It was the bosie, a ball which needs intense practice and often, in the wooing, is capricious enough to kill other natural talents. By hard and constant seeking, O'Reilly won his bosie and retained, also, his old leg-break and top-spinner loves.

The NSW Education Department did a gracious thing for the game of cricket and Australia when it recalled the big chap to city haunts. He returned as the 1930 Australian team came home from England, and returned with such venom that next year he played for Australia against South Africa. The following year he established himself for all time as a successful Test bowler against England. To be repetitious, just two years after O'Reilly had fought for bosie mastery in the back-blocks he became the No. 1 Australian bowler in a Test series against England.

Opportunity was kind to him at the eleventh hour. Nevertheless it was sheer ability alone which brought such progress.

Like all champions he was the compiler of his own text-book. In that he had much in common with Bradman, because, like that worthy, he risked everything on his knowledge and conception of his own art.

A Broth of a Bhoy – W. J. O'Reilly

The first day O'Reilly appeared among the Mighty at the Sydney Cricket Ground nets Mailey came to him and suggested that he should change his grip of the ball.

Mailey was Mailey. His word would have been gospel to most up-and-coming young bowlers, who would have hastened to do his bidding. But not O'Reilly. If there was one thing he possessed it was a mind of his own. Politely he thanked Mailey for his interest, but he had always held the ball that way and, if Mr Mailey did not mind, he would continue to do so.

That was not cheek. If somebody years before had gone to Mailey and suggested he should have changed his grip, Mailey undoubtedly would have done as O'Reilly did. Individual art is created and little moulding is needed. The essence of the champion is either inherent in the individual or it isn't, and he prefers to work out a destiny along his own lines.

Mailey twined his fingers around the ball and cracked his fingers and wrist when delivering as a stockman would his whip. O'Reilly cupped his fingers around the ball and rolled it out. Mailey was not renowned for his length, O'Reilly was; Mailey was a slow bowler, O'Reilly medium pace, and between the two was a fundamental difference in all things, even to temperament.

I recall no bowler who resembled O'Reilly. At medium pace he bowled a leg break, a bosie and a top-spinner. If the wicket took spin he could turn the ball the width of the stumps and more, as Jardine found to his amazement one Melbourne day in 1932; but generally his spin was modest and content to do all that was necessary – either miss the bat by a fraction or find its edge for catches.

He concealed his bosie as artfully as an expert cracksman would his fingerprints and therein was his great strength. There was some peculiar mixture of top-spin in his bosie that gave the ball a sharper rise from the pitch than his leg-break. This was the ball which brought many catches to his leg-trap. Unsuspecting batsmen played it with the bat the usual height from the ground. Bouncing higher, the ball kissed the bat higher up its face and, with the rising spin still operating, the ball flirted with the atmosphere long enough for the catch to be made.

But O'Reilly was not distinctive alone in the variety of balls he delivered. He had other rich gifts, none more tantalising to the batsman than his long, queer approach to the wickets. Edmund Blunden described it aptly when he wrote that O'Reilly's bowling began long before he got to the wickets. All batsmen like the bowler to come calmly and evenly in his run-up, but with O'Reilly a batsman's line of flight went up and down like a see-saw as O'Reilly came bobbing along like a kangaroo in the legs and a windmill in the arms. And then, finally, the ball hurtled at the batsman from a mass of erupting humanity.

All this was part of O'Reilly's technique and contributed to his greatness, but nothing in his make-up was of more importance than his temperament.

'I have never seen a bowler,' Constantine once told me, 'who seemed to suggest by his every action that he wished to goodness he was a fast bowler, a fast bowler who would carry every batting thing before him. That, all other things being equal, is the ideal bowling temperament to possess.'

Hot blood surged through O'Reilly's veins. It was quick to rise to the top, showing in veins that stood like whipcord over his temples if he thought he was being wronged by fate, umpires, conditions or cricket legislators – and I really think at no stage of his career did O'Reilly consider he and his bowling brothers were anything else but the victims of oppression. It might have been that the grudge he bore batsmen in the home paddock of his youth never really left him, but in his first-class career he always contended that bowlers were the playthings of the game, the legislators and the gates. The bowler was cricket's poor relation. He was a perpetual male Cinderella, always doing the interminable dirty work for his elder brothers, the batsmen and the legislators.

Such things worried O'Reilly. He was always cognisant of them and in that was vastly different, for instance, from Fleetwood-Smith, who never allowed to worry him the fact that doped and over-prepared wickets robbed him of his rightful spin. Fleetwood was the playboy of Test cricket. It was nothing in a Test match for him to squark like a magpie or whistle brightly as he ran up to bowl. In all the Tests I played with him, only once did I see Fleetwood do credit to his superb ability – in Adelaide in 1937, when he spun a Test for Australia out of a seemingly hopeless position.

O'Reilly's outlook on the game differed entirely. Cricket, to him, was something real and earnest. It was a job of work, put it that way, that just had to be done, and his broad shoulders seemed to attract responsibility. No job was ever too big for his heart, but that heart also had room in itself to house an extreme loathing for the type of first-class wicket on which, invariably, he had to bowl.

Those wickets would not take spin and that not because of any inability on O'Reilly's part. They were so smooth, so glossy from their preparation that the ball merely skidded straight through off them on an unchanged line of flight.

Veterans have assured me with glints in their eyes that Turner, Spofforth and others of preceding generations could spin a ball on any billiard-table wicket in the world. I have my doubts. I could not conceive anybody turning the ball by spin (not by bringing it back with body-break, mind you) on wickets I have seen at Adelaide, Melbourne, Sydney, Trent Bridge, Kennington Oval and Cape Town. The grass from those wickets had been shorn like hair from a convict's head; the substance remaining had then been rolled and rerolled into the ground.

Spin is abortive unless it has something to grip. It must have resistance, but on a modern typical Test wicket there was just no grassy top to grip the ball and allow the spin to do its work.

For hour after hour on such wickets O'Reilly was forced to fight the batsmen with length and variation of pace. He had to persevere until such time as his persistent length brought its own reward with a blade or two of grass resurrected from the marl to grip and embrace his spin.

Those were the occasions when your pernickety critic would say of O'Reilly that when he was not getting wickets he did not look to be in the highest world class. But what spin bowler did in such circumstances? Did Grimmett? Was not Grimmett, possibly the greatest slow bowler the world has seen, dropped from the Australian Eleven in his homeland in 1932–33 and not even considered in 1937, a year after a most successful South African tour, which made the Springboks think his slow magic was not of this world? And Freeman, who once took 304 wickets in an English season, was considered a slow-bowling gift on Australian wickets.

O'Reilly hated these wickets and he impersonally hated the batsmen who thrived on them. He started every such game with hate, and it showed in every ball he bowled. If his aged father had come to bat against him on such a wicket, O'Reilly would have recognised his inexorable enemies, the bat and the pads, before recognising his own flesh and blood and he would have shown no mercy. Indeed, there was no mercy in his make-up – not even to youngsters playing their first game in Sydney grade cricket. From the field I often shivered and felt for the poor tyro who came in to face O'Reilly when the 'Tiger's' dander was up.

He whose sense of humour was most marked off the field hung it up on the pavilion peg with his street clothes as he dressed for the cricket fray. The whimsical Mailey was the first to see the humorous side of it when some gasping batting fish, hopelessly unable to tell which way the ball was breaking, streakily snicked it between his legs and the stumps. Grimmett, too, often enjoyed himself hugely by keeping in some rabbit and tantalising him with his tricks. O'Reilly did not hold with such things. The middle of the ground was no place for fun or dunderheads, and he greeted indecent, inelegant snicks with a hollow, mirthless outburst which rubbed deep into the batsman his sense of good fortune and inefficiency.

He once wrote an article on bowling for his club report. It told you much of himself and I quote from it.

'Remember, you can never become a good attacking bowler if you do not develop a bowling "temperament". A happy-go-lucky, good-natured and carefree outlook is of no use whatever to an ambitious and competent bowler. He must be prepared to boil up inwardly on the slightest provocation, and opportunities are so common that there is no reason to cite even one.

'Conceal that desirable temperament from the public, but reveal it in all its force and fury to your opponent, the batsman. Spectators often imagine that a bowler is introducing sting or devil into his bowling when he is, in reality, merely working off a little of the surplus blood pressure caused by a "bowler's temperament".'

O'Reilly did not practise what he preached in this, for his state of mind was obvious to the public when he missed the stumps by a fraction, when he was no-balled or, worse still, when some worthy scrambled him away for a fortuitous four. Then O'Reilly really boiled and it was there for everybody to see. He clawed the air in his fury; he whipped himself into a grand old paddy and the batsman had to mind his p's and q's and his wicket, for an enraged O'Reilly was a terrible thing to behold.

There was method in such blatancy, of course, for it often gave O'Reilly a psychological advantage over the batsman. Such fire bluffed or bullied many a batsman into inferiority and dismissal, but when O'Reilly had worked himself into such a state no batsman could take risks with him. At such a time as that I have crept to within feet of Bradman, Hammond, Nourse, Ponsford, Compton, Hutton, Sutcliffe, Edrich, Taylor and the others at short leg and never felt I was taking an unusual physical risk. I knew nobody could hit O'Reilly hard to leg when his Irish was up; and I know of no other bowler I would have paid a similar fielding honour.

You could not retrieve your mistake against O'Reilly if you did not detect his bosie. His pace would not allow you to do that. A batsman could get out of trouble against Mailey's bosie at times, because that bosie often sailed through the air with a spin-thriftless disregard of length. O'Reilly's did not. It was always on the three-penny piece, so to speak, and it was made no easier for the batsman that O'Reilly aimed both his leg-break and the bosie at the middle and leg stump. His small amount of turn, a big asset in such circumstances, allowed him to do that.

His length was magnificent. It was mechanical and possibly it was because of this that batsmen on the short side in stature (Hassett, of Victoria, who made a century in each innings once in Sydney against O'Reilly and treated him harshly; Wallace, of New Zealand, in the only pre-war time he faced O'Reilly) found him less difficult than players of taller build. These two and Yardley, who collared O'Reilly at Cambridge one day in 1938 to execute the prettiest on-driving I have seen, were in my mind earlier in this chapter when I wrote that I could count on the fingers of one hand the batsmen who have really dealt harshly with O'Reilly.

His mechanical length would have been just a fraction on the short side to smaller batsmen, and this, I am inclined to think, enabled Hassett and Wallace to swing him to the on as they did. Brown, in 1944 in Australia, did much the same thing, but not against the O'Reilly of old.

On their day and not on his, others might have subdued O'Reilly, but even then very few took risks against him. His many duels with Bradman, all on Australian wickets, finished with honours about even. Bradman caned him in Adelaide in 1939, but O'Reilly wielded the big stick later that season when he caught Bradman on a relaid Sydney wicket that took spin, a wicket that O'Reilly would have liked to have taken with him on a world tour. Bradman gave O'Reilly more respect than any other bowler, Larwood, over a period, not even excluded.

Hammond devised the best method of combating O'Reilly. He recognised that O'Reilly's strong point was pitching at a batsman's legs, aiming at his blind spot and thereabouts.

In Australia in 1936–37 Hammond took guard on his leg stump to O'Reilly and even, at times, batted outside of that. This meant that O'Reilly, in attacking Hammond's legs, was taken wide off the wicket. When the ball came at his legs Hammond invariably tried to sweep it with what is known as a 'cow-shot'. On this angle, also, it is interesting that O'Reilly detested bowling against left-handers, possibly because he had to use his bosie incessantly if he wanted to attack their legs.

The Englishmen in 1938 generally batted on their leg stump and outside of it to O'Reilly, and I think this robbed him of some of his hostility. He was not then the bowler he was in 1932 or in South Africa in 1935, when he had Grimmett with him. O'Reilly often sent out a mental S-O-S that 1938 English season for Grimmett.

He was at his zenith in Australia in 1932, and I think never fully recovered from the burning out Woodfull gave him in that series. He bowled 383.4 eight-ball overs. His heart that season, indeed always, was too big. No captain asked him in vain to bowl, and he was a captain's delight in that he never sulked or needed cajoling if another spin bowler in the side was given the preference of bowling to a worn spot. O'Reilly could have used that spot as well as anybody and, because of his untiring efforts when everything was against him, richly deserved such a crumb, but he was first to realise a captain's difficulties and generously gave way to others.

I asked him once for his general opinions of wickets and those he had to bowl against. This is what he told me:

South African Wickets: I loved them. Probably it was because the South African batsmen were easier to bowl at than the English. The wickets took spin and were faster than those in England.

English: Will always be clouded in this. The memory of that Kennington Oval wicket in 1938 will take a lifetime to efface. When they were not overdone with that marl I liked them, although they were always slow and one had to push the ball through on them all the time. You will remember ordinary county wickets did not remain sticky for long. A half-hour or so.

Australian: The subject is tiresome. Covered wickets are anathema to me and so are the people who decree them. Batsmen administrators! Good on the fourth day for bowlers if bowlers have any energy left by then. More 'drongo' (an Australianism for indifferent) batsmen get centuries in Australia than in any other place in the world.

Ponsford: Greatest batsman I bowled against. Also the greatest concentrator. Like the elephant, he never forgot. I can never remember him taking a liberty with a good ball. Others did.

Bradman: Sat on the splice to me until he had me, and then proceeded to show how I should be dealt with. Always gave me the impression that he might, in his supreme confidence, do something not according to Hoyle. Have had him leg before wicket to a good length break on middle and off to leg.

Hammond: Grand player in all but the push shot away for a single off his toes, which was Woodfull's masterpiece. Do you remember the 'cow-shot' he brought to light here in 1936? I think he evolved that for my benefit. I got him several times using it.

Hutton: Has all the shots and one day will be persuaded to use them. A marvellous player, but not good enough to hold an all-time Test match record.

Nourse: A really good player, splendid in his footwork – but, do you know, I have almost forgotten all about Nourse. It was an extra good trip we had to South Africa, wasn't it?

O'Reilly's criticisms are like his bowling, full of pep and on the spot.

He had one secret ambition. That was to captain an Australian Eleven in an English tour.

O'Reilly would not want such a high post because of vanity. He did not know the meaning of such a word, but I think he thought the hard workers of the game deserved some such recognition, and he was anxious, too, to show that a bowler is as capable as a batsman of shrewd and inspiring leadership.

He was an inspiring leader. He was like Victor Richardson in that regard, bringing the best out of those under him. He showed that in Sydney grade games and in the last year of Sheffield Shield games before the war. Even more than this, however, England would have enjoyed him for his brilliant after-dinner speeches. English communities love a good, bright speaker, and in that regard O'Reilly stood on a pedestal among cricketers. He had a rich wit, choice of words and humorous satire that flowed naturally and graciously.

Off the field he was the ideal touring companion, full of history, conversation, good fellowship and an infectious Irish humour.

I recall his big moment when he travelled down a Johannesburg hotel lift with Gracie Fields, the only two in the lift.

Clamouring hundreds greeted them on the ground floor, Gracie having arrived in South Africa only a few moments before.

'Who's the big fellow?' asked somebody.

'He's Mr Gracie Fields,' said another.

And O'Reilly took a bow!

His best moments of all were in Ireland in 1938, when the O'Reilly's for miles around came to honour their Australian cousin. At Belfast they held the game up for some time while distracted umpires and a groundsman tried to shoo the O'Reillys from the field. They surrounded the big Australian and walked, chatting, to the very stumps with him.

A big cherubic grin never left his face all the time we were in Ireland. England might have doted on Bradman, adulating crowds cheering him on and off railway stations and following him up Piccadilly and the Strand, but O'Reilly went unchallenged in Ireland.

It was the only time I saw him generous to batsmen – indeed he complimented them on boundaries against him! – and the brogue he suddenly developed was more Irish than the Irish themselves.

''Tis a lovely plaice I'm in, to be shure,' he would say, 'and the O'Reillys are all the very naicest persins, begorrah!'

Apart from the bowling crease he was in his element most when conducting community singing on tour, which meant whenever there was community singing. He towered over the singers, dominating them. He glared at them like Beecham himself.

'We will now have Mother Machree,' he would announce. 'I want you all to come in together at the end of the down beat three. Now then. All ready. Right. One, two —.'

'Shure —,' I'd start to sing.

O'Reilly would stop and glare. 'Another peep from you before the downbeat three and I'll Mother Machree you,' he would threaten. 'We will now start again. For the benefit of the ignorant, we will have Mother Machree at the end of the downbeat three. Now, then. One, two —.'

'Shure —,' I'd start again and Barnett would launch off brightly into 'Bonnie Charlie'.

'Beecham' would down his imaginary baton, roll his sleeves and there would be trouble – plenty of it.

When the O'Reilly order had again been established he would take up the baton again.

'Now that it has been conclusively proved who is the best man around these parts,' he would say, 'we will have some singing. We will also have something Irish. We will have Mother Machree.'

And this despite the fact that we had been having 'something Irish' for the past half-hour or so!

A broth of a bhoy, indade, was the O'Reilly – and a man of giant stature in the game of cricket.

CHAPTER THREE   *From the Storehouse*

IT NEEDS LITTLE TO START THE ball of memory rolling. The cricketer who never rushes for a stump or the ball at the end of a Test, who fails to preserve with fitting autographs the bat with which he makes a Test century (or a humble double figures, even, in some club game), or who disdains at the tour's end to swop a cap or blazer – the cricketer who fails to do these things runs the risk of a cold old age devoid of many memories.

There will come an evening when Sam Sniffikins, whom Bill Blinkings has not seen since they trod a measure between the wickets together at Lord's many years ago, will make a call on Bill as he passes through his home town. The fire is cosy and Bill has a little something in the cupboard to warm the innards. The two are delighted to see each other; they are ready to reminisce and talk far into the night – but Bill, in his heyday, sniffed at Sam because Sam always had an eye cocked for souvenirs. As a result, Bill's walls and mantel-pieces lack an autographed stump, an inscribed ball, an action photograph, little odds and ends which keep the old days fresh and lead off into countless 'do you remember's?'. In consequence of the lack of promptings, Sam has to work hard to refresh Bill's mind because, with nothing before his eyes to refresh it, Bill has let his memory wander sadly downhill.

Perhaps, as I write, that rugged Australian, Ironmonger, sits before his fire and proudly points to the three stumps and bail suspended over the fireplace, sadly telling his neighbour, meanwhile, of the time when fate deprived him of the second bail.

What a story those stumps and the bail conjure! They stood mutely there in the Adelaide soil, together with their long departed brother-bail, as Ironmonger slowly wended his way to bat. Ironmonger was last man in, and though some Number Elevens might harbour within their breasts the feeling that their ability deserves a better batting position, Ironmonger was not one of these. He was of that type of last man in of whom it was written in the olden days that the horse instinctively backed between the shafts of the roller as soon as he made his appearance.

Ironmonger had played his shot of the series. That was in the preceding Test in Melbourne, when he came to the creases in his usual batting position with Bradman 98 not out. All Melbourne, inside and outside the ground or grouped about its wireless sets at the home or office, felt sorry for Bradman to be 98 not out with Ironmonger coming in No. 11. They knew their Ironmonger.

In view of his batting reputation, the remark which Ironmonger made that day as he passed Bradman on his way to the other end of the wicket should go down to posterity. In its sphere, it ranks with Nelson's dying remark to Hardy, Drake's at Plymouth and the like.

'Don't worry, son,' said Ironmonger, 'I'll see you through.'

And Ironmonger did. He planked his bat straight down the wicket as Larwood brought his arm over; he glued his feet in front of the stumps and never budged; he gave the teeming and wildly-excited thousands their greatest thrill in years as he saw it through for Bradman to get his century. When Bradman did that, Ironmonger then waved his bat with furious energy at one of Larwood's fastest balls and, miracle of miracles, the ball sped to the fence with the greatest and noblest cover drive of the series.

The position at Adelaide, then, as Ironmonger walked slowly to the wickets, was that Ironmonger had played his stroke of the series. The noisiest, stormiest Test of all history was within one ball of completion. It was not surprising Ironmonger did not survive one delivery; what was surprising was that in the hectic scramble for souvenirs at the end Ironmonger, who was clean bowled, got the three spread-eagled stumps and one of the speeding bails. He searched wildly for the other bail, but missed it.

He left the ground triumphant with three stumps, a bail and a bat rampant. He went under the shower a few minutes later with a piece of soap, three stumps and the bail. He boarded the express back to Melbourne that night still clutching his souvenirs. He walked up Collins Street, Melbourne, next day with his prized possessions still in hand.

With them over his mantel-piece, what a story Ironmonger could tell of that Test! All the incidents would flood back to him as he gazed at the stumps, silent witnesses in that Test to the Woodfull and Larwood drama, England four for 30 at lunch on the first day, and then recovering magnificently; Hammond bowled last ball of the day by a Bradman full toss; Oldfield put aside with a fractured skull; whispers of upsetting scenes in the dressing-room; the full-throated, angry roars of the Adelaide crowd; even the delectable scene when Leyland, primed with Jardine instructions, poked a stolid Yorkshire finger at Ironmonger and said, 'Eh, laad, thou'st using resin from pocket on ball.'

It is sometimes very necessary to have reminders to bring back the good old days. I called once upon an international who had played Test cricket years before me, and I was met at the gate by a handsome, friendly black sheep-dog that frolicked about my legs. 'Quiet, Ranji! Down, Ranji!' called my friend. I knew the association of the name, but the colour of the dog was incongruous. 'Ah, yes,' wistfully said my friend, 'the colouring is not quite right, but you should see his speed, his footwork in turning and chasing a ball. I see again all the quick movements of Ranjitsinhji's footwork.'

I had a bat once that stood me in good and long stead. It went with me into my first Sheffield Shield game and stayed with me up to my first Test. On the edge of it, high up near the handle, with youthful enthusiasm, I inked the scores I made with it; down the back of it I printed in small type the names of those bowling immortals who had looked my bat in the face. As I picked it up in my room of a night and ran a stroking hand over its face I could see again famous faces and recapture the many thrills those moments had given me. Sometimes – I was then very young, I hasten to add – I would even take it to bed with me on a cold wintry night when cricket and the sun were of another world.

I still remember the names I had written with preening pride on the side of the old warrior: Macartney, Kelleway, Mailey, Gregory, Oxenham, Blackie, Ironmonger, Wall, Grimmett, Constantine, Francis, Griffith, Quinn, Bell, Morkel, Vincent, McMillan! I had hoped it would live with me to give confidence against Tate (whom I desired it to meet most of all), Larwood and the rest of the 1932 English bowlers, but all the rolling, all the tender care and pious hoping could not smooth its cracked face nor recall to it the spring of young willow. As I fondle it in the years to come, I will always regret that it did not look Tate in the face, but as I licked wounds in my room on certain nights, I looked at my old friend standing remote in a corner and thought, perhaps, it was well it had not lived to see certain things.

Bradman was lavish in distributing souvenirs. Many a boyish

heart was gladdened by the presentation of a bat the champion had used in making a record. Sitting-rooms throughout the English-speaking world are studded with bats wielded by Bradman – in much the same way as the English countryside is dotted with beds in which Queen Elizabeth is alleged to have slept. It was right, perhaps, that Bradman should have given away hs record-making bats, for what a cluttering they would otherwise have made of his home!

In their palmy days most sportsmen do not give a second thought to setting up a reminiscing store for the morrow. Because they live so intimately with the great and their historic deeds, they pay no court to tangible associations, little realising that just around the corner is the remorseless day that will scatter their youth and their playing friends like thistle-down before a gale.

Yet lusty youth cannot be expected to see things in the perspective of experience.

There is the example of the Springbok Rugby footballers crossing the Indian Ocean in 1936 on their return from a highly successful tour in New Zealand – though, of a few Australian games, they lost one Test on a temporary lake on the Sydney Cricket Ground. Having decided that their playing days were at an end, the veterans of the team determined they would carry out a certain ceremonial in the middle of the Indian Ocean. Led by my very good and huge friend, Ferdie Bergh, they checked the ship's progress one night, solemnly met on the top deck and, all together, heaved far out to sea – their football boots! I wonder how many of them have since regretted their action, their fingers aching for the feel of oft-baptised sprigs in many a fount of Rugby endeavour?

On one of those days of tedious waiting at Old Trafford for the 1938 Test that never began, I was called aside by a kindly old soul. He humbly begged pardon for what he called an intrusion. I asked him not to regard it in such a light and, thus emboldened, he proudly took from a waistcoat pocket a little polished tobacco tin. In the way that memories will when twitted by association, my mind flew back to other days when gruesome little boys used to delight in scaring their fellows by producing a tin of the very same nature. They asked would you like to see the finger of a Turkish soldier, 'sent home to me by my uncle.' They opened the tin and there, on a piece of wadding, was a grubby little finger copiously treated with red ink. A hole in the bottom of the tin allowed the urchin to push his finger through. Red ink and imagination were supposed to do the gruesome rest.

There was nothing gruesome, however, in the tin of the Old Trafford veteran. He opened it tenderly and on a white piece of cloth were some strands of wiry black hair.

'From Dr Grace's beard,' said the old chap. 'My father had a barber's shop just across from Lord's and often clipped the champion's beard in the old days. I thought you might be interested.'

I certainly was interested. As I looked at the veteran's souvenir, I could almost see the Old Man walking down the steps at Old Trafford, rolling white sleeves up massive arms and grunting defiance through his beard.

Pavilions on Test days are full of reminiscences. Also at that time in Manchester I met an old chap in tall hat and morning dress, a Mr Paynter, I think, from memory, who presented me with a three-penny piece, on the back of which he had engraved the Lord's Prayer. He was then 82 years of age and will be remembered by many at Old Trafford. In his best days, he told me, he had added the Gloria to the Lord's Prayer for good measure, but sorrowfully he explained that one day at Old Trafford he got some dust in his right eye and it had never been the same since. It is difficult to reconcile dust with Manchester in any shape or form or at any time, but never would I have suggested to the old chap that, at 82, one cannot expect to do the things of former years.

By devious routes I return to what started me on this chapter. It is a pair of football socks unearthed in a drawer. The moths have paid them more attention in the past years than I, but not even gaping holes could dim the story they recalled with their red, yellow and black stripes. They represented the Wanderers Club in Johannesburg. This is their story.

It was early March and the end of a perfect cricket tour. That Australia had won every Test and every provincial game did not alone make the tour the memorable one it was. South Africa had beaten England in England a few months before our tour in the Dominion began, but the death of Cameron, the retirement of others, staleness inseparable from the aftermath of an English tour, the tantalising spin of Grimmett and O'Reilly – Fleetwood-Smith to a less degree – together with batting and fielding that headed the Springboks at every turn, were too much for the South Africans. Australia was unbeaten in an unforgettable tour of pleasures, friendship and delights.

The ending of the tour and the arrival in Cape Town of the mail-boat from England on its way to Australia did not synchronise by more than a week. We had time on our hands. Would we, we were asked, consider another match in the Transvaal to aid the Cameron fund? We would be delighted, of course, but lack of keenness for a game after playing it continuously for five months and the poor displays the Transvaal sides had previously given, with resultant lack of public interest, led us timidly to suggest a novelty. What if the Australians played the Transvaal at baseball?

The suggestion was not kindly received by the Transvaal cricket legislators. A successful South African baseball championship, in which Transvaal triumphed, had just been concluded in Cape Town. Baseball was a serious rival to cricket; publicity accruing to baseball from such a game could be to the detriment only of cricket.

Generously, however, though with misgivings, the Transvaal legislators gave way to the Australians. The baseball game became a fixture.

There were two baseball schools of thought in the Australian camp. McCormick, Richardson, Barnett and Darling had played the game in Australia. The team would be completed by five others who had never played the American game, and the schools divided on whether the intervening period should be spent in study of the rules or practice on the diamond, as the baseball field is called.

Grimmett, who had never played the game, but whose general theorising on sport was always profound, was unanimously appointed coach to the team, it being naively pointed out that in the circumstances there was a wide difference in being coach 'to' and not 'of' the team. Grimmett took his post seriously, even if no one else was inclined to do so. On the return trip from Durban to Johannesburg he conducted a blackboard lecture. With notebook in one hand, a piece of chalk in the other, he set determinedly about his coaching task, but banter and chaffing made it difficult.

A full-dress rehearsal came next day on the Wanderers. The scene in the dressing-room was ludicrous as players garbed for the field. O'Reilly was all legs in his baseball pantaloons; Richardson, McCabe, Oldfield and the rest, so at ease in their cricket flannels, looked guys in their baggy breeches, football socks and baseball blouse.

The practice was an unqualified success. Cricketing players who used to depart surreptitiously from the nets long before practice was over, now, as pseudo baseballers, became imbued with amazing practising zeal. They careered around the bases, twined their arms most scientifically behind their backs and threw curves, drops, the spit-ball (a very abstruse ball in which the thrower secretly covers one side of the ball with saliva, causing it to perform queer things in the air), and all the other mysterious throws known to baseball. They leaped wildly for 'flys' overhead, swatted home-runs, made double-plays and indulged in the chirruping bickering at each other which baseball not only allows, but, indeed, demands.

This baseball 'game' promised, indeed, to be the greatest piece of fun on the tour – but the morning newspapers took the smile off our faces at breakfast next day. Over-night the baseball game had developed most serious proportions.

'Transvaal's chance to atone for cricketing defeats' ran a streamer of big, bold type across the page. 'All sporting South Africa,' ran the article, 'will follow the baseball game at the Wanderers this afternoon with the keenest interest. The Transvaal team has a splendid opportunity of inflicting upon the Australians the first defeat of their tour. . . .'

This gave the baseball game, for us, a vastly different and a bitter taste. A game which we were regarding as a sporting novelty, a light finish to a long tour, had suddenly taken on a very different aspect. The joke was now very much on us. We had put out our chins, so to speak, and all that was left to us was to take it.

It was a far from chirpy band of Australians who gathered that Saturday afternoon in the familiar cricket dressing-room. The light banter of the previous day, as players dressed, was absent, and had there been any confidence in the team it would have quickly dissipated had anybody been courageous enough to look through the window at the huge crowd waiting to see the 'game'.

In front of the pavilion eleven or so white-knickered Transvaal men dashed hither and thither with bounds of confidence, performing incredible feats of throwing, hitting and catching.

Those of us who knew not the slightest baseball points began to take on a queer feeling in the stomach and also to ask agitated questions about the rules. We looked at ourselves in a mirror and realised how stupid it all was. We looked, and felt, abject fools in our pantaloons. If only we had listened to the cricket legislators – and one of them, dear 'Nummy' Deane, was mournfully reflecting at the doorway the incalculable harm this baseball game would do to cricket. I remember thinking that might be inconsequential to the harm it was now about to do us.

Sheepishly, very sheepishly, we slunk through the gate and ran on the field. The roar that went up circled around Johannesburg, and before it reached the Wanderers again we were already getting the 'bird' in approved baseball style. Any cricket barracking is childish in comparison.

And the opposition! Never could a team have looked more capable. They bristled with skill and efficiency, and to give the complete flavour had a full American battery – not full in any alcoholic sense, but in comprising an American pitcher and an American catcher. They would, we felt, simply blind us with American science and small talk.

We began to warm up, as one does before a baseball game. It might have been better if we had not, for catches were mulled, throws were wild, the barracking became even more intense, and it was quite obvious the American battery were sniggering at us.

We won the toss, went to bat and the 'game' was on. In as much time as it takes for an American battery to go through all the baffling mumbo-jumbo of nine throws we were out. Nine times did the American colossus turn his back on the battery, wheel about and let the ball go with the piercing speed of a bullet. Nine times did the Australian batters swing furiously at the ball and nine times did the ball go unmolested over the centre of the little white slab. Nine successive strikes, three batters out, side out!

The mobs howled their derision.

The Australians went to field, feeling all thumbs in their gloves. Cricketers who had never raised a nervous eyebrow before Test crowds of 60,000 felt wobbly in their pantalooned knees as base-ballers. A high soaring hit went out to McCabe at centre field. For one frightening moment he looked as if he would fling the glove aside and catch with his bare hands. Remembering, quickly, that the game was the thing, he did not. He went for the 'fly' in approved style and mulled it. Transvaal a man on second base. Brown let a ball go between his legs, a frightful mull, Transvaal one on first and third. A smashing three-bagger and Transvaal had two home in the first five minutes of the game.

Richardson doffed his catching mask and came out to give his men a pep talk. Transvaal coaches on the side line, as baseball entitled them to do, said rude and personal things, very rude and very personal, about Australians in general. Our reserves, O'Reilly and Oldfield, who should have been filling similar coaching positions and combating this propaganda from the side-line, crept further from view under the scoring bench. In this they had the envy of their comrades on the field.

Transvaal got no more home that innings. We got none home in our next three. If truth will out in the face of discomfiture, we did not even get a batter to first base. Curse that mail-boat, we thought, for not running in time! Curse ourselves for asking to play this fool game!

Then happened the miracle. I must preface its description by referring again to the American battery. Sly winks and nods and mystic signs ran from one to the other like Neon signs on Broadway. This was aided and abetted by the catcher, who expressed rather strong and pungent opinions about Australians and their antecedents directly into the ear of the Australians.

He went just too far. To a 'strike' against Darling, he held the ball forward under the Australian's nose and said something like this: 'Saay, you horn-woggled son of a guy! Help yer'self to an eyeful of this lil' white pill. Saay, dat's what youse suppos' to hit, guy. Wassa matter wid youse Aussie lallapoloosas?'

Let no one say that what followed was not cricket. It was not cricket we were playing, and what Darling did was evidently good baseball tactics. He gave the Yankee a contemptuous look, leaned over and spat viciously on the ball!

That marked the turning point of the game. The very next ball Darling made a mighty soaring hit far out over the heads of the out-fielders. Amid tremendous enthusiasm, he sped round the whole circuit. Australia, one home. Spurred by this, O'Reilly and Oldfield crept cautiously out from beneath the scorer's table and ventured to the coaching positions on the side-line.

'Keep it up, lads, keep it up,' quietly called O'Reilly. 'We can do it again, we can do it again,' apologetically cooed Oldfield, and, though decidedly poor, and not at all meaty, this at least marked a barracking beginning for Australia.

Barnett showed that the Australians could certainly do it again. In approved baseball style he moved into the next ball from the American pitcher. A full-blooded swing kissed the ball fairly and squarely with the juiciest part of the club and away, away, higher and higher soared the ball until it was almost lost to sight.

'Shades of Babe Ruth!' said the American pitcher. 'By the torch of the lil' ole Statoo of Liberty, what a heck of a smite,' said the American catcher.

Barnett did not have to dash helter-skelter around the bases. The umpire signalled him an undisputed home run and he ambled sedately along the circuit, touching his cap to the unstinted roars of applause. Australia two home!

A thousand pities there were no runners on bases to capitalise further two such beautiful hits, but that was forgotten in the next few minutes when the baseball rabbits came up to bat. There was not shivering at the knees now. Each came forward with supreme confidence.

McCabe drove one sweetly through the covers for a two-bagger; Brown hooked one gloriously for another two-bagger; I hit one over what would have been the bowler's head for a three-bagger; Grimmett tapped one to the covers for a quick single – pardon, a first base – Richardson played a magnificent on-drive for a two-bagger, and Australians scurried round the bases like ants about a disturbed ant-hill.

On their coaching mounds O'Reilly and Oldfield reached new-found heights of baseball barracking-cum-coaching.

'What a sissy lot of ball players, who taught you mugs the game,' roared O'Reilly. 'You'll never get us out, never get us out; put on a new bowler,' chanted Oldfield. In the excitement O'Reilly ventured on the field of play and was hurriedly removed to his mound by the umpire.

I shall not dwell much longer on that game. The further it went, the greater the heights the Australians found and the lower went the Transvaalers.

The cause was not difficult to discover. Cricketers who had had their eye trained all the summer applied cricketing tactics to base-ball. They fielded, threw and batted as if in a cricket game.

Only one mistake was made in the later stages, and that through ignorance. Another skier went out to McCabe at centre-field. Remembering his last dropped catch, McCabe placed his whole body between the ball and the ground. Determination was written all over him and when he made the catch he delightedly, in cricket fashion, threw the ball happily up and indulged in a series of little catches – the while a Transvaal player on first base moved to home!

In the seventh innings the pride and glory of Transvaal baseball struck their colours. Disgraced and dishevelled, the American battery gave way to another combination. They felt themselves able to cope with anything baseball sent along, but cover shots, pulls, drives and other cricketing shots had them nonplussed.

The end justified all that had gone before. A soaring hit went out to left field in Transvaal's final innings. A little figure twisted and turned, manoeuvring to judge the catch. It was coach Grimmett. We held our breath as the ball began to come down. Transvaal had two on bases. If this catch was mulled they might yet snatch the game out of the fire.

Grimmett was not dismayed. He gave not a thought to all the coaching he had given the team; not a thought, even, to the ethics of the game. He ignored his gloved left hand, shot up a bare right hand and made the most sensational one-handed catch of the cricket, baseball or matrimonial season. The game was over. Australia had won 12–3.

Going off the field, a dispirited but sporting American battery shook Richardson warmly by the hand.

'Your guys,' said the broken-hearted catcher, 'have put the big ball game back at least ten years in this here burg.'

Delighted Transvaal cricket legislators pressed us to keep our Wanderers socks as a souvenir. We accepted gladly. Next day from Perth, Western Australia, came a 48-word cablegram at 1/8½ a word asking us to play another baseball game there on the way east. We declined, as we did other invitations to play again in Cape Town. The Australian Eleven had played its first and last game of baseball. We knew enough about beginners' luck to recognise it when we saw it!

CHAPTER FOUR   *Style and the Man*

IF WE EXCEPT TENNIS, WITH Crawford as its masterly and graceful exponent, I think it would be difficult to refute that style and character belong more to the individual in cricket than in any other game known to man. If you see a class golfer play an approach shot to the flag, you have seen an approach shot as it should be played by most class golfers in any part of the world at a given time. The movements in a golf stroke are circumscribed; the feet are stationary because the ball is lying still, waiting to be hit in the one direction. To be true, there is a heel movement in the back-swing and the follow-through, but perhaps I could best illustrate my point by asking who would expect a Cotton to face about when addressing a ball, put his left foot on the wrong side of the ball and give it a leg-glance flick in the direction of the hole?

Similarly with Rugby. If a centre three-quarter breaks through in an international at Twickenham he does so by thrust, quick running, swerve or side-step, and that is precisely how a centre would go about breaking through in a match played, for instance, at Newlands, Sydney or Auckland. In cricket it is somewhat different. Thousands of people throughout the world bowl leg-breaks, but none do so with a style or delivery exactly the same. I once saw a pleasant fellow named Maynard bowl leg-breaks in the Victorian country town of Benalla. He began his run to the wickets from the direction of cover and, as if this were not baffling enough, he delivered the ball with his right hand from his left ear – that is, he bowled with his right arm across the back of his neck. This might sound very confusing, but not half so confusing, I'll wager, as trying to play a ball when unaware from which part of a man's anatomy it is going to emerge. Added to that, Maynard bowled a remarkably good length.

It is not with bowling, however, that I wish to make my point, though I could advance many rare individualists in O'Reilly, Grimmett, Larwood, McDonald, Tate and a dozen others. I was thinking more of batting and, particularly, the cover drive, for in such a drive by Hammond, Macartney, Kippax, Bradman or one of many others, including the merest tyro, you see a stroke that is at once the personal possession of the exploiter.

The fundamentals do not vary. Due observance must be paid to the niceties and the proprieties of swing, footwork, timing and the rest. The essentials of batting art just do not allow themselves to be put on one side, but it is in the execution and the interpretation of these parts that the whole becomes so vitally individual.

Hammond never looks anybody else other than the person set out in *Wisden* as Hammond, Mr W. R. (Gloucestershire), born in Kent, June 19, 1903. Put Hammond on an area with a hundred other batsmen playing a cover drive and you would know him immediately. So, too, with Duleepsinhji, Paynter, Woolley, Leyland, Sutcliffe, Robins (who plays a cover drive past square leg with more confidence than any batsman I know!) and a host of other Englishmen. All these, like the prodigal son, can be seen and recognised from afar.

If you were to come suddenly upon a game in Sydney from behind the towering concrete rampart that is the Members' Stand (withstanding the temptation, meanwhile, to look at the detailed scoring board, which even flares a light against the name of the fieldsman, contrasting with those in England, where the batsman is only a mere cipher). If, then, you were to happen upon a game in such a fashion, the merest glance at the batsman playing a stroke would tell you immediately whether he was Kippax, Bradman, Ponsford, McCabe, Macartney, Barnes or any of the Australians whose game has been bred upon individuality.

The style of such men lives and dies with them. This is not to say we will never see their equal again, for that is the trap in which many critics entangle themselves when they argue that a particular generation bred better cricketers than another. The point is that those who follow might in every degree be as graceful and as capable, but along different lines. It is because of this that cricket is so individual a game. Great players have their own interpretations and live their cricket lives according to themselves.

Once upon a time I played in a charity cricket game with Kippax. We were a team of fellows who had represented Australia, most of

us at the sophisticated stage when we could look back rather
humorously at the time when we took ourselves and the game
rather seriously. The good-natured chaffing in the dressing-room
contrasted with that laden atmosphere of grim and serious nationalism we all had known so well in our Test days, and, in between
creaking of the joints, there were those among us who fell pensively
to wondering whether the first ball might not be too straight,
whether the wicket might not prove too fast (it was notoriously a
slow one), whether our eyesight might not be too hazy, and then,
hope surging cheekily, whether fortune would be kind enough to
allow a stroke or two to revive the glories of other days.

Kippax was no stranger to me. I knew him more than passing
well, for he was in the full bloom of his artistic beauty when I came, a
diffident and tremulous youth, into the same club side. For many a
pleasant season after that I was privileged to enjoy from the other
batting end the close intimacy of his wristy stroke-making.

He was more than a dozen years past his best in this charity game,
but time had jogged along with him on friendly terms. He retained
his slim, willowy figure and spectators almost forgot the period of
elapsed time as Kippax moved down the pavilion steps and strode
out to bat with a characteristic little give in his right leg that faintly
suggested a limp. Characteristically, too, he gave his right leg-guard a
superstitious little tug in his first step on the ground, and even in the
manner in which he took block, marking it with a deft sprig in the toe
of his boot, there were all the evidences of his own particular style.

Kippax's stance at the wickets was an upright, graceful one. To
the very first ball sent him by an obliging bowler (this match was
first a charity one and then a friendly affair) he allowed the ball to go
almost into the wicket-keeper's hands before he glided across and
back, his bat sweeping down like a scimitar from the back of his
neck, and with a glorious, wristy, caressing flick he sent the ball
speeding down through the slips with a delectable late-cut.

The roar that greeted this stroke enveloped the ground. This was
the one stroke everybody wanted from Kippax; this was the stroke
for which he was famous on every Australian ground, the fast
wickets of which lend themselves so admirably to such behind the
wicket strokes, and here, off the very first ball, Kippax had given
every member of that crowd his heart's desire. Had he come back
into a game years later, even as a gouty, rheumatic old gentleman
(and heaven forbid such a fate awaits my old club companion!),
everybody who had known him in his heyday would expect, because
of the nature of things, that his first action at the wickets would be a
sweeping, graceful late-cut.

Kippax and this stroke walked to the wickets together in much the
same manner as did Walter Hammond and his magnificent stroke

185

through the covers off his back or front foot. Most hard-headed Australian batsmen were quite prepared to concede Kippax all the glory and the individuality of the late-cut (some also know this stroke as the back-cut, but I think the terms are synonymous). These other Australians reasoned, and with some logic to support them, that the late-cut was a risky business at the best of times, leaving the batsman open through a slight misjudgment to a catch at the wickets or in the slips and, also, to playing the ball on to his stumps. Then they added, and this with the finality of a man who expects the utmost value for his money, that the man invariably on the boundary at third-man generally turned the worth of the stroke into an insignificant single run. No, said these worthies. It is a pretty shot, and all that, but not a payable proposition.

Kippax was somewhat inclined to agree with them. When youngsters came to him, seeking an explanation of the mystery of his cutting art, his advice usually to them was to forget that such a stroke existed. He could not cut it off from his own stroke domicile, but, knowing its dangers and how often it had cost him his wicket, he was careful to see that through him others did not give it sanctuary.

It was true that the cut often did cost Kippax his wicket. A knowing bowler will deliberately bait a batsman on his strength, witness of this being the number of times McCabe has accepted and succumbed to the challenge on his powerful hook stroke. Tate was one who 'fed' Kippax on his cut, and it could be claimed, with figures to support it, that this liking for spectacular, behind-the-wicket strokes made of Kippax a rather indifferent Test performer. He made only one century against England, in 1928–29, and did not make any against South Africa.

He was never one, however, to set the huge score as his ultimate aim. Once he so far forgot himself as to make 315 not out against Queensland on his home wicket in Sydney, which he loved dearly; the next season he indulged himself in a phenomenal world's record last wicket stand of 307 with Hooker (Kippax 260 not out and Hooker 62), but generally Kippax was quite content to spend his riches lavishly without seeking in return the monument of a record. He assessed his innings by the pleasure it gave spectators and himself in the execution of classical strokes; he preferred artistic quality to mundane quantity, and it was because Kippax's game revolved in such a high classical sphere that it was torn to shreds so much by the bodyline holocaust. No Australian was more rudely upset in his style of play that season than Kippax. Even in ordinary club games he was unrecognisable from his real self. His style and conception of batting could not accommodate themselves to the realism of walking to the wickets with the ducking proclivities of the gentleman who offers his head at the fair for all and sundry to shy at it.

There is no better teacher or coach than emulation, and Kippax was at his best when a 14-year-old lad in A. A. Jackson began to play Sydney senior cricket in short trousers. The young of New South Wales have always been fortunate in their models. Summer comes earlier and with more resolution to NSW than it does to more southerly Melbourne, and players of the Mother State are revelling in warmth, with a resultant effect upon their stroke play, when their brethren down south are still endeavouring furiously to rout the cold of winter out of their limbs.

Down through the years the young of New South Wales have had a complexity of brilliant styles to emulate in the Gregorys, Duff, Trumper, Macartney, Taylor, Andrews, Kippax, McCabe, Bradman, Brown and the rest. Noble, Bardsley, Collins and others were on view for the more sober-minded, and New South Wales also moulded its youngsters by inviting promising players to share the cricket ground nets with the famous.

Jackson took Kippax as his guide and emulated him to such an extent that many considered he outshone his master. Jackson was only 19 when he made 164 in his first Test against England – two of the bowlers were Larwood and Tate and a third was the genial Somerset farmer, J. C. White, who baffled many with his charming simplicity and impeccable length. Possibly never has a Test innings exceeded Jackson's 164 for sheer artistry and wide variety of strokes.

I like to ponder on the beautiful yet poignant picture of the tall, slim Jackson in his first Test match – a mere slip of a boy, his fair, tousled hair waving in the slight breeze of Adelaide Oval, one of the prettiest of all cricketing grounds. He came with trepidation into his first Test match – every player does – but Jackson did not show it as he back, square cut and pulled Larwood, as he drove Tate and then glided yards up the wicket to hit White with lofty drives to the outfield. Bradman, a year older than Jackson, was also then beginning his big deeds against England, but Bradman went on to the heights, while the poignancy of Jackson is that death took rare and beautiful genius from the game when he was only 23.

Jackson died in Brisbane when the bodyline rumpus was at its height. His body came back to Sydney, his home city, on the same train as the warriors from the Fourth Imbroglio. Ill-health had denied his culture to the game for several years before his death, and England in 1930 saw only a shadow of the Jackson of Adelaide in 1929.

Of those English and Australian players who made centuries in their first Test, only R. E. Foster (287) and C. Bannerman (165 not out) exceeded Jackson's total, but he was the youngest in history to record the feat. Compton was 20, Hutton and Pataudi 22, Ranjitsinhji 24, Duleepsinhji and Foster 25, Leyland and George Gunn

28, Sutcliffe 30 and Dr W. G. Grace 32 (the latter was advanced in years when Tests commenced). It is to be noted that the three Indians who played for England succeeded in this most unusual feat.

Of the Australians, apart from Jackson, Duff was 22, Graham 23, Ponsford 24, Bannerman 25, Hartigan 29 and Collins 31.

Like Kippax, Jackson held his bat high on the handle, giving him a free, swinging bat with the very maximum of arc. Hardstaff, of Nottinghamshire, was the only other class batsman I noticed who held the bat so high (I exclude, of course, the out-and-out sloggers in the game), and this long swing induced Kippax and Jackson to play somewhat at the pitch of the ball – quite a necessary stroke in trade, I consider, on true true, fast Australian wickets, off which the ball rarely shifts, as the term has it. On their first tour to England together in 1930, Kippax accommodated his style to the different wickets, but Jackson was not quite so happy.

The similarity of style between Kippax and Jackson is shown by the photographs in this book depicting various players in their cover drive. That both played somewhat at the pitch of the ball is shown by the manner in which each has gone forward on to the heel of his left foot, throwing the body back from the pitch of the ball. This slight throwing of the body back gave Kippax and Jackson a bigger arc than others for their cover drive swing, and each picture tells truly how wrist-work has come gloriously into the stroke. This is noted best by the manner in which wrist-work has caused the face of the bat to change over.

The individuality of Macartney was fully shown in his cover drive, and it was the artistic individuality of the man that caused a ripple of delight to run around the ground whenever his name appeared on the scoring board. There is a photograph which shows Macartney leaving the Sydney Cricket Ground Pavilion on his way to bat. See there the enthusiasm which has brought men to their feet, their faces aglow with sheer delight at the prospect of witnessing their hero in thrilling action. Lucky is the man who can mean so much to his fellows, even in sport, and fortunate is the game which can produce such a man.

Macartney had wrists of steel. He was past his prime when I came to the game, but on several occasions in minor games I was privileged to be at the other end from him. I liked him best when he threatened the life of the bowler, the other batsman and the umpire by hitting the ball back straight like a bullet. He had a habit, I noticed, of twirling his bat aloft before settling down to his stance. It also seemed as if he were charging his piece of willow, for it came forward to meet the ball full of snap, punch and cheeky audacity. As I saw him, it appears to me that with such vital wrist-power he had no need to indulge in a long, raking back-swing to get force.

His photograph will show that he held the bat higher on the handle than Hammond and Bradman. He has moved up the wicket to make the ball of drivable length, getting his body over the top of the ball, and then he has got down into it, not so much with all his body, as Hammond does in his photographs, but with his wrists and powerful shoulders. The short length of the follow-through shows that where others relied upon the full swing of the arc to give them power, Macartney obtained this with the punch of his wrists.

I like to study this cover drive of Macartney, because I think it depicts perfectly the individual style of the man. Jackson, it will be noticed, is somewhat down in his cover drive, but I do not think I have seen any class batsman get down as low to his drive as this photograph shows Macartney doing – the one of Constantine, I think, shows more of a forward square cut than a cover drive.

The connoisseur will dote on these photographs, noting here and there the differences in which great men went about their work; but I challenge anybody to point out even a minute transgression of style in the photograph of Hammond playing a cover drive with Oldfield behind the wickets.

Once upon a time a good batsman, who possibly did not play for Australia simply because study took him from us to an English University, invited me to accompany him to the practice of the school eleven of which he was Headmaster. His plan was for us to bat in the middle against the boys, and he asked me to stop the game and lecture whenever I thought a happening warranted it.

He played a perfect off-drive. It cleaved mid-off and cover and cleaved the juniors, also, who were playing on a field afar off. It looked, at one stage, as if the ball might take a brick wall with it. This, indeed, was the perfect stroke. I hurriedly stopped the game and most enthusiastically lectured – a lecture, incidentally, which extolled the Head's virtues to the boys – on the timing, wrist-power, foot-work, application of weight and placing. I rather thought I did myself and the Head exceedingly proud.

At the end of it all the Headmaster inquired whether I had finished. I nodded. 'Well, now,' said he, 'I will tell you what was wrong with that stroke.'

That man was hard to please. I found it difficult to believe that a ball that had gone so sweetly, so fast and so far could have had anything wrong in its stroking, but not even my Headmaster friend (I hope I am sure) can fault this perfect photograph of Hammond in a cover drive. This, to my mind, has no peer in cricket photography, and ranks with the exquisite Beldam shots of Trumper in the full flight of his driving glory.

If a cricket lover never had the good fortune to see Trumper he could tell immediately by the Beldam photographs that here, indeed, was a classically artistic player. Trumper has jumped out to drive, different from the other strokes here portrayed, with the exception of Bradman's, and all batsmen will agree that this is the one stroke more than others in which there must be perfect co-ordination of mind, muscle and timing.

Trumper has gone some yards down to meet the ball. This, in itself, has made perfect timing more difficult and an absolute essential, but there is not the slightest suggestion of timidity with Trumper on this score. He has committed every inch of himself to the stroke, caring not a particle for the stumps and the wicket-keeper behind him. His swing is at its fullest, the wrists cocked at the top of his back-swing; his head and shoulders are on the perfect plane of balance, his eyes looking at the ball with one full eye and half the other, so that his shoulders are side-on and not full face to the ball. Note, too, how perfectly he has his weight at this stage of the stroke on his back leg, freeing the front leg to move to the ball.

The finish of the stroke is a dream – the perfect follow-through with the bat completing the full arc of swing, the head and shoulders still on the same plane, the erect body, with the bat hitting against the stiff left leg and the weight magnificently brought forward on to the front foot, the left toe pointing to cover and not up the wicket, for this would bring his left shoulder around, throwing his swing out of its groove. The moment of impact has to be imagined, but the photograph suggests it as clearly as day. The ball has been hit within a few bare inches of his left toe, Trumper's body and eyes over the top of it, his wrists clenching and stiffening at the moment of impact for the first and only time in his swing – and then the left hand taking the bat through.

The rhapsodies of the old-timers are not necessary to convince me that Trumper was the Prince of Batsmen. They might talk at length of how Trumper triumphed when his side needed him most or the wicket was at its worst, but cold figures on paper are drab things when considered in the light of immortality that these two photographs throw upon the cricket world. They speak truly, as mere, metallic figures fail to do, of Trumper's poetic grace and art. Such photographs should be framed and hung in every pavilion in the world for players to see and pay homage to, and seek inspiration from, as they take the field. A coach is incomplete without them.

So, too, should such distinction be paid to the masterpiece of Hammond, particularly, and Oldfield. If once you have seen Hammond make a cover drive the vision will live with you for all time. See Bradman, McCabe, Kippax, Hobbs, Jackson and the other stylists in a cover drive and there you have, in essence, the perfect demonstration of that player's skill and style, but none will show you the stroke at its greatest better than Hammond.

This photograph of him almost lives, so true is it a depiction of Hammond's grace, power, correctness and artistry. His feet are in magnificent position. His back foot pushes his weight against a rigid left foot, and note most carefully how he takes that weight like a dancer on the ball of his foot. His heel has nothing to do with the case, even being raised off the turf, which is as it should be, for a movement on to the heel throws the weight back. Wrist-power in its most glorious usage is seen in this Hammond stroke. The coach could talk for an hour on the lessons of this photograph, but it shows nothing better than Hammond's use of his powerful shoulders. His head and shoulders are on the perfect plane of balance, his body over the ball. By timing, balance, wrists (note how the face of the bat has turned over), shoulders and footwork Hammond has given the ball every ounce of his weight. One can almost hear the ball bouncing off the pickets.

The photograph shows also the art and grace of Oldfield behind the wickets. The angle of his fingers and thumbs and his graceful position, generally, contrast vividly with other wicket-keepers in the series. Oldfield's style is also shown admirably in the Macartney stroke.

The Bradman stroke is hardly a cover drive. His head suggests more an off-drive, but the stroke demonstrates his own particular individuality of style, a style of utilitarianism rather than flourishes and flounces. Like Hammond, his left leg is on the ball of the foot, though his weight is not so far forward. Unlike the others, it will be noticed that the face of Bradman's bat has not changed over in the follow-through, but there is the clear and unmistakable evidence of how Bradman has brought terrific force and speed into the stroke with his right hand and shoulder. Much of Bradman's power, in contrast with others, came from the velocity of his swing.

The Constantine photograph speaks for itself. He, also, has the long handle of Trumper, Kippax and Jackson. There is about this stroke a whiff of the refreshing personality which Constantine took to all places with him.

There is, as I wrote earlier, much to be said for emulation. Kippax moulded his style on Trumper and Jackson followed Kippax. Visual education has been given rapid recognition, particularly in military training, over the past few years. A boy will watch a movie with avid interest, whereas the coach's eternal 'Do's' and 'Don'ts' oftentimes bore him and kill his interest in a game. I have often wondered why the cricket powers that be have not collected a movie-picture library of the giants of the game in actual play (not at the nets), thus preserving for all time a visual record of the individual arts that have coursed richly through this game of ours.

CHAPTER FIVE

Snippets from an English Diary – 1938

Nᴏɴᴇ ᴋɴᴇᴡ ᴍᴏʀᴇ ᴛʜᴀɴ sʜᴇ. She had a hand in everybody's business, a finger and thumb, so to speak, in every pie. Let there be a murder, a suicide, a divorce entangling a peer and a chorus girl and off she would go, chattering and prattling away down to the merest gossipy and sordid detail.

Strange, I thought, that men should lavish such loving care and attention upon so inhuman a monster. She had no looks to speak of, was utterly devoid of soul, and yet no Cleopatra, no Lucretia Borgia or Juliet had man pay her more attention. Someone rushed to her if she uttered the slightest whimper; somebody was always at her beck and call, eager and ready to sense and decipher her every mood.

I had seen newspaper lords crowd over her and hang upon her every syllable, but that meant nothing to her. In her cold, rasping, metallic way she ambled on and on, not necessarily believing in what she said nor caring whose feelings she hurt.

I had often wondered at all this, never dreaming that some day she would mean to me what she so obviously meant to others . . . but now the time had come when she had me, too, at her mercy. I could not conceal my thoughts and feelings from her, and the wretched hag knew that she had me conquered. It was so obvious I was entreating her to speak the one magic word which would mean so much to me, the word which would open up a new world.

Lord's, Old Trafford and Canterbury; Cairo, Naples and London; dinners and receptions at the House of Commons, the Savoy,

Piccadilly and Mansion House; operas, theatres, dances and night clubs; St. Andrews, Wimbledon and the Riviera; Scotland, Ireland, the Mountain of Mourne and Glendalough; Buckingham Palace, Hyde Park, Regent Street, the Strand.

And that glorious English countryside of which Wells wrote, 'its firm yet gentle lines of hill and dale, its ordered confusion of features, its deer parks and downland, its castles and stately houses, its hamlets and old churches, its farms and rickets and barns and ancient trees, its pools and ponds and shining threads of rivers, its flower-starred hedgerows, its orchards and woodland patches, its village greens and kindly inns.'

All this to give or withhold and, yet knowing it, she continued on her idle way, chattering of markets and stock and such inconsequential trifles, or else lapsing into long spells of moody silence. Four years before I had been ignored; would it be the same again?

She began to speak. An attendant rushed to her. 'The Australian team for England was chosen in Melbourne to-day and it is —.' Like wildfire the news spread through the office and newspapermen came running from all directions. A special edition was waiting on this. 'Dah dit dit dah,' she said, and the slave who never left her wrote down B. She 'dah-ed' and 'dit-ditted' with great fury now and quickly, and ever so slowly, the tyro typed 'r-a-d-m-a-n, B-a-d-c-o-c-k, B-a-r-n-e-s, B-a-r-n-e-t-t, B-r-o-w-n, C-h-i-p-p-e-r-f-i-e-l-d.'

A pause, then, as if to emphasise that she had us completely in her spell. If she spluttered across from C to H all was lost, for no D was in the running and F was in between. Boating on the Thames, the ruins of Pompeii, snow-capped Vesuvius, the sunsets of the Indian Ocean, dancing on the boat-deck at night, Cambridge, Oxford, the Highlands of Scotland, the Lake district . . . !

She spoke again. 'Dah dit dah dit, dit dit, dah dit, dah dah dit . . .' We crowded over the operator. He typed F and an I and an N and a G.

We waited no longer. My acclaiming fellow-newspapermen and I turned our backs on the fickle and spluttering direct Press line from Melbourne. A toast was waiting across the way. A tour of England lay ahead.

Tales at Perth:

News of Hitler's march into Austria coincided with our entry into Perth from the east and the return of the Australian Rugby team from the west of the Indian Ocean. They painted lurid pictures of the state of unrest in Europe and looked their doubts that we would not get further on our tour than Perth, which, if the worst had to be faced, is the most hospitable and most beautiful city in Australia in which to be stranded. The Spanish Civil War blacked out their ship in the Mediterranean, which at that time appeared a fearful and ominous state of affairs. They went east, we went west to Europe – one tour-weary, the other tour-happy with an apprehensive eye on Europe.

On Playing at Colombo:

Many wilfully dodge the Colombo game. The thought of playing cricket as the equatorial sun streams over the pavilion brings an imaginary strain or convenient illness as the ship nears Colombo. There are frightening things to be read in the cabin about the dangers of the equator: (a) Every portion of the body must be covered from the insidious rays of the sun; (b) on no account must violent exercises be indulged in in the tropics; and (c) the shade must always be sought. Reading these and thinking ahead of the match at Colombo, one falls to wondering on how many burials one has seen at sea or, evading that, whether sunstroke brings on insanity.

It seems suicidal even to walk on the Colombo ground, let alone run. One goes to sleep the night before Colombo, convinced that one must wake on the morrow with an acute attack of appendicitis.

The strange peace of a ship at anchor after nine days of toiling up the Indian Ocean wakes you on the big day. A darting hand somewhat sadly tells a tale of no pain in the appendix region. A huge, red ball is just bursting itself in the magnificent splendour of a tropical sunrise over the Colombo hills, and floating up from below come the jabbering voices of natives as they paddle their craft to and fro. At the cabin door is a smart, smiling Cingalese tailor who wants to measure you – and does – for the silk tropical suit that will be back to you before the ships sails at midnight. And fits splendidly.

There is a sting already in the sun as, before breakfast, you stroll on deck and idly watch slips of native lads dive from the very top deck of the big liner for shillings thrown into the blue sea far below. The friendly members of the local cricket committee are soon on board, and with a resigned sigh you pack your cricket togs and trudge down the gangway. As the launch speeds off across the harbour you look back at the ship and wave, sadly, to the girl you danced with last night. She, you notice with some venom, does not venture even a toe out of the shade.

The caw-caws of hundreds of crows and the honk-honk of innumerable cars meet the launch at the jetty. Your first impression of the locals is that they drive with a foot on the accelerator and a hand on the horn, and the thought occurs that, if you don't mind your step, there is more than a fair chance of a car collecting you before the equatorial sun.

In quick time you have been fitted with a pith helmet for the game, visited the Galle Face Hotel and walked on to the beautiful Colombo ground with ten others of your party.

A lot of tosh is written about the Colombo game; a lot of old-wives' tales handed down from generation to generation. Brown and I husbanded ourselves over a century opening partnership, and then solicitously ushered ourselves back to the cool of the pavilion, content not to try or trust the majestical sun too far. Badcock and Hassett went further and made a century apiece – a feat unheard of in these Colombo games by tourists passing through.

The player who wilfully misses the Colombo game misses much. A huge awning breathes and sighs over glamorous and colourful Cingalese women, who alternate the wave of a fan with the flash of gleaming, smiling teeth. The grass at their sandalled feet is green with the luscious abundance of the tropics.

Colombo is the only ground in the world where the spectators barrack themselves and not the players. At least, it was so this day. If a dandy showed himself in front of the pavilion, dressed in his Sunday best, spectators began to chant in unison 'oi, oi, oi,' like the final 'oi' in the Lambeth Walk. The cry spread along the pavilion and around the ground until the strutting dandy suddenly lost his nerve and darted to lose himself in the crowd. The whole ground rocks with laughter.

It is grand fun and so also is it grand fun when the limb of a tree overlooking the ground suddenly wearies of the many using it as a free grandstand. The limb creaks in its splitting, there are agitated shouts and into the ground is catapulted a sprawling, heaving mass of youngsters. 'Oi, oi, oi' delightedly chant the spectators, and again the ground rocks with laughter, with none of the incoming spectators, happily, hurt.

Play at Colombo if you get the chance. And may you top the day off as pleasantly as Brown and I did when, with the young lady off the ship (later to become my wife), we wheeled quietly along that night to dance at the Galle Face. The soft pit-pat of the ricksha boys' feet was the only sound on the night, a night wrapped in stars and tied with a new moon.

On Passing Through Aden:

We passed through Aden this day – Allah be praised!

Cairo and a Guide:

It is odd to see familiar English faces and caps in a cricket game at the Gezira Club, half-way, so to speak, between England and Australia. The play suggested, as such touring teams so often find, that the visitors play cricket by day and play, in a sense, against the lavish hospitality of their hosts at night. It's hard to make both ends meet on tour. We were given a grand reception by an Egyptian guide at the Pyramids. 'Aussies? Well, strike me handsome! Too — right! Me spika da Aussie language, dinkum, bonza, strewth —' and a host of others not so fit for publication. He had not spoken the 'Aussie language', he told us, since the last War. He was so pleased at being able to speak it again that he charged us only three times the usual guide fee! When he was given it he looked somewhat sadly at us, as if to suggest we were not the men our fathers were. Perhaps we weren't!

'Ou est Papa?'

A strange team of hooded, long-cloaked Australians emerged gingerly from the funicular-railway at the top of Vesuvius. As protection against the cold, the garments were handed out on the railway. We looked like a procession of monks. It was bitterly cold, with snow on the Alps, and only a week before we had been steaming in the heat of the Red Sea. With many misgivings, we trod carefully along to the step-ladder and went into the crater to peer dubiously down the cone. We could not have trodden more carefully on the crackly surface had it been a sticky wicket, with us on the fielding side. Sulphur fumes and vapours caused by the mixture of hot and cold air gave a large French family of tourists many frights as it kept constantly losing Papa in the mist. Excited calls of 'Papa, papa, ou est Papa?' kept echoing around Vesuvius. It was difficult to know who looked most relieved at the end of the journey – the intact French family or the Australian Eleven. Pompeii was much more peaceful.

On Not Being Bradman:

Four truants, sitting on a Nice boulevard, sipped a light French beer and thought how pleasant it was not to be Bradman. At that moment he was sipping a cup of tea with the committee of the

Riviera tennis tournament. The tournament was not uninteresting.
King Gustav of Sweden played a stately game, and players of both
sexes contributed to a gay, bizarre atmosphere. The big attraction,
however, was Bradman. Nice made a grand fuss of him and escorted
him in numbers to afternoon tea. It was always the same with
Bradman. Wherever the team went he was the centre of attraction.
A crowd walked with him down the Strand, hundreds gathered at
railway stations just to catch a glimpse of him. Though the Australian team was invited to tea, four thought they would not be missed
and went on a tour of the Riviera instead. There were no language
difficulties. Four years before, in Paris, McCabe, O'Reilly and
Darling wanted to hire a taxi-driver to go to the races at Aux
Tromblee. McCabe tried his French first and failed; O'Reilly, a
school-teacher, took over with the air of easy assurance, but he, too,
failed. Darling, who knew no French, then gave a vivid imitation of
a jockey riding a close finish, saying, meanwhile, 'Aux Tromblee,
Aux Tromblee.' 'Oh, yes,' said the driver in fluent English, 'now I
understand. You want the racecourse.' We had a good day on the
Riviera – and not even our manager missed us from the tennis!

What's in a Name?

Badcock is dark in complexion, with gleaming black hair. Returning
in a bus from Monte Carlo with Barnes, Badcock was engaged in
conversation by an Italian. It was a one-sided conversation, as the
intruder, thinking Badcock was one of his countrymen, spoke in
Italian. Badcock's name for the rest of his cricketing life is 'Musso'.

Bradman and a Salute:

Governor Sir Charles Harrington and Bradman shared the salute at
Gibraltar. Sir Charles was a keen cricketing man, and we were the
envy of the ship one Sunday morning when a trim naval launch
pulled alongside and we were piped aboard with ceremony. Clear-
cut English faces and neat, service-like uniforms contrasted vividly
with those from across the Mediterranean way. Sir Charles invited
Bradman to stand with him as he took the salute from the Queen's
Own Regiment in a march past after church parade. It was a stirring
spectacle, particularly to Bradman. He was so carried away that his
hand shot up to his bared head and he, also, took the salute. 'I am
told,' he later apologised to the Governor, 'that I committed a
serious breach by saluting.' 'Don't you worry,' said Sir Charles, 'a
Bradman can get away with that.'

On Seeing England and London:

It is impossible to describe the effect that the mellowed English countryside with its soft lights, well-ordered hedges and fields and its countless hues of green, has for the first time upon Australian eyes long accustomed to gum trees, strong, glaring sunlight and paddocks undisturbed by fences for hundreds of acres. This soft, conserving light must surely be the reason why Englishmen still play the game when fifty. At that age the sap in the Australian has long since been chastened by the hot, drying sun of the Antipodes. The swift, noiseless train and the enchanting countryside carry on in a colourful dream to Waterloo – where the police erected barriers. The first step on London soil – station asphalt in this case – is the big moment in any Australian's life. It is good to see familiar English faces again, though those you knew in Australia have undergone a strange metamorphosis. G. O. Allen's face has lost the deep tan it had in Australia. He is clad, as are others, in the garb of the City – black coat, striped trousers, black Homburg hat and carrying a furled umbrella. This conventional London attire comes strangely at first to Australian eyes. R. H. Bettington, who went to Oxford from Parramatta, Sydney, and who was also in England at this time, tells the story of his wife, sister of the New Zealand captain, T. Lowry, and sister-in-law of A. P. F. Chapman, inducing him to celebrate his return to London by adopting the City garb. Bettington was somewhat dubious about it, but, going one day to pay a call to his old hospital, Guy's, he was inclined to tribute his wife's taste when the bus conductor paid him most unusual attention. At every opportunity the conductor made his way to Bettington and engaged him in conversation. Approaching Guy's, Bettington made to leave the bus and in a friendly manner told his new-found fan, so to term him, that he was just paying a visit to his old hospital. 'Old 'ospital?' said the conductor. 'Yes,' said Bettington, 'I trained here.' 'But, lumme, you ain't a doctor, are yer?' asked the conductor. 'Yes,' said Bettington. 'Lord luv us,' said the conductor, 'and 'ere ham hi thinkin' yer Victor McLaglen.'

On First Seeing Lord's:

A touring cricketer should jot down the impressions which crowd in on him when first he sees famous cricketing grounds. For years they have been delectable names to him, and as he reads about them, feeling intimate with their every characteristic, his mind boggles at the thought that some day he, too, will tread their sacrosanct turf. I grew up within five miles of the Sydney ground, and knew it well from the Hill as a youngster in the pristine days of Collins, Bardsley,

Hobbs, Gilligan and other heroes. We used to gaze in enthralment through the palings at the top of the Paddington mound as the players went to the nets on the Number Two ground and then, later, watched with an almost overpowering awe the umpires and players as they emerged for play from the mysterious and hallowed depths of the Members' Stand. Melbourne and Adelaide, which I knew first as a player, have each their own individual atmosphere, Adelaide, with its hills in the distance and immediate parklands and cathedral spires, possessing a beauty all its own among famous grounds. Brisbane is the sad sack of all Test grounds, lacking in everything but a paradise of a wicket. Johannesburg, Durban and Cape Town sparkle with distinctiveness – the latter surrounded by the incredible beauty of trees and Table Top, with a brewery peeping into the grounds for good measure – but it is Lord's, of all grounds, that holds most interest for the touring cricketer. I could not imagine cricket without Lord's; it is truly, as has been so often acclaimed, the mecca of the game, and one is filled with reverence and tradition as he enters the ground itself. Some have told me that they have been disappointed on first seeing Lord's. I cannot imagine why. To be true, it lacks the huge concrete stands of the Melbourne amphitheatre, and the Australian is at first struck by the absence of the towering scoring boards so common to all first-class Australian grounds. Everything that goes before in the trip through London – from Trafalgar Square, through Admiralty Arch, past Buckingham Palace with its Royal Standard and red-black attired sentries spanking it along the side railings, through Hyde Park – all this prepares one for the majestic grandeur and old-world charm of Lord's, dozing in the watery sunlight of a late April afternoon. Its Mound Stand is immaculately white; from the nursery nets in the distance comes the soft music of ball on willow to play around the aged face of the Long Pavilion, pleading with it to rouse from its winter hibernation and give its hoary benediction and indulgence to yet another cricket season. It must be grand to play in Lord's first game of the year. At this time the tourist is down in Worcester, listening to the peals from the adjacent cathedral. Lord's is all I ever expected it to be, brimful of years, tradition and ghosts. I hope it never changes, not even to taking unto itself a modern scoring board. I could not imagine, for instance, the huge Adelaide scoring board towering over Lord's. It would make the ground out of proportion. I listened to a very brilliant speech one evening at Lord's by our Right Hon R. G. Menzies, in which at a dinner, presided over by Lord Baldwin, he cleverly twitted the MCC for its unmodern conveniences. Most English grounds stand in need of useful scoring boards, but, please, not at Lord's! The clank-clank of the printing machine as it slowly turns out its scoring card, identifying batsmen and bowlers with their numerals on the meagre board, is part of the general Lord's set-up. I walked slowly around Lord's, looking into every nook and cranny, feeling even a familiarity with The Great One, Grace, as I peered down into the depths of the aged baths. With what vigour must he have splashed away here at the end of a long sunny day at the creases, a hundred or two behind his name – sorry, his number – and plenty of bathing room to take his bulk. I walked the Lord's outfield and saw not a soul in sight. I put a foot on the unprepared square of wicket and immediately groundsmen, messengers, net bowlers, printers and gentlemen in the dress of the city appeared gesticulating from all quarters of the ground. I saw no harm in what I did, testing the spring of the turf as a captain does when he pokes a forefinger into the wicket, but Lord's is Lord's and the wicket is holy, untouchable ground. I explained to an impressive looking gentleman that in Australia the wickets are torn to shreds in the off-season by football boots. He was not impressed. I left Lord's – very impressed. Nothing is more English than the manner in which the spectators parade the ground during the luncheon interval, gazing long and intently at the wicket, which is guarded off by ropes. A bell rings, everybody goes back to his seat (which is never molested, as far as I could see), and not a scrap of paper is left on the ground as the umpires and fieldsmen walk out. I am rather afraid this would not be practicable in Australia. Some spirit would be bound to attempt taking a piece of the wicket as a souvenir.

Bradman and an Admirer:

Bradman, who develops at each rising more and more into a magnificent speech-maker, told the story at a Royal Empire Society dinner in London of a letter he received from a West Indian admirer. 'Please allow me to make your acquaintance in the absence of a third person and in the presence of this letter. I have waited your advent to the West Indies with wild patience. I made your acquaintance ten years ago by reading about you in a newspaper. One day in an examination they asked: What is Australia famous for? I provoked laughter in the class-room by answering "cricketers".' Bradman's modesty would not allow him to quote more of the letter. One sentence ran: 'Mr Bradman, I love you. Will you promise in turn to love me?'

How McCormick Went Deaf:

Two records at Worcester in the opening match may never be broken. Bradman made his third successive double-century in the usual opening game of the tour against Worcestershire, and, for the other record, McCormick had the dubious feat of bowling 35 no-balls. Eight came in his first over, nine in his second. Nothing is more galling and annoying to the average bowler when, after putting all his cunning and spirit into a delivery, he hears the merciless no-ball call at his back. The hearty swing which the batsman makes might give him just the little spirit which he needs. Watch the average bowler if he is no-balled several times. More likely than not, he glares furiously and most ostentatiously paces his run back from the wicket. There was nothing like that about McCormick. He apologised profusely to umpire Baldwin. In the next game but one, against Leicestershire, McCormick bowled 15 no-balls. The opportunity provided by such an unusual happening was too good for one particularly fertile newspaper mind to pass. He wrote that Larwood made a special trip to Leicester to try and remedy McCormick's run to the wicket. That was untrue. We never saw Larwood at all in England, but why worry about facts if some faked story can be written with an unusual slant! McCormick probably got into his no-ball habit in the practice at Lord's before the tour started. He cut his run down while bowling at half-pace and found his steps all astray when it came to the real thing. Royal Worcester people gave Bradman a glorious piece to celebrate his three double centuries. The same firm also gave each member of the team a magnificent piece of plate, on which the signatures of the team were inscribed in gold lettering. A touring team receives many splendid gifts in England, nowhere more so than Worcester, home of china and gloves. McCormick, one of cricket's greatest wits, often after the Worcester match stared straight ahead when he was addressed by one outside the team. A fellow-Australian would explain that McCormick had gone deaf. To the solicitous enquirer, the Australian would further explain that the repeated call of 'no-ball' at Worcester had affected McCormick's hearing. All this time McCormick would stare ahead without the glimmer of a smile on his face.

High Jinks at Oxford:

Substituting as wicket-keeper against Oxford at Christ Church ground when Walker retired injured, I stumped three batsmen. It should have been only two. With the last man in and running eight yards from home, Bradman sent me a perfect return over the stumps. I caught it, ignored the stumps and threw the ball back to the bowler, Fleetwood-Smith. Bradman was nonplussed and wanted an explanation. 'I think,' said I, with inflated ego, the previous stumpings having quite obviously gone to my head, 'that I can stump this chap.' And bless me if I didn't, the very next Fleetwood-Smith ball! Retaining the ball, I asked my Oxford victims if they would oblige by autographing it, as I, myself, might have difficulty in believing this in the years to come. E. D. R. Eagar signed first and put an exclamation mark after his name; W. Murray-Wood signed next and put two exclamation marks; R. E. Whetherly, the last man in, signed last and put three exclamation marks. Which, I think, summed up the position nicely. The strangest sight I saw at Oxford was young men playing bowls on Magdalen green; the prettiest was a punt with two girl undergrads emerging from underneath the bridge on the winding Isis.

Cambridge Phenomena and Baths:

There were some magnificent spectacles at Cambridge , none more interesting than the 6 ft 3 in. O'Reilly trying to bathe in the smallest bath we had ever seen. Hassett was so impressed that he took a photograph of it. The Australian in England looked for showers, which is the national Australian bathing pastime and probably accounts for so many cricketers being bald. With the exception of Old Trafford and the Moore Park Golf Club, we looked in vain. The one at Moore Park was discovered by some explorer who wandered deep into the cloisters. When the shower was turned on the first contribution was dead and dusty insects. That shower had not been used much, which is not so strange if one knows of the English custom of baths. On most grounds it was a case of first off the field and undressed had the best bath. It was a wise man who made a bath reconnaissance before play began. Few grounds had more than two baths, and, as it usually took fifteen minutes to run the bath and as long to empty it for the next, it will be seen what a clamour there was for baths. There were two magnificent baths at Lord's. One mounted on a dais to descend into it, preparatory to locking the door against the knocking horse if he wanted his bath in peace and reflection of the old heroes who had used this bath down the years. Contrasting with Lord's, Sydney has six showers and two baths for each team. Other Australian grounds are not so well equipped. The custom at most English hotels is to ring for the chambermaid and order a bath. Ethel, our popular chambermaid in the London hotel, was run off her feet running baths for us and never ceased to wonder why we had daily baths. She told us it was nothing uncommon for guests to stay a week at the hotel and not order a bath. Which reminds me that on the Continent a bath is usually charged extra. There are only two or three baths to most hotels, and taking a bath is quite a parade. The rooms generally contain a hand-basin, and one Australian was explaining one day how easy it was to take a tub from that. 'You just stand in front of the basin,' he said, 'and wash down as far as possible and up as far as possible.' 'Yes,' said a listener, 'but what about possible?' . . . To return to Cambridge. No better batting on tour was seen than Yardley's 67. He made 50 in an hour, with eleven fours. He treated O'Reilly contemptuously at one stage, and Brown and I were obliged to edge further and further away from O'Reilly's in-field. Gibb is the batting counterpart of Sutcliffe – similar style and mannerisms. He must have copied his style on moving pictures of Sutcliffe. . . . Another phenomenon happened at Cambridge. I asked Charles Fry a question and he did not know the answer. Some bird sang gloriously in a Cambridge Oak, but Fry could not tell me what type it was. The prettiest and more varied greens in all England are to be seen in a corner of the Clare quadrangle.

Dining With the Savages:

A night out with the Savages is a red-letter night. To become a member of the Savage Club one must first have done something worth while in the worlds of literature, art, science, music or drama, and it is not difficult to conceive what a collection of bright people it brings when the Savages meet. Two Australians, Harold Williams and Malcolm McEachern, the latter the Jetsam with Flotsam, combined to give the Australian team a dinner at the Savages in Carlton House Terrace. No better evening was spent on tour. I doubt whether any theatre in London at the period could have provided such a wealth of turns as kept popping up from all corners of the Savages that evening. I can recall, among others, George Stampa, of *Punch*, David Low, the two Harkers, Billy Leonard, Parry and Trefor Jones, Robert Easton, Norman Allin and George Baker. The choir which Harold Williams was leading towards the end of the night was full of magnificent music, happy fellowship and a plethora of encores. One dear old chap, over the dining table, quite convinced me that Dr W. G. Grace was the greatest batsman who ever lived. I've forgotten how he worked it out, but it was good – so was the dinner! Harold Williams, incidentally, played with the same Sydney Club (Waverley) as Kippax and myself. Perhaps his best feat in the cricketing world was scaling up the Kennington Oval pavilion to gain entrance into the Australian dressing-room after a somewhat officious Australian manager had barred the festive door after a victory which won the Ashes.

A Team of Personalities:

J. W. A. Stephenson is the best cricketing personality in England who has not visited Australia. He would have been tremendously popular in our country because of the unlimited enthusiasm and energy he puts into everything he does. Like Constantine, he ranges constantly in the field, being here before the shot is played and there to receive it. No fieldsman is more upsetting to a batsman. You can never trust him to stay put. Steve looks the sorriest man on the field when stumps are pulled for the day. This jack-in-the-box was at his top in the Australians' first game at Lord's, against the MCC. He worried Bradman immensely at the beginning of a 278 innings with balls which moved in the air at the last moment and nipped with venom off the pitch. With such a ball he caught Bradman a painful whack on the instep. A passing aeroplane at that moment was showing an advertisement with the advice to 'rub it in'. Batting at the other end, I pointed it out to the hopping Bradman, but he did not seem to be in the mood to enjoy the most unusual coincidence. Stephenson bowled Badcock, and before the disturbed bails had settled on the ground Stephenson was out with cover-point, explaining it all to him. What a magnificent team of touring personalities England could choose! Stephenson, Jim Smith (who causes the Long Pavilion to shiver in the slip-stream of his colossal swings for six), Wellard, Gimblett, Bartlett, the Hon Charles Lyttelton, Freddie Brown, Mitchell, Levett, Nichols and a few others. These men have cricket personality – on and off the field. They would deal limitless Tests a smashing blow if they were playing on a ground opposite such a game. Stephenson, a permanent Army man, brings the smartness of the parade ground into his batting movements.

'Mild' Barracking at the Oval:

Kennington Oval is a huge, drab ground, surrounded by gasometers, which are inflated on Saturday and down on Monday after London has cooked its Sunday joints. It is a ground on which players and spectators barely get to know each other because of the distances between. Bradman was severely roasted here for not making Surrey follow on. Had that barracking been in Australia, the cables would have run hot; as it was at the Oval, *Wisden* was constrained to term it a 'mild demonstration'. I should like to be present to hear what *Wisden* would term a wild demonstration. It should be worth hearing. An Australian team in England has a difficult task. A tour consists of 36 games, and because of the importance of the gate all the opposing teams expect the Australians to field their Test side. This is a natural expectation. I have been with an Australian team that was jeered off a railway station because Bradman, who was resting, was not with the team. It is impossible, because of injuries and especially when staleness sets in towards the end of the tour, for the Australians to do themselves full justice in all games. This sometimes gives rise to feeling against the Australians. Bradman did not make Surrey follow on because he had to conserve O'Reilly's vigour with the first Test drawing near. Our team must have been one of the weakest in bowling Australia ever sent to England. It relied almost exclusively on O'Reilly and, to a less extent, McCormick in the big games. I fancy Ebeling, Nagel and Grimmett could have made it a magnificent bowling side. Fishlock played a remarkable innings in Surrey's second attempt. He made 95, while Gregory made five and Squires four. Fishlock, I think, should have been a permanent English fixture in this and the last series of Tests. I wonder whether he comes from the wrong side of the Thames? He is a left-hander and Australian spin bowlers do not like left-handers. He would have handsomely repaid Allen, I think, had that English captain pinned more faith on him in Australia in 1936–37.

Over the Waves at Southend:

Essex provided a natural wicket at Southend, perhaps too natural, because there were more waves on its surface than on the adjoining Thames Estuary. The wicket developed 'spots' on the first day, and it was not surprising that the game finished in two days. Australia scored 145 and 153, Essex 114 and 87. Brown and McCabe played splendid innings. Essex turned on the best attacking bowling of the counties with Farnes, Stephenson and Nichols. No more charming sportsman plays the game than Farnes. A feature of his bowling is a terrific grunt, which he delivers with the ball. I always liked taking strike to Farnes in a Test, because his first few balls are only medium fast. It seemed that he was anxious to strike a length first. An exception to this happened in the third Test at Leeds when he warmed up before the game. I think somebody advised him to do this. His first ball at Leeds was of surprising and terrific speed. . . . The Southend game coincided with a public holiday and Southend was invaded by swarms of Londoners. The seaside was certainly bright and full of colourful personalities. I never ceased to wonder how rollicking holiday-makers, full of more than the holiday spirit, suddenly straightened up and walked the proverbial straight line as soon as a policeman's uniform hove into sight. The respect for the English police uniform is most marked. . . . It was depressing to wake in Southend of a morning and look out, as far as vision went, on a sea of bleak-roofed tenement houses. What contrasts there are in England! . . . (Postscript in 1946: Through death on active service in the Global War, England lost not only two magnificent bowlers in Kenneth Farnes and Hedley Verity, but two cricketers whose personality endeared them to the Australians. Farnes was the most handsome Test cricketer of his age, a movie star in looks, but better than his looks was his modest, cheerful and cultured company. Hedley was of the same quiet type, immensely popular with the Australians, none of whom resented the fact that Verity, with fingers cupped to mouth, appealed more for leg before wicket than any other known bowler. After such appeals he used to smile wryly and wink to the batsman in between runs, as much as to say: 'I just want the umpire to feel that he is in this game as much as you and me.' I don't think that Hedley ever recovered from the heart-aches he suffered in Australia in 1936–37, when rain gave England two wet wickets in successive Tests and he never bowled a ball! To such left-handers a wet wicket is indeed a gift from the heavens, but the incongruous Australian system of covering the approaches and not the pitch enabled the fast bowlers to become positive terrors when it rained. A strange and intensely sad thought that we shall never again see the lilting, loping run of Verity to the wickets nor the rugged fury of Farnes. I pay tribute to them as two of cricket's most likeable characters.)

An Enthusiastic 'Baby':

It was not until the first day of July that Barnes, the baby of the team, played his first match. He broke his wrist on the liner a few days out from England and chafed unmercifully as he was forced to sit back and watch the team play month after month without him. Never was such unbridled enthusiasm let loose on a field than with Barnes at Swansea. He chased balls to the boundary with the speed and vigour of a Rugby winger. No chase was too hopeless for him, and at the end of one he sprawled over the ropes and lost himself deep in the crowd. At the end of the day's play a wrathful Welshman presented a bill to manager Jeanes for a pair of trousers which Barnes had sprigged in his wild dive. The Welshman was paid! The best story of Barnes was on the occasion he had made well over a century and was met coming in by his inseparable pal, Badcock, going out to bat. Badcock congratulated him. Barnes snorted. 'What's up with you,' said Badcock, 'you got a century, didn't you?' 'Yes,' said Barnes, not at all pleased, 'but I can't afford to get out.' Badcock almost collapsed in merriment.

On Making a Test 'Pair':

In Sydney, at the end of the Australian tour by the English team of 1936–37, the English captain, G. O. Allen, talked to me of young Australians. He did not think Badcock would be a success on English wickets and based that assumption on the manner in which Badcock played back, moving across the wicket. Allen, like most English amateurs, made a deeper analytical study of the game than many Australian players. So far as Tests were concerned, Allen was right. Badcock had a miserable Test run and never once made double figures. At Lord's he suffered the depressing experience of making a 'pair' in a Test – at Lord's, of all places! The Australian dressing-room was glum as Badcock set out from the wicket on his trek back through the Long Pavilion and up the stairs. No Australian was more popular with his team-mates. We were all ready with expressions of sympathy, but Badcock beat us to it. His smiling face burst through the doorway and he doubled up in roars of laughter. He is the first batsman I have known who has seen the funny side of a 'pair'. I know I did not feel like laughing when I collected the 'honour' against England at Adelaide in 1932–33. . . . Writing of G. O. Allen – what a pity he never played against us in 1938. He looked on at Scarborough. He is a great favourite with Australians. Larwood's feats dimmed those of Allen in Australia in 1932, but he was a really splendid fast bowler, little inferior to Larwood. And what a delightful vocabulary when he bowled a bad ball!

Hassett the Naturalist:

The Grindleford hills of Derbyshire have had a strange effect upon Hassett. He came to the country inn late one night pulling a wet, muddy and complaining goat, which he said he had found out in the hills. He particularly insisted that Bradman should see the goat. The next night everybody locked their doors, which was just as well, because Hassett found a hedgehog. Despite his plaintive pleas, nobody would open up to look at his find. He brought it down to breakfast next day. . . . It was at Grindleford that Bradman received news that the Australian Board of Control would not relax their rule on wives travelling with the team and allow Mrs Bradman to journey to England, arriving at the end of the tour. Bradman was justly incensed, saying he would never come to England to play again after this tour. The Board later relented and allowed all the wives to trip across.

Royalty at Lord's:

Cricket must remain unchallenged as the greatest of all games simply because of the Lord's Test. For atmosphere, tradition and setting, no game can offer a spectacle to come within cooee of these most glorious of all sporting days. One can visualise planters, mining men, service men and those others whose life has taken them to far-flung outposts of the Empire, planning for years ahead so that they will reach Home again on furlough in time for the Saturday of the England–Australia Test match. This is the day when friends meet again after a lapse of years, each hastily and anxiously making his way to the rendezvous which has always produced the other; this is the day when staid, respectable gentlemen fling themselves unashamedly at the world in flaunting ties, ties whose bizarre colours the eyes of the in-going batsmen will do their best to avoid as he makes his way out through the Long Pavilion. Saucy ties, as Robertson-Glasgow once wrote, reticulated and streated, of the sort that man puts on when he is going to kick life a good one from behind. These, if you care to term them so, are the wearers of the Old School ties, but let there be no supercilious sneer at their wearing on Test day at Lord's. The gaudy MCC tie itself; old Etonians and old Harrovians; the bilious pink gin and vermouth colours of the Free Purchasers; the Old This or the Old That. All have their affinities and associations, all members most honourably bound to sport their colours at Lord's on this great day in English sporting history. The seeker, prepared for facial and physical surprises after the interval years, peers no further if the tie is not of his kind. The warmth of handshakes hearts the Pavilion. . . . After lunch comes the inspiring moment when the Royal Standard is run up over the Pavilion. The King has arrived. The players stand in two lines on the field, His Majesty walks out from the Long Pavilion and all Lord's stands to attention, men baring their heads, as the King meets the players. The game goes on, the Royal Standard fluttering in the breeze as the warm sun envelops Lord's. Hammond poises majestically on his back foot and crashes a ball through the covers to the ropes and all Lord's is delighted. There can be nothing in British history more essentially British than this setting. One glimpse of Lord's on such a day enriches the heart and memory. Lucky is the cricketer who plays in such a game and thrice lucky, also, is the cricketer who, on this Saturday afternoon when Lord's exudes good fellowship and warm feelings, plays a bright innings, crashes down the wickets or performs some spectacular feat in the field. . . . The late King George V came to be regarded by Australians as England's greatest upsetter of Australian partnerships. His arrival at Lord's was invariably followed by the breaking of some stout

Australian partnership. King George VI kept up the Royal tradition, though in a different manner. Before lunch McCormick had
produced a devastating piece of bowling that put England's stocks at
3–31. Then came His Majesty, Hammond and Paynter. The next
wicket fell at 253! . . . The story is told of the players being
introduced to King George V at Lord's. He stopped opposite
Mitchell and the former coal-miner, but now England's slow bowler, was introduced. Mitchell leaned across to the King and in a
sincere, confidential voice asked: 'And how is Her Majesty to-day,
Sir?' 'Thank you, Mr Mitchell,' replied the King, 'she is very well
indeed, and I shall tell her to-night you enquired after her.' . . . I
should like to see a Test at Lord's, not play in it. It would be
comforting to enter a Test ground again without that little ball of
nervous anticipation or emotion that tosses apprehensively in the
player's stomach. It is delicious, I grant, to fling oneself on a Test
green at the fall of a wicket and smell the sweet nectar of the grass,
but it makes one slightly envious to look up at the Lord's boxes,
boxes like those at an opera house, and see the family butler
dispensing cool drinks to the occupants. If I see a Test at Lord's
again and witness batting in keeping with the double centuries of
Hammond and Brown, the century of Bradman, the elegance of a
Compton or a McCabe, the fighting qualities of a Paynter, the
languid bowling cunning of a Verity or the fury of an O'Reilly,
McCormick or Farnes – if I see things to equal these, I will be more
than satisfied. And, though my beard be grey, I pray I bore nobody
with tiresome comparisons of the good Old Days! All cricketers
should either grow old gracefully, like F. S. Jackson, or be penned
in an enclosure by themselves.

Disappointment at Swansea:

A pleasant occurrence half-way or further through the English tour
is a rainy day. Most members of the team are 'flannel-happy' by this
stage and warmly welcome a day's rest from the game. Swansea was
an exception. There was such enthusiasm for the game with Glam-
organ and the Welsh made such an appeal to the Australians that
the whole side was sorry when rain cheated a crowd of 25,000 of its
money's worth. Both sides did their best to get a game going on the
saturated wicket, but further rain ruined all prospects. . . . I did not
begrudge my wicket to Wooller, the Welsh Rugby International. I
was rather hoping somebody would suggest a game of Rugby in lieu
of cricket. We could have turned out rather a handy side, and as
Swansea is where Wales plays some of its Rugby internationals, we
might have had the opportunity of hearing the famed singing of the
Welsh Rugby crowds. . . . Recent Australians who have been

internationals in cricket and Rugby are J. M. Taylor and Dr Otto Nothling. . . . Mailey, touring with the Australians as a newspaper correspondent, arranged a picnic for the Swansea week-end. The younger players entered into it with great heart; the others, knowing a little of Arthur's managership, fought shy. One of the older players asked one of the picnickers that night how it all went. 'It started very brightly,' he said. 'We had several cars, some very nice lasses and there was nothing wrong with the day. We got well out in the country and Arthur picked a grand spot. We all agreed it would be a lovely spot in which to have lunch and then Arthur said "Good Lord, I forgot all about the picnic basket."' Arthur is a little forgetful at times. . . . Brown and myself went bathing over the week-end. We had quite an audience as we shot a few breakers; that is, swimming down the crest of the wave as it curls and then shooting shorewards with the broken wave. It is an old Australian custom, but it seemed to be a novelty on the Welsh beach. What amused us was the popular style of undressing for the water. A person draped a huge towel about himself like a cape, furious shufflings and wrigglings went on underneath and then emerged the costumed body for the water. . . . Across the lane from the hotel stood a four-storeyed tenement house. The place swarmed with children. I counted five in one room. There could be nothing more gloomy and disheartening than the walk I took through Swansea slum areas. And yet just outside Swansea, on the way we took up to Scotland, there are miles of the most glorious countryside imaginable. It is difficult to believe that Swansea areas and areas in the industrial north of England belong in the same land as palatial homes and castles into which we were invited.

Scotland St Andrew's:

What the Scottish lack in cricket ability they more than atone for in hospitality. It is amusing to see the reactions of Australians when they enter the land of their antecedents. They become more local than the locals. Barnett, for instance, who went up to Scotland ahead of the team, greeted his fellows in dazzling kilts, tartan and glengarry. He did not mind the chaffing at all. One half of the team failing to interpret the Scottish burr of a railway porter where we changed trains for Dundee, only half the team arrived in that historic city. The others came later, wiser in the Scottish dialect. I awoke the next morning to the lovely music of a conversation between two painters daubing the wall outside my window. . . . Accepting an invitation after the game, McCabe and I motored down with new-found friends to St Andrew's, where we had a delicious Scottish supper and then played nine holes on the famous golf course. The long English twilight almost opens up another day when cricket is ended. It is difficult to imagine St Andrew's, because of the course itself, as the home of golf. The holes run quite amiably and unpretentiously along with houses, roads and the railway yards. We both sacrificed a ball in trying to carry the railway yards in the dog-leg hole. We could also understand how a fellow Manly (NSW) member of ours in Ferrier came to get into such grief on the Road hole in the British Amateur Championship in 1936. Our hosts told us that St Andrew's belongs to the people, who pay nothing to play on it. It is not uncommon, they said, to see a woman going a-shopping with a few clubs and a ball, dropping the market-baskets as she players her stroke. Our hosts drove us down to Glasgow that night. If Scotland played cricket in keeping with its hospitality our tour there would not have been so easy. . . . Playing over the burns at St Andrew's reminded me of that delectable golfing story which concerns the Scottish minister of religion. One of the holes was across a burn and when he carried the water he would happily address the ball in flight, 'Ah, away ye go over yon bonnie burn.' When he didn't carry the burn but plopped into it, he would mutter, 'Down you go into that bloody sewer again.'

On Not Playing at Manchester:

Somebody once wrote (I think it was Neville Cardus) that all self-respecting newspapers keep the phrase ready in slug form, 'Rain at Manchester – No Play'. Rain there for four days and four nights washed out completely the Fourth Test. It looked, as we were leaving Manchester, that it was out to out-Noah Noah's 40 days and 40 nights. Many hard things have been said of the Manchester weather, and as far as the 1938 Australian team could see they are well deserved. The silver lining to the weather was the huge strawberries served up for lunch each day at Old Trafford while everybody sat about and waited for the clouds to roll by. The English strawberry has to be seen and tasted to be believed. Of all the stories told of Manchester, this, I think, takes some beating. The fussy passenger poked his head out of the carriage window and addressed the guard. 'Hey, Guard, why have we stopped so long in this tunnel?' 'This is no tunnel,' replied the Guard, 'this is Manchester.' In not playing that 1938 Test at Old Trafford, I think we missed a lot. The 1938 tourists never really got to know the Manchester folk. History repeated itself in our tour. Not a ball was bowled at Manchester in 1890. The Test in 1912 was confined to one day's play.

211

On Bradman's Popularity:

I was taking a walk, in civilian clothes, around the Leeds ground
when Bradman was clean bowled by Bowes at 103 in the fourth
Test. The reaction in the crowd to Bradman's dismissal was amazing. Everybody I looked at sported the widest of grins. They shook
hands and thumped their neighbour's back. Perhaps most of this
crowd saw Bradman make 334 in Leeds in 1930 and 304 in 1934 and
considered that his going at a mere 103 was a cheap piece of work.
Perhaps it was. If it were possible, Bradman seems to be more
popular in England than Australia. An electrical current runs
through the crowd whenever he makes his appearance. I wonder
just how much he has put into the coffers of the game. He is cricket's
undisputed crowd pleaser and attractor of all time, but, that game
apart, Bradman must also rank high in the world's list of box-office
personalities of all ages. A hard to please connoisseur might quibble
at this or that in Bradman's technique. The hard-headed masses,
wanting honest visible value for their money, know nothing of that
nor do they worry about it. They can follow every move of Bradman's feet and bat, and, what they like most about him, he gives
them plenty for their money. No quick entrances and exits with
Bradman and time is not allowed to stand still while he is at the
wickets – though the 1938 Bradman, in this regard, nods only in
acquaintance with the 1930 hero.

Opinions on a Bowling Theory:

Most English counties in 1938 carried a type of bowler who is a
menace to cricket. He is the leg-theory bowler – not to be confused
at all with bodyline. He mostly bowls around the wicket and gives
the ball spin from the off. He aims at the leg stump or outside of it
and he packs the leg-field with fieldsmen. This is by no means an
extenuation of boring innings I and others played in England, but
this type of bowler does much harm to cricket in that he is often
responsible for negative and dreary batting. He does not threaten
the stumps and the batsman is in no danger of dismissal. All he does
is to provide the batsman with the opportunity of taking all the risks
if he wants to make runs. If the batsman does not want to enter into
this rather one-sided affair, the cricket palls beyond measure, but it
will be found that most critics take the batsman to task rather than
the bowler. I admit that this theory demands the utmost accuracy in
length and in that I concede it its only merit. I have never seen it
bowled in Australian or South African cricket. No English team to
Australia has included such a bowler, to my knowledge. He would
be at a disadvantage on our wickets in that he would get little or no

turn off the wicket. It would be interesting to know why it has become such a standard work in English cricket. It is usually bowled by men rather long in the cricket brain who have reservoirs of patience, but what is the reason for it? Too many matches, too much time to play with, a bowler's natural reaction of complaint against doped wickets? If legislators can analyse that correctly and remedy it they will do the game a great service. Another thought in this trend is that the English make runs harder to get than the Australians. They place the field with more intent and their bowlers conduct their deliveries accordingly. The Australians, with spin, play true to the national trait of gambling, and are prepared to toss along the odds of a few full tosses and long hops to get a good winner. For that reason an Australian team must always score heavily for victory.

Rugby and Australian Rules:

They play a form of football called Australian Rules in the south of Australia. That is why the principal topic of argument in any Australian Eleven on tour is the respective merits of Rugby and Australian Rules. By their States shall ye know them! When somebody produced a football at Harrogate, Yorkshire, the matter came to a head in a most glorious rough and tumble of associated rules. And this on the eve of the fourth Test at Leeds! Luckily no arms or legs were broken and that not because of a lack of spirit. In 1932 in Australia Jardine came down with a heavy hand on some of his team playing golf. He made them stop it. It is wrong to play serious golf or tennis in the midst of a serious cricket tour. The swings and general principles are entirely unrelated, but a little relaxation in another game on the eve of a Test is magnificent medicine. Perhaps, though, Rugby-cum-Australian Rules is a little rich!

Crowds in the North:

Crowds in the north of England, particularly Leeds and Sheffield, have more humour and character in their make-up than those in the south. They are more spontaneous and friendlier. Cricketers react to the crowd's mood, and it was true that games in the north produced a better type of cricket than those, generally, in the south. An exception to this was at Canterbury, the loveliest and friendliest ground on which we played in England. The old tree which grows inside the boundary, the President's tent and those of the others with gay colours flying, the fields of crops waving in the distance made up into a delightful cricket scene. The Kent ladies and men are also of a happy, friendly type – the ladies also beautiful! J. R.

Mason, the old Kent and England player, was host to Brown and myself for several days at Cooden and we had no more enjoyable time in England. It was at Canterbury that Woolley took his farewell of the Australians. His innings was true to style – elegant and beautiful. I shall never lose a boyish memory I have of Woolley crashing Gregory through the covers at Sydney for a matchless boundary.

Putting Edrich in His Place:

A little Cockney newsboy recognised Bill Edrich as we were driving back to Trafalgar Square from the Oval one day when we were 'bushed' in London. Edrich called the lad across and asked the way. 'Garn,' said the lad, 'I don't think I oughta tell ya. Why ain't yer making more runs?' Edrich, a magnificent batsman, who made his thousand runs in May, could not strike it rich at all against the Australians in the Tests. The selectors persevered with him, and rightly so, throughout the series, though it was difficult to reconcile this with their action in dropping Barnett for the last Test. Perhaps Barnett was too dashing a batsman for a limitless Test! The younger generation of English cricketers, Edrich, Compton, Griffiths, Hardstaff, Yardley, Levett and others, made warm friendships with the Australians. They are bringing a delightful spirit into the game, a spirit the very opposite of that prevailing in the bodyline years – and, as will be noticed elsewhere, I by no means blame Englishmen alone for that earlier feeling.

So Passeth All Earthly Glories:

A sad sight at Leeds to see Tate on crutches. No Englishman has been more popular with Australians than the big-hearted Sussex bowler, and no bowler in this series (as O'Reilly, I think, is past his best) approaches his skill with the ball. There is always something pathetic in the manner of a big figure going out of the game. He is soon forgotten by most people. I remember a morning at Port Augusta (South Australia) railway station after a horde of schoolboys had raided the train for English and Australian autographs. Just outside my cabin several of them were discussing their gains. One fellow said: 'J. B. Hobbs? J. B. Hobbs? I'll cross him out. I only want cricketers in my lot.' A familiar sight with Tate was when he engaged in conversation on the field with an opposing player. It looked most secret and confidential, but generally I found Maurice was passing some friendly remark about the weather or the wicket. Many people often ask what batsmen talk about in the middle of the wicket. I recall one day when Bradman and I had a discussion.

Bradman said: 'We have kidded to Robbie long enough. Leave him to me now and I will carve him.' The joke was on Robins. In playful and secretive manner he crept up behind us, pretending to listen to the conversation. He did not hear it, of course, but Bradman did 'carve' him.

Festival Games:

So far as the Australians are concerned, the three Festival Games at the end of a tour are misnomers and unpopular. They come at the end of over four months of hard play, six days a week from eleven in the morning to six-thirty in the evening. Each Festival side, also, amounts to an English Test eleven. It must be remembered that the Australian plays no more than six or eight first-class games in an Australian season. An English season of 36 is exceedingly hard work and all Australians become stale and tired of the game long before the tour ends. A week's entire holiday from the game during the middle of a tour would do much to brighten the play of tourists, who consider that far too much cricket is played in England for the good standard of the game. These Festival games would approach more to the nature of their name if the competitive aspect were dropped and players mingled for the choosing of two teams. One other thought on English cricket – the umpiring is truly magnificent. In all the 36 games I cannot remember a single decision that was bad. English umpires also bring a friendly and personal touch into their game. They are as much part of the game as the players.

McCabe's Pinnacle:

The best innings of the tour was that played by McCabe at Trent Bridge in the first Test, when he made 232. People who saw it and are in the position to judge refer to it as the best in the history of Tests. From 6–194 in reply to England's 8–658 (dec.), McCabe took Australia's score, with the help of indifferent batsmen in Barnett, O'Reilly, McCormick and Fleetwood-Smith, to 411. McCabe made his 232 out of 300; he made 72 of a last wicket stand of 77 with Fleetwood-Smith in 28 minutes. The figures tell one story of McCabe's innings; his brilliant, effortless stroke-making and domination of the game tell the real one. I would place Charles Barnett's 126 in the same game as the next spectacular innings in the series (Barnett is a much better bat than England thinks); then follows Hammond's 240 at Lord's. Bradman, strangely enough, did not turn on any Test fireworks. His batting was marked by complete soundness at a time when that was most needed by his side. His 103 at Leeds on a sporty wicket was the innings of a champion. His 144 not out against the clock at Trent Bridge, for which he hardly received a clap from a most unsporting and ill-mannered crowd, and his 102 not out at Lord's were the innings of a fighting captain. Paynter, a charming little fellow, chockful of courage, was feared as much by the Australians as any other Englishman. His 216 not out at Trent Bridge and 99 at Lord's placed him third on my batting list to Hammond and Bradman. I could not separate Hutton and Brown for the next position. Hutton's 13 hours and 20 minutes at the Oval for 364 is the epic of its kind for all time. Brown was the series' most dependable batsman, his 206 through the innings at Lord's being a masterpiece. After these, in my mind, came Compton. Possibly only McCabe's innings at Nottingham was better in real merit than Compton's 76 at Lord's in the second innings. I have a tremendously high opinion of Compton. And what a charming lad he is! Bowlers on both sides had an uncommonly lean time. O'Reilly's ten wickets at Leeds was the only star bowling effort of the whole series. Bartlett's 157, his century in 57 minutes being the fastest of the season, stands clear as the most spectacular innings played against the Australians. He is a powerful left-hander, hitting six sixes and 18 fours. His sixes did not just clear the ropes. They soared over with yards and yards to spare on the big Sussex ground at Brighton.

A Voice for Voce:

If the Australians had the job of choosing England's Test eleven, one of the first chosen would be William Voce, of Notts. The MCC selectors do not seem to regard him highly for games in England, though he made two trips to Australia and was most outstanding. Voce bowls a magnificent ball which runs away from the batsman. He makes it talk on the average English wicket. (Postscript in 1945: The loss of Verity might well mean the return of Voce to the English Eleven as a spinner. He was fast in his prime, but he should have no difficulty in settling down to the Ironmonger type of left-handed spinner. I give the tip to the MCC selectors for what it is worth!)

A Good Companion:

An opening batsman is fortunate if he hits it with his partner. W. A. Brown is an ideal partner. He is thoroughly unselfish, answers every call and is most reliable in his own calling. Best of all, he has a delectable sense of humour – and opening batsmen need that, particularly when the barrackers are at them. It is odd, though you take it for granted, how used two batsmen can become to each other. For instance, Brown and I never call. I can tell by his attitude if he wants to come for a run; and he does the same with me.

Left, 'The Straight Drive
Completed to Perfection' (Victor
Trumper)
Below, Kippax and His Style. He
was quite content to spend his
riches lavishly without seeking
in return the monument of a
record.

Top, Power, Punch and Audacity. The individuality of Macartney was fully shown in his cover drive.

Below, The Artistry of Jackson. A mere slip of a boy, his fair, tousled hair waving in the slight breeze of Adelaide, one of the prettiest of all cricketing grounds.

Above right, Hammond and Oldfield. It almost lives, so true is it a depiction of Hammond's grace, power, correctness and artistry.

Below right, Bradman jumps out to lift one to the boundary. Duckworth is the wicket-keeper.

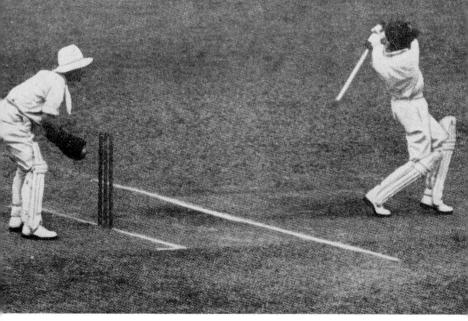

Speaks for Itself. There is about this stroke, a whiff of the refreshing personality which Constantine took to all places with him.

Left, Spin Unlimited. Slow-bowler McCool ties himself in as many knots, almost, as he did the English batting. Umpire Scott stoops in the background.

Right, Australian fast bowler, Ray Lindwall, whose three wickets in four balls at Adelaide was the best stump-shattering effort of the series. In this photograph, he has undoubtedly dragged over the line, with the ball far from being delivered.

Above, Hutton and the Bumpers: The English star falls prone to the ground as Miller gives him a bumper in Sydney in the final Test. One slip is out of the picture. Compare this field with that shown in the bodyline picture of Woodfull ducking a Larwood bumper in Brisbane.

Right above, A Leg-Bye off the Skull: Washbrook gets hit on the head when batting on the Brisbane 'sticky' wicket. Notice his cap falling to the ground. Bradman is in close on the leg-side.

Right below, Umpire Scott's hand is on the way up in this much-debated decision in Melbourne. Bowler Lindwall and Tallon are shown in the appeal rampant; batsman Edrich almost in the gesture supplicatory.

Bradman's Fourth: The tense moment in Adelaide when Bedser clean bowled the Australian champion for nil. It was Bradman's fourth score of nought against the English in Tests. Note how Hammond, who is at first slip, crowded the Australian with two men close in at leg.

Peculiarly enough, the first time we batted together in first-class cricket he was run out through a misunderstanding. We had a phenomenal run of successes in South Africa, having a century opening partnership, at least, on nearly every occasion we went to the wickets. In this English tour we were not so fortunate. His form was poor at the start, mine good; he rose to his top midway through the tour, while I lost form. There is no more conscientious cricketer in the game than Brown. He trains hard and by terrific practice made himself a class fields-man. I count my association with him as one of the best things that happened to me in cricket. Had he been a number four or five batsman I think the game of cricket would have known few better stroke-makers. Opening an innings is a deadening business.

Honour for McCormick:

Great excitement when McCormick is made a Purchaser. You have to do something notoriously foolish to become a member of this select London club. For instance, a well-known Englishman returning to England from India was settling down in his cabin. He made a bundle on his berth of his money, notes, and odd papers to be thrown out the porthole. Everything tidied, he opened the port-hole and threw out – his money! He was elected a Purchaser instantly. McCormick was elected because of his no-ball feat at Worcester. King Purchasers are people who do something unbeliev-ably foolish. Members save all Queen Victoria 'bun' pennies, minted in the early part of her reign and showing a bun hairstyle. These are handed in on club festive nights. Hospital cots are thus endowed by the Purchasers, who have the great distinction of being able to laugh at themselves. The story is that the Bank of England keeps the bun pennies in circulation purely because of the Purchasers.

Come Back to Erin:

The playing of two games in Ireland, one at Belfast and the other at Dublin, was an experiment. Other Australian teams of long ago had played in Ireland, but ours was the first to go there for a long time. The experiment was so successful that every team in future is bound to include Ireland in its programme. The Belfast people arranged a glorious tour one day, which took us out through Downpatrick to Newcastle, running down the side of the Mountains of Mourne, along the boundary of north and south Ireland and back up to Belfast. The glorious Newcastle golf course did its best to make us feel at home. The caddies staged a strike while we were there! In a lonely, thatched cottage on the side of the Mourne Mountains an aged Irish woman talked remarkably of world politics. The September crisis was nigh. Her anticipations of world events were to be proved true, and her home was so remote that one wondered how tales of the outside world would ever penetrate there. And we saw a lovely Irish wedding and the happy couple jolting along to the honeymoon in a jaunting cart. Captain Lindsay, of Belfast, was a magnificent Irish host. The standard of cricket there is not quite up to first-class, although one, Ingram, was a good bowler. I think I can claim that I got the best 'bite' of the tour at Belfast. A typical guide was showing us over the lavish North of Ireland Parliament. He was pointing out in the Chamber where personalities sat. 'And where,' I asked, 'does de Valera sit?' The guide almost exploded. We left Belfast with regrets and entered Dublin with anticipations that were fully realised. How could a team fare otherwise with an O'Reilly in its midst! Dublin we loved with its green trams, green telegraph posts, green telegram forms, green on everything that would take green. And the lovely, soft, rich voices! Ah, begorrah! The game at Trinity was an unqualified success and nearly every spectator there seemed to go down to the wharf to farewell the team when it left by boat. Spontaneously, as the ship pulled out, the crowd began to sing 'Come Back to Erin'. Hassett and I, who stayed on in Ireland for ten more days, sang with the crowd. It was one of the most moving scenes I have witnessed. Future Australian teams will indeed go back to Erin, and if their stay is as enjoyable as ours was, they will be fortunate.

Having a Dhrop of Phorter:

Samuel Roach, a Carlow legal man and our host, took a few days' holiday to show the two of us the beauty spots of Ireland. Glendalough and the wayside picnic we will never forget. One day Hassett and I took the maids' cycles and rode into Carlow. We had been told a lot about the Irish porter and decided to sample it. We walked into the village inn, drew up a stool apiece, tasted the porter and liked it. While we were in that inn we were the only ones who sat on the business side of the bar. The locals sauntered in, went round to the back of the bar, poured their drink, put their money in the till, took their change and everybody seemed happy. A lovely touch, you will agree, but perhaps not applicable to many countries.

Farewell to London:

Our last evening in London, appropriately enough, as it was our most popular London rendezvous throughout the tour, was spent at the Sports Club in St. James' Square. Colonel James Foley, our guide, philosopher and good friend, was host at a magnificent dinner. Colonel Foley, Tasmanian born, went to Nigeria at an early age and stayed there in mining, with the exception of the trips he made to England to coincide with the visit of an Australian cricket team. His hospitality to the players, as he travelled with them on most of the tour, was a byword. Through him we made firm friends with many of the Sports Club, particularly Angus Butler, Geoffrey Oliff, Bayliss Smith, Davey, Walter Wynn, Harmon Hargreaves and the author, Bruce Lockhart.

The spirit of the September crisis hung heavily over London. Mr Chamberlain, at that time, was at Munich, but everybody put on a bold face at the dinner, and O'Reilly, in a magnificent speech, gave it added flavour. Hassett, who would make an ideal advertising agent, was always singing my singing praises, and at this dinner induced a well-known musical critic to give me an audition. I would have none of it, but Hassett is most persistent when he likes. The setting was ludicrous. Hassett insisted on conducting and the critic stood patiently by. Embarrassedly, I did my poor best. The critic did not say a word at the finish, but melted quietly away. Hassett, who is nothing if not loyal, insisted that he could not understand how such a one came to get a name as a musical critic. . . . Our last view of London next day was through the carriage window, O'Reilly still wearing the tall hat presented to him for his speech.

A Dear Old Lady on Shipboard:

She was, without doubt, a dear old lady though rather critical, perhaps, of Australian cricketers. It was one dreamy afternoon in the for'ard lounge when the ship was gliding down through the tropics. The for'ard lounge was a place for the older members of the ship passengers; the aft was frequented more by the younger and noisier personnel. The ship's orchestra was playing Chopin and Bach, old ladies either read or plied gently moving knitting needles. I was an intruder because a fellow-passenger had loaned me Douglas Reed's latest book for the afternoon, and I wanted to make the most of it in the best atmosphere. At the end of a number a gentle soul nearby clapped enthusiastically. 'Ah,' said another, 'you liked that?' 'Indeed, yes,' said the other, and, with a pleasant look across to me, whom she knew, 'I would clap the orchestra just as enthusiastically as I would the Australian cricketers.' It was not, it seemed, a tactful remark. The other old lady, it seemed, did not like the Australian cricketers. She said so with decided feeling. 'Mind you,' she said, 'I have not met any, but I have heard of them. Would you believe that the other night six of the young hooligans appeared at the fancy dress ball as six young ship-wrecked maidens? Disgraceful!' I was sorry to hear that. I was one of the six and I thought we rather looked the part, though O'Reilly, possibly, was rather a gawky maiden. The rest of us, particularly Hassett, Brown and McCabe, I thought, looked particularly fetching in our made-up wigs and loaned nightgowns. A shipwreck, after all, is a shipwreck. My friendly old lady was too embarrassed to stop. She got up and walked away, as did Mrs Fleetwood-Smith. The critical old lady turned to me. She was warming to her subject. 'They are not fit, sir, to travel with people like you and me.' I bowed with what I thought was grace befitting a person who makes the ideal travelling companion. 'Mind you, they are not all alike. Take Mr Bradman now. He is a gentleman. Indeed, yes. He has a lovely home in Adelaide.' I failed to see what this had to do with it, but who was I to interrupt? 'No, sir. Don't talk to me of the Australian cricketers.' I tried to look as if nothing was further from my mind. I kept right out of it, even to the point of not telling her that I was one of the team. After all, she was rather an old lady, and what did it matter, anyhow? The team loved the story and the dear old lady never afterwards failed to nod kindly to me as we passed on the ship.

CHAPTER SIX   *Snippets from an*
                    African Diary – 1935–36

Ｎothing is more pathetic, yet amusing, than the presiding gentleman at a sporting function who, knowing little of sport, insists on making a sporting speech. He trots out all the hackneyed sporting phrases and looks most pleased with himself; he receives his greatest applause when he makes an unconscious blunder. This happened almost at the beginning of the journey by the Australians to South Africa in 1935. We were travelling on the Trans-continental railway line in Western Australia and were given a civic reception at Kalgoorlie. Richardson, the captain, was leading a happy band of men and the beginning of the trip, after we had assembled at Adelaide, was marked by much jollity and friendship. 'And now,' said the Kalgoorlie Mayor, finishing his civic speech of welcome, 'I want to wish you and your team, Mr Chipperfield, all the best of successes at the Olympic Games!' No speech on tour was better received. It was reminiscent of the blunder the Brisbane Mayor made in 1928, when he welcomed Chapman and his MCC team. The Mayor said how pleased he was to see old faces in Sutcliffe, Hobbs and others. 'I also want to give a very warm welcome,' said the Mayor, 'to Mr Mead. We knew his father very well out here in 1911.' Phil Mead blushed and tried to look as if it really was his father who came to Australia in 1911. His team-mates enthusiastically 'hear-hear-ed' the Mayor who appeared delighted with himself.

Bad News from Africa:

The liner carrying the Australians to South Africa was in the middle of its long dreary run from Fremantle to Durban when the wireless brought news one day that Horace (Jock) Cameron had died in Johannesburg on November 2, 1935. His sad and totally unexpected demise made a big impression on our party, because Cameron had been a popular figure in our land and those of us privileged to have his friendship were looking forward to meeting him again in a few days' time. In the face of adversity, when his team followed one disappointing display with another and yet another, Cameron showed himself in Australia in 1931–32 to be a big-hearted captain, who kept the game in its true perspective. He was, also, one of the best punishing batsmen in the world, and I saw no peer to him as a wicket-keeper. Such tragedies have been too common in South African sport. It was approximately a year previously that the accomplished left-handed bowler, Neville Quinn, died suddenly.

On Pulling Into Durban:

There can be few more delightful ports in the world than Durban. The old inhabitants say they have seen elephants and hippopotami roaming the suburbs, which might or might not be leg-pulling, but there is nothing imaginary about the dozens of monkeys which scamper in the trees at Stellawood. The huge Zulu ricksha boys, with cow's horns butting out from their feathered-topped heads, never ceased to draw our interest. The tourist walking out of his hotel is met by a long line of these grinning, huge-muscled fellows, who prance and jump about to advertise themselves as strong pullers of the ricksha. There are 60,000 Indians in Durban and a grotesque sight is when rain comes to Kingsmead, Durban's main ground, and a long centipede of tarpaulin will emerge from the pavilion to cover the wicket, the tarpaulin being carried by Indians in their native white dress. A huge crowd met the liner at the Durban wharf, waiting to give us a typically warm Springbok welcome, but the earliest welcome came from a lone signalling figure off a headland when the liner emerged from the early morning mist. She was Miss Ethel Campbell, known to every Australian soldier of 1914–18 who went to Europe via South Africa. Miss Campbell was revered by the Australian Digger, who referred to her as the Signaller, because she thus met and farewelled every Australian troopship from the headland. Her hospitality to our men was famed throughout Australia. W. A. Oldfield, wicket-keeper of the original Australian Imperial Forces team, was with our side, and Miss Campbell, true to her record, was there to welcome him.

The Sick Stockrider:

It was a happy coincidence that the Australian team was in Durban on November 17, the anniversary of the death of the great Australian bowler, Jack Ferris, at Durban in 1900. We visited his grave, where a few of his friends had erected a tombstone. The breath of Australia keeps him company in Adam Lindsay Gordon's lines in 'The Sick Stockrider':

'Let me slumber in the hollow where the wattle blossoms wave,
  With never stone nor rail to fence my bed;
Should the sturdy station children pull the bush flower on my
    grave,
  I may chance to hear them romping overhead.'

Our Manager Introduces Himself:

Harold Rowe, manager of the Australian team, was a first-class cricketer in our land. I believe he would have played for Australia had his West Australian home not been separated by some two thousand miles from our hub of Test cricket. No better or more popular manager sailed, and this Australian team, from the manager down, was particularly keen to make a good name for itself off the field in the first full-scale Australian tour of South Africa. The bodyline era had left both English and Australian cricket under a cloud. Events had shown cricketers of several lands that there was just as important a game to be played off as on the field. Manager Rowe, therefore, arose with eagerness at our first big reception in Durban to create a good impression. Like all good speakers on such occasions, he tossed in the inevitable humorous cricket story. It was about a former well-known Australian captain whose immense bulk was world famous. This fellow was playing in an up-country game in Australia, and the poor yokel bowler, when he saw the other take up his huge stance at the wicket, complained to the umpire that he could not even see the three stumps.

'Never mind that,' said the country umpire 'you just bowl the ball up. If it hits him on the legs, I'll give him out leg before wicket; if it hits him on the rear, I'll give it a wide!'

The audience was a male one, and the manager, naturally enough, used perhaps a more expressive word than rear. Mr Rowe sat down, pleased with the reception of the joke and his speech. Victor Richardson leaned across and touched him on the arm.

'That peculiar little thing in front of you, Harold,' said Richardson, 'is a microphone. That joke of yours should go well over the air!'

Poor Rowe was horrified. The players afterwards teased him on tour by inducing sweet young things to say to him, 'Oh, Mr Rowe, I listened in to your first speech. I thought it was just wonderful!'

One Fresh and One Jaded:

The coincidence of the Australian and South African season is a blessing for a touring side. It comes fresh after the home winter spell, whereas an English team visiting Australia and Australians and South African teams visiting England do so at the end of a full summer at home. It is impossible to retain skill and enthusiasm for a game if that game develops into a solid round of duty. In this regard, the South Africans were at a disadvantage against us. They had just finished a tour of England, in which Rowan and Nourse, for instance, had played 54 and 53 innings respectively and Langton had bowled almost a thousand overs. Anybody who plays 54 innings or who bowls six thousand balls in a short English summer has been not on a sporting so much as a business tour. Some day somebody will realise just how damaging it is to the sport and the individual to play cricketers and tennis players into the ground over a short period. South Africa had beaten England at Lord's in the only Test finished. Mitchell 164 not out, Cameron 90, Balaskas 5–49 and 4–54 and Langton 4–31 were the Springbok heroes. As Australia had beaten England in 1934 the clash in South Africa was virtually for the world's title. Bradman, because of ill health, had declined the tour. In 19 Tests to that date, South Africa had beaten Australia only once.

Away to a Good Start:

Fortunate is the touring side which gets away to a good start. The same applies to the individual. Confidence in cricket is a peculiar and almost indefinable quality, terrifying the individual when it is lacking and being taken for granted when it is present. The man of experience knows it does not do to take confidence too much for granted, because it is easily lost. Success alone begets confidence. Of those who have been through the mill and known days of lean fortune, who does not recall his wretched feelings of hopelessness as he comes to the wicket after a run of poor scores? It reminds me of a cartoon I once saw, entitled 'The Batsman's Nightmare'. He was defending stumps three times their usual size, at his back loomed the biggest pair of wicket-keeping hands ever seen, and on all sides he was surrounded by grinning, leering fieldsmen with giant hands ready for the catch. In all this the wretched batsman's piece of willow had dwindled to a mere tooth-pick . . . Richardson's Australian team was fortunate in starting well in its first game at Durban.

We had a week of practice on excellent wickets, and in this regard South African wickets are much superior to the general run of practice wickets in England. The Kingsmead wicket was as true as an Australian one, though slightly slower, and the weather was like an Australian summer. Richardson closed with 5–522 after all the Australian batsmen had shown form. Brown made 148, myself 121 (the opening partnership was 215), Richardson 75, McCabe 65, Chipperfield 60 and Darling 26. We had four Springbok internationals against us in Herby Wade, Siedle, Nourse and Dalton. Nourse made a magnificent century, as did Harvey, who later won his international cap, and Siedle also had a good look at our bowling with 21 and 68. The amazing Grimmett, whose career has been marked by scarcely a loose ball, took nine wickets in the two innings and Australia won handsomely. The first ball Grimmett bowls when he reaches the cricketers' heaven is bound to be of immaculate length. Usually, with a slow bowler, the batsman knows he will get a few loose deliveries to begin with, but Grimmett knows not the term. On reflection, I like the expression I have used regarding Siedle – 'he had a good look at our bowling'. Siedle looks harder at a bowler than anybody I have seen. As he settles down for the strike, he extends his eyes to their limit, grimacing with his face meanwhile. Then his eyeballs protrude as he stares so intently up the wicket to interpret everything the bowler sends along. Siedle was chosen to come to Australia in 1931, but could not make the trip. Judging by the contortions of his eyes, he was anxious to catch up in this one game with what his fellows had learned of Grimmett and O'Reilly in Australia. A feature of the match was that O'Reilly failed to take a wicket in 17 overs.

Obsequies for Newlands:

'Where,' asked our humourist and fast bowler, Ernie McCormick, after he had bowled for an innings on the Cape Town wicket and sat in the dressing-room caressing his bare, sore feet, 'can I get a wreath?' 'Whatever for?' we asked, puzzled. 'I want to lay it on this Newlands wicket,' replied McCormick, 'it is the deadest thing I have ever struck.' The genial Bob Crisp, South African fast bowler, agreed with McCormick. Newlands certainly is a lifeless wicket, probably the slowest in the world. Out batsmen liked it and so did our spinners. Fleetwood-Smith made the Western Province batsmen turn all manner of astounding capers in taking 12 wickets for 103. What a bowler this chap is when he likes, but the job of any captain with Fleetwood is to get him to take the game and himself seriously . . . I doubt if there is a prettier ground in the world than Newlands. It is English-like in the crop of trees under which spectators sit, and always the game moves on with the huge, bulky Table Mountain serving as a backcloth. Table Mountain seems to rise sheer from the ground at long-off. The many colours far up the mountainside throw off the glinting rays of the sun, and hour by hour the huge mass of rock takes on a different character. I liked Table Top best when its summit was shrouded in cloud – the Devil and an old Dutchman competing, as the old fable has it, to see which is the better smoker.

Up in the Air at Cape Town:

The average Cape Town (or Kaapstad) citizen takes his aerial railway very much for granted. This runs from Adderley Street (so called because of Adderley, the member of Parliament, who vigorously opposed the English plan to dump convicts in the colony), to 3,582 feet high Table Mountain. The trip takes twenty minutes and the thrill is impossible to describe. The cage in itself seems a flimsy little thing, the sides reaching possibly to one's hips; but the flimsiness of it becomes more apparent as it goes on up and up, climbing the slender, steel hawser, which loses itself far up in the mountain above. The feeling in this cage is altogether different from that in an aeroplane. The whirr of the propellers gives a feeling of solidity in a 'plane, but there is no noise in the cage, just a seemingly endless going upwards, a slight oscillation and the ground beneath fading away into a fairyland in which the tops of trees look like pin-points. And only mere floor-boards between you and this vast space! To go up in it by day or night is the thrill of a lifetime. It stops when the weather is windy. It made us giddy to be told of the attendant who sits where the cage is joined to the cable and calmly oils the cable for its entire length.

High Up at Johannesburg:

The City of the Second Chance, as somebody with a sense of humour once termed Johannesburg, was a plateau of waving grasslands when Dr W. G. Grace had long passed the zenith of his career. The Old Chap, therefore, knew nothing about the good batting light and the perfect wicket of the Wanderers, which, in addition to being the best fielding ground in the world, also rates as the best Scotchman's Hill. I should explain the latter term. It is usually applied to a high vantage point, where unpaying spectators outside the ground can see the play. The Oval in Kennington is a gift to such spectators with its surrounding tenements, but the towering skyscrapers around the Wanderers provide excellent and better grandstands. Binoculars flash from all directions when there is a Test on at the

Wanderers. . . . The fielding ground is superb, meticulously level with fine grass, in which the fingers sink to receive the ball. And to throw from the boundary on the Wanderers is ridiculously simple, because the ball sails on and on through the rarified air. This air is most deceptive for gauging catches, and players coming upon Johannesburg from the sea level find themselves panting for breath or in some instances bleeding freely from the nose. Sport in Johannesburg, I should think, asks a lot of a person's heart, and there is something in the air which seems to make Johannesburg a favourite haunt for many of the Union's best sportsmen. Good jobs seem to be there in plentitude. I once saw a golf match on one of the city's magnificent golf courses, in which a car magnate saved his game against a butchering business-man by sinking a long putt on the last green. The bet was a car against a side of beef! . . . This vivid city of towering sky-scrapers and picturesque castles of gold dumps was doubly interesting to the touring Australians.

In the early days the government of the Transvaal Republic asked an Australian gold digger named Armfield to report on the Witwatersrand, a field from which £50 million sterling was being annually taken in this year of 1935. Our Australian compatriot calmly announced that the field was not one for the prospector! In 1886 an Australian gold digger named Harrison did something to retrieve our national reputation. He modestly reported that his long experience on the Australian fields led him to think that Oosthuizen's farm was a payable gold-field! The Johannesburg gold people held nothing against us because of this slur cast on their fields by our predecessors. After we had gone down to sea-level on the East Geduld mine, the manager offered us the week's recovery – in the shape of a brick – if we could pick it up with one hand. We certainly tried hard enough! At this mine was the impression of Gracie Fields' shoe on the wet concrete, stoutly barricaded to preserve it for posterity. . . . O'Reilly took his first wicket, Mitchell clean bowled, in this third game of the tour against Transvaal at the Wanderers. This was exceedingly strange for O'Reilly, who is intensely difficult for batsmen who have never seen his wares before. He took four wickets for 109, ordinary figures to be true, which did not suggest the tremendous difficulties the South Africans were later to have against him. Mitchell, Briscoe, Foley and Langton made handy scores. By this third game all the leading South African batsmen, with the exception of Rowan, had had a good look at the Australian bowling. Later games and the Tests especially were to prove that instead of improving against our spinners they went sadly off. It was in this game that we 'fluked' a double leg trap for O'Reilly's bowling, a trap that was later to torment and tantalise the Springboks beyond measure, and which incited at least one critic to urge the South Africans to smash this 'insult to their manhood'.

At home in New South Wales I had always fielded at short or silly leg to O'Reilly. Richardson, our captain and the best 'silly' fieldsman it has been my pleasure to see, took over the job in the early Union games. I loved fielding, but became very bored when placed in the old gentlemen's positions. No captain was more approachable than Vic Richardson, a factor which contributed towards his greatness as the best Australian captain I knew, and I put it to him at Johannesburg that I would like a bigger fielding finger in the pie. 'Come up with me, then,' said Vic, and I moved up to silly square leg. It would be impossible to estimate how much sting that double 'suicide' trap took out of the Springboks. O'Reilly's peerless length and unusual pace for this type of bowling allowed us to sit on the Springboks all the season and pick their bats for catches. We took decided risks and the South Africans threw their wickets away often trying to drive us out. Few English batsmen allowed us to worry them so much. They played the 'dead' bat better than the South Africans. After dodging injury all the season, Richardson and I smiled wryly when one newspaper critic towards the end seriously advocated that it was unfair of us to field so close! . . . It was disappointing to read in early 1945 that the sumptuous Johannesburg railway station was not satisfied with its £750,000 expanse and intended to gobble up the Wanderers. There is no better club spirit anywhere, I think, than at the Wanderers. Even a Test match does not stop the ground being given over on Friday night to the Dogs – a sport which came to South Africa from Australia, as did the wattle and gum trees which abound in the Union. And now grimy coal trucks are to be shunted across a field which many generations of all lands have hallowed. I am disappointed, Johannesburg! Is business so real that sentiment counts for naught?

Talking at the Wickets:

Rowan, of the Transvaal, was the slightest player in the Tests and the most talkative. The vast majority of batsmen abhor talking while they are batting, the suggestion being that it upsets their confidence. Many have a little social chat about the game or some outstanding incident between overs, but nearly everybody is as mute as the Sphinx during an over. I remember in my earlier days that there were suggestions that this wicket-keeper or that had a habit of 'talking batsmen out', the idea being, for instance, to compliment a young batsman on his footwork or advise him that the best way to play a certain bowler was to go down the wicket after him. The talkative wicket-keeper was thus supposed to open up opportunities of stumpings for himself. I never came across such a wicket-keeper, and always found that as a race keepers kept their tongue to themselves – outside of appeals, of course – unless they were invited by the batsmen to join in on some topic.

Rowan was different. He kept up a happy running conversation with everybody within earshot on the particular merits and demerits of the ball bowled, the stroke played, the good or bad fortune of affairs, the health of the in-fieldsmen's families and so on. A very bright lad, Eric Rowan! He stayed with us long enough to top score with 66 in the first innings of the first Test at Durban and then left for the pavilion, still full of chirpy chat. . . . When Dudley Nourse made a century against us in the first match of the tour, all the Australians wrote him down as a top-notch batsman. It was not the century he made so much as the manner in which he made it. His 91 in the second innings of the Durban Test, therefore, was no surprise. He is glorious in his footwork. He moved yards down the wicket to Grimmett, and ranks second to Bradman, I am inclined to think, in the speed of his feet. A beautiful driver, he plays the square cut gloriously, but is not, I would say, a great lover of the fast stuff. . . . Moods in a cricket game are largely actuated by the weather. Players react quickly to surroundings, sun and rain, but never could a Test have been played under more dismal conditions than one day of this first Test, when an 84 miles an hour hurricane swept the open Kingsmead ground. Players and umpires chased the bails all the afternoon, and it was difficult for the batsmen to keep their feet, let alone maintain their balance at the creases. It was just as bad for the bowlers and fieldsmen as the batsmen. Despite all this, McCabe and Chipperfield made magnificent centuries. McCabe always appears to open a tour, season or a series at the top of his form. Kingsmead was delighted with his skill. . . . Kingsmead is unique of all the grounds I know in perpetuating Test deeds. The maker of a century or the taker of five wickets in an innings is invited to plant a tree in an avenue on the ground, which bears many famous names. The Australians, who won the Test by nine wickets, sent off a fair contingent with spades at the end of the game. McCabe, Chipperfield and O'Reilly planted trees, Fleetwood-Smith missed fame by a wicket and Grimmett by two. The South Africans were not represented. Nourse missed by nine runs and Langton by one wicket.

Nourse and McCabe:

South African cricket took on a new lease of life against Australia on 27th December, 1935. On that day Dudley Nourse took Grimmett, O'Reilly and Fleetwood-Smith by the scruff of their bowling necks and rubbed their faces in the lush grass of the Wanderers. He made 231, the highest South African score in history against Australia, the previous best being Faulkner's 204 in Melbourne in 1910–11. These two alone have topped the double century against Australia, but it is interesting that on the same ground as Dudley performed his magnificent feat, his father, Dave, made 111 in 1921–22 against a hot bowling side, which included Jack Gregory, McDonald and Mailey. Dave made his century on an ant-bed, matting wicket. This 1935 innings by his son was a classic, with vigorous, clean strokes which cleaved the field in all directions. Nourse's innings was just the tonic South African cricket needed. The tantalising spin of Grimmett and O'Reilly, to this stage, had made the Springboks feel very sick, and it did not help those with the job on hand to be given all manner of gratuitous advice from the Press-box on how to deal with these Australian monsters of spin. I write this not unkindly, because I admired his style of play and knew he was past his best when he came to Australia in 1931, but Herbie Taylor criticised rather harshly in his Press articles from the pavilion. Why is it that most sportsmen who have run their race usually fall into the role of severe critics? Is it because they are resentful of the fact that life is passing them by, that they begrudge to youth the fields which they once trod themselves nobly and well? Youth is much more tolerant of age in sport than age is of youth. I recall an old Australian international who was forever reminding me when I came across him that none of my generation would have made the international grade in his day. I knew another who derived much self-satisfaction from telling me that Tate, Grimmett and O'Reilly were 'just bowlers'. What does it all matter? The point is that all are trying to play the game to the best of their ability. And I remember that Taylor, now so profuse in his advice, did not cut too glorious a figure himself against our spinners in Australia.

It is well, always, to appreciate the difficulties of the one who has the job on hand. Not one Australian batsman envied the Springboks in their terrific job against Grimmett, O'Reilly, McCormick, and, to a lesser extent, Fleetwood-Smith. They had wickets which took spin and they were supported by brilliant fielding. All three Australians had entirely dissimilar spinning methods. Grimmett and O'Reilly were masterly exponents of length, and Fleetwood-Smith, on his day, was a baffling problem. Possibly no Test side in history walked on to the ground with a better spinning combination. There was no peace for the Springboks. If they struggled through an O'Reilly over they had to face Grimmett at the other end. Our spinners were quickly taking the heart out of South African cricket, and thus it was good to see Nourse play his glorious innings. All South Africa rejoiced and the Australians did not begrudge it one little bit. Nourse had made none in his first innings and had a terrific battle to make his first run in the second. . . . On the same pinnacle of greatness was McCabe's 189 not out in Australia's second innings. We were 1–16 when McCabe came to bat and when play ceased the score was 2–274. McCabe's 189 not out had dominated the play. The wicket had powdered badly and in the mid-afternoon there blew up a black, mineral-laden storm, which made the light wretched. Despite these disabilities, McCabe treated the bowling and the position as he liked. South Africa began our innings with Test victory in the air. Herby Wade took the most unusual course of appealing against the light from the field, on which seeming victory had turned into pending defeat. It was one of McCabe's three historical innings. Fortunate is a ground which witnessed the Nourse and McCabe innings in the same Test.

A Chapter of Accidents:

McCabe will not soon forget the third Test at Newlands (Cape Town). He sat in the pavilion with the pads on for hours while the Australian openers made the record score of 233. He walked to bat stiff and cold, as a batsman does who has been sitting and waiting so long for a wicket to fall. He really opened his score when he snicked a ball fine to leg. Quite understandably the umpire gave it as two byes and next ball McCabe was caught and bowled for a 'duck'. He lost a presentation fountain pen that day, and on the way home to the hotel was booked for speeding. McCabe left the car in front of the hotel and that night there was a terrific rainstorm. The water short circuited the horn and there was a terrific din in the middle of the night. A traffic policeman tracked down McCabe, had him out of bed and 'booked' him again for parking in the wrong place. O'Reilly lent McCabe moral support next day when he went to interview the traffic police. They left the station with an armful of autograph books and plenty of good advice about the Cape Town traffic rules. As McCabe and O'Reilly drove along the Cape Town streets thereafter, they took the salute from every traffic cop they passed.

On Temperament:

The fundamental difference between Australian and South African batsmen seems to be temperament. Up to the end of the third Test there had been 25 South African scores against Australia exceeding 20. When a batsman reaches 20 it usually means that he has played himself in, has had a good look at the bowling, knows the wicket and is gaining confidence. The Australian reasoning is that once a batsman reaches 20 he should go on to a big score. Yet on those 25 occasions when South Africans had reached the twenties only one, Nourse, had gone on to three figures. The average Australian batsman solidifies a good start; the average South African by contrast allows indiscretions to creep in. Instead of digging in against Grimmett and O'Reilly and playing them ball by ball, the Springbok invariably went in for the kill, and that was no simple matter against such bowlers. Most South African wickets fell in the attempt to hit our spinners of their length (sometimes before the ball was bowled) or to hit our suicide fieldsmen out of position. Comparing the Australian batsmen, of the 17 scores of over 20 in the first three Tests five had gone on to centuries. There had been three sixties and two fifties. Richardson stampeded the South Africans in the first innings of the third Test by putting Grimmett on while the ball was practically new. South Africa never recovered from 4–29.

On the Bloemfontein Mat:

Once upon a time all South African cricket was played on matting. The exception now is the rule, and we struck only two on the tour – Bloemfontein and Bulawayo. We liked the mat tremendously, because the ball came through truly, it favoured on-side strokes and it gave bowlers a chance, the ball gripping the coir for spin. I am inclined to think that a good matting wicket on ant-bed is as good as the average first-class turf wicket. In Australia we are prone to advocate turf wickets in country districts, but unless properly prepared a turf wicket is of more nuisance than benefit, leading to many batting and bowling evils. Bloemfontein welcomed us with an earth-shake. Even better than his bowling feats on tour was O'Reilly's record in getting from the second-floor of the hotel into the street outside. The shake lasted only a few seconds, but O'Reilly was outside before it finished. O'Brien and McCabe made centuries on the mat, Australia closing with 4–361. Grimmett and O'Reilly took ten and nine wickets respectively during the match.

The Story of Nupen:

Wherever went went in South Africa we heard the story of E. P. Nupen, which invariably finished with a sigh and on the note of what a pity it was we never saw him bowl on matting. It was not our business to tell the South Africans their business, but in their Nupen lament they have fooled themselves over the years and, against us, at least robbed themselves of a bowler who should have had a position in every Test. Nupen, as I understand the story, made his name on matting wickets and, going to England with a Union team when young, did not succeed there as expected. Nupen came home and South Africa was inclined to shake its cricket heads when his name was mentioned and say, 'Ah, what a glorious bowler on matting wickets!' They were then prepared to forget all about this tall, well-built, medium-paced bowler. That impression seemed to have seeped into Nupen's cricketing soul. He gave us, too, the impression that he considered himself no good on turf. He came to bowl rather apologetically against us at the Wanderers for Transvaal and later in one Test. He spun from the off and flipped one back now and then from the leg, but he was never pushed to the front with the ball at the beginning of an innings as if his skipper had faith in him. His skipper, his side, the spectators and Nupen himself seemed to be saying with every ball, 'Ah, if this were only a matting wicket!' The point is that we were pleased Nupen did not play in the whole series. We considered him a real danger, but these things are discussed only in the dressing-room.

A Beer or Not a Beer?

The first and only tiff we had with South African officialdom was at Kimberley, home of diamonds, Cecil Rhodes, Beit, Barnato and the Big Hole. Bowling under the hot African sun was hard work, and one or two of our bowlers usually left orders with the 12th man that when he brought out drinks he was to bring out a small glass of beer. They found that such a stimulant stood them in good stead. At Kimberley, however, one of the official hierarchy of South African cricket put down a prohibition foot and refused to allow such a drink to go on the Kimberley field. I do not know what the tough miners of other Kimberley days would have done, but our 12th man, Chipperfield, himself a teetotaller, complained bitterly and came on the field to see Richardson about it. Our skipper walked off, said a few well-chosen words to the official about men having a man's mind, the drinks came out with small beers among them, and that was that. We were fortunate in having with us, through the tour, a South African manager from Cape Town in W. F. Lambrechts. 'Lammy' was 'one of the boys' and intensely popular with the team. He did much to make our Union progress so successful. The story is that the Kimberley ground was built, with a tremendously long pavilion, out of the diamonds found on the field when it was decided to turn it into a sports-ground. When our Rugby footballers played there in 1933 the ground was all ant-bed. In our time there was a circle of green grass running within a radius of the wicket, with the outer field ant-bed. Because of the nature of the ground the ball was stitched with copper-wire. Our spin bowlers did not like it. A youth named Helfrich had a good double against us with 64 and 59. He played

O'Reilly with more confidence than many of the Test men. I thought he was bound to become an international.

This lad, who was only 16 when he played against Australia, died soon afterwards before having a chance to prove his worth. His death is a further instance of how South Africa is unfortunate in losing its stars from a small population.

Whether the 'beer incident' or the atmosphere got into our blood it is hard to say, but between wickets the Australians put on a little game of that other national game of ours – two up! It must be difficult to get an illicit diamond out of Kimberley. That opinion impressed itself upon us after seeing the Native compound, hearing of the X-ray and other treatment for the natives when they leave, seeing the high voltage barbed wire which encompasses the compound and the packs of Alsatian dogs which stand guard. The pulsator machine which pounded and crushed the blue rocks was a wonder to us, and there was a tremendous thrill in watching the dirt spill down with water over vaselined trays. Every now and then a diamond hit the vaseline and stayed while the dirt swirled past. Vaseline, like a pretty woman, has an affinity for diamonds.

Boys of the Old Brigade!

On their way through South Africa to the 1914–18 War, the Australian troops evidently made the most of their stay in the Union. We heard tales of them throughout the Union. One evening in Johannesburg, Darling and I knew what was coming when a guest at dinner started out on the old, old story.

'We always knew when there was an Australian troopship in port,' said this guest. 'Mother would make us all come inside, Father would lock the doors and we would put out the lights.'

This was rather thick, but Darling and I kept a stiff upper lip.

'Ah, yes,' I said, 'I suppose you lived in Durban?'

'Indeed, no,' she replied. 'We lived forty miles out in the country from Durban!'

Returning home that night, Darling and I comforted each other with the thought that possibly the present generation is not as good as past ones.

The Colour of South Africa:

South Africa will never lack a huge tourist trade, for new wonders of the human race and the gigantic lavishness of nature meet one at every turn. It is vastly dissimilar to anything Europe has to offer, and though on the same degrees of latitude as Australia the two countries differ entirely. As a patriotic Australian I winced when told that the Union imported wattle trees as well as gum trees from our land, and then promptly began to export wattle bark back to us! The gold mines, which run deep under the city, honeycombing it as the catacombs did early Rome, are full of romance and provide the city with a thrill every now and then as a big fall in a mine causes the sky-scrapers above to give a gentle totter. Visitors look askance at this; the local folk do not notice it. The gold mines are part of the world's wonders. People at all unwell are advised against going down the mines, and rightly so, for the speed of the drop in the huge lifts causes the ears to go deaf. Thousands of feet underground one emerges into a city-like labyrinth of concrete roads running in all directions, a huge power-house and gutters of swirling waters. To hear an explosion from miles along the level echoing along the tunnel is an experience never forgotten. So also is the spectacle of two huge natives, torsos bare, sweating and vibrating as one plunges a pneumatic drill into a small opening, while the other leans his back against him, giving support. There is no greater spectacle in Johannesburg than a native dance of a Sunday morning at a mine compound. Hundreds of natives dress in football jerseys with fantastic head-dress, and following their leader, a man of huge physique, who is garbed for the occasion and usually with a whistle, they go through amazing dances in splendid rhythm with the vast array of drums and native-made xylophones. They work themselves up to a terrific frenzy, stamping the earth until it reverberates. The din is terrific, and every now and then there are peals of laughter from the native watchers as the funny man of the team imitates the doctor or the manager of the mine.

Very generously one Sunday morning the South African Government placed a huge aeroplane at our disposal and at dawn we left Johannesburg for the Kruger National Park, the two hundred miles long and forty miles square area in the Eastern Transvaal which belongs exclusively to one million wild animals, lions, elephants, buffalo, giraffe, crocodiles, hippos, zebra and many varieties of beautiful buck. Hundreds of miles of good roads run through the Reserve. These were used by only three cars when the Reserve was opened in 1927, because it was difficult to convince people that it was safe to travel among so many wild and ferocious animals in a mere sedan. Because of the danger of malaria the Reserve is open only during the winter and spring months, but the Government most generously stretched a point for us. It was an unforgettable trip. We came round a bend in the road upon a party of ten or a dozen lions and lionesses enjoying their midday meal of buck. The lions merely stared at the car, and are now so used to the sight of them that they do not even wander away. The elephants, too, seemed friendly enough, but strict rules forbid people to emerge from the cars to see just how far this seeming friendliness goes. That day ranked as our best in South Africa, not least being the excitement of the natives at seeing their first aeroplane. An improvised strip had been made for the occasion.

Johannes and His Snakes:

Except the match against Eastern Province, all else faded into insignificance beside the Snake Park. The Australians quite frankly were scared of snakes from the first day they put foot in South Africa. On the Pietermaritzburg station one day O'Reilly and I, after many misgivings and assurances that it was harmless, accepted a baby snake from schoolboys on an opposite train, and very warily took it back to our train to frighten McCabe and the native attendant so much that they locked themselves in cabins. We played golf often in the Union, and whenever the ball went into dangerous looking rough we were invariably inclined to regard it indifferently and say it was only an old ball, anyway. The mambas, particularly, had us scared, and entering a barn in an up-country home one day I was quite certain my last few minutes had come when I was bitten on the nape of the neck. The 'mamba' proved to be only a hornet, although the period waiting for this to be proved was quite exciting. At Port Elizabeth hundreds of mambas, pythons, adders, cobras and boom-slangs slither and wriggle and swim in a small enclosure and, horror of horrors, into their pit walks Johannes the Native, calmly takes two handfuls of the writhing creatures and drapes them around his neck! Then, for good measure, Johannes the Native takes a particularly nasty looking reptile, grabs it at the jaw and them firmly strokes its fangs with a piece of stick until the poison drips slowly off. Ugh! Johannes got his job when his predecessor ran off to sea. The only other snake farm is in Sau Paulo (Brazil). The best snake story concerns three young white lads, 15, 13 and 10, who caught snakes and supplied them to the farm. Thinking they could make their money much easier, they broke into the farm one night, and while two kept watch the other, bare-legged, dropped into the pit, heaved out the reptiles to his friends and they sold them back to the farm next day. Those lads deserved something better than the caning they got from the local magistrate.

A Plum for Bradman:

An Australian Eleven cricketer away from his business position and home for six months in a foreign land does not exactly become a millionaire on the out-of-pocket expenses he is allowed. He has his financial commitments at home, in addition to the many and varied expenses on tour and six months' loss of time in his job. We were allowed out-of-pocket expenses of about £300 each for the South African tour. Most, if not all, lost money on the tour, and it did not help when a leading South African official blandly told us at Johannesburg that Bradman had been offered £1,000 as a bonus to make the trip. Bradman, as I have explained elsewhere, was too ill to tour. Had he made the tour under those special conditions it is not difficult to conceive the resentment others would have felt at this singling out of an individual. As it was, we had decided views on the offer.

Bulawayo and the Falls:

Up from Kimberley and through Mafeking, the Kalahari desert and the Bechuanaland Protectorate, we came to Southern Rhodesia, land of the Matabeles and the Mashonas, Bulawayo, the Matapos, the burial place of Rhodes, the Everlasting or Resurrection plant and the famous Victoria Falls. Being a touring cricketer is a good way to see the world, and the Australians were indebted to our hosts for giving us a magnificent holiday spell at the Victoria Falls. We first saw the breath-taking Falls by night, blundering along wet, slippery rocks, the imminence of which to the sheer drop over the side gave us misgivings when we saw them again next day. Livingstone was the first white man to see 'scenes so lovely as must have been gazed upon by angels in their flight.' A hunter named Baldwin was the second and Chapman the third. Chapman wondered at the spoors of elephants, rhinos, buffalos and hippos at the very brink of the precipice. 'It makes one's hair stand on end,' he wrote, 'to see the numerous indications of their midnight rambles at the very verge of eternity. Here they come at the dead, dark midnight hours to drink the spray and wallow in the mire; and on asking a native how it was they were not afraid, he asked me in return: 'Didn't they grow up together?' And this was where we rambled at midnight! From a staging we took a motor-boat trip up the Zambesi River and landed on a jungle island inhabited by monkeys. It was rather interesting to reflect what would have happened had the engine of that motor-boat cut out! . . . Our game at Bulawayo was also on the matting. We were again perfectly at ease. Darling made a brilliant century and Brown played a classical innings for 97. The Rhodesians were making merry with 4–157 when rain washed the game out. O'Reilly did not take a wicket. . . . One should not leave Rhodesia without mentioning the 'sun-downer'. It seems to be an old Rhodesian custom. History says that whisky was the first commodity the white man brought with him into the land of the

Mashonas and the Matabeles. The Rhodesian claims that the 'sun-downer' is the antidote to malaria. Years afterwards, in Australia, I placed in water a dried sprig of the Resurrection Plant I had brought with me from Rhodes' lonely grave on the Matapos. Slowly and miraculously it took on again the green and russet colours it had known when it grew on those lonely, desolate hills which mark the grave of Rhodes, a grave known simply by the name on it, 'Cecil John Rhodes'.

Record for Grimmett:

With 23 wickets in the last two Tests, C. V. Grimmett took his total for the series to the dizzy heights of 44, a record for any Australian bowler in a series. Grimmett's total of Test wickets stands at 216, made up of 106 English, 77 South African and 33 West Indian victims. This is the record, the previous best being 189 by S. F. Barnes for England. I never cease to wonder at Grimmett's control and variation of pace and height. Like O'Reilly, the South African wickets suited him admirably. They gave him enough turn to beat the bat and yet allow his top-spinner to come through with pace for a clean bowled or leg before wicket. O'Reilly, also, had a magnificent Test season, claiming 27 Test wickets at a cost of 17 each. O'Reilly is the type of bowler whom captains bless every minute of a game. Like all class bowlers, he is temperamental, but he is most unselfish in aiding a skipper should there be a 'spot' at a particular end of the wicket. O'Reilly will suggest to the skipper that he should give it to the other man, though nobody is better suited than O'Reilly to capitalise the gift of such a 'spot'. An instance of this was in the last Test at Durban, when he gave way to Grimmett. The slow bowler took 13 wickets in the match; O'Reilly four.

Richardson Catches:

There was no finer feature of the tour than Richardson's fielding. He took 26 catches in positions ranging from slips to cover, but he was particularly deadly in the leg trap to O'Reilly. He took almost miraculous catches there. I have never seen a catch going in Richardson's direction without knowing that the batsman was as good as out. He brackets in my mind with Hammond in possessing the cleanest pair of catching hands I have seen. In the final Test at Durban, Richardson caught half the South African side out in the second innings. He took his catches off Grimmett in the most unusual fielding position I have seen – two yards away from the bat, at gully slip, standing almost alongside the wicket-keeper. Grimmett was spinning the ball furiously and Richardson helped himself to catches as they curled off the bat. After this game at Durban, following the usual Natal custom, Mitchell (five wickets), Grimmett (seven and six wickets) and myself (118) planted trees, Grimmett two. It would have been fitting had Richardson been invited to plant one because of his five catches.

Unusual Crop of 'Pairs':

One of the most remarkable features of this series was the inordinate number of 'pairs' made in the Tests. Bob Crisp had the rare distinction of getting two sets of pairs, Nicholson and Balaskas a set apiece.

A Veteran Makes Good:

The final match of the tour at Cape Town showed that South Africa might have done worse than play the two Nourses in the series. Dudley's father, Dave, played a capital half-century innings against us. It was a grand performance, despite the fact that Grimmett was not playing. The rest of the Australian bowlers were keen to dismiss Nourse Snr cheaply. A present generation does not like a preceding one to show it up. Dave Nourse gave an object lesson to the young Springboks on how to play against class bowlers. He played each ball quietly and with a spirit of determination – it was obvious with many younger ones during this tour that they had made up their minds what they were going to do with O'Reilly and Grimmett before the ball was bowled, and therein lies batting suicide. Some day I hope to see South Africa give Australia a terrific Test hiding. We have had it too much our way, and when that other day dawns I hope Australia will take its hiding with as much cheerfulness and good-natured sportsmanship as that exhibited by these charming South African fellows in two series of Tests, in which one galling disappointment followed the other. It is easy to be good sportsmen when with a winning team. The other is the real test.

A Word for the Skippers:

No harm can come to a game when the skippers are of the Richardson and Wade calibre. In that the 1935–36 series in South Africa was fortunate. Wade took defeat after defeat (and the fourth Test at Johannesburg was over in two humbling days) in as gallant a manner as Cameron had done before him in Australia. Each side took pleasure in the individual successes of the other, and that is how cricket should be played and will always be played if the two skippers are of the right type. No Australian on that tour has anything but the highest praise for Richardson. He was not chosen originally in the team, but came in as captain when Bradman had to decline the trip because of ill-health. Richardson is a captain in a hundred. His personality on the field is inspiring, yet withal he manages to impress his players that they are representing their country and not themselves. A good captain is a rare species. He does not bustle his men, he has little to say, he gives them credit for knowing the game, and he does not upset them by any fanciful alteration in the batting or bowling order. Richardson and Hammond are alike in their calm leadership. One of the greatest attributes a captain can possess is good-humoured optimism, and nature richly endowed Victor Richardson with that! He is the most admirable captain I knew.

CHAPTER SEVEN   *The Genius of McCabe*

T HE CRICKET GENIUS OF MCCABE
merges itself without fuss or bother into three epochial events –
Sydney (1932), Johannesburg (1935) and Nottingham (1938). Like
a renowned general whose name is closely followed by that of the
battlefield on which he wrote pages into history, McCabe could well
go down to posterity as McCabe of the Sydney Cricket Ground,
McCabe of the Wanderers and McCabe of Trent Bridge. At each of
these three citadels of cricket he played a Test innings of immortality. All three were so brilliant and monumental that those who saw
them hesitate to say that any one was greater than the others.

Unlike many other immortal innings which probably do not
reveal their value on paper, McCabe's three immediately stand out
when set down in relation to his team's total, for they tell clearly
how he dominated the play and monopolised the scene. At Sydney,
against the full fury of Jardine's bodyline tactics, McCabe made 187
not out in a total of 360; at Johannesburg, in deplorable light and on
a badly worn wicket, he made 189 not out of his team's 2–274; at
Trent Bridge he made 232 of Australia's 411 after the five other
acknowledged batsmen of the side, including Bradman, had fallen
for only 151.

In all these games Australia had its back to the wall, a point worth
particular notice, because in such circumstances McCabe showed
out in his best colours. At Sydney, with Bradman standing out of the
Australian team through illness, McCabe came to the wickets with

the scoring board showing 4–87. Larwood had taken three of the four, and bodyline had paralysed most of the Australians in preceding games. At Johannesburg he came to the creases when Australia needed 382 runs with nine wickets in hand on a tattered wicket that had already produced 898 runs. At Nottingham, on the Trent Bridge wicket, when McCabe attacked the English bowling with one of the most vicious innings known to the game, Australia was facing ignominy with 5–151 in answer to England's mammoth total of 8–658 (declared).

These facts prove, therefore, that McCabe was a great man in a crisis. He played all his cricket in the time of Bradman and much of it in the period of Ponsford – which is another way of suggesting that had there been more crises it would be reasonable to assume there would have been more McCabe epics, for it can never be assessed how the dominating brilliance of Bradman, in particular, dimmed the glory of McCabe.

A good instance of this was the Australian tour of England in the conciliatory and appeasing year of 1934. Even though the indiscreet Larwood and Voce had been stood in the Test corner for the season, the batting of some of the Australians had been given such a rude shock 18 months before in Australia that two of them, Bradman and Ponsford, did not find their international feet until the fourth Test. Until that game Bradman's Test figures were 29, 25, 36, 13 and 30 and Ponsford's 53, 5, 12 and 30 not out. During these initial games it was mainly McCabe who held the Australian batting together with 88, 65, 34, 19, 137 and 33 not out.

Then came the Leeds and Oval Tests. Bradman and Ponsford jumped into form and confidence together, and for hour after hour McCabe, who was next batsman in, doodled and fidgeted in the pavilion while Bradman and Ponsford put on 388 at Leeds and 450 at the Oval. McCabe followed these paralysing partnerships and made only 27 and 10.

Only those who have experienced it know how dismal it is to sit in the pavilion for long hours with pads on, gloves and bat handy, and with the limbs, at first aching and eager for action, becoming colder and colder through inactivity.

Such long inactivity chilled McCabe's ardour. Many batsmen would have delighted in walking to the wickets after the opposing bowlers had been thrashed unmercifully, but McCabe was not of these. He preferred to sniff battle as he walked to the creases, not lifeless bowling corpses. He liked to do his own taming, his own mastering, and he was never one to chase big scores when they were there for the simple asking and staying at the wickets.

In this outlook on the game he differed from most other batsmen of his generation. He differed from practically all in that never once in his career did he allow the stultifying atmosphere of limitless Tests to dim the bright lights of his brilliance. Outwardly, at least, it cost Hammond no appreciable effort to bundle up his beautiful artistry and leave it behind him in his locked Sydney or Melbourne hotel room while he walked out with his tradesmanlike ones, twos and occasional fours to do battle in a limitless Test. McCabe, on the other hand, plied the one type of batting in all classes of game, picnic, grade, Sheffield Shield or Test. It was based on attack.

He came to the wickets usually about Number Five, and by this time the game had assumed a definite character. If his side was in trouble, McCabe reasoned that the best way to attempt to extricate it was by attack; if his side was on top, he told himself that his part was to try and force home that advantage by aggression. Thus, you see, whichever way the game went McCabe always played the same brand of cricket, and it was typical of him that, unlike the vast majority of batsmen who fall to the lure of three figures, he never got down to a low gear as he neared the century. Rather did he try to accelerate, because he did not hold that a century or a double century was a holy Mecca that should be approached by slow, plodding, deliberate footsteps of deference.

This complete disregard of a century was a characteristic of his outlook on the game. It first became noticeable at school at St Joseph's College in Sydney, where he was a useful performer at both batting and bowling, but it was his school captain, Cullen, who gained publicity with a string of centuries, while McCabe barely merited mention in the newspapers of the day. His greatest sport renown at school was won when he disregarded a chronic appendix, played in a Rugby final and distinguished himself with thrilling diving tackles.

He left school and returned to the country town of Grenfell, for, like Bradman, O'Reilly and Allsopp, the latter a glorious crowd-pleaser of those days, McCabe was essentially a country product and first learned to bat on a concrete wicket. This, I think, is a better nursery wicket than turf pitches because of its even pace, height and trueness, and it was on the concrete he learned those pull and square cut strokes which lit the cricket world with artistry wherever he went. On spacious country grounds; also, across which magpies and kooka-burras flutter and from which sombre, blue mountains can be seen some fifty or more miles away in the distance, there crept into his play a light-heartedness of spirit, an outlook on the game which is not always easy to capture on city grounds hemmed in by space, industry and critics.

He might have been born to blush either unseen or late in the first-class sphere, wasting his sweetness on the Grenfell air, had not opportunity come to him in the guise of an Easter visit to his home town by a Sydney team. The players of that team liked the look of McCabe. They carried the gossip of his prowess back to the city, and McCabe embellished his good name when he came to Sydney in one of those magnificent Country Week carnivals which put life-blood into cricket in Australia.

This is the week which is marked off on the calendar of all young country cricketers. For several months they almost burst themselves in endeavour, riding far and wide on horses, in buggies and cars to catch the eyes of the selectors, because this week in Sydney, Melbourne, Perth, Brisbane or Adelaide is a week in a lifetime. Cow-cockies from the coastal belt; jackeroos and boundary-riders from the hot, parched plains of the West; cattle drovers and timber cutters from the sun-baked north; wheat-growers, squatters, musterers, shearers, fruit growers and pickers from the Riverina – from all parts of the State they converge on the capital in a do or die spirit for a week crammed full of cricket, camaraderie, movies, dances, sight-seeing and general excitement.

Spirit alone is left to these footsore, magnificent young Australians at the end of their week. Another day or two and they will be riding far over the ranges after sheep, chuckling merrily at the many good times they had with their cobbers down in the Big Smoke, as countrymen affectionately term the city. With becoming modesty it never enters their minds that they will be remembered in the city, and thus there was sensation one day in the placid south-western New South Wales town of Grenfell when a wire came for S. J. McCabe asking him to Sydney to play with the Sheffield Shield Eleven.

There is not much secrecy about wires in the average Australian country town. They soon become common property, not, of course, through the agency of the person to whom they are addressed, but because any link with the outside world is considered to be news belonging to the community. An invitation to one of the townspeople to play first-class cricket not only made Grenfell history, but it was decidedly hot news.

What concerned the town's inhabitants most, however, was whether the selectors had chosen the correct McCabe. There were four brothers, three of them outstanding at cricket, and many in the town wondered whether the McCabe the selectors meant to choose was not S. J. but his older brother Leslie. Stanley Joseph himself thought that the one they wanted was Leslie.

And so, somewhat diffidently, S. J. returned to Sydney and joined the Sheffield Shield ranks. He did not set the Sydney Harbour on fire, nor the Torrens nor the Yarra when he toured to the southern States. Bradman came into the fold with a great flourish, making a century in his first Shield game, but McCabe slipped in quietly and unobtrusively. He did well enough the first season to hold his place with a few runs one day, a wicket or two the next and always a neat, smart fieldsman.

The following season was 1930 with a team to be chosen for England. McCabe did not make the headlines, which were monopolised almost entirely by Bradman in making 1,586 runs at an average of 113.28. Set beside Bradman's mammoth world's record that season of 452 not out, McCabe's scores of 35, 46, 77, 3, 69, 70, 70, 50 not out, 15, 60, 81 and 29 seemed poor meat. They showed, however, that McCabe was consistent, that he got his runs brightly, and might indeed have approached Bradman's five centuries for the season had he attached more importance to three figures.

He slipped into the Australian Eleven in as quiet a manner as he had into the New South Wales side. His entire innocence of centuries denied him publicity and made him seem a most surprising choice. Good judges appreciated his promise, but there was no great hubbub about his choice. Most of the attention was focussed on the dropping of Ryder, who comprised with R. L. Jones (NSW) and C. E. Dolling (SA) the selection committee which chose the tourists. There was gripping drama in this thrusting aside of Ryder by his co-selectors. He had captained Australia the year before against Chapman's team, was in many quarters considered a certain choice for that post again, and in that Australian season had imposing figures. In between the choosing of the team one night and its announcement next day Ryder strode to the wickets under great stress and made an unconquered century, but not even this grand feat swayed his two colleagues from their judgment.

The publicity given Ryder took much attention from the selection of the 19-year-old baby, McCabe. The surprising feature of his selection was that he was chosen to go to England principally as a batsman without ever having made a century in a first-class game.

Four years before Kippax had the colossal average for the season of 112 (colossal because this was 2 BB – two years before Bradman). Kippax had played cricket of exceeding charm and promise for several years before 1926, and on the eve of selection he made a magnificent Shield score of 271 not out. The team was announced on the morrow, but, like Abou Ben Adhem, Kippax's name was not on the list. Neither was that of Victor Richardson, who had been carrying the South Australian batting on his manly shoulders for some years. Richardson averaged over fifty that 1926 season, but not even his superlative and unsurpassed fielding – and a champion fieldsman is almost of the same value to a side as a good bowler – not even his charming cricket personality and courage in a crisis could gain him an English trip when his ability was at its full flower.

Opportunity is sometimes more than half the winning of the battle of recognition. Bradman, Jackson and McCabe were more fortunate than Kippax, Richardson and others in the time they came into the game. Those who waxed successful just before and after the 1914–1918 War still held the stage in 1926, and did not draw on their retirement slippers until about 1930. The door of opportunity, therefore, was ajar in 1930, but, even so, the selectors of that time deserve acknowledgment for their discernment and courage in choosing the colt McCabe.

He was following in the distinguished footsteps of Clem Hill, who was 19 when he made his first trip to England in 1896. S. E. Gregory was 20 when he made the first of his eight trips to the Mother Land, and Victor Trumper was 22.

Bradman, of course, put all other Australians out in the cold in England in 1930, but, even though McCabe was not an outstanding success on his first English tour, he made modest scores when they were needed and he played his cricket with bright courage. His first seven English innings yielded a paltry 51 runs and much doubt as to his ability. Woodfull rushed him in first one day against Oxford and he made 91. Against Cambridge he made 96, his highest score of the tour, because he was destined not to make a century on that visit to England.

His highest Test score of 1930 was 54, and his subsequent Test innings in Australia against the West Indies and South Africa – in neither series did he make a century – barely prepared the cricket world for the first of his three epic Test innings.

It was Sydney of late 1932 and the first Test of the bodyline series. Woodfull and Ponsford had commenced in sure orthodox fashion against orthodox fast bowling, but, when Larwood suddenly switched across to legside tactics, the star of Australia took a quick dip towards the horizon. Four wickets had fallen for 87 with Bradman out of the game when McCabe came to the wickets. The prospects were poor.

As if to show her capriciousness and how surely she held destiny in her hands, Fate permitted McCabe when five to play a ball from devastator Larwood towards Voce in the gully. The ball flew high off the bat and came to earth a few inches short of Voce's clutching fingers. In such manner does Fate toy with history, granting or denying favours by the flimsiest of margins. Did not A. W. Carr write the first page of an immortal chapter when he dropped His Excellency, Charles Macartney (known far and wide as the Governor-General because of the way in which he lorded things at the wicket), when he was two at Leeds in 1926? Had Carr taken that chance cricket would have been infinitely poorer by the loss of an innings which yielded a century before lunch, a century out of the team's total of 131 in eighty minutes, and an innings everywhere acknowledged as unexcelled in the history of the game for sheer artistry and brilliance.

So, too, had Voce got his fingers to the McCabe shot in Sydney the game would have lost one of its gems. McCabe first had to master an English attack which included Larwood at the very apogee of his greatness. After the attack had been mastered, McCabe switched to defiance, taking the crowd of fifty thousand enthusiastic Australians from the depths of despair to the heights of happiness.

How the crowd surged into ecstasies that day at the temporary slaying of the giant Larwood! To that time Larwood's deeds had been a challenge not only to Australian cricket, but to Australian manhood. He flowed in an unforgettable current of rhythm to the creases like a wave gathering itself smoothly up before crashing down on the beach. Larwood's speed, his physical danger to the batsmen were such as to strike awe into the hearts of those watching from over the fence, but McCabe first checked him, then cheeked him, and finally laughed at this English colossus – though be it noted that the Englishman had most of the other laughs with McCabe in that 1932–33 season.

With Richardson, whose share was 49, McCabe put on 129 for the fifth wicket, the most able and impressive of all Australian partnerships of that series. With Grimmett, who made 19, McCabe added 68, and with Wall, whose contribution was four, McCabe added 55 for the last wicket. This amazing last wicket partnership, in which McCabe guided Wall away from the strike and himself hit boundary after boundary, was the one which caused the record crowd of that Sydney Saturday morning to burst itself and the picket fence (though some said the hundreds of pickets were pulled off the fence to give the crowded spectators a better view) in uncontrollable frenzies of acclamation.

When stumps were drawn at the end of the first day's play Australia was 6–290; when the innings finished before lunch of the next day the total was 360, of which McCabe was 187 not out.

Considering the terrific odds he had to face, I am inclined to the opinion that this Sydney innings was McCabe's greatest, but as soon as one tries to become dogmatic on this subject there floats before the vision the epics of Johannesburg and Trent Bridge. I saw all three innings, batting for a long period with him at Johannesburg, and it was here he had to face disabilities unknown to him at Sydney and Trent Bridge. At each of the latter places he batted on a glorious wicket, the type of wicket a batsman dreams about. At Johannesburg, on the contrary, he did duty on a dusty wicket, a pitch worn cranky and irritable by 898 runs, and of all wickets, even a wet and sticky one, none is more difficult than that off which the ball shoots and bites.

McCabe ran to a flowing century before lunch, joining Macartney and Bradman in the feat, but in the afternoon, if it were possible, he pulverised the South African attack even more into dust. The Springboks had a plenitude of bowlers to take advantage of the conditions. Langton and Nupen were splendid medium-paced spin bowlers, and Mitchell and Balaskas found that the wicket greatly exaggerated their spin and also hurried it through.

McCabe never put a foot or his bat in a false position. To me, at the other end and fully aware of the difficulties of maintaining even a defence on such a wicket, McCabe's batting bordered on the miraculous. He made 100 in 91 minutes, 150 in 145 and in that total was the amazing tally of 24 boundaries.

In the middle afternoon lightning flashed with startling vividness in the mineral-laden Johannesburg air. Peals of thunder rolled over the Wanderers, but not even the wretched light of the impending storm could dim the Australian's brilliance.

No better compliment could have been paid McCabe than this. With Australia still 125 runs behind and three hours to play, Wade, the South African skipper, did the most extraordinary thing of appealing against the light from the field. It was quite apparent that the pending heavy rain would stop the match at any moment. There was thus no fear that South Africa could be beaten, but Wade was nonplussed, mesmerised and indeed stampeded by the profuse profligacy of McCabe's boundaries. Some said that there was the flavour of unsportsmanship in Wade's appeal, but Wade was one of cricket's gentlemen. I knew from close quarters that McCabe had woven a spell over him.

Trent Bridge differed somewhat from the others, because here McCabe had to contend with strictly orthodox tactics on a perfect wicket.

'Come and see this. Do not miss a moment of it. You will never see the like of it again,' called Bradman on the balcony of the Australian dressing room during the McCabe epic at Trent Bridge; but again I would not care to say that this innings was greater than the others.

The Trent Bridge circumstances were similar to those of Sydney in the sense that McCabe, bereft of class batsmen, had to fight the Englishmen in keeping the 'rabbits' away from the strike. Not even the peerless and graceful flow of boundaries (he played his shots with less effort than any other batsman) showed more genius in McCabe's innings than the manner in which he circumvented Hammond's captaincy and the wiles of the English bowlers and fieldsmen to keep him away from the batting end. McCabe's score was 232. Those of the others who came to the wickets with him were Ward 2, Hassett 1, Badcock 9, Barnett 22, O'Reilly 9, McCormick 2 and Fleetwood-Smith 5 not out.

McCabe took the complete strike during eight of the last ten overs of the innings. In a last-wicket stand with Fleetwood-Smith, of 77 in 28 minutes McCabe scored 72. He hit 34 fours and one six, and 16 of the boundaries came in the ten overs just mentioned.

All three innings, Sydney, Johannesburg and Trent Bridge, will live in a warm memory, and they will serve to prove that not even the all-powerful Bradman could deprive McCabe of his rightful place in cricket's annals. The writers of the game searched their Thesaurus to do justice to him. 'The glittering, undimmed morning star of the first Test . . . and what of the visionary monster Larwood now? This Siva with a necklace of skulls? . . . a matter for history in Test cricket . . . here is a cricketer who is a true son of sport. The heart and youth of Victor Trumper beat again in the cricket of McCabe . . . with the grace and verve of a lithe-limbed ballet dancer . . . cheers rolled like thunder as he stood there, the noblest young Roman of them all, whipping England's bowlers as with the scourges of the Seven Furies, with all the calmness of an old warhorse before the battle; with all the abandon of confident youth. . . . Test cricket has seen no more immortal innings.'

In such manner did the writers strive to do justice to McCabe on these various occasions. It was convenient for them, perhaps, that McCabe's career saw fit to distribute one epic innings to each of the three great cricketing lands – England, Australia and South Africa.

This is not to suggest that he knew no other big moments in the game. He had a Test century in Manchester in 1934 with 137; he played brilliantly for 149 in a Durban Test in 1935, and he registered a Test century in Melbourne in the last game of the series against G. O. Allen's team in 1937.

As I pointed out previously, however, McCabe was never one to measure success by the yardstick of three figures. I never met a cricketer who cared less about three figures, and he was never one to cast miserable and anxious eyes at the score-board to watch his approach to the century. Had McCabe been hundred hungry caution would have given him a longer list of first-class centuries, for dismissal came to him often in the seventies, eighties and, indeed, the nineties.

I once saw him given out in the nineties in a Test against England in Sydney. Even from the balcony of the dressing-room it looked a bad decision. There was a distinctive snick before the ball hit his pads, but not one of the huge crowd was given the slightest suggestion by McCabe that the umpire had given a doubtful decision. He skipped away quickly from the wickets with a little characteristic he possesses, whereas, I fear, some Test batsmen might have shown human disapproval in one way or another. Some might have hesitated at the wicket, others might have given their bat a slap to denote a hit, expressed themselves fully and obviously to the first fieldsman they passed on the way out; but not even the disappointment of dismissal in the nineties of a Test could upset McCabe's natural good sportsmanship.

Nor was this a pose on the ground. In the dressing-room his quiet reply to the inevitable question was: 'I think I hit it.' At such a question many a disgruntled batsman, giving vent in the privacy of the dressing-room to his pent-up feelings, would explode: 'Hit it? Of course I — hit it!'

There was another occasion when he showed out in gallant colours. At Scarborough in 1934 Sutcliffe hit a ball to square leg and called Wyatt for a run. The ball accidentally hit the umpire's foot and went off at a tangent to a fieldsman, who returned it smartly to McCabe, who was bowling. Wyatt was stranded yards down the wicket, but McCabe quietly caught the ball and walked back to begin his bowling run, while Wyatt, very relieved, scrambled home to his crease. There was no fussy ostentation about McCabe, nothing to show the public that he was 'playing the game'.

It is no easy matter to give McCabe his proper position among the batsmen of his generation. It could be said of him, I think, that he was not a reliable Test batsman in the meaning of the term. Whenever I saw Leyland and Paynter walk on to a Test field I knew instinctively that there would be no stuff and nonsense, that each would have to be dug out by the roots like a century old oak tree. Test cricket to these two and their like was Test cricket first, last and in the middle, and each Test ball was met with a stiff upper lip, a bat straight up and down the line and a head above it crammed with admirable and magnificent north of England resolution and canniness.

It was not in McCabe's nature to look upon cricket as such a life and death business. Bowlers did not get him out in Test matches so much as he got himself out by taking risks. He could never refuse a hook shot.

I really think he hated Test cricket, particularly towards the end of a series. He could not bring himself to play the cautious, canny type of game which Tests demanded, and he begrudged the nervous toll a series exacted. He showed this once in Adelaide when Robins set an exaggerated field to give him a single so that he could operate against the batsman at the other end. Most Test batsman would not have been worried by the field which Robins set. They would have played the slow bowler quietly, looking for twos and an occasional four, but McCabe jumped immediately to the challenge and tried to hit the ball over the heads of the deep fieldsmen. He failed, as he failed in the other innings of the match when a fast bowler dropped one short, feeding McCabe on his favourite hook stroke. Here again most batsmen would have been content with an ordinary four, but McCabe tried adventurously for six and was caught as the ball was sailing over the fence.

He brought criticism on his head on both occasions. Critics said these strokes were fit and proper in carnival or village green cricket, but not in a Test. In this, I think, was the essence of McCabe's dislike for Tests. In keeping with the advice of Polonius, he wanted always to be true to himself. His nature did not permit him to regard cricket in any other light than a game which should be played chivalrously and cavalierly, whether in a Test, Sheffield Shield or up-country fixture.

Nothing in cricket gave him more enjoyment than his many tilts with Grimmett. They were firm friends, and always the same conversation would proceed in a dressing-room before the game and when McCabe came to the wickets.

'I'll give you the cane to-day, Grum,' McCabe would say as he was getting his line of direction from the umpire.

'I don't think you will,' the Fox smilingly would answer from the other end. 'I have saved myself specially for you.'

And in truth it did seem that Grimmett bowled better against McCabe than any other Australian batsman. A little skip, a little hop and over in its low trajectory would come a Grimmett ball full of spin and guile, pitching, for a certainty, on the blind-spot and forcing McCabe feverishly on the defensive.

Grimmett came out of these duels with major honours, but he had a calmer temperament and a field to help him. McCabe might send him soaring out over long-off or long-on, but Grimmett would motion his men back and back and McCabe always accepted the challenge. There were days when McCabe triumphed, but it was not uncommon to see Grimmett trap him, and then friend Clarrie would double up with merriment at McCabe's expense.

'You sly old Fox, Grum,' McCabe would gaily call as he walked out; 'but wait until the next innings. I'll get you then.'

That was how McCabe loved to play, freely and adventurously, not feeling that the Sword of Damocles hung over his batting head at the wickets. He was always ready to take risks, blatant risks. There are many Australians who claim that they would much rather see a good innings by McCabe than a good one by Bradman. That was purely a matter of opinion. Each was a powerful force in the world of cricket and played his own individual and essential part. It is to be remembered that Bradman's genius was infinitely more consistent, reliable and on longer view than that of McCabe. It is possible also, I suppose, by overindulgence to become blasé about the choicest wine.

McCabe will be remembered in a different category from Bradman. He is assured forever, because of his three scintillating innings, of immortality in the cricket hall of fame.

CHAPTER EIGHT   *A Sly Old Fox*

Iɴ ᴀɴ ᴀꜰᴛᴇʀ-ᴅɪɴɴᴇʀ sᴘᴇᴇᴄʜ Charles Dickens declared that genius was an infinite capacity for taking pains. No cricketer I met could better illustrate the truth underlying the dictum than Clarence Victor Grimmett. It does not deny that 'genius must be born and never can be taught', as Dryden insisted. It breathes the absolute necessity for cultivation if high reward is sought.

It is obvious that Grimmett had natural talent and he had, moreover, an innate love of cricket. Without incessant and assiduous concentration, however, his mere devotion to the bowling art would never have earned him his seat among the mighty.

C. T. B. Turner, 'the Terror' of the nineties, who once spreadeagled and nonplussed 314 heroes in an English season, ascribes much of his success to constant early practice with the object of gaining mastery of length and spin. He marked the spot on the country wicket of Bathurst where he used to practise before Sheffield Shield and Test honours came his way, and kept pegging away until he was satisfied with his control of the ball. It is said of the Victorian Albert Trott, who subsequently became a consistent all-rounder with Middlesex for a decade, that it was his custom to place a fruit case in front of the stumps in order to develop his capacity to turn the ball round it on to the stumps.

Grimmett was such a student. Born in New Zealand, he admits having played no other game save cricket until he was 22, except for a little Rugby at school. He played a little baseball after migrating to Sydney (a migration brought about, I believe, by a hankering after cricket and opportunity), but Grimmett glories in the fact that he practically lived for cricket. He practised every available opportunity, even through the winter.

The Grimmett practice was never aimless. It was always with a set purpose, and the proper manner of greeting this charming, smiling little fellow after a winter's hibernation was not to enquire after his health or his family, but to seek knowledge of what new bowling mystery the winter had produced.

Neville Cardus tells the story of when they met in Rundle Street, Adelaide, during the dark days of the war and the conversation fell into lugubrious channels.

'This is a terrible thing, this war, Neville,' said Grimmett.

'It is, indeed,' readily agreed Cardus, 'when we think of all the art and culture it has destroyed. The lovely old historic buildings of Europe; the—'

'Yes, yes,' hastily cut in Grimmett, 'but I was thinking particularly of a new ball I have discovered. I'll never have the chance now to try it out against the class batsman.'

His ambition was to perfect new deliveries, and he was always experimenting with his wrist at this and that angle at the moment of delivery, his shoulder at varying heights or his body at different angles to the batsman. To this end the last particular special he used took him about twelve years to control sufficiently to be introduced in a match. That is the delivery now known as Grimmett's 'flipper', because of the click of his fingers as he released the ball. He bowled it with a leg-break action and the ball, making pace off the wicket, came in from the off. Batsmen in neighbouring States warned each other of Grimmett's 'flipper', related what it did, and then said: 'You can't very well miss it. You'll know it by the flick of the old chap's fingers.

You were inclined to feel sorry for this frail little chap, whose perpetual task at the bowling creases over the years had given him a rounded right shoulder. Twelve years to perfect a delivery, you told yourself, and then betrayed by the flick of his fingers! It didn't seem fair, somehow, and it seemed rather poor that batsmen should be in such a hurry to pass on trade secrets. Poor Clarrie Grimmett!

But not for nothing did my esteemed friend Clarrie come to be known as the Sly Old Fox of Cricket. He knew what batsmen said about him in the pavilion, and he knew their plans to overcome him, and so with his lovely little aimless hop and skip at the beginning of his run he jogged up to the wickets to bowl against the knowing batsman.

Grimmett's right arm took its little swing back; the ball flew away with a low trajectory, and with it went the unmistakable flick of fingers.

Zounds! But from the pavilion you could see the smirk on the face of the batsman as he went forward confidently to meet the ball. The flicker, indeed, he seemed to say. Just watch what I do to this flicker of —. But the ball has not turned from the off. It has come the other way and there is a pretty mess, with the batsman's feet in the wrong position and the ball hitting them and not the bat, an appealing finger in the air from Grimmett, an acknowledgment from the umpire and off to the pavilion goes a sad and not very wise batsman. Who said this flicker of Grimmett's came from the off?

You were fortunate, in such circumstances, if you were fielding with Grimmett's side and close to the wicket. The little chap would come across, his right foot seeming to slink in a distinctive manner, and across his face would spread an impish smile of mischief. And then it would all dawn on you.

'Why, you old fox, Grum,' you'd say. 'I do believe you bowled a leg-break with your right hand and flicked the fingers of your left.'

Grimmett would never admit anything. He would just rock with silent and inward merriment at these batsmen who knew all about his flicker, who passed on their trade secrets. It was their wits against his, and he had been in the bowling business a long, long time and what he learned he had learnt the hard way. Life was like that.

He was a master of detail and worked everything out according to plan. Long study of traffic down King William Street, in Adelaide, for instance, taught him that it paid to wait ten seconds after the green light had flashed for traffic to move. Cars behind tooted Grimmett impatiently, but he could not be flurried. He waited his ten seconds, drove off at 20 miles an hour and then found that he caught all the rest of the traffic lights down King William Street. He was, you see, observant and a master of detail. In such a manner did he also work out his bowling plans of campaign.

Such thoroughness is part of the Grimmett make-up. It emphasises his whole outlook on cricket and bowling. Without perfect control, he avers, bowling 'ceases to interest me'. To attain that control he placed a piece of card about eighteen inches square on the pitch, used one stump only, and never tired of experimenting.

There was reason behind all his actions. From the time he entered the Interstate sphere he avoided bowling to batsman at practice as much as possible, because he wanted to concentrate on control of length and direction without distraction from other players and against batsmen, as often happens in the nets, who want to chance their eye and play strokes they would not attempt against him in a game. Such practice had no appeal for Grimmett.

He was a migratory soul. He came to Sydney from New Zealand, left there for Melbourne and found his permanent residence finally in Adelaide. It was while he was in Melbourne that he secured a load of Merri Creek soil and laid down a full length pitch at his home. From Merri Creek comes the black soil traditionally associated with the famous Melbourne Cricket Ground. He practised on his home-made pitch at every opportunity – and his sole fieldsman was a fox terrier.

The 'Sly Old Fox' had a number of balls and taught the dog to lie down until he wanted them back. On Sunday mornings neighbours came for a regular practice, and it was interesting that one of the visitors should have been Ponsford at the time he was about to break into the big news.

Grimmett had one paramount idea at his self imposed and self conducted practices – the attainment of length and direction as the solid foundation of his bowling. He continue to experiment with all kinds of spin. He used a tennis ball, observed the results and came to the conclusion that speed off the pitch was the ideal to strive for. With characteristic thoroughness he decided to discard, except for demonstration purposes, those spin deliveries which did not fizz off the wicket.

He learnt how a ball swerved according to the kind of spin imparted and how the arm movement also had its effect on the flight of the ball. But while he was experimenting he was building according to his own solid specifications what he calls his 'stock ball'. His practices always ended with ten minutes of two deliveries and nothing else, the stock ball (a slight leg break of perfect length and direction) and an ordinary straight through delivery with leg break action. At any time Grimmett could pick up a ball and pitch it almost exactly where he wanted it. A batsman set in his task welcomes the advent of a slow bowler, because there is almost sure to be a few full tosses or long-hops until the bowler feels his fingers, so to speak, but there were no such benefits from Grimmett. With top-spin or side-spin, his very first ball was always religiously on that length which causes a batsman's feet to twitter.

Hobbs completely underestimated Grimmett's pertinacity when, after the South Australian's sensational eruption into Test history, he predicted failure for him on English pitches. In that Test debut against Gilligan's men on the Sydney ground in 1925 Grimmett took eleven wickets for 82. His victims were Hobbs, Sandham, Woolley, Hendren, Hearne (twice), Whysall (twice), Kilner, Gilligan and Strudwick.

Mailey had been the slow spinner in the four previous games of the series. With Grimmett wreaking havoc among the knights of

England's batsmen of that day, Mailey's services were scarcely called upon in that match.

Mailey gave the ball plenty of air, plenty of time for the spin to take effect and the batsmen to muddle their stroke. Grimmett was faster through the air and had a low trajectory – a different type altogether to Mailey. Perhaps the pom-pom effect following the high explosives from Mailey, against which they had constructed their defences during previous clashes, contributed to the shock the English batsmen suffered on that occasion.

Hobbs' estimate, however, was quite wrong (as was the Ponsford estimate when first he batted against Larwood and there appeared in the Press under his name the opinion that 'Larwood wasn't really fast'). Grimmett was destined to prove he was much more of a menace on English than Australian pitches. The capture of all ten wickets of a team on his first tour provided the hall-mark, particularly when it is remembered that the county he demolished was Yorkshire, almost as difficult to rout as the English Eleven.

Like every other bowler of note, Grimmett has definite views on the over preparation of pitches and sympathy for his fellow strugglers. He, too, like O'Reilly, considers that batsmen have been pampered, and unresponsive wickets give the bowlers so little encouragement that they become understandably disheartened.

Of the first-class wickets in Australia he rates that on the Sydney Ground, since it was ploughed up some years ago, the best for a spin bowler (O'Reilly once said that he would like to take this particular wicket with him on a world tour). The Melbourne wicket, in Grimmett's opinion, is tough for the bowler, and Brisbane and Adelaide main pitches are somewhat alike – easy for the batsmen. South African wickets, he thinks, are too easy paced (though Grimmett had a devastating tour there in 1935–36), and he ascribes the variation among English wickets to the climate, the incidence of wet and dry weather.

He came to the conclusion that one can bowl with more energy in England, that the ball can be made to do a bit more in the atmosphere and that the wickets, generally, were more responsive to spin than in other lands. His one qualification is the hard wicket greasy on top after rain, which, during that period, is heartbreaking for a bowler.

Grimmett admits he does not know how the old-timers would fare as regards the ability to turn the ball on some of the modern over-prepared pitches. The only one with whom he had experience was the late J. V. Saunders, the medium fast left hander of the famous 1902 Australian Eleven.

'He could certainly turn the ball a lot and at a fast pace,' declares Grimmett.

If one wanted a true assessment of a bowler, what better source of information should be available than a great batsman who has faced him. The converse should apply with equal effect, and here are Grimmett's views on the relative merits of the contemporaries against whom he pitted his cunning.

'Hammond,' he told me, 'is a wonderful batsman, not quite as strong on the leg-side as the off. I always bowled at his toes. He was inclined to jump away into position to drive to the offside and in doing so occasionally "lost " the ball. I would like to have had Hammond field in slips to me throughout my career.'

'Bradman, of course, stands on a pedestal as a rungetter, but from my point of view he was never as difficult to bowl to as batsman like Hobbs, McCabe, Kippax, Andrews, Hassett and many others I could name. He was nearly always troubled by accurate spin bowling and was never comfortable against O'Reilly. Hassett, on the other hand, was one of the best batsmen I ever bowled against, and handled O'Reilly better than anyone else I've seen.

'McCabe is a great batsman, and I doubt if there is anyone who times a ball with such effortless ease. His footwork and technique are faultless.

'Dudley Nourse, of South Africa, is a smaller edition of Hammond, but he is much stronger in his on-side play than England's captain. Talking of on-side play, George Headley, of the West Indies, is the best I have seen. I never tired of watching his beautiful footwork. And don't infer that he could not play on the off. He made glorious shots all round the field.'

These are generous tributes, but from one who laboured so diligently to achieve his ambition they ring with truth, although his opinions of Bradman will cause many an eyebrow to twist in wonder and disagreement. Interspersed with his many fruitful harvests of wickets were one or two periods of drought. Two magnificent seasons in England in 1930 and 1934 did not stop Australia from making little use of him in Australia in 1932–33 and no use of him at all in 1936–37, although the season before the South African Tests bore witness with 44 victims that he was at the top of his form. In 1937–38 season Bradman's preferential use of Ward over Grimmett for South Australia suggested only too plainly that Grimmett's sun had set, and the little fellow, still thinking his form was as good as ever (and his deeds the next Australian season certainly upheld him), cut a strangely sad and forlorn figure on Australian grounds. He was the second string to the South Australian slow bowling bow, and this for Grimmett was heartbreaking and passing strange, because often in his career he was the carrier of that side.

On those other occasions Grimmett must sometimes have felt with Edison that there is another definition of genius – one per cent of inspiration and ninety-nine per cent perspiration – but he never wilted as the score mounted. His persistence rivalled that of an irritating gnat. Deliberately he adopted standover methods, wheeling into the attack like a flash, giving the batsman not a split second to prepare for the next stinging delivery. The average Grimmett over was of less duration than that of any other bowler I can recall.

Withal 'Scarlet', as he was known to his Australian friends and a cognomen apparently acquired because of the elusiveness of his deliveries, has a keen sense of humour. This trait of his quick swing into attack recalls a story he loves to tell of Phil Mead, the aldermanic proportioned left-hander who made two trips to Australia.

Every batsman has his mannerisms. They may be reflected in his stance awaiting delivery or between strokes, his approach to the wicket, his method of relaxation. The peculiarities add personal spice.

Mead's mannerisms were unique. They became ritual prior to every delivery he faced. First grounding his bat to take strike, Mead would shuffle up to it left, right, left, right, left, right with short elephantine steps – always the six steps. Then he would look round to square leg, at the same time touching his cap as if in salute to the umpire. Once upon a time, I fear, some enterprising captain hastily despatched first slip to fine leg on Mead, who there and then vowed that he would never again be caught napping – hence his final look to the leg side.

All this ritual performed, Mead would then be ready for the bowler to commence his run. Grimmett's particular delight was to time his approach at the most disconcerting time for Mead. Not too early, was the thought running through Grimmett's mind. If the ritual is interrupted Mead will draw away from the stumps.

And so Grimmett bowled at a time when Mead, true to his superstitions, had to hurry through his shuffling and his salute. Mead was not by any means the only batsman who found no peace from Grimmett.

His cunning was never better exemplified than in one passage with a noted New South Wales batsman. Grimmett appealed for leg before. The umpire said 'No.'

Retaining his stance, the batsman called 'Clarrie,' and with index finger pointed in a straight line from the intercepting pad up and down the pitch.

There was not the flicker of a smile from the Fox. He wheeled into the next delivery. Again the ball struck the pad.

'How's that?' was Grimmett's quiet address to the umpire.

This time the fateful hand went up.

As the crestfallen batsman turned pavilionwards he had two

words from the Master. They were 'Excuse me.' The other turned and saw Grimmett's venomous index finger pointing up and down the straight line between stumps and stumps.

A rare cricketer was my old friend Clarrie. I count it as great an honour to have played in the same Test side as him as any other man I played with or against. Happy is the lover of the game who retains the mental vision of a little, round shouldered bowler pegging away, pegging away for over after over, for this vision is one, indeed, which shows cricket subtlety, cunning, ability and great-heartedness at their very richest and best.

It seems unreal that a first-class ground will never know him again, for over the years he seemed perpetual, the Peter Pan of cricket. 'I fear,' he wrote to me of recent days in a letter, 'that old age is creeping on me.' Only those who knew the reticent, delightful Grimmett will realise what pain it must have cost him to write in that strain, for he loved cricket dearly and over the years he kept on bobbing up and bogging up, this year reputed to be finished, next year to be proved better than ever.

Of one thing I am certain. Cricket never looked a greater game than when C. V. Grimmett was bowling.

He played cricket as a science, a game of infinite skill, and when the day's play had ended he was never one to join in a mad, swirling dash to be dressed and away. He loved the atmosphere of the dressing-room, he loved to talk over the day's happenings and natter, as they say in Yorkshire. Best of all he loved the friendship of his fellow-man.

'Come, Clarrie,' would say one of his fellows, probably Victor Richardson, for whom Grimmett would do anything, 'we can't possibly go until you sing the song that made you famous.'

Grimmett would need some cajoling – but not very much. With the happiest of smiles on his face he would sing:

> 'She was a sweet little dicky bird,
>   Tweet, tweet, tweet, tweet, she went.
> She used to sing all day
>   Till my money was spent.'

> 'She was always sighing,
>   I thought she was going to die,
> But she was one of the early birds,
>   And I was one of the worms.'

The applause from his fellows which always greeted this brought as much cheer to the heart of Clarrie Grimmett as when he took all ten of Yorkshire's wickets. What a lovable little cricketer and gentleman – the Peter Pan of the game or else, as he secretly loved to be called, a Sly Old Fox!

CHAPTER NINE   *Our World Eleven*

Oᴜʀ ꜱᴇʟꜰ-ɪᴍᴘᴏꜱᴇᴅ ᴛᴀꜱᴋ ᴡᴀꜱ
no easy one. We consoled ourselves with that thought as, dinner
finished, we drew up deep chairs, filled our pipes and gazed with
pleasurable anticipation into the broad, cheery depths of the leap-
ing log-fire.

We were to choose a World Eleven from our contemporaries,
cricketers we had played with and against. That decision we made at
dinner and, having made it, we put it aside like some tasty morsel for
full and undivided attention later. It would not necessarily be a
World Eleven of the best and most successful players, a team such as
enthusiasts choose in pavilions throughout the world when rain
holds up play. Our team was to go on a mythical world tour at the
end of the Global War, its purpose to put cricket back on its pedestal
by showing all the graces, the art, culture and personality, on and off
the field, that the game had to offer. This made it clear, therefore,
that our team was not to be one for the prime purpose of winning
matches – though its calibre would be such that it would not lose any
– but its principal and indeed its only object was to show, by
representation, the elect of cricket that had flowed through the
game in our time.

And now the moment had come to commence the job. The
atmosphere of the Australian bush, in which I had happened across
my companion for the first time in years, admirably lent itself in its
loneliness to thought and memories. Rain outside was beating a

cheery symphony on the corrugated iron roof before it gurgled along the guttering and dropped with many a musical plink-plonk into the storage tank; from the distance, on the sharp winter's air, came the complaining note of an express train as it hauled its load up the steep grade of the range. It would be half an hour before it emerged hissingly triumphant at the bottom of the homestead paddock, and I wondered how far advanced we would be then on our team. I fell to musing that also along this same railway track had gone speeding in nights gone by all the cricket elect of Australia, England, South Africa, West Indies – speeding backwards and forwards between Sydney, Melbourne and Adelaide to write pages of indelible deeds in the history of the game.

My companion turned the wireless down on a lilting Strauss waltz. He dropped a huge box-log on the fire, sending myriads of sparks chasing up the aged, blackened chimney, and as he resumed his seat I scribbled down the first name on my pad.

'Ah,' said he, with a twinkle, 'not so fast, not so fast. You have written down a name and you will now tell me that we want ten more. The name you have written is Bradman; I am now going to suggest that you cross it out.'

I smiled indulgently at him. 'The peace of these haunts has turned your mind,' I said to him. 'I admit the name I have written is Bradman, but surely you are not objecting to him. I do not choose him so much as he chooses himself. He is an automatic selection.

'We must have system in this selection,' he replied. 'We will begin by choosing our opening batsmen. Further, I am not so sure that Bradman will be in my side.'

I smiled at him.

'No, I am serious in this,' he maintained. 'The point we stressed at dinner, remember, was that our team was not to be one to win matches. If that were so, Bradman would be the first chosen – "I dips me lid" to Bradman as a match winner. I acknowledge also his concentrative powers and stamina, two abilities he possessed above all other batsmen. He was a gigantic amasser of runs, but did Bradman have any cultural grace not possessed by other batsmen? I don't think he did.'

'His footwork was unequalled in our time,' I replied. 'I also saw nobody come near him in making the placement of a field look futile. Also, I can't think of a quicker scorer. He never made his big scores by sitting on the bowlers; he made them by going out after them.'

'I agree with all that,' he said stolidly, puffing away at his pipe. He was a determined customer, this fellow, and he showed that best in the manner in which he had never admitted cricket defeat. He paused a long while, meditatively poking the fire, before he spoke again. 'We will consider Bradman and his position now and I want to sum him up by saying this: For the purposes for which we want this team, Bradman is too good. That sounds illogical, but it isn't really. I think other batsmen had graceful batting contours not possessed by Bradman, but that is not quite the point, because Bradman was nothing if not a crowd-pleaser. But leave art and tradesmanship on one side. Bradman is too good for my side because he is too dominant, and, being too dominant, he defeats a principal objective. In an afternoon's play by our team I want to see on show many varied batting styles. What I am afraid of is that Bradman would bat all the afternoon and swamp the others.'

'I agree up to a point,' I answered. 'Bradman in a team had a depressing effect upon the play of others. The best example of that was McCabe, who rarely did his genius justice in big cricket. But what of Ponsford? I want him in my side and he also was a monopolist.'

'I would choose Ponsford, under orders. He would bat with those orders to be opened if and when he reached a century. They would remind him that he made 110 in his first Test innings – and 110 is a good enough score for any man. If Ponsford paid no heed to those orders, we would have another standing by for the next game.'

'Why not give Bradman orders also?' I asked.

'You know as well as I that orders did not enter into Bradman's cricket. He was his own law. I don't think he would take notice of orders.'

'Well,' I said, 'I will surprise you perhaps by agreeing to leave Bradman's name out for the present. I agree on only one condition, which I will mention later.'

I crossed out Bradman's name.

'Ponsford?' I said.

'Agreed,' he replied. 'A magnificent opening batsman, not altogether a lover, though, of express bowling. Had a weakness there. However, not alone in that. Had all the strokes; splendid in his forcing strokes to the on.'

We both wrote Ponsford down.

'We should define the limits of choice,' I said. 'I once played with Hobbs in a Press side. Does that entitle him to consideration, because if it does I will not look further for the other opener. Then what of Woolley and Macartney? We both played either with and against them.'

'We played against Dave Nourse Snr in South Africa, also,' said my companion, 'and at various times we played against many others of that time. Carter, Bardsley and so on. No, I don't think we can consider them, because we can't judge them, not having seen them in their prime. I think we must confine ourselves to people we played against in Tests.'

The express just then went roaring past the homestead. I pulled the curtain aside to see the streaming blaze of lights speeding on into the night. We had not got very far in that first half-hour and I wanted to speak at some length on opening batsmen.

I wrote down these names and showed them to him: Headley, Hutton, Brown, Mitchell, Jackson, Barnett, Walters, Sutcliffe, Woodfull.

'That's not a bad collection of opening batsmen,' I said. 'With the exception of Woodfull, and possibly Sutcliffe and Mitchell, they are also gifted stroke-makers, and in this regard I want to make a point. How brilliant would some of these have been had they gone in later down, say, about number five, the pick batting position of all? I ask that question particularly of Jackson and Barnett.'

'I don't grasp your point,' he replied.

'I will try to explain it. The opening batsmen in a Test have terrific responsibilities. They go to bat when bowlers and fieldsmen are freshest, the wicket unknown, the ball new, shiny and lively. The atmosphere in itself is a test. Well, now! What is the frame of mind of the opening batsman? Is he ready to fling his bat at the ball in all manner of strokes or does the importance of his position impress him most? I can give you one example. By glorious cricket Charles Barnett made almost a hundred before lunch in the first Test in England in 1938. Barnett could not hold his Test position in the final game, because what was wanted was an opening batsman who could be judged by time and not by runs or strokes. Indeed, the English powers in 1946 have not yet forgiven Barnett for making almost a hundred before lunch in a Test. He's still on the outside looking in. Wish Australia had him.'

He gave a prodigious yawn. 'I don't see what all this has got to do with the case,' he said, 'but the floor is still yours if you want it.'

'It has a lot to do with *my* case,' I came back warmly. 'Most of those opening batsmen I have mentioned could play a drive with the best of batsmen, but when such a ball came along early in a Test innings, caution often got the better of most of them. Had they gone for the drive it would have come off in most cases. The lurking fear always, however, was for the ball which would swing, with the opener being caught in the slips. "Ah," the critics would then say. "he is not an opening batsman. He has a weakness in the slips".'

'I suppose,' he said, with rather a bored look, 'you are coming to some point?'

'Yes,' I replied, 'and this is it. I instance only Jackson, though it could apply to others. If Jackson cannot get in as an opener, can he as number five? Would Jackson have been more brilliant than others had he gone in that sheltered number five position, where the ball does not swing and the position is set for stroke-making? Sometimes I batted lower down and was struck by the change in difficulties.'

'Do you remember Brown at Bulawayo?' he asked.

'Indeed, I do. Neither you nor I have seen a more magnificent stroke-making innings. That illustrates my point. Opening an innings has curbed the ability of many a player. Bradman once took on the opening batsman position and soon gave it up.'

'There were also many times,' he countered, 'when Bradman came to the creases as a virtual opener, after the opener had failed.'

I busily stuffed my pipe and pretended not to notice that. I let it go by, like a ball outside the off stump.

'But I also remember McCabe in Sydney against the New Zealander, Cowie,' he said. 'McCabe opened with you and twice had his stumps knocked by a ball which swung late.'

'Yes, I think McCabe changed his ideas about opening after that experience. Those two deliveries might have put paid to any opening batsman,' I continued, 'but that illustrates the type of ball always likely to come along to an opener. He must play his game accordingly.'

'I think,' said he, with a look at his wristlet watch, 'if we are to get anywhere with this team to-night we ought to choose another opening batsman. I will give you first say.'

'Headley,' said I. 'Right,' said he, and down went the West Indian's name. We both knew we had a champion in Headley, brilliant in his footwork and glorious in on-side strokes; maker of Test centuries in both England and Australia, and, best test of a batsman, maker of runs when his side needed them most.

'Mind you,' said he, 'if it were limitless Tests we were setting out to play, my choice might be different. I would not so lightly dismiss Woodfull, Hutton and Sutcliffe.'

'If we are to get anywhere with this team to-night —' I began.

'I was just going to say,' he said hurriedly, 'that we have chosen two men and have already dropped the two Test record breakers, Bradman and Hutton,'

'I would not use the term "drop" for Bradman,' I said; 'I want to come back to him later.'

'My next is Hammond. Any comment?'

'None, only to say that nobody in flannels looked more the perfect cricketer. Best slip field in the world, had the best cover stroke in the world, and a deadly bowler when he felt like pushing himself into it. Limitless cricket will never live down the shame that sometimes in Australia it made Hammond a dull player.'

'He was playing to orders.'

'Not so much orders as the nature of a limitless Test. Hammond standing at the wickets, waiting for the ball, is one of cricket's masterpieces. It is excelled only by that crashing cover drive off his back foot.'

'The critics argue he was a poor on-side player. What do you make of that?'

'I would say that he did not indulge himself in on-side strokes. The reason for that, I think, was his cover shot off the back foot. To that ball other batsmen would play the hook or pull shot. Hammond got himself into the cover habit. His foot went straight back to a short ball, whereas others put it across for the pull. It was a great pity that with his glorious shoulders and powerful wrists Hammond did not indulge in the pull shot. The crowd loves a good, honest, cross-bat pull.'

'Remember his soaring sixes over the long-off in the fifth Test in Sydney in 1933?'

'I do, indeed. I also remember that Woolley in 1938 wrote there were about 30 players of Hammond's standard in English cricket before the 1914 War. Woolley also thought that Hammond would have had difficulty in getting into an English team of that time.'

"Green hills look greener from afar." We cannot dispute what Woolley says, but it is a point to remember that Woolley then was looking at older players with a young and impressionable mind. I remember the veneration I had as a youngster for certain Test players, but when, in after years, I came to play with and against them I found they were blood and bone, the same as anybody else. If there were 30 players of Hammond's standing at any one time in English cricket it must have been the English Golden Age.'

'Many say it was.'

'I would not be afraid of sending our team against a World Eleven of that time or any time.'

'I would not dream of it without Bradman.'

'Neither would I – but we are choosing this team for another purpose, not to play England of 1912.'

'For the next wicket down, Duleepsinhji. There was in the lithe Indian's sleek stroking something beautifully artistic and full of cricket's grace. If Duleepsinhji were not in this team, it would be lacking in something. Also, a great slip fieldsman.'

'He suits me. The only trouble is that we are storing up an embarrassment of riches for the final batting position.'

'Let us run through them,' I said. 'Have you anybody to add to these: Nourse, Kippax, McCabe, Compton?'

'Compton in that class?' he asked.

'Certainly. A classical stroke-maker. The three series of Tests cancelled out by the War would have seen him rise, I think, to

266

superlative heights. I think Compton will still prove a greater batsman than the three we have bracketed him with. More reliable than McCabe or Kippax; at his best when things are tough, and good on a bad wicket.'

'I think that about our Barnes.'

'Yes, indeed. He would have been a heavy scorer in Tests. His ability had about it the brilliancy of McCabe's stroke-making and Bradman's consistency.'

'Not a bad combination! and I nominate Barnes as the best square-cutter in the world to-day.'

'We can't deal with suppositions, I'm afraid,' I said. 'Another sad point about our team is that we can't consider Indians, as we never played against them. Amarnath and Amar Singh appeal to me on performances and repute. I exclude, of course, Duleepsinhji and the Nawab of Pataudi, who played for England against us.

'An interesting thing about that,' I continued. 'Three Indians have played for England against Australia and all three made a century in their first Test innings. Duleepsinhji, Ranjitsinhji and the Nawab of Pataudi.'

My friend threw another log on the fire.

'Picking this team is like a limitless Test,' he said. 'You take it quietly for the first three or four hours. Let me see – McCabe, Kippax, Nourse, Compton. Kippax was an artist, but an indifferent Test performer, and if Kippax is advanced I will bring Jackson forcibly in for this batting position, even though he did open. Good judges considered Jackson the closest approach to Trumper. He made 164 in his first Test against an English side, including Larwood and Tate.'

'True. England did not see the real Jackson in 1930 because of ill-health,' I said. 'But we can't logically consider and assess opening batsmen for a number five position. I think we should confine it to lower down batsmen.'

'McCabe stands alone,' he said. 'In his 232 at Trent Bridge, 187 not out at Sydney and 189 not out at Johannesburg, he played three of the greatest innings known to Test cricket.'

'Any one of those innings was good enough to win McCabe his place in my side,' I said.

'Nourse was good to watch. Fast, clean footwork. His 231 against Australia, with O'Reilly and Grimmett, in 1935 at Johannesburg was a classical innings. But he was not in McCabe's class of brilliancy.'

He wrote down McCabe and our side now stood:–

Ponsford	Duleepsinhji
Headley	McCabe
Hammond	

The next was a wicket-keeper. We had an abundance of talent in Oldfield, Ames, Cameron, Duckworth.

'If Oldfield had not gone to South Africa in 1935–36, I might not hesitate in this,' said the other. 'I cannot forget the hash he made of taking Fleetwood-Smith. He did his reputation no good with the South Africans by that trip.'

'Fleetwood-Smith certainly made a mess of Oldfield on that tour,' I agreed. 'Mind you, Fleetwood was not the easiest of bowlers in the world to take, pitching on the leg stump and then breaking away quickly and sharply. Bradman's Test score of 334 would still stand as the record had Barnett not missed a stumping of Hutton off Fleetwood-Smith when he was 40 at the Oval in 1938. And Barnett was a specialist in taking Fleetwood. Hutton made 364, if you remember.'

'Are we likely to forget that in a hurry? Neither will Ben Barnett.'

'Even forgetting the South African phase of Oldfield's career, I'm inclined to plump for Cameron. I have never seen eclipsed the standard of his keeping in Melbourne in one Test in 1931. Oldfield, quick and stylish, missed a few chances not always apparent to everybody, and I don't think Cameron suffered in comparison with him as a keeper. In addition, Cameron was one of the best punishing bats in the world.'

'Remember the story they tell of Hedley Verity and that Yorkshire bundle of good humour, wicket-keeper Wood? Jock Cameron had hit Hedley for three sixes and three fours in one over. "Keep it oop, keep it oop, Hedley," said Wood at the end of the over, "thou hast him in two minds." "What do you mean?" asked Verity. "Well," said Wood, "he's not quite sure whether t'hit thee for four or six".'

'Ames was a handy man, breezy with the bat when he felt like it.'

'Yes, but lacking the polish of the others behind the stumps.'

'And "Garge" Duckworth. People would come from miles around to see and particularly hear Duckie. He'd be a great draw-card. Should "Garge" concern us?'

'Hardly – not with a Cameron to consider first and then an Oldfield.'

Cameron's name went down on the list.

Next we wanted an all-rounder. We had few to choose from, and whether this was because of a periodic shortage or the difficulties of bowling on modern, doped wickets we found it hard to decide. My friend thought the average cricketer who had both batting and bowling pretentions found it best to concentrate upon one or the other, as attention to both might have made him ordinary in both spheres.

He instanced Hammond, who could, he claimed, have been an

outstanding medium-paced off-spinner, with whip off the pitch, had he given everything to bowling. I agreed with him, because I had batted against Hammond after he had made an infrequent failure with the bat and found him of Tate-like hostility. He made the ball stand up off the wicket higher than anybody I knew.

'We never saw Amar Singh, the Indian,' I said. 'The Indians had some good all-rounders on paper, at least. But I cannot think of anybody to rival Constantine. He was not an imposing Test batsman on figures against the Australians, but I think it unwise to judge his batting on that. I put him down as the cleanest and hardest hitter I saw. What do you think?'

'Bartlett, of Sussex, hit pretty hard against us at Brighton one day. A century in 57 minutes is rather rapid progress, eh?'

'Trumper once made fifty in five minutes in a Sydney grade game. But to return to all-rounders. It is not quite right to say there has been a paucity of all-rounders in recent years. Jas, Langridge, M. S. Nichols, J. H. Parks, George Pope, Sinfield, Todd and Wellard are Englishmen who have performed the double feat of a thousand runs and a hundred wickets in the years just before the war. Jim Smith, of Middlesex, was also a handy man. Australia has been lean in all-rounders since Jack Gregory. But Pepper and Miller will rise to heights. They are two glorious all-rounders, good to watch. They are other youngsters whose cricket the War hit to leg. Denis Morkel was the only all-rounder Springbok I can remember.'

'Possibly Langton. But none of these in Constantine's class,' said my friend. I agreed. A slashing batsman, beautiful bowler and a dream of a fieldsman in any position, Constantine walked into our side. A cricketer, moreover, full of personality.

The hour by now was very late. Two more divisions of the express had passed by, the rain had stopped long since and we still had the bowlers to choose. Luckily, I could see few disagreements in view in this direction, but as he had been a tried and proven Test bowler I was ready to sway to his judgment in this regard.

'The fast bowler picks himself with me,' said he. 'Right,' I said and we wrote down the name without even mentioning it.

'The same goes for Tate. Stood in a class of his own as a medium bowler.' We wrote again.

I mused for a while. 'Do you know,' I said, 'I think our fast bowler would have been one of the best batsmen of his age had he not been a fast bowler. I'll never forget his Test innings in Sydney, and how he drove on the off. A glorious batsman – but let's get on.'

'The spinners must be all Australian,' said he. 'Amazing that the country which produced Bosanquet, the father of the spin, one might call him, has not since produced one to take the cricket world by spinning storm. Freeman, Tyldesley, Brown, Mitchell, Sims,

Robins, Peebles, Wright and the rest. Fair to good performers, but nothing at all sensational. The same with South Africa. They had a good one in olden days in Schwarz, I understand, but McMillan and Balaskas could not compare with Mailey or Grimmett, for example.'

'Has it got anything to do with climate?' I asked. 'Do our chaps spin better here because of the warm sun and its influence on supple fingers? I'd hate to spin a ball in England during May. It would take me all my time to feel my fingers, let alone the ball.'

'Sounds feasible, but South Africa has a climate similar to ours. Again, if we except Mailey in Australia in 1920–21 and 1924–25, when English cricket was at a fairly low ebb, our spinners did better in England than Australia. Grimmett is the classic example. He was far from being a Test fixture in games in Australia, remember.'

'Freeman played in only two Tests in Australia and, most remarkable, never in a Test against Australia in England.'

We turned up Freeman's figures in *Wisden*. They staggered us. In 1928 he took 304 wickets at an average of 18; in 1933, 298 at 15; in four consecutive seasons, 1928–1931, he took 1,122 wickets, and in eight successive seasons he took over 200 wickets. And never a Test for England against Australia at Home!

'Freeman's figures on English wickets, which do help spin, should encourage generations of slow bowlers in England for years to come,' said my companion.

'Two bowlers to go,' I said, recalling his mind to the job.

'Grimmett and O'Reilly,' said he. 'Grimmett, unquestionably, as the exponent of slow cunning, allied with an impeccable length. I have never seen a better length bowler than Grimmett. O'Reilly, not far behind Grimmett in control of length, was something unusual in the bowling world. A type of his own, a style and approach to the game of his own and something else that must nearly be of his own – a century of wickets in only four series of Tests against England. And that on mostly heart-breaking wickets!'

'No arguments to offer and none to put against either of them,' said I. We wrote down our final names.

'As to the captain,' said I. 'I liked Hammond in this guise. Not the shrewd man Jardine was in detecting a batsman's weakness, but no fussiness, and he allowed each man to play his own game. Few Test captains do that. Have you any suggestions?'

'I was thinking of Cameron, but this side will captain itself. Hammond suits me.'

'And now,' said I, 'to return to Bradman. I am not dropping him from the side. He comes with it for two or more express reasons. It is a touring side. I agree that if Bradman played with this side we would not see from some the cricket we would otherwise witness. He would swamp them, as you say. That was one of the features of his intense individualism, and we cannot blame him for that, not that we want to. But as this mythical tour is to recreate interest in the game, what could offer more interest than the Bradman of the 1932 season playing against the Larwood of the 1932 season, with no bodyline? All the cricket world would want to see the outcome of that.'

'I was just looking,' he said, 'at Test averages in this copy of *Wisden*. I see, even with bodyline thrown in, that Bradman averages 91.42 per Test innings against England. Clem Hill is 35.46; Armstrong 35.03; Trumper 32.79, and Syd Gregory 25.80. These are the Australians who have scored over 2,000 runs. Bradman has scored 3,840 runs in 46 innings; Trumper 2,263 in 74 innings. Probably different times, circumstances and outlooks, but those figures are certainly staggering.'

This was now our touring combination:–

Ponsford	Constantine
Headley	Larwood
Hammond (captain)	Tate
Duleepsinhji	Grimmett
McCabe	O'Reilly
Cameron	Bradman (for the opposition)

'Frank Chester as umpire. Add "Fergie" as baggage-man and scorer and away it goes,' said he.

'It is not a bad side,' I said. 'I would see it do battle with confidence against any team of any time – but, from those left behind, it would not be difficult to choose another good team.'

'Cricket between the wars seems to have depended largely on a few big personalities. Perhaps there was something in what Woolley said, after all.'

'This team of ours lacks just a few little things,' I began. 'No specialist in the field at cover. In fact, not a champion fielding side at all. No left-handed batsmen. Paynter and Leyland, good redoubtable Test men, but neither a stylist. No left-handed bowler. Verity and Quinn —'

'What of Ironmonger?' he cut in. 'We have forgotten the best left-hand bowler I saw. He would have taken 200 wickets on any English tour. The person who first put about the tale of a doubtful action kept Ironmonger out of several trips. He would have been unplayable at times in England.'

'I agree whole-heartedly,' I said. 'But he cannot displace any of my four bowlers. One other thing this team lacks. A batsman of the like of Sutcliffe or Collins, who can put his back to the wall and play for time. That is one of cricket's greatest charms. It also includes no

Yorkshireman – and I'm afraid a world team without a dash of Yorkshire lacks something.'

'How they love a fight!' he soliloquised, and then, 'But I suppose it is impossible to have everything, and we can compromise with Yorkshire by playing the County at Bramall Lane – where the best and fairest cricketing crowd in the world lives.'

'I think we might have started something with this team,' I said, exhibiting some diffidence.

'What matter,' said he, 'we can take it. After all, it is our side. Others can agree to differ and pick their own. We did play with and against these chaps.'

'Well, then,' I said, 'now to bed, to sleep – perchance to dream.'

'If only we do dream,' he came back enthusiastically, 'how would you like in your dreams to see this team against one, say, of the 1905 period?'

'What a dream!'

'Somebody like F. S. Jackson, who knew both periods, knows the game and players so well, with their faults and virtues, should write an account with scores of such a game as he sees it unfolding in his mind's eye.'

'Might do it myself, some day. G'night.'

'G'night.'

CHAPTER TEN

On Gossips and Critics

I OFTEN WONDER WHETHER cricket enthusiasts continue to hold meetings such as those delightfully gossipy and intimate ones which captivated us every Saturday evening of those seasons just past. Conway and I had a ritual that filled every blissful hour of those Saturdays. We were the youngest members of the Second Eleven, and long after our elders had hurried home to their families after the day's play, we would sit ensconced in the little shop at the corner with passion-fruit ice-cream on a dish in front of us and the latest edition of the afternoon newspaper, open at the cricket page, propped before us.

I can almost imagine the flavour of the passion-fruit on my tongue again. We used to roll it caressingly around our mouths as our eyes took in every detail of the five or more columns of scores. Those were the newspaper days when even a shire cricketer had his place in the scheme of things. His fortunes for the season might have continued poor, but custom did not rob him of his Saturday mention in six-point type with one whole single line to himself, though the line of dots running across from his name to the end of the column often ended in an ignominious '0'.

But it was the Saturday evening, when the club representatives gathered on the corner, which really provided the critics with their best gossiping, analytical moments. Sometimes, if the seniors had had a good day (and they had many in those years), we might even be honoured by the presence of some of the First Eleven. Perhaps the international Carter, making his way with characteristically quick steps to his office in an evening call, would stop by to make some happy quip or pass judgment on the day's play. We hung on every word that fell from the great man's lips; we accepted it all as gospel, and, indeed, from thenceforth quoted it as our own opinion.

We made a great array those Saturday evenings as we strung along the side of the footpath or formed little independent caves in the entrance to shops. We were, apart from the omniscient and slightly aloof firsts, a good cross-section of the seconds (rather lordly people if there were not too many firsts present), the thirds (closer to earth), the fourths (humble) and the shires (very humble); but though, as I say, we were many in number, there were occasional evenings after the club had been through a particular lean day when the cynics came to scoff at the few brave enough to make an appearance.

The whole of the day's play with its teeming incidents had to be discussed. Players would come from all directions (many of the younger ones with urgent views and news to impart, because, Saturday night being Saturday night, there was also a sweetheart in the offing), and sometimes, an hour or two after the main party had assembled, would come the stragglers, bats and pads still importantly in hand, who had been travelling long from distant fields. They gave their stumps scores. Then followed in rapid succession the particulars, the highlights, the analysis of this and that, the criticisms and the prophecies. They came out in a quick jumble, several talking together, but once delivered they were there for the evening's dissection and for possible recapitulation in after years to the discomfiture of some over-enthusiastic or immature critic.

Chief Justice of the corner was Ernest Williams, friend and helper of every up and coming cricketer in the district. Points of cricket law, the merits or demerits of some particular innings or bowling effort, all made their way to Williams for final and incontestable judgment. He was a bosom friend of Carter's; he had been a personal friend of Victor Trumper; he had seen the great 'W. G.'; he could quote chapter and verse of the doughty deeds of every cricketing immortal, and this, scathingly, to the rout and discomfiture of some young innocent who had vain ideas of the ability of the moderns.

Another stern critic in the set was Edward ('Not Out') Kent. A distinguished umpire (withal a difficult man, I remember, to convince that your conception of a straight line between wicket and wicket coincided with his), he also had the distinction of living in our district. A very proper umpires' committee, therefore, not wishing to place in his way the temptation of drawing a slightly more elastic straight line between wicket and wicket to the advantage of the men of his home suburb, Kent never officiated in a game in which our club was concerned.

But nothing, of course, could have shaken Kent's view of what constituted leg-before-wicket. He was as unshakable in that as Einstein in his theory of relativity. There was, in Kent, nothing of that renowned umpire, officiating in a very close game, who gave the last batsman out in a doubtful decision, shouting meanwhile: 'Out! Out, you beauty, and we've won. Hooray!'

Looking back, I am inclined to think that the great strength of our club in those days was brought about by the keen interest and competition for places, which, in turn, was stimulated by club gossip and chatter. This intense playing over of the game again, the keen analysis and expression of different viewpoints, constituted the very life-blood of the club, because cricket, I'm sure, is never so strong as when it has in its wake a stream of knowledgable critics, dreamers of the game and well-wishers.

Williams was a case in point. His fanatical love of the game had a most practical expression. I was one of a number of pre-work youths to whom the club's entrance fee of 10/6 was quite a consideration, but at the beginning of the season Williams would come quietly among us and leave us infinitely the richer for a little cardboard notice of membership. Then, too, were the occasions when Williams, Bob Holm, Carter or Stevens – all district stalwarts and encouragers of the young – would give a bat, a pair of pads or gloves to some aspiring lad who had performed out of the ordinary.

A kindly man can do his name no greater service than to go among the youngsters – preferably youngsters whose environment will not permit such luxuries – and leave with them the implements of sport. Such deeds begin many a Test player of the future on his road. The world takes on a new meaning for a talented lad who suddenly finds himself the possessor of a chaste, white-faced, unmarked new bat. A new bat and his own property! He takes it to his bedroom, plays a few strokes (he is in a Test match, of course); he never wants to let it out of his sight; hurries home to it from school, and so, apart from gladdening a youthful heart, the aim of ambition is pinned.

A friend of mine, A. W. Wells, of Bloemfontein, South Africa (whom I know only through correspondence), once wrote a charming cricket story called 'The Last Over'. It was of an Englishman who went to South Africa, made a cricketing name for himself and returned to his home village in England to play what was to prove his last match. He was the hero and he motored home that evening sad in the knowledge that this was his last game. He pulled up to watch a contest in which street urchins were playing with improvised implements. He made them the supreme gesture. He tossed them his cricket kit!

One of the best stories I know of Dr Herbert Evatt, the Australian statesman, concerns some schoolboys. He was waiting one afternoon near the Rose Bay (Sydney) flying base to welcome the New Zealand Prime Minister, Peter Fraser. As he waited, he was engrossed in a school cricket game. Suddenly he became frightfully upset. A natural left-hander was bowling over the wicket and the pitch was taking spin! The Doctor, shifting from one foot to the other, could stand it no longer. He made a megaphone of his hands and roared out across the field: 'Hey, bowler! Hey, bowler! Change to round the wicket. Round the wicket, not over.' And the bowler promptly did, vetoed a cropful of wickets and will never know, possibly, who his distinguished adviser was.

Dr Evatt is a cricket gossiper. He loves to chat on and on about the game, expressing strong opinions which are also solid ones. In that category, also, is R. G. Menzies. I don't think I have met a better judge of the game or a more supreme lover of the game – i.e., to my mind, he is cricket's most delightful after-dinner speaker, followed in that regard by the South African Minister, Jan Hofmeyer. Often after a Press political interview in Canberra with Mr Menzies, he has bidden me stay behind to discuss, as he put it, 'some important matters.' Why didn't the English selectors appreciate the ability of Charlie Barnett and Edrich; was Australia sufficiently prepared for the coming Tests; what about the Australian captaincy? The best cricket dinners given in Australia (and the only ones, so far as I know, to first-class cricketers) are those by Mr Menzies to the Victorian Eleven when it wins the Sheffield Shield. Cricket legislators note!

Mr Menzies was not born with a silver spoon in his mouth. I like the story he tells of himself as a lad when he set out for the Melbourne Cricket Ground when Victoria was playing England. He went early, with his lunch, not so that he could get a good seat around the arena, but that he could get the seat underneath the particular tree in the parklands outside the ground which gave him a view of the scoring board. No good Samaritan came along to buy him into the ground; from beneath the tree, as he puts it, he saw every run of Warwick Armstrong's double century go against his name. There was love of the game if you like. R. G. Menzies should be an Australian selector. He not only loves the game – he knows it.

Warwick Armstrong, like most former cricketers, was a severe critic. I remember once meeting Armstrong at the Randwick racecourse, and with several cricket enthusiasts in the party he took the chance to express his views of the moderns. A few days before O'Reilly had taken 8-23 and 6-22 against Queensland, but

Armstrong would not agree that O'Reilly was anything more than 'just a bowler'. He would not have it that he was a great bowler. He thought the same about Tate, though he passed Larwood as being in the Great Class.

When O'Reilly's name was mentioned, Warwick reeled off a string of famous bowling names of the past with such spirited rapidity that one could almost imagine O'Reilly (W. J.), doing odd jobs for their souls in Valhalla, and being glad of the privilege.

'He didn't turn a single ball against the Queenslanders. I was behind the wickets with glasses, and I should know,' said Warwick.

'But the Queenslanders —' I began to advance.

Warwick snorted, and when a twenty-two-stone man snorts it's hard to hold out against it.

'I could bowl the Queenslanders out even now,' he said.

I remembered that there was always a doubt whether Warwick, himself, really turned the ball. His leg-breaks were reputed to be top-spinners.

'Jack Hobbs once told me that you —' I began.

'Did you see Trumble bowl?' asked Armstrong.

'No.'

'Griffen?'

'No.'

'Howell?'

'No.'

'Noble?'

I felt, by this, like asking whether Warwick himself had ever seen Bill the Conqueror, but he gave me no opening.

Armstrong did not believe Bradman stood on a pedestal alone. Trumper, Duff, Syd Gregory (he did mention a fourth, but I have forgotten him) were all as good as Bradman.

'Tyldesley, Shrewsbury, Ranji, Fry —' started off another member of the Reminiscing Squad.

It looked like a memory test, with honours to the man who could go back the furthest. The eyes of the Old Timer glistened as he leaned on his stick in the corner.

He went back to the first Australian aboriginal team, which toured England and gave an exhibition of boomerang and spear throwing after each game. 'Dick-a-dick, Nulla Nulla—' he started off – but he did not have the floor for long.

'What a marvellous cricketer Warwick was himself,' said a friend of mine, Tom Howard, in an aside, and I quite agreed, because I think Armstrong was one of the really great personalities in the game of all time. They say that when he was the Australian captain he brooked no nonsense. His word was law. I could well understand that.

'No two cricketers in Australia to-day are up to Test standard,' was Warwick's first criticism.

'It would seem, then,' I observed, mostly to myself, 'that the players of to-day are not as good as they were.'

'No,' said a meek little chap in the other corner, who had not spoken before, 'they never were, my boy, and they never will be.'

I wrote what I thought was a human interest story of that friendly little discussion, but my Editor, a timid soul, who knew nought of cricket, withdrew it in haste after the First Edition. He thought Mr Armstrong might object to it! He didn't know Warwick, of course. Warwick was a man of firm conviction, and he didn't care who knew what he thought.

I recall that Armstrong story by way of passing on to the observation that players are not always the best critics. I am not claiming that Armstrong was wrong in his opinions. The very distinguished position he occupied in the game entitled him to express such opinions – which might have been perfectly correct – but there have been others whose opinions have been forced back down their throats. A fellow Test player once wrote that Bradman was not up to Test standard; another that Larwood was not really a fast bowler.

The truth is, of course, that playing cricket and writing about it are poles apart. One does not qualify a person for the other; indeed it makes it all the more difficult. Each is a specialised job, and the once-famous player who finds himself converted overnight into a journalist writing in judgment on the game and its participants is usually in a most invidious position. He lacks that experience which enables a professional journalist to write about it and about. The cum-by-night journalist feels that he has to be critical to justify himself, and so he goes to it. In his playing moments he has been so steeped in the grim, remorseless concentration of Test cricket that many aspects of the play have passed him by. He has been a doer, not an observer, and thus he knows nothing of the humorous figure he has cut when, possibly, in his most serious moments.

The proper old gentleman of the game he meets as he comes into it will adjure him to pay no attention to the crowd; to ignore it entirely for fear its remarks might upset his play. Once upon a time a stuffy captain mildly rebuked me because I so far forgot myself and the dignity of first-class cricket as to indulge in a few little pleasantries with some schoolboys over the fence. In the Leeds Test of 1938, while fielding on the boundary, I was on the verge of offering my arm to a portly, humorous Yorkshire woman who had to scurry across a portion of the ground each time to a new position when the sight-board was moved – but I didn't dare. You see, we are a very serious lot of fellows, we Test cricketers. We move in a little satisfactory world of adulation, and are inclined often to put on airs and graces.

I once had a very good experience of the fickleness of success. I top-scored for Australia in a Test in Melbourne and was right royally dined and wined by a very prominent Australian. Life was magnificent. Two weeks later I distinguished myself by making a 'pair of blobs' in the next Test. Walking the street next day, I saw my distinguished friend coming towards me. He saw me – and crossed to the other side of the street!

But that by the way. What I really wanted to impress was the necessity, for the good of the game, to have unlimited gossipers and as many qualified critics as possible, and by critics I do not mean those who tell you that in so many minutes such-and-such a batsman made so many runs with so many boundaries, and when he left the score was so-and-so.

This type of writing is an insult to your true lover of the game. He can read all the details he wants in the scores. He does want to know, if a batsman makes a score or a bowler takes wickets, what quality of performance it was and what was the calibre of the opposition; how much good fortune was in the innings and how much art. He wants pen pictures of the players, the setting, and the crowd. He wants to be as intimate as he can with it all, and it is in this that critics like Neville Cardus and Robertson-Glasgow, to name two, are so invaluable to the game. They lay cricket and its principals bare open to their readers, because they analyse with a microscope and understand every little mood and humour of the game. Cajole Cardus into reminiscing, with actions and dialect, on Yorkshire and Lancashire heroes in the game, and there you'll have several hours of rare cricketing humour.

One of the best writings I have read was penned by Cardus concerning an England–South Africa Test – and he never saw a ball bowled! With the weather screaming no play in the morning, Cardus left London and returned to Manchester. To his dismay, he opened the evening newspaper and found that a thrilling day's play had taken place. Nothing daunted, he got the necessary bare essentials from an agency and wrote a piece that will live in cricket literature. Only a true, gifted cricket writer could have done that. Cardus knew to the minutest detail the men he was writing about; he knew, if they made a score or took wickets, just exactly how their individuality would have taken them about it. Apart from the salient facts, there would be no difference to your expert who knew Bradman in Bradman making a century in Adelaide to Bradman making a century in Manchester.

I once made a century at Lord's, a century that gave me great satisfaction, because, for once, I had got a move on, and this was at

Lord's. But the reason for my pleasure was principally because I had promised Cardus that some time in England I would play an innings specially for him. I picked Stephenson, Hammond and Macindoe fine and square to the leg boundary; I connected with what I thought were rather nifty cover drives. I was 82 of the side's first 100. This, I thought, might please even Cardus, but of course, he never saw it. He told me later that when he saw me coming to bat he found he had to leave the ground early!

I like the manner in which Robertson-Glasgow (himself a first-class bowler) describes the character and whims of players. Take this delightful study of Phil Mead: 'He was number four. Perhaps two wickets had fallen cheaply; and there the cheapness would end. He emerged from the pavilion with a strong, rolling gait – like a longshoreman with a purpose. He pervaded a cricket pitch. He occupied it and encamped upon it. He erected a tent with a system of infallible pegging, then posted inexorable sentries. He took guard with the air of a guest who, having been offered a week-end by his host, obstinately decides to reside for six months. Having settled his whereabouts with the umpire, he wiggled the toe of his left boot for some fifteen seconds inside the crease, pulled the peak of a cap that seemed all peak, wiggled again, pulled again, then gave a comprehensive stare around him, as if to satisfy himself that no fielder, aware of the task ahead, had brought out a stick of dynamite. Then he leaned forward and looked at you down the pitch, quite still. His bat looked almost laughably broad.'

And Edmund Blunden on Warwick Armstrong: 'He made a bat look like a teaspoon and the bowling weak tea; he turned it about idly, jovially, musingly. Still he had but to wield the bat – a little wristwork – and the field paced after the ball in vain. It was almost too easy.'

Some first-class cricketers chafe when the critic takes them to task. They demand to know what this same critic has done himself in the game; how high did he rise, and so on. Going further, they talk of presenting a bat to the critic and asking him to oblige by demonstrating what he means. But your true critic is not upset by these fulminations. The point is that the player has his field, the critic his, and, except in very few circumstances, the wise man will not try to invade the other's domain. I would never think, for instance, of asking Neville Cardus to trundle his slow, round-arm, off-spinning wares (plenty of air and usually width, too!) on a first-class field, but I do think that Cardus will live in cricket history as much an adornment to the game as Victor Trumper.

Contrariwise, the Test-cricketer-turned-writer, like the man with the wheel-barrow, has the job very much in front of him. His long experience on the field has led him to take for granted happenings which are of vital interest to the ordinary followers of the game. Moreover, his movements on the field are mostly functional; much of interest passes him by. When I perched at silly-leg to O'Reilly's bowling, I knew absolutely nothing of what went on behind my back. I had my attention focussed on the batsman. (When I smothered up as the batsman made a full-blooded swing in my direction, there were times when I knew nothing of what was going on in front of me, either!)

But now I must leave this, observing finally that it will be a poor day for the game when it ceases to attract the men of literature and the gossipers. The slow, tranquil trend of the game, its tactics and movements obvious, lends itself admirably to their purposes. And we players can serve our purpose best by suffering the critics gladly, even though we disagree with them.

Last year I watched a game in Sydney from the Members' Stand. I was surrounded on all sides by THE critics and thus should have known better, but, involuntarily, as a fieldsman gathered the ball ten yards from the stumps with the running batsman still five yards out of his crease, I uttered the words, 'Have a throw.' When the fieldsman didn't, I expressed condemnation – and four gentlemen in front turned on me as one, made it obvious that they regarded me as a fool, and their spokesman said in withering tone: 'How ridiculous; had he done so and missed there would have been four overthrows!'

I answered not. I remembered my place in time. I thought, however, that had I been the fieldsman and the game a Test, with four runs separating England and Australia with the last Englishman in, and the destiny of the Ashes hinging on the result, I certainly would have run the risk of four overthrows.

All that illustrates is that the player, the critic, or the observer cannot possibly hope, like the old man with his son and the donkey, to please everybody. The famous Sarah Bernhardt proved this once after she had been watching a Rugby game for half an hour. 'Ah,' she gushed, obviously trying to say the right thing, 'I do so love this game of cricket. It is so essentially British.'

CHAPTER ELEVEN   *Kick-backs from 1946–47*

SINCE THE WRITING AND PRINTING of two editions of this book the first post-war series of Tests between England and Australia have been played, and, unfortunately, they take the general story of bodyline further along its way. In the first instance, no series of modern Test matches other than the bodyline one knew such an abundance of bumpers. Secondly, these bumpers were bowled almost exclusively by the Australians and that, without censure, in the presence of Scott and Borwick, two umpires who in other seasons had officially frowned on fast bumpers. Borwick no-balled the aborigine, Gilbert, and Scott in Adelaide in 1937, called all the pace bowlers into an ante-room before the Grimmett–Richardson testimonial match and described where a fast ball could justifiably be pitched. Finally, even many Australians detected in the captaincy of Bradman in the 1946–47 Tests an element of mercilessness that recalled memories of Jardine. One point, however, must strongly be stressed. At no time was there the faintest suggestion of extra men being placed on the leg side.

England wanted to postpone this 1946–47 tour. It was thought too soon after serious and disruptive events to attempt a recapturing of the standard and glamour of former days, but Australia strongly favoured a quick return to the series. Official Australian circles also allowed it to be known at Lords that international sport would not be unwelcome as a means of settling people back into ordinary life again, and, at the very least, a Test series would take the public mind off industrial and other upsets inseparable from war's aftermath. Then, too, the game in both countries stood in need of money.

In 1944 at the London Guildhall the Australian Prime Minister, John Curtin, had spun his superb phrase of the British Commonwealth of Nations defending the 'last 22 yards', and he also had readily listened in 1944 to a Lords plea for assistance in the early resuscitation of the game in England. He promptly had additional Australian servicemen-cricketers posted to England from Australia and the Islands for 'special duty'.

John Curtin loved cricket. For him it was life's greatest relaxation from high office – office which eventually killed him. In his press interviews at Canberra and elsewhere he often used a cricket tag to illustrate his meaning or define some particular situation. I could well imagine the look on his face in 1944 when Winston Churchill told him that cricket left him cold. The Prime Ministers were spending a consultative week-end at Chequers, and D. K. Rodgers, secretary to the Australian Prime Minister, had telephoned a message that the Royal Australian Air Force Eleven had won a most exciting game at Lords by a wicket. Later, in conversation, Mr Churchill told of his knowledge of the telephone call and musingly observed that that same telephone line had brought news of the fall of France and other momentous events of that time!

Doctor Evatt, the Australian statesman, supported the MCC tour to Australia. Shipping berths were as scarce as sunlight in the average English winter, and I mention this and Dr Evatt's good offices because some sought, unkindly and unappreciatively, to misplace blame when the MCC team fell below expectations. Before a game was played in Perth it was suggested by Englishmen (not belonging to the team) that the tour was before its time. In the grim and unyielding conception of modern Test cricket the 1946–47 tour undoubtedly was before its time. There were many difficulties to be overcome in England, although in the numerous games against the Australian Services team and the Indian tour of England in 1946 the MCC selectors had more to guide them than their Australian counterparts.

But this is immaterial. Such considerations are valid only when the winning of the game is paramount. For the players and the enthusiasts in the British Commonwealth the all-important feature of the 1946–47 tour was that international cricket between two great rivals should even be possible again, and if at the end of the series there was a sense of disappointment and disillusionment, the fault surely was not with those who had laboured to make the tour possible, but perhaps with some who trod the sward and just as much who pricked with the pen.

The MCC team was far from being a good one. The selectors (probably through no fault of their own) committed the cardinal error of including too many players near the end of their tether, and, apart altogether from the greater likelihood of strains, the player who already has one foot and a toe or two of the other in the pavilion has neither the capacity nor the incentive of the younger man on tour to rise above misfortunes. The MCC team of 1946–47 knew these contradistinctions. Because of the perils and tribulations of the Homeland during the war, no previous team had so many ardent well-wishers in Australia, and no English team to Australia in the twentieth century could possibly have been so lacking in technique and incentive. Hammond's team played like a war-dulled side, as undoubtedly it was. At the end of the tour it had the worst record of any English team to Australia since Stephenson brought the first side in 1862. It won only one first-class game. This 1946-47 team lost in almost everything but behaviour on the field – and I am not unmindful of the several occasions when some players showed obvious disagreement with umpiring decisions.

Hammond wisely made no claims for his team the day Australian pressmen crowded on board the liner to interview him at Fremantle. The press immediately dubbed him 'poor copy'. Never voluble at the best of times, he refused to discuss his team individually and committed himself to no more than the hope (which he shared with all Australia!) that Bradman would play Test cricket again. Manager Howard was also a man of few words. The horde of newspapermen, their principals in the East clamouring for copy, found it difficult to justify the expense of being sent to the West, and, further, found it difficult to justify themselves in the month, almost, which the MCC team spent in Western Australia.

It was in this period that 'scandal' writing made its first appearance of the tour. Many modern newspapers have developed an insatiable craving for the sensational and the critical in sport, politics, international and everyday affairs. The principle seems to be not to waste space in analysis, knowledgeable criticism and praise if somebody else can be slang-banged and that in a double-barrelled manner which assaults the reader in 30-point type at the same time. And if the sub-editor hears a murmur that the reader is the best judge of news, why, he'll make it 40-point type!

The advancement in type and newspaper make-up has much to do with the sensationalism of sporting copy. When the make-up sub-editor receives the dummy of his page with the advertisements placed, he plans his page for display, which includes attractiveness and balance. As large splashings of type in the headlines are deemed to make for a page which attracts the eye, the sub-editor allows for a streamer, say, of 40-point type which extends the whole width of the page, with the story breaking down to three or four column heads. To balance such heads, the first body of the type must be set in 12-point or 10-point (the main body of type is mostly seven- or six-point), and so, even before a story has materialised, it is destined for lavish display – and very, very often when the worth of the story does not merit its splashings. Then enters the sub-editor to build up or garnish the story.

Sport, together with other every-day happenings, receives such treatment in most modern newspapers, and the reader, instead of being helped, must make his own evaluation of the story. Further, modern cricket now knows the player-writer (who seems to be highly valued by newspapers), and to compete with this type the professional journalist, eager to justify himself, has his typewriter and his news-sense always cocked for a story out of the ordinary. Add to these the other type of journalist who will stunt anything, and the foregoing will give some explanation why the 1946–47 cricket season knew more than its share of newspaper publicity.

This tour was the first I had made as a non-player and I discovered many things. First, that many players resent (as I undoubtedly did!) the slightest criticism, which is taken personally, or analysis; secondly, and more importantly, as a non-player I found myself much closer by correspondence and conversation to the keen follower of the game than I had ever been as a player. This man in the street, this ordinary onlooker, is no fool. He has a shrewd and generally correct conception of what goes on in front of him. He's not gulled by what he reads or hears, and is most capable of putting his own interpretation on players and their actions. Thus he knew that much mischief on this tour was created by the stunt press, and he knew also that feelings between the teams at the end of the tour were not exactly 'cricket'.

Compton, Hutton and Edrich gauged the pace of Australian wickets in the first week; Hammond, after the first fortnight, looked as great a batsman as ever. The long stay in Perth delighted the batsmen in their chances of practice, but it caused many a bowler's brow to pucker in distasteful thoughts of his future on Australian pitches. Bedser and Pollard, in England, could cut and seam the ball off the wicket; they found in Perth they could barely move it, and it was further upsetting for them that in the bright sunlight the new ball hardly moved at all in the air. At Northam, in one of the two additional second-class games, Voce knew the ignominy of being hit for six over long-off with the new ball by a youngster.

This was an example of the knowledge of one who wrote for a prominent newspaper. It happened at Perth:

'"Fergie", how did that batsman get out?'

The long-suffering Ferguson, who is scoring and has been answering such questions for countless tours, replies: 'Stumped.'

'Who stumped him?'

And from high in the press-box a scornful voice calls down: 'The man at fine-leg, I guess.'

Of early interest in the tour was the request by A. Randall, the Western Australian member of the Board of Control, that the Australian barracker should behave himself in the coming tour. This request was made at the first official welcome to the MCC team and made many squirm. It was most unnecessary. The barracker during the preceding tour by G. O. Allen's MCC team had been exemplary and, further, the request at an inopportune moment revived memories of Jardine's tour. Again, such a plea, which came from a relatively junior cricket State of the Commonwealth, presumptuously proposed to teach the Australian barracker his supposed place, and Australians usually react oppositely when so stung.

No Australian tour by English cricketers could possibly have known less barracking, though the bespectacled, professorial Gibb, who had an unhappy tour in performances, was singled out for much banter. At Bendigo, famous for its gold yield, he was giving his mark on the crease a terrific and typical pounding (Gibb usually put more gusto into this than his strokes) when a wag called out: 'It's no use, Gibb. We got all the gold out of there years ago.'

The general barracking was insignificant. A remarkable feature of the tour was the manner in which usually partisan Australians warmed to this MCC team and wished it well. The most spirited piece of barracking of the whole tour was levelled at Barnes in Sydney when he made continuous appeals against the light, and there were further murmurs of Australian disapproval in Adelaide and again, later in the season, in Sydney. Many onlookers demurred in Adelaide at the prolonged continuance of Bradman's tactics in keeping so many men on the fence against Compton, and when Australian fieldsmen (Compton, in shielding Evans, refused to run singles) ran alongside the ball for yards without attempting to pick it up. In Sydney, finally, many did not approve of what they considered an overdose of bumpers by Lindwall and Miller.

This general absence of barracking over the series highlighted two things – the lack of necessity for the snub on Australian barrackers at the beginning of the tour, and the welter of barracking during the Jardine tour and the reason for it.

It was fitting that the first appeal of the tour should have come from George Duckworth. Sitting this time in the press-box, he couldn't resist the temptation in Perth when a batsman put his leg in

front of a ball. Duckworth's appeal, in his best voice, led those on
the field below. He looked most crestfallen when spectators turned
in amazement. He was strangely coy later in the tour when, playing
in a Press team which enjoyed every minute of its cricket, a
spectator over a loud-speaker offered £5 to the particular charity
fund if George would once demonstrate his famous appeal.

It was obvious in Perth that there was a pronounced weakness in
the MCC team against slow bowling. Dooland, just released from
the Commandos, turned the side inside out one day when bowling
into a fine-leg breeze which allowed him to dip and swerve his
break. Dooland's form that day would have worried the best
Australian batsmen, but the weakness in the touring team was also
shown once in the Perth nets when Grimmett, also to work in the
press-box, had a turn with the ball and badly bamboozled some of
the tourists.

At this early stage of the tour the Englishmen were much
interested in Bradman's future. The Australian champion would
not commit himself and there was much speculation in the press.
Many things concerned Bradman. He had his own brokerage
business in Adelaide and ill-health had caused him to be discharged
from the army some years before. Even if health and business
permitted Bradman to play, he had the prickling decision to make
whether he retained sufficient of his former skill to do himself
justice. Cricket could offer him nothing he had not experienced to
the brim before. He had only the preservation of his reputation to
gain and much to lose – as Hammond could ruefully have told him at
the end of the tour!

Bradman led South Australia against the MCC, but if Hammond
was eager to know whether the greatest scoring medium of all time
retained his ability, he managed to conceal that eagerness. It was
not until the third of the four-day game that Hammond declared,
and in this game – as, indeed, in all games against the States – the
MCC team did not reveal the slightest desire to achieve a win in four
days. This might have been because the Englishmen realised they
were not good enough to win in four days, but the acceptance of a
drawn game – and that sometimes even on the first day – is to be
noted. An Australian team often found itself roasted in the long
English season when it did not vigorously pursue victory in the third
day of a three-day game.

Bradman, gingerly at first, went to the peace of mind of 75 in this
first innings against Hammond's men. This innings revealed: (a) he
was still a grand batsman, but not now likely to be a record breaker;
(b) the clock was never again likely to be beaten by him; and (c) his
agile mind had not yet conceived that his footwork, like the old grey
mare, was not what it used to be. Twice he was caught in attempting

to drive. His mind was quicker in getting to the ball than his feet, but he adjusted this as the season advanced.

In Adelaide Hammond mocked the gods and never afterwards obtained forgiveness. Possibly bored by the slow batting of his preceding men (Hutton and Washbrook batted all of the first day for 237 runs) and probably satisfied with his century and double century in the West, he most un-Hammondlike rushed down the pitch to the first ball ever bowled at him by Dooland. Hammond was stranded and stumped by yards. Of all the batsmen I've known, none usually took more pains than Hammond to have a probing look at the wares of a new slow bowler. Hence the surprise in Adelaide to see him take Dooland so casually.

And so to Melbourne. No finer century in the season was seen than Hutton's in this game against Victoria. The pitch had not long been topdressed and the surface had caked in preparation. A look at the pitch after the match showed it to be the ugliest dry-wicket imaginable – a spiteful business of exaggerated spin and bounce. Yet Hutton played immaculately. A six over the long fine-leg fence was the stroke of the match, and the superb, upright, swinging Hutton of this day was in contrast later as he fell prone on the pitch against bumpers.

In the next Melbourne game, against an Australian Eleven led by Bradman, it was Compton's turn to provide a dream-like century. England's batting stocks at this time should have been high with Compton and Hutton in such glorious form, but in this same game the English batsmen, generally, shivered in the first of their long series of McCool tremors.

McCool bowls leg-breaks somewhat in the Grimmett style. His delivery is slightly round-arm, but he differs from Grimmett in that he tosses the ball higher, is slower through the air and turns the ball more. He concentrates his attack upon the off-stump, and Bradman, with astute captaincy, teased the Englishmen in Melbourne by setting a strong off-side field with an inner and outer cordon. It was almost impossible to find a gap. Hard drives went straight to a man. In such circumstances most class batsmen take power off their drives and look for singles in an attempt to bring the field in. Then, if this is achieved, the batsman goes for his drive again or perhaps lofts the ball over the infield.

Oddly, it was not until the second Test in Sydney that the Englishmen began to do this against McCool. When drives couldn't pierce the field in the early games against McCool, the Englishmen tried to loft him, and Hammond, Hutton and others were either out to catches or stumpings, a higher tossed ball meeting with phenomenal success in deceiving the Englishmen in length. Then, too, Hutton and Washbrook began to play McCool from the crease – and there is no more palpitating or unedifying sight in cricket than a batsman who anchors one foot in the crease while stretching to the utmost with the other.

Edrich was one English exception. Rarely, if ever, was he at fault against McCool or other Australian slow and spin bowlers who tied his comrades in knots. He played in copy-book style, without any blots.

Before the first Test in Brisbane slow Australian bowling had caused a mental blight, accompanied by some form of foot-rot, to descend upon the MCC men. The average Australian batsman (and especially upon Australian wickets, which give little turn) makes an involuntary forward movement as the slow bowler brings his arm over. If he is in error, he considers he has plenty of time to correct his mistake, but to the eve of Brisbane, excepting Edrich, the Englishmen did not seem to move either way until the ball was half-way down the pitch. Why is there this variance in national styles of play? It might be said that the average Englishman, much bigger in the foot than the average Australian (Bradman could have got both his feet into one of Tate's boots), is slower footed by nature, but probably a factor is that the ball shifts and moves off English turf and the natural movement there is back to counteract the turn.

Many successful leg-twisters in England – Freeman, Tyldesley, Robins and Brown, to name some – had difficulty in turning the ball the length of an eyelid in Australia on our best wickets, and once a batsman knew this, he knew, also, that he could play up the wicket with little fear of being nobbled by the break.

Probably Hammond, who in his three previous tours of Australia owed about 75 per cent of his runs to his treatment of slow bowlers, tried to impress this upon his newer batsmen, but the evidence, to Brisbane, was that the English tactics were to play back, and, unaccountably, the stay-at-homes by Brisbane included Compton, as gifted in the art of footwork as anybody. The know-alls began to talk of preconceived tactics and orders – which, if true, were fatal. A slow bowler, because of his natural inclination to inaccuracy, is played in the air and not from the dressing-room.

In those three previous tours I have mentioned, Hammond added to his belt the scalp of a promising young Australian slow bowler. He got to them on the full or at the pitch and drove like fury; when they wilted under that and dropped the ball short, he hit it even harder off the back foot with that delectable stroke which will keep his memory alive forever. Many a slow bowler, previously, did not know whether he was coming or going against Hammond, but in 1946–47, in the eastern States, it was Hammond who was nearly always going and those who had lived with him in his days of pristine glory began to shift uncomfortably whenever he came to bat. A sad spectacle. Hammond retained much of his greatness, but the Dame showed him her back completely, and the batsman out of luck in cricket spends most of his time in the pavilion.

For Hammond pity and excuses took the place of adulation – invariably the lot of one who slightly overstays himself in a game – but if I had never seen Hammond play some of the loveliest innings in all cricket creation I would remember him, always, for the two classical innings he played on the Brisbane 'glue pot' in the first Test of this series. In such circumstances, the score sheet is a fraud and a humbug. Hammond's scores in this Test were 32 and 23 – comparative failures in the cricket book of time – but on a pitch where the ball bites, kicks and does everything but pull faces (and I'll swear it does that at times) the test of a batsman, as he fights in the hope of better things to come, is not runs but time.

Had events swung England's way just a little in the first Test, Hammond and his men would not have had to bat twice on a wet wicket. In no previous game had Gibb looked the part of an All England keeper, and when Evans was seen fully attired at practice the day before the Test began, it was immediately assumed a change had been made in a plan long apparent to play Gibb as keeper. Gibb is bespectacled. That seems an immediate handicap for a Test stumper, and, probably because he did not sight the ball quickly, his movements did not have the smooth flow of a natural keeper.

Gibb had the misfortune to miss Hassett behind the forties and McCool at two. Hassett made 128 and McCool 96, but, costly as these misses were, the 'Bradman incident' was the feature of the game. Obviously nervous in his first post-war attempt to maintain his phenomenal record, Bradman was ill at ease in timing and judgment and sneaked the ball very streakily through the slips until he reached the twenties. At 28 a ball flew to Ikin at second slip. There was an awkward pause on the part of everybody concerned and then Ikin broke it by appealing for a catch. Umpire Borwick answered with a shake of his hand.

This 'incident' was the most discussed of the series. Former Test cricketers in the Press-box involuntarily shouted 'he's out', and that was the general Press-box opinion, an opinion, of course, which is not infallible. Inquiries made some weeks afterwards, however, provided conclusive evidence that it *was* a catch Ikin made, and not, as Bradman obviously thought, a bump ball.

Now, in all my experiences with Bradman, I never once had the slightest reason to doubt his sportsmanship. If tales are true, Dr Grace was sometimes a shrewd bluffer and was not above trying to put one across if he thought he could get away with it.* There was nothing of that about Bradman. At this time in Brisbane he was playing poor cricket, possibly the poorest of his Test career. His mind was troubled and probably he could not realise that he had given a catch. Had he thought so, he would have walked out immediately, not waiting for an appeal. Had the catch gone to Hammond his very action in taking it and tossing it to someone else would have left no doubt in anybody's mind, but the doubt arose when Ikin, seeing Bradman stay at the wicket, appealed to the umpire with the ball held aloft. This, seemingly, brought doubt to the umpire's mind and he gave Bradman the benefit of it.

The Englishmen had no doubt this was a catch, and as the game is only a game, not a life and death business, it should be admitted that an unfortunate mistake was made – though the series has never happened yet which has been free from umpiring errors. This was unfortunate, however, in that the principal was Bradman and that he went on to 187. This huge score gave him much needed confidence and it meant that England was forced to bat twice on a wet wicket. Had Bradman gone for 28, Australia certainly would have had at least one turn on the wet wicket, and a chill blast blows in the pavilion door whenever Australia has to bat on a wet wicket. And, further, an innings on a wet wicket would have taken some form and confidence from the Australian batting, as it did to England's.

Apart from Hammond, Edrich, Ikin, Compton, Yardley and Washbrook were splendid on this glue-pot. Washbrook once ran a leg-bye off his skull and this from a good length ball! Two tropical deluges on successive days, the second putting the whole ground a foot under water at one stage, sealed England's fate, but the side won undying honours by its plucky, tenacious batting. Toshack, a left hander, playing in his first Test, took 9 wickets for 99 runs, but he was still soundly twigged by the critics. With an average of four critics to each Test player, it was hard to please everybody.

All this batting on the bad wicket at Brisbane ran the MCC men, with the exception of Edrich, very much out of form in Sydney for the second Test. Hammond won the toss and the side seemed to be out soon afterwards. An orthodox, old-style slow bowler in Ian Johnson tied the Englishmen in knots with off breaks, and again did the Englishmen, always excepting Edrich, refuse to get up the pitch. The tail, Bedser, at ten, and Wright, at eleven, gave most of the head a lesson in using their feet, and these two played the Australian

* This is an alleged instance of his shrewdness. He would allow the opposing captain the honour of tossing. Then, invariably, he would call, 'The Lady,' with the coin in the air, and, on strolling across to look at it on the ground, would exclaim, 'And the Lady it is.' As the head of Queen Victoria was on one side and Britannia on the other, it could hardly be anything else but 'the Lady'!

bowling with ease, having the satisfaction of seeing McCool taken off for the first time against England.

There was much jiggery-pook about the light in this match. It rained on the second day and when play was resumed the ball came through without venom off a pitch wet on the top. Barnes, a splendid batsman, was enjoying himself immensely, but almost as if he had suddenly picked up a message on his radar, he began to appeal against the light. And Barnes does nothing by halves. His first appeal refused, he appealed again two balls later. This, so to speak, being set aside, he called on privilege and took the subject up again in the flash of another two balls, and at every appeal the umpires came solemnly together in the middle of the pitch, peered about as if for pickpockets, and then motioned the game on. It was recorded, officially, that there were eight appeals, but this might have been more or less, as Barnes put the question with the rapidity of a chairman when Parliament is in the committee stages of a Bill with the 'guillotine' in operation.

The spectators howled in fury, but, custom being exactly custom, the umpires had to confer each time an appeal was made. Barnes upset officialdom at the end of the season when he made a broadcast in Perth to the effect that he appealed because he did not want Australia to lose any more wickets that afternoon. That was candid enough, but perhaps he had instructions. The fault was not his entirely, because rules are bad which permit such stretching. Possibly something will be done about this vexatious rule, but it was most noticeable that the Englishmen refused (with the exception of once by Hutton in Sydney as the tour was ending) to appeal against the light or rain for the rest of the series – batting on in semi-darkness and rain in Melbourne when facing defeat in the third Test. Bradman, as fielding captain, was forced to make the first move.

Theorists have often suggested that there should be a machine to give a light decision, but I think this is impracticable, as the light must often be determined by background, and this differs on all grounds. In Sydney, for instance, the background of the Paddington grandstand is a bad one in dull light and the ball from the bowler goes high above the sight-board. The world's leading umpire, Frank Chester, raised a hub-dub at Leeds in 1947 when he was alleged to have told Melville, the South African captain, and Yardley not to use their fast bowlers in the dim light. It was claimed by many that Chester had acted outside his duties. Perhaps he had, in the strict interpretation of those duties, but Chester has individuality as an umpire, and I can understand the spirit in which he gave such information. Many a captain will refrain from using his fast bowler in a doubtful light because it usually brings an appeal against the light. Perhaps Chester was doing nothing else than letting the captains know his opinion that he considered the light fit against medium and slow bowlers, but not for the fast men. To sum up, the light rule stands in need of some enlightenment.

The Australians gave not even a kind look away in this Test. Barnes and Bradman sat almost immobile on the English attack for much of the third day. In 300 minutes they scored 225. They continued their squatting on the fourth day for several hours, and then they both opened out in a blaze of delightful batting, each scoring 234, and thus sharing the Test record score for Sydney. Bradman was his old devastating self in his final fifty runs. On the morning of the fifth day Australia was 316 ahead, and all the critics had no doubt Bradman would close. He didn't. This gave him charge of the wicket, and though the grass after the rain of the Saturday looked like the early stages of a wheat crop, he refused to have it cut and used the heavy roller. If the pitch was about to crack, this would help it on its way – shrewd reasoning on Bradman's part – but the English batting cracked even more than the pitch, and Australia ran out easy winners.

Hutton was an interesting study in this game. His superlatively brilliant 37 in 24 minutes in the second innings had the old-timers recalling Trumper; but one always sensed it could not last, though he was out in a most peculiar manner. His left hand swung off the bat, and, with control lost, the bat carried on to the stumps. Early in the innings almost the whole Australian team appealed for a catch behind off Hutton. Umpire Borwick refused it. The Australians were just as confident about this as the Englishmen in Brisbane about Bradman. A difference was that Hutton did not go on to a huge score, otherwise there might have been another rumpus.

Miller gave Hutton a goodly dose of bumpers. Right through the season the Australians were to exploit the contention made earlier that Hutton did not like bumpers. Indeed, on this tour, Hutton showed less liking for bumpers than any class batsman I've seen.

I think his dislike for bumpers was aggravated by an injured arm. On the trip across the Australian Desert he showed me one day his badly scarred left arm, broken during war training. This arm was much shorter than his right and had known 45 stitches in the two operations on it. It carried grafted pieces of bone from both legs, and I think this injured arm was always in Hutton's mind as he ducked bumpers. He insisted that his arm did not worry him, but I often noticed him giving it a furtive rub out in the middle.

I'm sure bumpers greatly upset Hutton's style of play and turned him into a batsman of moods, one day consistently brilliant, the next spasmodically indifferent. The tour knew nothing better than his stroke-making, and had Australia not been rich in fast bowlers, he would have made colossal scores. Bradman never deterred his fast men from bowling bumpers, but it must be clearly understood that at no time did Bradman have more than the orthodox number of men on the on-side. But, because of his war injury, there were times when Australians thought a little generosity or chivalry towards Hutton would not have been misplaced.

The MCC team was at sixes and sevens for the third Test in Melbourne. Hammond's batting form had left him; Bedser, spoken of as a second Tate, could do little off the wicket; and Wright, though bowling with execrable luck, was his own worst enemy with a deluge of no-balls. There was, too, a melancholy note about Hammond's captaincy, which was lacking in drive and, sometimes it seemed, thought. Wright and Bedser often went from the bowling crease to the boundary between overs, while Hammond sailed like a schooner from slip to slip anchorage with hardly ever a consultation with his bowlers and fieldsmen. And most marked still was the mental determination of most batsmen to play from the crease.

The Australian picture was one of brightness. Bradman was full of batting confidence and he had welded the Australians into a splendid all-round fighting force, strong at all points. He had such a wealth of bowling talent that Johnson, the hero of Sydney, barely made contact with the bowling crease in Melbourne. Tallon was sensational – and vocal – behind the stumps; Barnes ran into his best form in Sydney; McCool, Miller and Hassett were making runs, and the fielding was grand – the team, in short, a tribute to Bradman's inspiration.

The Melbourne Test will long be remembered as the Umpires' Upheaval. The stir over the umpiring and alleged mistakes swept the cricketing world, and one London correspondent solemnly testified to the mark on the edge of Edrich's bat as evidence of a wrong decision – the spot marked x, so to speak. No one can be too dogmatic about happenings when viewed from an acute side-on angle (as at Melbourne) and from far away, but sometimes one who has been through the mill will get an impression of an event, and some did think that Edrich faintly snicked the ball to which he was given out leg before.

Umpire Scott, who was singularly free of trouble during the series, gave Edrich out. It was a tight decision, on which the best possible umpire could have erred, though the argument of the mark on the bat's edge was a weak one, because this could have happened at any previous time in the innings or at the nets.

The other decision was the Compton one, and Scott also gave it. They followed soon after the Edrich one and the two combined caused the type-writers to clatter – a few of the loudest being those of correspondents who had been gently slumbering. Compton's state of mind was important in this happening. The manacling of his footwork had made him look an ordinary batsman again, and successive failures, by Melbourne, had him in that state known to players as the 'horrors'.

Only a disturbed mind could have allowed Compton to do what he did against Toshack. A tall left-hander, Toshack was bowling over the stumps, and Compton brought his two legs around to the ball and made no attempt to play it with the bat. Compton's guard was between middle and leg stumps. Strangely, only Hutton used against Toshack a device which the Englishmen had used with great success against O'Reilly (which was to shift guard from middle-and-leg to the leg stump and even outside it), so that, all considered, Compton was guilty of an error of judgment in playing with his legs a ball so obviously close to the line.

As soon as the ball hit Compton, he jumped aside. Photographs, with Compton looking down at his legs, were taken from immediately behind the stumps, and they show Compton's legs clear of the stumps. This evidence was readily accepted in some quarters, and then Compton's reactions to the decision further pointed the bone at Scott.

Compton looked down at his legs and then up at the umpire. He looked down at his legs again and then, obviously dissatisfied, walked away from the wicket. Five yards away, he turned again and took one last long, lingering look of farewell – like Goldsmith's exiles – or of disgust.

I give these particulars in no unkind manner against Compton. I do so to emphasise the substance upon which many sensational newspaper stories are based. Compton is one of the loveliest characters in the game of cricket. He was intensely popular with Australian crowds. He made many friends along the pickets, and I am sure that had he not been in the throes of misfortune he would have slapped his leg with the bat in characteristic and self-admonishing manner and skipped off to the pavilion.

The rankling over a decision soon dies. A friend once told me of his schoolboy impressions of the tumultuous Hill-Crockett decision in Sydney in 1903. Hill was run out when Australia was making a thrilling uphill fight.

'Don't ask me,' said my friend, 'whether Hill was truly out. I was a kiddy (I had wagged it from school for the day) in an Australian crowd that thought Hill was in. Anybody on the Hill that day who thought our hero was out was guilty of implied treason, heresy, schism and all uncharitableness. Also, he would have been stoned.'

And so the Hill merged in a bitter chant against Crockett of 'Crock, Crock, Crock,' that went on for ages. Hill, too, showed displeasure with the decision – but in 1936 my friend met Hill in Adelaide and he said he *was* out. Thirty-three years had passed, and Clem Hill had gathered the wisdom of subscribing to the cricket doctrine, 'The umpire, right or wrong.'

The umpiring in this series was not quite up to Test standard. That is not meant unkindly, but umpires, like players, must be judged on their deeds, and no critic has hesitated in criticism of a player's misdeeds. Umpiring is not an easy task, and it is also a thankless one.* Generally, Australian umpiring is not on the same English plane of excellence, where the ranks include many top-notch players of other days, whereas Australia has need of only eight umpires in a first-class season. Possibly Australians are too inclined to give their decisions immediately (G. O. Allen mentioned this as a fault at the end of his Australian tour in 1936–37), and I think the general Australian habit of turning with the bowler and then squatting almost to the height of the stumps is apt to lead to an error every now and then. The squatting is for a close decision for lbw on whether the ball would clear the stumps, but this sighting along the line of the stumps does not give as good a view for some decisions as an umpire looking down on his job.

At the end of the Melbourne Test the Englishmen asked for a change in umpires. A Board of Control sub-committee of three appointed umpires, and, without any ado, should have agreed immediately to other umpiring names being submitted to their guests. But publicity had played the very deuce with Test umpiring. Scott and Borwick had their names mentioned as often as Bradman and Hammond, and so, perforce, up arched the bristling backs of nationalism and the Englishmen were asked for particulars of alleged umpiring mistakes. This, naturally, they refused to do – and thereupon the sub-committee sternly and officiously appointed Scott and Borwick again for Adelaide.

The umpire never lived who did not make mistakes. No Test series has happened without mistakes being made, and these errors usually even out over a series, but in this particular season terrific publicity centred on some decisions. Gestures on the field or whispers from the dressing-room did not leave the press-critic to

---

* The Right Hon A. W. Fadden tells a story against himself which illustrates the thorny path of the umpire. A team of Australian aborigines from Pine Island, off the coast of North Queensland, annually played Rugby against a Townsville team and almost annually took a hiding. In this particular season, however (a season in which Mr Fadden, who refereed the game, was one of His Majesty's high Cabinet Ministers in Australia), the Pine Islanders won by 10–nil. Down the Townsville main street that night an aborigine, who had spent the day elsewhere, asked another how the game had gone. 'Oh, we beat dat w'ite trash,' said the second aborigine, with disdain: 'we beat dem ten ter nil – and dey wouddna got da nil only dat plurry Artie Fadden was Empire!'

rely on his own impressions alone. The Bradman decision in Brisbane made a big difference to England. The Hutton decision Sydney might have evened this up, but didn't; Edrich was generally conceded to have snicked the ball on to his pads in Melbourne, and, later in Adelaide, the allegation was that Tallon did not make a catch off Washbrook, but scooped it up on the half-volley.

So much for the general story of the umpiring. Scott and Borwick are both splendid characters and any mistakes were certainly honest ones, but, as the Australian selectors, Bradman, Dwyer and Ryder, saw all players and umpires in action in Australia before the Tests began, they, and not the Board sub-committee, were in a better all-round position to suggest umpires. At all events, this remains. When the Englishmen suggested a change in umpires, it should have been done immediately as a courtesy, with no questions asked.

At one period of the Melbourne Test, with Lindwall, McCool and Tallon pulverising the English attack, it almost seemed that the roll call of all time had been called and 'Croucher' Jessop, Bonnor, Jack Gregory, Constantine and all others were in attendance. One huge driving six by Lindwall over long-on will never be forgotten, but in the ecstasies of such clean smiting the critic found himself asking what had happened to Hammond's captaincy. At this stage it seemed shot to shreds. He persevered with the same bowlers and adhered to the orthodox fields while boundaries were whizzing in all directions.

There was one other signal feature of this drawn game. It was apparent that the Englishmen had tired of being on the receiving end of the multiplicity of Australian bumpers, and as soon as Bradman came to the wickets in the first innings, Voce rolled his sleeves higher and bounced the ball short. Bradman was not exactly at ease. He executed several very hurried movements and twice the ball went to unexpected places, but Voce was only 23 years of age when first he bowled bumpers in Australia. In 1946 he was 38. Ping went a muscle in his groin after three bumpers and off the field limped Voce, a victim of himself and the English desire to curb this Australian monopoly of the bumper.

This grim fight in Melbourne, watched by a world's record crowd for a Test, was not all confined to the middle. One of the most spirited was in the ladies' grandstand, where, mostly, occupants came just after breakfast with their knitting and peas to be shelled for dinner, and sat stolidly to the end of the day. One day there was a great twitter before lunch. In the middle of the grandstand one lady was sitting – and as if she meant it – on another lady's lap! It appeared that Lady No 1 had been sitting for much longer than she thought necessary very much behind a post. All the morning she had pleaded with Lady No 2 to move up, but she, tight-lipped and grim, was like a Test opening batsman – no suspicious moves or unseemly vigour for at least the first two hours. And so, finally, with great determination, Number 2 arose and planked herself down on her neighbour's lap – and resolutely refused to budge. Uproar and much laughter by all in the grandstand with the exception of the two women, who saw no humour in the situation (especially the one underneath, the one on top being no light weight). A diffident constable eventually put No 1 firmly back in her seat, and so they sat for the rest of the day – huffy and unspeaking.

A probing, pawing tom-cat brought light relief and interruption to the field in Adelaide after the cricket and the weather had got most people down. This particular game was one of the worst possible advertisements for Test cricket. For six intensely sultry and oppressive days (and midnight in the city was as intolerable as high noon) the players moved on to high scores and prodigious individual feats, but at the end of this long period of time the game was drawn – a result foreshadowed some three days, at least, before the contest finished. In this game Bradman and Hammond seemed intent on not yielding a single point to the other, and, for his part, Bradman gave obvious signs that a drawn game, giving Australia the Ashes, would satisfy him.

In all cricketing time before only three Test cricketers in Bardsley, Sutcliffe and Hammond had made two separate centuries in a Test match, but the Adelaide game almost provided three more. Morris and Compton made two separate centuries and Hutton made 94 and 76.

Morris and Compton are most accomplished batsmen, and Hutton, in the second innings, revealed that strange streak of inconsistency so characteristic of his batting on this tour. This time, against the bumpers, he stood upright and swept them for superb boundaries. Morris, whose two centuries in this game followed upon one in Melbourne, will come to rank with the great left-handers of the game, but, apart from the centurions and the usual Adelaide story of a lifeless, soulless wicket, the most interesting story of this game belonged to the hitherto despised Hardstaff, who, coming unexpectedly into the MCC side overnight, showed his comrades how slow spin bowling should be played.

Like the Australians, Hardstaff began a forward move as the slow bowler's arm got to the top, and the result was that he had no difficulty in getting to the ball on the full. McCool and Dooland, whose wiles had looked of another world in preceding games, immediately took on an earthly hue. And Hardstaff's tactics led Compton back to his natural game, with the result that, in this Test and the final one in Sydney, he looked and was the really great batsman he is. To Adelaide, Edrich alone had consistently seemed the typical English Test batsman, although Washbrook, in Melbourne, particularly in his treatment of Toshack, also looked his country's part, but as Hardstaff got much further up the wicket than Edrich, due praise must be given Hardstaff for showing the way to his fellows against the slows.

In the first Adelaide innings Bradman made nothing after Lindwall had provided the most sensational piece of fast bowling of the series – he clean bowled three Englishmen in four balls and missed the hat-trick by a coat of varnish. Bradman came to bat with little time remaining in the day, and Bedser clean bowled him with a 'trimmer', one of good length which pitched on the off and hit the leg stump. I liked, too, the manner in which Hammond crowded Bradman with two short legs as soon as he came in. They were excellent tactics. This was the fourth score of nil that Bradman had made against England.

The 'Old and Bolds' sniffed about the fourth day that Bradman would be content with a drawn game in this match. Following on wins in Brisbane and Sydney, a draw would give Australia the Ashes, and Bradman, naturally, was out to achieve just that. It was his tactics late on the fifth day that gave the critics cause to strum their harps, and need I add that the army of critics on this tour, the largest in cricket history, and most of us playing better cricket from the grandstand than we ever had played in the middle, wanted but little to surge into action. This was the period when Evans took 95 minutes to score his first run for England. On this same ground, 26 years before, Charles Kelleway made 147 in limitless hours against England – a feat which led Parkin to tell him as he passed at the wickets, 'You'll be a great player in eternity, Charlie. Time's of no account there.'

England was facing defeat when Evans joined Compton, and the more gifted batsman, Compton, naturally tried to keep the strike. Bradman retaliated by stringing his men deep towards the fence, making singles about Compton's only possible scoring stroke. In turn, Compton refused to run for the singles even when the ball was fielded near the boundary (the Adelaide ground is very short on both sides). Bradman's tactics were obviously the correct ones in trying to draw Compton away from the strike, and, furthermore, when a batsman is trying to keep the strike he is always liable to do something foolish.

In a large space of time, with these tactics, the game got exactly nowhere, and it took on a ludicrous note when some Australians ostentatiously ran alongside the ball for some yards without attempting to field it. The tactics obviously went on for too long and, furthermore, they were continued again the next morning, when, if Australia were to win, attack should have been coming from all quarters. Possibly Bradman thought that if the Englishmen were in no hurry to take risks and get runs, that suited him, as a draw clinched the Tests issue.

Then, too, this had some sort of counterpart when Australia was batting, and Miller, after a beautiful century, was made to look like a tradesman again when Hammond put up the shutters and clamped them on him with a large dose of leg-theory. Bradman evidently remembered this. In a welter of newspaper criticism after the game, he wrote to an Adelaide newspaper that he could not protect himself 'at the moment' against criticism, because it would entail charges against the opposing side's tactics.

All this was interesting, even if it only supported the view of the 'Old and Bolds' that feeling had arisen between the two captains, but the taste left in the mouth of the public was that a competitive game, begun a week before, had fizzled out into a tame draw, with Australia having nine wickets in hand at the close of play. And in the last hour, with Bradman batting, Australia scored at the rate of a run every two minutes.

In his hey-day Bradman might well have had this game won at five o'clock. At 38 years of age, however, he could not summon up the deeds of old that knocked complacency off the face of the clock. He had a hard struggle to get off his 'pair' – he did it eventually off a no-ball – and other games had shown that the dashers of this side were the younger brigade, Miller, Lindwall, McCool and Tallon. It was a pity Donald G. did not give the young Australian bloods their heads on this last day. Thousands were leaving the ground at 5.30, something I'd never seen before with Bradman batting, and they were grumbling in no uncertain manner. A wild dash for runs that day would have done cricket, and Test cricket, much good – but possibly Bradman could reply to this: 'Yes, and what a caning I'd have got from the critics if I had lost the game when a draw was all that was necessary to win the Ashes!' A Test captain must often feel like the man in the parable of the donkey and his son, and a Test captain can do little better than have the series won by the fourth Test, when all is said and criticised!

One final word about this Adelaide wicket. Top-dressings over the years have made it a mattress. Even after six days it was still stolidly asleep. Like Trent Bridge and the Kennington Oval pitches it should be dug up and, with the Veto, dumped far out to sea.

In Adelaide most of the batsmen were content to wait for the runs to come. In Sydney, in the final Test, with the spinners whistling a beauty across the pitch every now and then, most batsmen decided to be up and doing in the stroke-making business. This Sydney Test was a glorious and thrilling business, which came at a time when many ardent enthusiasts were thinking they could well afford to stay away from Test cricket, that it failed appreciatively to warrant the excessive publicity it had been given.

England could well have won this game. Some of the Australian batting whales on plus-perfect pitches proved to be minnows when the spinning ball demanded a sound technique, and had Edrich, on balance, seeing the ball all the way and receiving it truly into both hands, not dropped Bradman in the slips at two in the second innings, England might have gone on to victory. Bradman made 63, his most attractive innings of the series. This put Australia almost on top (Miller was to clinch it), and the setting and atmosphere as Bradman returned to the pavilion were in every way worthy of a Test exit from the game of the greatest run-scoring machine in cricket history. He was cheered all the way back from a pitch on which he had known so many remarkable triumphs, one the world's record score of 452 not out. Bradman doffed his cap halfway to the pavilion and was received by the members with tumultuous cheering. In every way was it a fitting farewell – but Bradman said at the finish he had no intention of retiring.

Grace made one thousand runs in May when in his 47th year – a feat which gained the bearded gentleman £9,073/8/3 in subscriptions, a sum possibly unequalled by 99 per cent of players in a lifetime of professionalism. But Hammond, at 43, with fibrositis denying him a last chance of atonement on a ground on which he had risen to the heights, was a tragic instance of an immortal who had dallied too long on cricketing earth. In a delectable print entitled 'No Flowers For Hammond', Robertson-Glasgow observed that many things would happen in cricket again that had happened before, but not Walter Hammond. How true! All that a pitiful season did for Hammond in Australia, a season in which fortune refused him even a single flirting wink, let alone a smile, was to separate the chaff critics from the wheat. Australian cricket will always have a warm spot for Hammond.

In every respect, may it be claimed, did this last Test support the contention that four days, on a not over-prepared pitch, is sufficient for a game, and, further, that on such a pitch the game develops its finest characteristics. It is a strange thought that those pitches which provide the best Test cricket, cricket which sends blood pulsating through the game again, are accidental. It was so in Melbourne in 1932–33; it was true of the 1938 Leeds Test, and it was the case in 1947 in Sydney. Rain kept the groundsmen indoors for much of the few days preceding the Test, and thus it began with the critics admonishing the bowlers, as if to guard against them getting any false ideas of their ability or their future, that the pitch would favour spin bowlers.

Of course it favoured spin bowlers – but it also favoured the game of cricket, and it did not leave out on a limb those batsmen whose technique could cope with a turning ball. O'Reilly's greatest complaint against Australian pitches is that they allow too many second-class batsmen to make first-class centuries. An over-prepared pitch debases and humiliates a bowler before it leads him to the final slaughter by batsmen who are encouraged in every way to be run-gluttons. I make this point. On such pitches, it is the pitch, and not the batsman, which first defeats the bowler.

Had it not been for this final Test in Sydney, this 1946–47 series would have gone into the records unmourned, not very much honoured and somewhat discordantly sung, and all doubly so because the series was dubbed a 'goodwill' one. The final day did much to erase other matches when Miller, after Bradman's delightful innings, threw aside caution and determined that the game would be won by six o'clock. With one day washed out and one day untouched, this game finished in four days and on a note which I loved. McCool hit a ball wide of mid-on with Australia needing three to win. With all the players ready to swoop for souvenirs if this proved the winning run, Miller snatched a bail from one end as he turned from the single, uprooted a stump as he turned from the two at the other end, and he ran the winning run with bat, stump and bail all in hand. In this gesture of boyishness was a grand contempt for all the deadly seriousness and grim-lipness of modern Test cricket.

Miller, like Compton, is brimful of cricket personality. I would willingly swop the thousand runs I miserly hoarded in Test cricket for half a dozen of those glorious off-drives of his, one of the loveliest sights the game has to offer. Cricket needs much more of his spirit of adventure and risk, and Test selectors would do well to lean to this type. But let me observe, too, that many a so-called stodgy batsman could well have run to strokes in Test cricket had it not been borne in upon him that his purpose in the international sphere was to play the waiting game.

More so than any other game, I think, cricket is brimful of individuality. I readily grant that much 'hot air' is written and spoken about the game. In the darkest days of the war this appeared in an English magazine: 'Few things, apart from war, can be more nerve-racking than the anxiety of a distinguished parent about the development of his son's cricket;' but, the super-enthusiast aside, it is undeniable that cricket is a game of art and culture, of science and character, and that it has a tranquil peace of immense value in a noisy world.

Miller bats, I feel sure, as Trumper did. In 1902, in England, Trumper made 13 centuries and his highest score was 128. I am not underrating Bradman nor the high place he will always hold in the game. He marks an epoch – Grace, Trumper, Hobbs and Bradman – but as surely as Bradman did out-Ponsford Ponsford, so, too, some day will youngsters arise with the ambition to out-Bradman Bradman. Where bodyline was conceived to upset the highly developed piece of mechanism that was Bradman, the next Bradman will require atomic energy to upheave him.

Records played a large part in the individuality of Bradman. He was always fascinating to watch. He made his runs well and in good time, but it is trite to observe that the super-excellence of wickets helped him large in his huge run-getting. This huge run-getting, however, has dominated the game in its most recent period, and in this tour of Australia we had the strange experience of Compton denying his better parts, trying to submerge his individuality, in an attempt to play the waiting, run-getting game.

Possibly Compton was not altogether a free agent in this. It was said at Perth that he 'trod the carpet' in explaining why he was stumped at 98, after having narrowly escaped stumping in precisely the same manner at 12. The reasoning, possibly, was that one lesson should have been enough, and particularly when his team was up against it, but Compton should be the last person in cricket to receive official tinkering. Time will prove him, I think, the greatest English batsman since Hobbs, with the facility, also, to excel on wet wickets; but the point is that Compton, with his own particular temperament and genius, is an individualist who should be allowed to play cricket as nature intended him to do.

Test cricket, if it is to recapture the spirit of the game, must cater for individuality. There must be more adventure in it and less of the spirit of the fate of the world depending upon the outcome of a mere game with bat and ball. I think the young generation has this spirit. There are two other essentials, a new conception of the preparation of pitches being a prime one. The other is revolutionary. It is the scrapping, or ignoring, for a trial period at least, of records and statistics.

As for the spirit, I don't think the 'goodwill' series helped one iota, and in this Bradman must accept his share of responsibility. He was a good and a shrewd leader, but not a generous one. The strength of his side over that of England's was most pronounced. The Australian batting averages were the highest in history, and England's bowling was headed by Yardley, practically unknown as a county bowler before the team sailed. It was Bradman's job to win for Australia, undoubtedly, but he could have made one or two gestures to such an opposing side. Particularly should he have ordered his fast men, Lindwall and Miller, to cut down the big crop of bumpers. It seemed to me, however, that Bradman, when confronted with an MCC cap, could neither forget nor forgive the bodyline tour.

Late in 1947 we saw a different Bradman. In two of the early games against the Indians in their first tour of Australia, Bradman played an entirely different brand of cricket to that which we saw against Hammond's MCC team. He had about him again an atmosphere reminiscent of the Bradman who enjoyed so hugely his first few seasons in international cricket. As with others, we must always remember with Bradman that bodyline gave him an absolute sickener of Test cricket, and, indeed, cricket for some years.

To the Indians went the signal honour of being the opponents for Bradman's hundredth first-class century – and that is an honour. For most of his playing life Bradman's health was dubious, but in this year of 1947 he was the sole Australian of his cricketing generation left in the game. Often, while a contemporary of Bradman's in the New South Wales or Australian teams, I had listened in the quiet seclusion of the dressing-room, when play had finished, to the conversation of those who sought to mollify, after a huge Bradman score, their own feelings or the feelings of those who had gone before. Bradman was never one to linger on in gossip after the day's doings, and so those left behind could discuss him frankly.

I hear again the sentiments of an older player. 'Don's a young man now. He's got eyesight and footwork out of the ordinary, but wait until he gets older and see how quickly he comes back to the field then. He can get away with unorthodoxy now. But the time will come when his eyesight and footwork leave him. You mark my words.'

I permit myself a whimsical smile. As I write, he's the only one of our Australian generation left to the game. While we sedately push perambulators around the district or play straight drives at aphids on the roses with a poison spray, Bradman goes on and on making centuries. And off the field he's no sluggard either. He's a family man with two children; he is head of his own brokerage business on the Adelaide Stock Exchange; as president of an Adelaide association of businessmen, he makes speeches on national affairs which impress visiting Prime Ministers; he's a member of the most exclusive body of sporting men in Australia – the Cricket Board of Control – he's an Australian selector, he plays a family game of tennis at the week-end, and plays it well, too, and he is champion of his golf club.

I have mentioned before the colossal number of centuries we could have expected from Bradman had he enjoyed a similar number of first-class innings as, for instance, Hobbs and Dr Grace. The scene on the Sydney Cricket Ground, his first home ground and where he scored the world's record of 452 not out, will never be forgotten as Bradman made his century of centuries against India on November 15. The next Dominion century maker to him is Bardsley with 53. Many Australians figure in the forties with centuries, and Dave Nourse heads the South Africans with 38. These figures prove this: Bradman is twice as prolific a scorer as the best of all other cricketers. One rare occasion, indeed, when figures can be believed.

These early games against India in Australia in 1947 showed that Bradman, to an extent, had recaptured some lighter thoughts on the game, but against Hammond's MCC team he was always the stern realist, who made the winning of the game his prime objective.

In this last Sydney Test, with the Ashes won, Miller once gave Hutton three successive head-high bouncers. Lindwall, also, was very much in the bouncing market. In playing a bumper, Compton trod on his wicket, and the feeling over the Australian tactics was easily sensed.

Now, in this analysis of the period of cricket which I played and observed, I would not like to be considered just another of those once-active players who, activity over, sits down with the long-beards and bemoans and berates the game and its players. Possibly I might be thought to have a bodyline or bumper bee in my bonnet, but one could not possibly overlook (or, as one who had been through the original bodyline fracas, regret) the large part which bumpers played in the Australian fast attack – though the leg-field was never packed.

These bumpers were essentially intimidatory. There are no stumps in the vicinity of a batsman's head, and, as in 1932–33, bumpers were responsible for feeling between the teams. I have not hesitated to claim that an occasional bumper, which could lead to a catch at fine leg, is part of the legitimate stock of every fast bowler, but there comes a time when bumpers move out of this category and into the intimidatory one. Such a time is sensed by the experienced and, indeed, was provided for by the instructions which the MCC gave to umpires to cover county matches and the tour of the Australians in England in 1938.

Rule 43, making the umpires the sole judges of fair and unfair play, embraces these instructions, and in 1945 the Australian Board scrapped all its laws and embraced the English ones. Thus this law was operative in the 1946–47 Australian season. One must wonder, therefore, why the umpires did not enforce the special rule to cover bumper bowling, particularly as each Test umpire had moved before in Australian cricket against short-pitched balls.

So badly did Hutton shape against the bumpers that Bradman must often have wondered, as others did, how this English batsman (who had taken the world's record Test score from him) would have fared against the Larwood–Voce onslaught in 1932–33. As a captain, Bradman rightly insists on having his finger in all affairs that concern his team, and as he made no visible move on the field to curb Miller and Lindwall in their short-pitched deliveries, it must be accepted that he concurred in them or even suggested the policy. In the final Test at Sydney Miller bowled three successive head-high bumpers at Hutton. Fielding at cover-point, Bradman seemed somewhat amused at Hutton's attempts to evade the bumpers, but nobody – Bradman, Miller or the umpires – gave anybody the impression that anything untoward was happening. O'Reilly wrote of these tactics in the last Test that they were overdone. The 'Sydney Morning Herald' critic wrote: 'I think that most sober-minded onlookers must have regretted the frequency of the bumpers.' One other critic, a noted participant in the bodyline era, thought most strongly against the Australian bumpers, but, recalling memories of other days, thought it polite not to enter another controversy.

Now, it might be thought that I am contradictory in my attitude towards bumpers. Possibly I am. I recall that, in earlier editions of this book, written before this recent series, I wrote that no prim compromise between the MCC and the Board would have deterred Australian fast bowlers from exploiting the theory in 1940 (had not war intervened) that Hutton had a weakness against bumpers. I wrote also: 'If a batsman does not like bumpers that is all the more reason why a bowler should bowl a bumper every ball if he feels like it.' That may seem a twisty 'bosie' to play now, but we have to consider this in the light of what might have happened in the unborn tour of 1940 and what did happen in the 'goodwill' one of 1946–47. This recent one should have been built around goodwill and a family spirit, and bumping sauce for Hutton in Australia in 1946–47 could well lead to bumping sauce for Bradman and others in England in 1948, and so on and on into cricketing time.

It is all very well to pelt bumpers down at an opponent's head, but it is wise to keep in the attacking head the thought that there is always another day when the advantage might have shifted. I am not so certain that the principle established in this series isn't that all future touring teams should go equipped with the cricket equiva-lents of gas and atomic bombs, to be used in case of necessity or advantage, or their mere possession meant as a warning that funny business will beget funny business. And that surely (this phrase has a familiar ring) would not be cricket!

Index